CONSTRUCTION ACCOUNTING

A GUIDE FOR ATTORNEYS AND OTHER PROFESSIONALS

Patrick A. McGeehin, Edward G. Benes,
Patrick J. Greene, Jr., and Wm. Cary Wright
Editors

FORUM ON THE CONSTRUCTION INDUSTRY

AMERICAN BAR ASSOCIATION
Defending Liberty
Pursuing Justice

Cover design by ABA Publishing.

The materials contained herein represent the opinions and views of the authors and/or the editors, and should not be construed to be the views or opinions of the law firms or companies with whom such persons are in partnership with, associated with, or employed by, nor of the American Bar Association or the Forum on the Construction Industry, unless adopted pursuant to the bylaws of the Association.

Nothing contained in this book is to be considered as the rendering of legal advice, either generally or in connection with any specific issue or case; nor do these materials purport to explain or interpret any specific bond or policy, or any provisions thereof, issued by any particular franchise company, or to render franchise or other professional advice. Readers are responsible for obtaining advice from their own lawyers or other professionals. This book and any forms and agreements herein are intended for educational and informational purposes only.

© 2010 American Bar Association. All rights reserved.

No part of this publication may be reproduced, stored in a retrieval system, or transmitted in any form or by any means, electronic, mechanical, photocopying, recording, or otherwise, without the prior written permission of the publisher. For permission, contact the ABA Copyrights & Contracts Department at copyright@abanet.org or via fax at 312-988-6030.

Printed in the United States of America.

14 13 12 11 10 5 4 3 2 1

Library of Congress Cataloging-in-Publication Data

Construction accounting : a guide for attorneys and other professionals / Patrick A. McGeehin ... [et al.], editors.
   p. cm.
  Includes index.
  ISBN 978-1-60442-832-2
  1. Construction industry—United States—Accounting. 2. Construction industry—Accounting—Law and legislation—United States. I. McGeehin, Patrick A.
  HF5686.B7C583 2010
  657'.869—dc22

                                                        2010011168

Discounts are available for books ordered in bulk. Special consideration is given to state bars, CLE programs, and other bar-related organizations. Inquire at Book Publishing, ABA Publishing, American Bar Association, 321 North Clark Street, Chicago, Illinois 60654-7598.

www.ababooks.org

Library
University of Texas
at San Antonio

CONTENTS

About the Editors	*xiii*
About the Authors	*xvii*
Introduction	*xxxi*
Patrick A. McGeehin	

Chapter 1
Basic Financial and Accounting Concepts   1
Dennis L. Allen and Richard E. Gavin

Accounting Standards	1
Financial Accounting Standards Board	*1*
American Institute of Certified Public Accountants	*3*
Standards Other than GAAP	*4*
Auditing Standards	4
Generally Accepted Auditing Standards	*5*
General Standards	5
Standards of Field Work	5
Standards of Reporting	5
Types of Audits	6
Financial Statement Audit	*6*
Fraud Audit	*7*
Internal Audit	*7*
Government Audit	*7*
Contract or Project Audit	*8*
Operational Audit	*8*
Basic Financial Statements	9
Balance Sheet	*9*
Income Statement	*11*
Statement of Cash Flows	*12*
Notes to Financial Statements	*14*
Supplemental Schedules to Financial Statements	*16*
Project Accounting and Revenue Recognition	16
Conclusion	17
Notes	17

Appendix 1–A
Supplemental Schedule of Contract Revenues, Costs, and Earnings   18

Appendix 1–B
Supplemental Schedule of Contracts   20

Chapter 2
Revenue Recognition and Other Construction Accounting Issues   23
Jeffrey B. Charkow and William D. Guernier
   Introduction   23
      GAAP for Construction Contractors   23
      Revenue Realization, the Matching Principle, and Conservatism   24
   Completed-Contract Method   25
      Example   *25*
      Loss Contracts Under the Completed-Contract Method   26
      When Can a Contractor Use the Completed-Contract Method?   27
   Percentage-of-Completion Method   28
      Determining Costs   *29*
         Incurred Contract Costs   29
         Estimated Cost-to-Complete   30
      Determining Revenue   *31*
         Unpriced Change Orders   32
         Claims   32
         Unpriced Change Orders and Claims Accounting—
           An Example   33
      Measuring Progress   *34*
         Input Method of Measurement   35
         Output Methods of Measurement   35
         Which Measure to Use?   36
   Other Information in the Construction Audit Guide   36
   Miscellaneous Issues for Attorneys   37
      Purchase Price Disputes   *37*
      Financial Statement Disclosure of Litigation Strategy   *37*
      Accounting Disclosure Disputes   *38*
   Conclusion   38
   Notes   39

Chapter 3
What Sureties and Owners Look for in Contractors'
     Financial Statements   41
Jay Bernstein and Jeffrey E. Fuchs
   Introduction   41
   Surety and Owner Concerns Regarding Contractor Finances   41
   The Three Cs   43
      Assessing the Contractor's Capital   *44*
      Assessing the Contractor's Capacity   *44*
         Work in Progress   45
         Job Cost Reporting   45
         Equipment   46
         Personnel and Management Team   46
         Work History   47

Business Plan	47
Bank Line of Credit	47
Assessing the Contractor's Character	47
Integrity Perceived During the "Meet and Greet"	48
Letters of Recommendation and References	48
Third-Party Reports	48
Financial Statement Documents and Supplementary Schedules	48
Financial Tests, Measures, and Ratios Derived from the Contractor's Financial Information	51
Sample Analysis of a Contractor's Financial Statements	55
Conclusion	57
Notes	57

Chapter 4
Booking of Claims for Financial Reporting Purposes — 59
Kevin D. Dennis, Scott D. Gray, Thomas R. Lynch, and Robert J. Symon

Introduction	59
GAAP Requirements for Booking Revenue and Claims on Long-Term Construction Contracts	60
General Requirements for Recognizing Revenue on Long-Term Construction Contracts	60
GAAP Guidelines for Recognizing Revenue on Change Orders or Claims	62
Liabilities Associated with Attorney Opinion Letters Related to Claims	65
Liability of Lawyers and Accountants for Statements Made in the Scope of Client Representation	66
Primary Liability	67
Primary Liability Under Federal Securities Law	67
Primary Liability Under State Law	70
"Secondary" or "Aiding and Abetting" Liability	71
Conclusion	72
Notes	72

Chapter 5
Navigating a Construction Contract Audit: Standards, Rights, and Obligations — 75
John A. Becka, Shannon J. Briglia, and Colin A. Daigle

Introduction	75
Public Sector Audits	76
Introduction	76
What Is the DCAA?	79
When Does DCAA Conduct Audits?	80
DCAA Audit Procedures	81
Audit of REAs and Claims	82

The Role of the DCAA Auditor in the Procurement Process	83
Consequences of Noncompliance: Exercise of Auditor Discretion	84
Reduction of Payment Request via Notice of Intent to Disallow	85
Suspension of Payment	85
Interest and Penalties for Unallowable Costs	85
Liability for Fraudulent Claims for Payment	86
Private Sector Audits	86
Introduction	86
Comparison of Private and Public Sector Audits	87
Types of Commercial Audits	87
Contractual Provisions Addressing Audit Rights and Accounting Records	89
Audit Rights Clauses—Implications for Contractors	90
Informational Requests by Auditors	91
Audit Frequency	93
Job Cost Systems and Accounting	93
Auditor's Role versus the Architect's Responsibilities	94
Construction Project Auditors	95
Auditing the "Reasonable"	97
High-Risk Areas Subject to Contract Audit	97
Labor Costs	98
Incentive Compensation—Bonuses	98
Off-Site Labor	99
Costs Subject to Prior Owner Approval	99
Equipment Costs	99
Miscellaneous Costs	100
Related Parties	100
Subcontractors	101
Contract Allowances	101
Discounts, Rebates, and Refunds	101
Conclusion	101
Notes	102

Appendix 5-A
DCAA Contract Audit Manual (CAM) DCAAM 7640.1 — **107**
    Notes — 108

Appendix 5-B
Audit Guidance and Audit Management Guidance Memorandums for Regional Directors (MRDs) — **109**
    Notes — 117

Appendix 5-C
Directory of Audit Programs (AP) and Other Audit Guidance (OAG) Documents — **119**
    Notes — 128

Appendix 5-D
Department of Defense Policy for Resolving
    Contract Disagreements   129

Chapter 6
Types of Financial Reports and Opinions Issued by CPAs
    and Applicable Professional Standards   133
Paul M. James, Stephen B. Shapiro, Anita M. Sheckells, Claudia R. Wolter, and Wiley R. Wright, III

Introduction	133
Financial Statement Reporting and Applicable Standards	133
Financial Statements	*133*
Audit, Review, and Compilation Engagements	*134*
Audited Financial Statements	135
Reviewed Financial Statements	140
Compiled Financial Statements	141
Table Comparison: Audit, Review, Compilation	143
Going-Concern Issues	143
Special Report Engagements	*146*
Consulting and Expert Services	149
Consulting Services	*149*
Consultations	150
Advisory Services	150
Implementation Services	150
Transaction Services	151
Staff and Other Support Services	151
Product Services	151
Expert Witness and Consulting Expert Services	*151*
Discovery of Testifying and Nontestifying Experts	152
Admissibility of Evidence	153
Privilege Applied to Consulting Experts	154
Conclusion	155
Notes	156

Chapter 7
Contract Types and Accounting Issues Related to Changes in Price
    and Cost Reimbursement   157
Michael R. Benes, Jeffrey G. Gilmore, and Douglas A. Trueheart

Introduction	157
Contract Types, Forms, and Performance Issues	
Related to Costs	158
Firm-Fixed-Price Contracts	*158*
Economic Price Adjustment	158
Cost-Reimbursement Contracts	*159*
Selected Forms for Cost-Reimbursable Contracting	*160*

Contractor's Duty to Notify Owner of Increased Costs Under Cost-Reimbursement Contracts	*161*
Audit Rights	*162*
Cost Accounting Issues Related to Cost-Reimbursement Contracts and Changes Under Fixed-Price Contracts	162
Labor Costs	*162*
On-Site Construction Workers	163
On-Site Supervision and Administrative Personnel	164
Off-Site Personnel Providing Direct Project Services	164
Home Office Personnel	165
Wages and Benefits	166
Insurance	*170*
Equipment Pricing	*171*
Rate Books	172
Actual Contractor Cost	173
Ownership Costs	174
Operating Costs	175
Pricing Sheets or Lists	176
Small Tools	*177*
Computer Charges	*178*
Conclusion	179
Notes	180

Appendix
EJCDC Article 11: Reimbursable Costs — **183**

Article 11—Cost of the Work; Allowances; Unit Price Work	183
1.01 Cost of the Work	*183*
1.02 Allowances	*186*
1.03 Unit Price Work	*187*

Chapter 8
Government Contract Cost Accounting Issues Affecting Construction Contractors — **189**
Edwin C. Giddings, Matthew R. Krafft, and Patrick A. McGeehin

Introduction	189
Contracting Methods	190
Cost or Pricing Data and FAR Part 15, Contracting by Negotiation	190
Cost or Pricing Data Certification	*192*
Cutoff Dates and Cost Sweeps	*192*
Practical Considerations	*193*
Unallowable Costs Under Government Contracts	194
FAR Provisions Specifically Relating to Construction Contracts and Advance Agreements	*199*
Specific Cost Areas	*199*
Company-Owned Construction Equipment	199

General Conditions—Field Overhead Costs	201
Entertainment	203
Self-Insurance (31.205-19)	203
Travel	204
Legal Fees	204
Volume and Other Discounts	205
Construction and Architect-Engineer Contract Requirements (FAR Part 36)	206
Payment Provisions	206
Progress Payments	*206*
Itemization of Amounts Requested	206
Subcontractor and Additional Information	207
Retainage	207
Reimbursement for Bond Premiums	207
Final Payment	208
Prompt Payment for Construction Contracts	*208*
Cost Accounting Standards	208
Background and Purpose	*208*
Coverage and Exemptions	*209*
Standards	*209*
Certification of Indirect Costs and Related Penalties	212
Conclusion	214
Notes	215

Chapter 9
Pricing of Construction Claims — 217
Paul J. Gorman, Daniel Kwon, Paul A. Varela, and David B. Wonderlick

Introduction	217
Construction Costs	218
Contractual Considerations in Pricing Claims	219
Changes Clause	*220*
Force Account	*220*
Differing Site Conditions	*220*
Quantity Variations	*221*
No Damages for Delay	*221*
Liquidated Damages	*222*
Notice of Claim Requirements	*222*
Disputes Clause	*222*
The Project Record	223
Pricing Methods	223
Discrete Pricing Methods	*224*
Specific Identification	224
Discrete Pricing of Time-Related Costs	225
Measured Mile	*225*

Global Pricing Methods	*226*
Total Cost Method	226
Modified Total Cost Method	227
Quantum Meruit and Jury Verdict	228
Inefficiency Claims	228
Sample Measured Mile Calculation	*229*
Measured Mile	229
Challenges to Measured Mile Analyses	232
Industry and Academic Studies	*232*
Trade Organization Studies: Mechanical Contractors Association of America and National Electrical Contractors Association	233
Overtime-Related Inefficiency Studies: Army Corps of Engineers and Business Roundtable	234
Change Order-Related Inefficiency Studies: Leonard and Ibbs	235
Delay Claims	235
Extended Field Overhead	*236*
Home Office Overhead	*237*
The Eichleay Method	238
Challenges to Home Office Overhead Costs	240
Acceleration Costs	*240*
Types of Acceleration Costs	240
Entitlement to Recover for Acceleration	240
Change Order Claims	241
Change Order Pricing Generally—Direct Costs and Markup	*241*
Cumulative Impact of Multiple Changes	*244*
Equipment Cost Claims	244
Equipment Rental Costs	*245*
Equipment Ownership Costs	*245*
Equipment Rate Manuals	*246*
Other Claim Elements	246
Documents Required to Support Claimed Costs	247
Cost Documents	*247*
Original Bid Estimate	247
Change Orders	248
Job Cost Reports	248
Detailed Transaction Reports	248
Labor Distribution Reports	248
Productivity Information	249
Applications for Payment	249
Additional Documents	249
Schedule Analysis—Related Documents	*250*
Conclusion	250
Notes	250

Chapter 10
**Discovery and Use of Accounting Information
and Accounting Experts in Construction Litigation
and Arbitration** 257
Colin A. Johns and John W. Ralls
   Introduction 257
   Discovery of Accounting Information 257
      Identifying the Need for Discovery 257
      Developing a Discovery Plan: A Checklist 258
      Discovery Vehicles 259
         Document Production Requests 259
         Depositions of Fact Witnesses 263
         Interrogatories 264
   Use of Accounting Records in the Proof
      and Disproof of Damages 265
   Using and Opposing Accountants as Expert Witnesses 266
      When to Retain an Accounting or Other Cost Expert 266
      Challenges to Expert Accounting Testimony 267
         Legal Standard 268
         Financial Damages Expert Testimony 268
         Recent Cases 269
      Deposing Accounting Experts 271
   Conclusion 272
   Notes 272

Appendix
**Contractors' Cost and Accounting Records to Consider
      Requesting in Discovery** 277

Chapter 11
Accounting Issues in Fraud Investigations 281
*Brandi N. Kleinman, Steven J. Kmieciak, Alan F. Nagorzanski,
Rodney W. Sowards, and Daniel P. Wierzba*
   Introduction 281
      Definition of Fraud 281
         Accounting Definition 281
         Legal Definition 282
      Legal Elements; Penalties for Fraud 282
      Organizational and Performance Fraud 283
         Organizational Fraud 283
         Performance Fraud 286
      False Claims Acts 289
         Criminal False Claims Act—18 U.S.C. § 287 289
         Civil False Claims Act—31 U.S.C. § 3729 290
      Recent Examples of the Consequences of Fraudulent Activity 291

Contents

Uncovering and Detecting Fraud	292
Opportunities for Fraud in the Construction Industry	292
Job Cost Reports	292
Payment Applications	293
Bonding Process	294
Contract Performance	295
Red Flags or Badges of Fraud	*296*
Off-site Storage or Delivery of Materials	296
Excessive Front-End-Loading	297
Out-of-Sequence Work	297
Excessive Productivity	298
Related Business Entities	298
Questionable Journal Entries	299
Numerous Bank Accounts	301
Fraud Prevention and Detection	301
Precontract Project Controls	*301*
Ongoing Project Analytical Procedures	*302*
Conclusion	303
Notes	304
Table of Authorities	*307*
Index	*317*

ABOUT THE EDITORS

Patrick A. McGeehin, a CPA and Senior Managing Director with FTI Consulting, Inc., consults on construction and litigation matters, providing contract claims assistance and litigation support services relating to the calculation of and approach to damages, such as delay and disruption, inefficiencies, breach of contract, lost profits, and fraud-related issues. His primary focuses are in the construction and government contracts industries, although he has experience consulting and testifying in other business sectors.

Mr. McGeehin provides expert testimony in contract disputes and cost accounting matters, and has testified in both court and board forums, including appearances before various Federal and State Boards of Contract, and various U.S. District Courts and State Circuit Courts, and in International Arbitrations settings. He has written articles published in the American Bar Association's *Public Contract Law Journal* and in the *Construction Business Review*, among other publications, and has authored a chapter on Lost Profits in *Business Valuation Resources*.

Mr. McGeehin received a Bachelor of Science in Accounting from the University of Scranton (summa cum laude), and was awarded a Master of Business Administration degree from The George Washington University. He has been a guest speaker on construction industry topics for many organizations over the span of his career.

Edward G. Benes is Senior Counsel for AECOM Technology Corporation. AECOM provides professional technical and management support services to a broad range of markets, including transportation, facilities, construction, environmental, and energy. Mr. Benes is responsible for AECOM's legal matters in the Midwestern region of the United States. His responsibilities include preparing and negotiating design and construction contracts, addressing corporate legal issues, and managing professional and general liability claims and disputes. Mr. Benes is also responsible for addressing AECOM's intellectual property matters, which includes preparing and negotiating licensing agreements, prosecuting patents and trademarks, and enforcing AECOM's intellectual property rights.

Prior to becoming an attorney, Mr. Benes practiced engineering for over eight years. He gained experience in chemical process, waste treatment, and storm water design. In addition to being a licensed professional engineer, Mr. Benes is admitted to practice before the United States Patent and Trademark office.

Mr. Benes received his engineering degree from Purdue University in West Lafayette, Indiana, and his law degree from Loyola University in Chicago, Illinois. He is a member of the ABA Forum on the Construction Industry, the Richard Linn American Inn of Court, and the American Intellectual Property Law Association.

Patrick J. Greene, Jr., is a partner at Peckar & Abramson, one of the premier firms representing the construction industry, and heads the Government Practice Group in New York and New Jersey.

In more than 25 years of practice, Mr. Greene has advised some of the nation's largest construction contractors regarding performance and compliance issues in contracting in the public and private sectors, including, especially, federal government contracting. He has prepared, litigated, and resolved multiple complex extra work, delay, and impact claims on domestic and international construction projects. Notably, Mr. Greene successfully presented the seminal case concerning the New Jersey Construction Lien Law before the New Jersey Supreme Court and recently tried one of the largest, most complex cases in the history of the US GSBCA.

Mr. Greene has presented numerous seminars involving construction litigation and government contracting. He has been recognized as a leading construction lawyer by *Best Lawyers in America* and *The International Who's Who of Construction Lawyers*, and as a New Jersey and New York Super Lawyer. He is the current co-chairman of the Construction Litigation Committee of the Litigation Section of the American Bar Association and past co-chairman of the New Jersey State Bar Association Construction and Public Contract Law Section.

Mr. Greene is a graduate of St. Peter's College and the Georgetown University Law Center.

Wm. Cary Wright is a Partner with Carlton Fields in its Tampa, Florida office. He is board-certified in Construction Law by the Florida Bar, and has extensive experience representing clients in construction disputes including construction claims, defective products, water intrusion, mold, construction liens, bond claims, insurance coverage matters, and risk management issues. Mr. Wright also has substantial experience in contract drafting and contract review including the preparation of owner-contractor agreements and contractor-subcontractor agreements. He has also spoken and written extensively on construction-related issues.

Mr. Wright is active in the American Bar Association Forum on the Construction Industry (Forum), the Real Property Probate & Trust Law (RPPTL) Section of the Florida Bar, and the Hillsborough County Bar. His present and past positions include Chair of Division 7—Bonds, Liens and Insurance of the Forum (2008–present); Past Chair, RPPTL Construction Law Committee

(2007–2009); Co-Vice-Chair, RPPTL Construction Law Institute (2009); Co-Vice Chair, RPPTL Real Property and Liability Insurance Committee (2009); and Past Chair, Construction Law Section, Hillsborough County Bar Association (2005–2007).

Mr. Wright is listed in *Chambers USA Guide to America's Leading Business Lawyers* (Construction) 2007, 2008, and 2009 editions. He was selected for inclusion in *Best Lawyers in America* 2007–2010 editions, and selected for inclusion in *Florida Super Lawyers* 2006–2009 editions.

Mr. Wright received his Doctor of Jurisprudence from Stetson University College of Law (cum laude), in 1990, where he was the Managing Editor of the *Stetson Law Review*. Mr. Wright graduated from the University of Florida with a Bachelor of Science in Accounting (with honors) in 1985.

ABOUT THE AUTHORS

Dennis L. Allen is Senior Vice President in charge of Hill International, Inc.'s construction consulting and claims operations in Washington, D.C. Mr. Allen has more than 35 years of experience working with contractors, owners, and developers in overall project development, preparing and monitoring project cost controls, and helping to manage risk throughout the construction and operational processes. As a litigation consultant, he has served as an expert witness on some of the largest construction and real estate claims in the United States and overseas, analyzing issues such as labor and equipment costs, acceleration costs, lost profits, cumulative costs of changes, insurance claims, and delay costs.

Mr. Allen has a broad background in all subjects concerning construction and real estate, having worked for a major contractor, two developers, and an institutional lender in the development of construction and operating cost systems; the analysis of project construction and operating results; and the development or review of project budgets, construction estimates, operating budgets, and financing plans.

Mr. Allen received his Bachelor of Business Administration in Accounting. Mr. Allen is a Certified Public Accountant, a Certified Construction Industry Financial Professional, and a Certified Fraud Examiner.

John A. Becka is a Director in the FTI Forensic and Litigation Consulting practice and is based in Bethesda, Maryland. Mr. Becka has 35 years of professional experience in financial and accounting operations management. His experience includes positions with several large federal government contractors in both the manufacturing and professional services business. He was responsible for financial planning, financial reporting, financial analysis, pricing, contract administration, regulatory compliance, and audit interface (internal, external, and DCAA). He has extensive experience with federal government contracts, including the development of complex indirect rate structures within the confines of cost allowability and allocability provisions of the Federal Acquisition Regulation.

Mr. Becka received a Master of Business Administration degree in Government Procurement and Contracting from George Washington University and a Bachelor of Science degree in Finance from the University of Maryland. In addition, he has completed executive-level courses in finance and management at Harvard, Wharton (University of Pennsylvania), and Darden (University of Virginia) business schools.

Michael R. Benes is Director of Consulting Operations and a Partner in the accounting/consulting firm of Benes & Krueger, S.C., Waukesha, Wisconsin, which provides services almost exclusively to construction industry clients throughout the nation. Mr. Benes is a Certified Public Accountant licensed in Wisconsin, is Certified in Financial Forensics, and has a Master of Business Administration degree.

Mr. Benes' background encompasses experience as a management consultant where he has helped contractors select and install computer systems, develop operational improvement plans, create business and strategic plans, design continuity plans, and resolve complex construction disputes. His dispute resolution practice focuses primarily on the analysis of construction claims where he works for owners, contractors, architects, and engineers.

Mr. Benes has served as consultant and an expert witness for numerous clients throughout the country and internationally. He has provided testimony in federal and state courts as well as arbitration proceedings. Mr. Benes has been a guest lecturer for various professional groups including the Associated Builders and Contractors, Associated General Contractors, American Subcontractors Association, and various state and local Bar Associations.

Jay Bernstein is Assistant General Counsel to the Real Property Division of the General Services Administration, where he represents the government in complex litigation brought before the Civilian Board of Contract Appeals. His areas of expertise include government contract law, surety law, litigation, and dispute resolution.

Prior to joining GSA, Mr. Bernstein represented contractors, subcontractors, and sureties in private practice, and handled performance bond and payment bond claims as Managing Director of a major surety company. He also served as Deputy Counsel to the Contract Litigation Unit of the Maryland Office of the Attorney General, where he litigated claims before the Maryland State Board of Contract Appeals.

Mr. Bernstein received a Bachelor of Arts degree from Yeshiva University in 1979, a Doctor of Jurisprudence from New York University School of Law in 1982, and a Master of Art from the Baltimore Hebrew University in 1994.

Shannon J. Briglia is a Founding Member of the construction law firm of BrigliaMcLaughlin, PLLC, where she concentrates her practice in the resolution of public and private construction disputes. With more than 20 years of experience in the construction industry, Ms. Briglia represents clients in federal and state court trials and appeals, in arbitration and mediation, and before commissions and boards of contract appeal.

Ms. Briglia is a member of the American Bar Association, Forum on Construction, in addition to the Public Contract Law Section and the Fidelity & Surety Law Committee. Ms. Briglia is a frequent author and speaker on construction and surety issues. She has written and spoken on scheduling, delays, inefficiencies, changes, differing site conditions, terminations, payment, and surety bond issues to a variety of audiences, including other lawyers as well as contractors and sureties. *Chambers USA 2007* described her as receiving hearty client praise as "always extraordinarily prepared and articulate." She was selected as a Virginia "SuperLawyer" in 2008 and 2009 and a Washington, D.C. "SuperLawyer" for 2007, 2008, and 2009 in the area of construction law.

Ms. Briglia received a Bachelor of Science degree from Virginia Tech, and a Doctor of Jurisprudence from George Mason University School of Law.

Jeffrey B. Charkow is a Partner with Stein Ray Harris LLP. His practice encompasses construction law as well coverage work on behalf of policy holders. Mr. Charkow has represented owners, EPC contractors, design professionals, design-builders, and general contractors/subcontractors concerning building defects, delay/inefficiency claims, and most significant issues involved in the construction process. He has worked on litigation from projects such as the expansion and renovation of Notre Dame Football Stadium, a power plant in Central America, and the City of Chicago's Emergency Communication System. He is admitted to practice in Illinois, the United States District Court for the Northern District of Illinois, the United States District Court for the Central District of Illinois, and the Ninth Circuit Court of Appeals.

Mr. Charkow graduated from Washington University School of Law in 1993 where he was a member of the *Washington University Law Quarterly* and graduated Order of the Coif. Mr. Charkow received his undergraduate degree from the University of Wisconsin-Madison in 1988.

Colin A. Daigle is a Managing Director and Construction Consulting Practice Leader with Marsh Risk Consulting. He has served as a financial damages expert for a variety of project types and has testified as a construction financial damages and claims pricing expert at trial, as well as other dispute forums. Mr. Daigle has analyzed financial impacts related to lost productivity, extended and added general conditions, improper billings, disputed changes, escalation, equipment claims, and home office overhead, among other areas. He has implemented project controls and construction accounting best practices and has conducted project audits to improve transparency, accountability, contract compliance, and early dispute resolution.

Prior to Marsh, Mr. Daigle worked in the accounting division of Miller & Long Concrete Construction and the advisory and dispute sections of PricewaterhouseCoopers and KPMG.

Mr. Daigle is an active member of the construction industry as an author and speaker, as well as through various organizations. He is a member of the ABA's Forum on the Construction Industry and the Construction Financial Management Association and a past member of the CFMA's National Accounting and Reporting Committee. Mr. Daigle is a licensed Certified Public Accountant (CPA), Certified in Financial Forensics (CFF), a Certified

Information Technology Professional (CITP), and Forensic Certified Public Accountant (FCPA). He received a Bachelor of Science in Business Administration from La Salle University.

Kevin D. Dennis is a Managing Director with Navigant Consulting. Mr. Dennis specializes in assisting clients with the accounting, financial, economic, and management aspects of disputes, particularly as they relate to construction, commercial contracts, intellectual property, financial institutions, and bankruptcy matters. Mr. Dennis's construction-related experience dates to the early 1990s and includes roadway and bridge projects; residential/commercial developments; senior-living facilities; chemical, oil, and gas facilities; power plants; manufacturing plants; hospitals; airports; and wastewater treatment facilities. These projects have involved both ongoing and completed construction projects, including the performance of change order analyses, contract cost audits, documentation reviews, claims development, and claims analyses.

Mr. Dennis has also been a court-appointed Examiner and has assisted Trustees with analyzing complex, multiparty transactions and relationships. He has provided expert testimony on construction and other matters in depositions, arbitration hearings, bankruptcy proceedings, and state and federal courts. Mr. Dennis received his Bachelor of Science degree from Florida Southern College and his Master of Accounting from the University of Florida. Mr. Dennis is licensed as a Certified Public Accountant in Florida and California, holds the AICPA's Certified in Financial Forensics designation, and is a Certified Management Accountant.

Jeffrey E. Fuchs is the President of Delta Consulting Group. He has construction contracting and consulting expertise based on over 28 years of experience in the engineering and construction industries. His expertise includes construction management and project oversight; analysis and resolution of contract disputes, including delay analyses, damage calculations, and productivity impacts; forensic engineering and accounting; litigation support and expert witness testimony; project and corporate cost accounting; and property cost segregation studies. Mr. Fuchs's prior experience includes positions as Area Director for Ernst & Young's Construction Industry Consulting Services for the Mid-Atlantic region; Vice President of Operations for a commercial construction company; Director of Environmental and Contract Management for a large government agency; and Project Engineer for a large general contractor. Mr. Fuchs has the proven ability to quickly assess problems encountered by owners, developers, contractors, engineers, and government and financial institutions based on his involvement with numerous, diverse projects totaling billions of dollars.

Mr. Fuchs received a Bachelor of Science degree in Civil Engineering from the University of Maryland in 1982, and a Master of Science degree in Construction Engineering & Management from the University of Maryland in 1987. He is a retired Civil Engineering Officer in the U.S. Air Force and a registered Professional Engineer and Certified Public Accountant.

Richard E. Gavin is a Partner at Grassi & Co. and is the construction industry niche leader. He began his career more than 25 years ago and has extensive experience in operational reviews, business forecasting and projecting, business valuations, human resource advisory services, overhead analysis, internal control evaluations, and strategic tax planning.

Mr. Gavin is a frequent lecturer on tax issues, financial statements, analytical reviews, fraud prevention, and internal control development, and is an adjunct professor at Columbia University teaching a graduate-level course in finance and accounting for construction contractors. He has numerous published articles on family business succession planning, best practices, and joint ventures.

Mr. Gavin is active in the Construction Financial Management Association, Long Island Contractors Association, and the Construction Industry Council. He is an active member of the American Institute of Certified Public Accountants and the New York State Society of Certified Public Accountants.

Mr. Gavin was one of the first individuals in the country to attain the designation of Certified Construction Industry Financial Professional. He has a Bachelor of Business Administration degree from Hofstra University.

Edwin C. Giddings is a Director in the FTI Forensic and Litigation Consulting practice. He has over 30 years of experience in the government contracting industry. Before joining Rubino & McGeehin, Mr. Giddings served as the government contracts compliance officer for two Fortune 500 companies. He provided regulatory and financial guidance to executive management regarding compliance with federal procurement laws and regulations (FAR, CAS, DFAR, and TINA) and established and managed compliance and internal control programs. Mr. Giddings's experience also includes positions with several other large government contractors where his responsibilities included government compliance, contract administration, financial reporting, proposal development, and government audit liaison. Prior to his government contractor work, he held positions at two large CPA firms. Early in his career, he worked as a senior analyst with the Office of the Inspector General of the U.S. Department of Defense, where he planned and supervised operational and program results reviews, and the U.S. General Accounting Office, where he served as an agent for the Congressional Joint Committee on Internal Revenue Taxation.

Mr. Giddings is a member of the American Institute of Certified Public Accountants, the Institute of Management Accountants, and the Professional Contracts Management Association. He received a Bachelor of Science degree from East Carolina University.

Jeffrey G. Gilmore is the Chair of Akerman Senterfitt LLP's National Construction Practice Group. His practice emphasizes domestic and international construction law involving a broad range of public and private matters, including EPC/design-build projects, healthcare, multifamily housing, power generation, petrochemical, and infrastructure projects (transportation, water, and public safety). In addition, he has been recognized for his experience in construction matters in *Chambers USA* (2008, 2009); *The Legal 500 US 2009*, Recommended in the Southeast for Construction; *The Best Lawyers in America for Construction Law* (2008, 2009); a Virginia "SuperLawyer" in 2010 for Construction Litigation; and the Virginia Business Legal Elite (2008, 2009) in the Construction category. Mr. Gilmore is admitted to practice in the District of Columbia, Maryland, and the Commonwealth of Virginia. He received his law degree from the College of William and Mary School of Law in 1982, and a Bachelor of Arts in Economics from Miami University in 1979.

Paul J. Gorman is a Principal in Exponent's Construction Consulting practice. He has broad experience in the review and analysis of construction costs and the preparation of construction claim damages. He is familiar with all categories of construction costs and has analyzed these costs on behalf of owners, both public and private, general contractors, and subcontractors. Mr. Gorman has construction experience in a variety of industries including transportation, heavy/civil and highway, manufacturing facilities, prisons, power plants, and commercial buildings.

Mr. Gorman has provided expert testimony on the subject of damages and construction cost analysis on several occasions in federal, state, and city courts, and in arbitrations. He has also participated in mediations as both an expert witness and as a mediator.

Mr. Gorman received a Master of Business Administration degree from the State University of New York at Buffalo in 1979, and a Bachelor of Science in Business Management from the State University of New York at Buffalo in 1977.

Scott D. Gray is a Managing Director with the Miami office of Navigant Consulting, Inc. Mr. Gray has over 26 years of consulting experience, including the analysis of costs and damages incurred on over 200 construction projects and government contracts. He has analyzed claims for owners, developers, general contractors, subcontractors, A/E firms, and sureties for projects ranging from EPC contracts to build-to-print construction projects. Issues addressed in these claim analyses include damages arising from acceleration, changed work, contract termination, cumulative impact, deficient design, delay, losses of efficiency, subcontractor default, and others.

The majority of Mr. Gray's engagements involve some form of delay damages, including extended site overhead costs, unabsorbed home office overhead, extended equipment costs, and labor/material escalation. He has often analyzed and calculated daily cost rates to quantify such delay damages.

Mr. Gray has provided expert testimony in litigation on several occasions, in ICC arbitration proceedings, the U.S. Court of Federal Claims, the General Services Board of Contract Appeals, federal district court, state court, and AAA arbitration and mediation proceedings.

Mr. Gray received a Bachelor of Arts degree (with honors) in Economics from Colgate University, and a Master of Business Administration from Georgetown University.

William D. Guernier is a Vice President of The Kenrich Group in its New York office. Mr. Guernier's career includes nearly 10 years as a financial officer in the real estate and construction industry and over 20 years as a consultant. Prior to joining The Kenrich Group, he was a partner at a "Big Four" accounting firm, a Managing Director at an international consulting firm, and a Vice President of Tucker Alan Inc.

In his 30 years of experience, Mr. Guernier has provided expert consulting services on financial, accounting, economic, and damages matters in numerous areas including construction, government contracts, real estate, and commercial bankruptcies. He has testified on damages issues in various courts and in arbitrations. He has also assisted counsel and clients in numerous extensive settlement negotiations, as well as in mediation.

Mr. Guernier received a Bachelor of Business Administration degree in Accounting from the College of William & Mary, and a Master of Business Administration from The George Washington University.

Paul M. James is a Partner with the national Construction Industry Practice Group of Holland & Knight and works in the firm's Boston office where he serves as the Regional Practice Group Leader. Mr. James concentrates his practice in construction law and litigation and alternative dispute resolution. He represents a range of construction industry clients in both the private and public sectors, with a focus on the representation of general contractors, at-risk construction managers, and design-build contractors. His practice includes structuring project delivery methods and reviewing, structuring, and negotiating construction, design, and construction management contracts; advising clients on contract interpretation and contract and project administration for commercial, institutional, and public building projects and public works projects; claim avoidance counseling; public procurement laws and bid protests; construction industry labor and employment issues; OSHA matters; change order management; project close-out management; assessment, preparation, and defense of claims; litigation and arbitration of construction-related disputes; and providing general business advice to construction industry clients.

Mr. James received his Doctor of Jurisprudence from the Boston University School of Law, and Bachelor of Arts (cum laude) from Providence College.

Colin A. Johns is President of Hemming Morse Inc., and a Director in the Litigation and Forensic Consulting Services Group in the San Francisco office of Hemming Morse, Inc. He has more than 30 years of experience in the field of public accounting in the United States and the United Kingdom. He has also worked as an auditor, consultant, and expert witness. Mr. Johns has handled a diverse range of litigation issues, including construction claims, accountants' liability, and contractual disputes, and has testified in state and federal courts. A member of the American Institute of Certified Public Accountants, he is one of the authors of the AICPA's Practice Aid 06-4 Calculating Lost Profits and is Certified in Financial Forensics by the AICPA. He is also a former Chair of the California Society of Certified

Public Accountants Litigation Sections, Economic Damages Section, which provides education and a discussion forum for more than 200 CalCPA members throughout the state, and is a member of the Litigation Sections Steering Committee. Mr. Johns is also a member of the Association of Certified Fraud Examiners and the Institute of Chartered Accountants of Scotland. He holds a Bachelor of Arts in Economics, with an emphasis in Accounting and Business Finance, from the University of Manchester, England.

Brandi N. Kleinman is a Principal with the Veritas Advisory Group, Inc. She provides financial, accounting, and economic damage evaluations involving complex commercial disputes.

Ms. Kleinman has assisted clients and counsel in matters pertaining to breach of contract, infringement of intellectual property rights, business interruption, bankruptcy, securities fraud, breach of fiduciary duty, insurance disputes, white-collar fraud investigations, construction claims, and various matters related to the valuation of businesses and disputes. She has significant experience in the banking, construction, energy, manufacturing, and real estate industries, among others.

Ms. Kleinman's construction claims experience includes cost analyses performed on behalf of owners, contractors, and subcontractors. She has consulted on a variety of projects including airports, power plants, stadiums, public works/infrastructure, and commercial and residential buildings.

Ms. Kleinman earned her Bachelor of Business Administration degree in Finance from the University of Texas at Austin and her Master of Science in Accounting and Information Management degree from the University of Texas at Dallas. Ms. Kleinman is a Certified Public Accountant, licensed in the state of Texas, and is a member of the American Institute of Certified Public Accountants.

Steven J. Kmieciak is a Partner in the Washington, D.C., office of Seyfarth Shaw LLP. He regularly engages in counseling on commercial and government construction contract matters and specializes in the avoidance and resolution of disputes. He has represented contractors, subcontractors, and owners on many types of projects including industrial facilities, dredging, above-and below-ground heavy rail mass transit systems, bridges, buildings, airport facilities, container seaports and wharves, and civil works. He also has significant experience resolving claims arising from U.S. government contracts other than construction. He has had significant experience on a variety of international projects. Mr. Kmieciak has developed expertise in contract drafting and interpretation, contract administration, ADR, and litigation.

Mr. Kmieciak received a Doctor of Jurisprudence from the University of Maryland School of Law in 1979, and a Bachelor of Arts from the University of Notre Dame in 1975.

ABOUT THE AUTHORS

Matthew R. Krafft is a senior managing director in the FTI Forensic and Litigation Consulting practice and is based in Bethesda. He has provided consulting services and expert testimony in a variety of situations, including construction and government contract claims, partnership disputes, employee noncompete disputes, bankruptcy examinations, Qui Tam (False Claim) Actions, lost profit disputes, and fraud investigations. He has testified in Federal District Court, bankruptcy court, and state courts as well as dispute resolution boards and mediation proceedings.

Mr. Krafft has extensive experience in government-contract-related matters. He regularly provides consulting services in areas such as indirect cost rate determinations, cost allowability reviews, assistance with DCAA audits, and preparation of claims and equitable adjustments in accordance with the Federal Acquisition Regulation.

Mr. Krafft has a U.S. Department of Justice security clearance as an examiner or trustee and has served as a court-appointed Chapter 11 examiner.

He received a Bachelor of Science degree (cum laude) from Washington & Lee University and a Master of Business Administration degree with a concentration in managerial accounting from The George Washington University.

Daniel Kwon is a Senior Associate with Exponent in its Construction Consulting Practice. Mr. Kwon specializes in preparing claims related to all types of construction impacts and delays, and has prepared cost and schedule analyses and narrative reports for many different types of construction projects. He has analyzed cost information; created and analyzed as-built schedules; developed graphs, charts, and other visual aids for presentation purposes; and served as an on-site scheduler for a general contractor, providing cost and scheduling services for active construction projects. Prior to joining Exponent, Mr. Kwon was a project engineer at a major general contractor, where his projects included construction of a presidential library and a landmark public high school.

Mr. Kwon received a Master of Science degree in Civil and Environmental Engineering from the University of California, Los Angeles, and a Bachelor of Science degree in Civil and Environmental Engineering from Stanford University.

Thomas R. Lynch is an Associate in the Washington, D.C., office and practices primarily with the Construction & Procurement Practice Group. He represents general contractors, subcontractors, and sureties on private and public construction projects, and his experience includes matters in both state and federal courts.

Mr. Lynch received a Doctor of Jurisprudence from Georgetown University Law Center in 2006, and a Bachelor of Arts from the University of Puget Sound in 2001.

Alan F. Nagorzanski is a Vice President with the Veritas Advisory Group, Inc. and a founding member of the firm. He has over 25 years of consulting experience in matters involving financial, accounting, economic, construction, scheduling, and statistical issues.

Mr. Nagorzanski has consulted with counsel and clients on matters such as securities fraud, investigative accounting, accounting malpractice, business valuation, lender liability, business interruption, lost profits, bankruptcy, intellectual property, breach of contract, construction claims, surety bond claims, and fraud investigations. He has substantial experience in developing, analyzing, and defending against complex financial, accounting, economic, and statistical models in business litigation matters.

Mr. Nagorzanski has significant experience in assisting in the preparation of and defending against contractor claims, analyzing cost overruns, calculating loss of efficiency, and quantifying impacts and schedule delays in the construction of projects such as airport terminals, light rail projects, central libraries, power plant modifications, convention centers, performance halls, stadiums, high-rise office buildings, hotels, and sports arenas.

Mr. Nagorzanski received his Bachelor of Science degree in Mechanical Engineering from the University of Notre Dame and his Master of Business Administration with a specialization in finance from the University of Chicago. He is a licensed Professional Engineer in the state of Texas, a member of the Institute of Management Accountants, and a Certified Management Accountant.

John W. Ralls is a Partner in the San Francisco office of Howrey LLP. Mr. Ralls specializes in construction claims, disputes, and counseling. He represents contractors, owners, design professionals, suppliers, and construction managers in trials, arbitrations, mediations, and negotiations. Mr. Ralls also provides contract, dispute, and licensing advice before, during, and after construction projects. He has provided these services on a variety of projects, including convention centers, wind energy projects, hospitals, and industrial facilities.

Mr. Ralls has been listed in *Who's Who Legal, California Who's Who of Business Lawyers* (2007–Construction) and as a Northern California Super Lawyer by *San Francisco Law & Politics Magazine* (2005–2006, 2008–2009—Construction Law). He is the Editor (2008–present) and was the Associate Editor (2004–2008) of *Construction Lawyer*, the quarterly journal of the ABA Forum on the Construction Industry.

Mr. Ralls received his J.D. from University of California, Berkeley, School of Law (Boalt Hall) in 1990, and his undergraduate degree from the University of California—Berkeley (A.B.) in 1987.

Stephen B. Shapiro is a partner in the Washington, D.C., office of Holland & Knight LLP. Mr. Shapiro is a Board Member of the Associated General Contractors of Metropolitan Washington, D.C., and serves on the NAVFAC, Corps of Engineers, Federal Acquisition Regulation, and Project Delivery Committees of the Associated General Contractors of America. He is also a member of the American Bar Association's Public Law Section and Forum on the Construction

Industry. Mr. Shapiro received his B.A. from the University of Maryland and his J.D. degree from The George Washington University Law School. He has been in the private practice of law specializing in construction and government contracts law for more than 22 years. Mr. Shapiro represents public contractors and government entities in public contract matters throughout the United States.

Anita M. Sheckells, CPA, CIFP, a Shareholder with KatzAbosch, joined the firm in 1984. She currently serves as Co-Chair of the firm's Audit and Accounting Services Group and is past-Chair of the firm's Construction and Real Estate Services Group. As past-Chair of the Maryland Association of Certified Public Accountants' Construction Accounting Committee, she organized two of the annual construction conferences. Ms. Sheckells holds the prestigious distinction of Certified Construction Industry Financial Professional, a certification held by less than 15 professionals in Maryland and less than 700 professionals in the United States.

Ms. Sheckells specializes in services to the construction and real estate industries including special accounting and tax issues, bonding and banking issues, business advisory services, tax planning, and accounting and tax services for closely held businesses.

As a current board member and past President, she is very active with the Construction Financial Management Association. In addition, she is a member of the Associated Builders and Contractors, Women in ABC Committee, which promotes careers in construction and hosts various charitable events.

Ms. Sheckells received a Bachelor of Science, Business Administration degree with a Concentration in Accounting from the University of Baltimore.

Rodney W. Sowards is a Vice President in the Dallas office of Veritas Advisory Group, Inc. and a founding member of the firm. His litigation-support practice focuses primarily on financial, accounting, and economic damage evaluations of complex commercial litigation disputes.

Mr. Sowards has over 20 years of experience in consulting with clients on a variety of managerial and dispute resolution matters. Over the course of his career, He has performed and supervised hundreds of investigations of businesses in a variety of industries including banking, construction, energy, manufacturing, and real estate. He has served as the court-appointed Claims Administrator and Distribution Agent for numerous securities fraud disputes and has worked for receivers, examiners, and other agents of the court. Mr. Sowards has also rendered expert testimony in state and federal courts as well as arbitration proceedings.

Mr. Sowards is a frequent guest lecturer at the University of Texas on accounting and financial topics to undergraduate and graduate students.

Mr. Sowards is a Certified Public Accountant, licensed in the state of Texas. He is also Certified in Financial Forensics. Mr. Sowards is a member of the American Institute of Certified Public Accountants and the Association of Certified Fraud Examiners. He is a graduate with high honors from the University of Texas at Austin with a Bachelor of Business Administration with an emphasis in finance.

Robert J. Symon is a Partner with Bradley Arant Boult Cummings and practices in the areas of construction and government contract law. Clients routinely seek out Mr. Symon's advice to assist in such matters as negotiating contract language, interpreting the Federal Acquisition Regulation prosecuting claims under the Contract Disputes Act, and ensuring export compliance under the International Traffic in Arms Regulations, to name just a few. He has litigated disputes throughout the country in state and federal courts involving a wide variety of complex construction claims. Mr. Symon has also enjoyed considerable success prosecuting and defending bid protests at the Government Accountability Office.

Mr. Symon received a Doctor of Jurisprudence from the University of Baltimore School of Law in 1992, and a Bachelor of Arts from Washington & Jefferson College in 1988.

Douglas A. Trueheart is a Senior Vice President with CapAnalysis, an affiliate of Howrey. Mr. Trueheart has over 35 years of experience in providing accounting and tax consulting services. Working closely with the Corporate and Transactional practice of Howrey, he provides consulting services to clients relating to the structuring of corporate transactions including mergers, acquisitions, and the structure and restructure of new and existing business ventures. He also provides tax controversy services, including representing clients before the Internal Revenue Service at both the examination and appellate level and has assisted with tax cases argued before the U.S. Tax Court and the U.S. Court of Claims. Working closely with the Securities Litigation, Government Enforcement & White Collar Defense practice of Howrey, Mr. Trueheart provides consulting services to clients with respect to the proper accounting and tax treatment for transactions as well as the professional responsibilities of accounting and tax advisors. He has played an active role in internal investigations for corporations under examination by the SEC in connection with the accounting treatment of transactions and for an international accounting firm in connection with tax services rendered to a public company.

Mr. Trueheart received a Bachelor of Science in Accounting from the University of Virginia in 1973. He is a Certified Public Accountant, Virginia.

Paul A. Varela is a Senior Partner at Watt, Tieder, Hoffar & Fitzgerald. He counsels clients in contract planning, administration, and dispute resolution matters nationwide in the engineering and construction industry. His broad range of legal experience includes roads, bridges, high rise buildings, nuclear and conventional power, environmental remediation, biomedical centers, energy and chemical projects, airports, professional sports stadiums, telecom, pharmaceutical, mass transit, and other heavy construction projects, as well as embassies and all types of general building design and construction. Mr. Varela has extensive claims negotiation and prosecution experience with private as well as state and federal government entities, and his expertise includes design-build, P3, government contracts, and suretyship. He has represented clients across the country in jury and bench trials, mediations, arbitrations, boards of contract appeals, and state and federal court for both domestic and international disputes.

Mr. Varela's honors include *Chambers USA* list of Top Construction Lawyers—2005, 2006, 2007, 2008, 2009; *Best Lawyers in America*, Construction Law category—2009, 2010; *Washington D.C.'s Best Lawyers*—2009, 2010; and Virginia's Best Lawyers—2010.

Mr. Varela received a Doctor of Jurisprudence from the College of William & Mary in 1989, where he was a member of the *William & Mary Law Review*, and a Bachelor of Arts from the University of Virginia in 1985.

Daniel P. Wierzba is an Associate in the Government Contracts Practice Group of Seyfarth Shaw LLP. His practice focuses on bid protests, white-collar defense, construction law, and commercial litigation. Before joining Seyfarth Shaw, Mr. Wierzba practiced in a construction law/government contracts boutique firm in McLean, Virginia. Among his notable cases is a federal court trial where a subcontractor client was awarded nearly seven figures in damages for its pass-through contract and Spearin claims against a government entity. Mr. Wierzba is a contributing author to the *Construction Claims Advisor*, and was co-author of an article that was presented at the 2008 ABA Forum on the Construction Industry/TIPS Fidelity & Surety Law Committee's Joint Midwinter Meeting in New York.

Mr. Wierzba received a Doctor of Jurisprudence from Georgetown University Law Center in 2005, and a Bachelor of Arts from the University of Arizona in 2000.

Claudia R. Wolter, CPA, a Shareholder with KatzAbosch, joined the firm in 1988. She has played a major role in leading the firm into the twenty-first century with cutting-edge initiatives, including the transition to and managing of a paperless environment. She serves as co-chair of the firm's Accounting and Auditing Committee and is also a member of the Construction and Real Estate Services Group.

Ms. Wolter provides a full range of accounting, tax, and consulting services for clients, including auditing and accounting, construction and real estate planning, tax planning, job cost systems evaluation, business succession planning, software consultation, and obtaining bonding and financing.

Ms. Wolter received a Bachelor of Science in Accounting (magna cum laude) from Towson State University.

David B. Wonderlick is an Associate with Watt, Tieder, Hoffar & Fitzgerald, L.L.P. Mr. Wonderlick focuses his practice on construction litigation and government contracts. He has represented contractors, subcontractors, suppliers, owners, developers, sureties, and public agencies on projects involving the construction of conventional and nuclear power plants, wastewater treatment facilities, highways and bridges, professional sports stadiums, mass transit systems, hotels, military facilities, and housing complexes. Mr. Wonderlick also has experience in drafting contracts for the procurement of construction, architectural, and engineering services.

Mr. Wonderlick received a Doctor of Jurisprudence from the College of William & Mary in 2004, where he was the Managing Editor of the *William & Mary Law Review* and a Graduate Research Fellow. He received a Bachelor of Arts (summa cum laude) from Susquehanna University in 2001.

Wiley R. Wright is a Senior Managing Director in the FTI Forensic and Litigation Consulting practice. Mr. Wright's work includes preparation and evaluation of claims for damages; fraud and false claims investigations; assessing the adequacy of accounting systems and indirect cost rate methodologies of governmental agencies; determinations of ability to pay; and expert testimony on specific damage and cost accounting issues. In addition to his litigation and expert witness services, Mr. Wright has many years of experience consulting on construction and government contract matters. He has testified as an expert witness before numerous state and federal courts, Boards of Contract Appeals, and in domestic and international arbitration, and has participated in mediations and settlement negotiations.

Mr. Wright co-authored "Professional Standards Applicable to Litigation Support," published in the Maryland Society of Certified Public Accountants' *CPA Statement*, and has given presentations on construction damage issues before a variety of professional groups. Mr. Wright is a CPA and is a graduate of George Mason University.

INTRODUCTION

PATRICK A. MCGEEHIN

Construction attorneys frequently struggle with the financial, accounting, and pricing issues that arise in representing a contractor, owner, or other construction project participant. A common refrain heard from attorneys is "I went to law school because I didn't like math," or its equivalent. It is not surprising that many lawyers do not get excited by accounting and cost issues—preferring to focus on more interesting legal issues and the key facts that will establish entitlement. It is all too true as well that accounting and pricing texts are often written in a highly technical form geared to accountants, making it difficult for lawyers to get their arms around specific aspects of construction accounting even when the spirit is willing.

But in both construction contracting and construction disputes, financial and accounting issues, such as those involving costs, pricing, and overhead allocations, play a major role. Proving entitlement does no good for the client if the damages claimed are unsupported by the cost records and, many times, detailed and well-grounded expert testimony from an accounting professional. Additionally, detailed cost-allowability issues often need to be addressed in negotiating contracts in order to avoid disputes later. An active construction lawyer, like it or not, will have many occasions to put to good use a clear understanding of construction industry accounting and financial reports and practices.

For these reasons, we set out to put together a book that would be straightforward enough to assist even the most "numbers-challenged" construction law practitioner, written more in lawyer's language than the terse and sometimes impenetrable language of accounting, yet offering enough detail and specificity to provide a useful reference on the more detailed and complicated financial topics that a construction lawyer may be called upon to understand and deal with. Under the general umbrella of Construction Accounting, we have addressed a wide range of topics: from Generally Accepted Accounting Principles (GAAP) and Generally Accepted Auditing Standards (GAAS) to understanding a contractor's financial statements; from what a surety looks for in a contractor's finances to the peculiar cost and pricing rules applicable to government contracts; from claim pricing issues, to audits, to detecting financial fraud situations; as well as discovery and trial issues relating to accounting and damages experts.

An early decision in planning the book was our concept for selecting chapter authors: We paired experienced accountants who have a construction-industry perspective with construction lawyers interested in and experienced with cost-accounting issues. This was done to help ensure that the chapters would address the concerns of and actual problems faced by construction lawyers, and be written in a manner more familiar to lawyers. Hopefully, the resulting book will serve a variety of purposes, chief among them to provide lawyers with an in-depth resource on the construction accounting and pricing issues that are relevant to the construction industry.

As with all Forum on the Construction Industry publications, there were many people who committed vast amounts of their time and energy to making this book a reality. The original idea for the book came from Adrian Bastianelli, who was at the time the Publications Committee chair, and currently is serving as Chair of the Forum. My co-editors, Ed Benes, Pat Greene, and Cary Wright, all worked hard to wrestle the chapters to the finish line, one by one. The authors and other contributors, too numerous to mention individually here, responded cheerfully to short deadlines, and to the editors' gentle nudges and requests for supplementation or rewrites. The ABA Publications staff, particularly Sarah Forbes Orwig and Amelia Stone, as well as Amy Phillips, provided helpful advice and guidance throughout. My thanks go out to you all. You have a book that you can be proud of as a result, one that should have a useful place on many a bookshelf.

CHAPTER 1

Basic Financial and Accounting Concepts

DENNIS L. ALLEN
RICHARD E. GAVIN

Accounting Standards

The financial statements of a business entity are prepared and governed by the guidance and application of generally accepted accounting principles (GAAP). GAAP is the term used to refer to a standard framework of guidelines for financial accounting. GAAP includes the standards, conventions, and rules accountants follow in recording and summarizing transactions and in preparing financial statements. Even within GAAP, there can be some different presentations of financial data, since financial statements reflect information for different types of companies; however, all financial statements must adhere to certain overall concepts and principles. Some GAAP requirements are formal and specific, while others are guidance, based more in tradition or history, or more general concepts and principles. In all cases, the goal is to make financial statements usable to the third-party reader. Such standards are important to the efficient functioning of the economy, as investors, creditors, auditors, and others rely on credible, transparent, and comparable financial information as part of their various evaluations of the financial data presented by a business entity.

Although there are a number of organizations and publications that issue or contain guidelines, there is no single source or manual one can refer to when determining GAAP. As can be seen below, GAAP stems from numerous sources, depending on the individual issue or application.

Financial Accounting Standards Board

Since 1973, the Financial Accounting Standards Board (FASB) has been the designated organization in the private sector for establishing standards for financial accounting. Those standards govern the preparation of financial statements. They are officially recognized as authoritative by the Securities and Exchange Commission (SEC) (Financial Reporting Release No. 1, Section 101, and reaffirmed in its April 2003 Policy Statement) and the American Institute of Certified Public Accountants (AICPA) (Rule 203, Rules of Professional Conduct, as amended May 1973 and May 1979).

The mission of the FASB is to establish and improve standards of financial accounting and reporting for the guidance and education of the public, including issuers, auditors, and users of financial information. The FASB develops broad accounting concepts as well as standards for financial reporting. It also provides guidance on implementation of standards.

On June 30, 2009, the FASB issued FASB Statement No. 168, The FASB Accounting Standards Codification and the Hierarchy of Generally Accepted Accounting Principles—a replacement of FASB Statement No. 162. On the effective date of this standard, the FASB Accounting Standards Codification (ASC) became the source of authoritative U.S. accounting and reporting standards for nongovernmental entities, in addition to guidance issued by the SEC. The ASC significantly changes the way financial statement preparers, auditors, and academics perform accounting research, and are effective for financial statements issued for interim and annual periods ending after September 15, 2009.

This new standard flattens the GAAP hierarchy to two levels: one that is authoritative (what is in the FASB ASC) and one that is nonauthoritative (items not found in the FASB ASC). Exceptions to this two-level hierarchy include all rules and interpretive releases of the SEC under the authority of federal securities laws, which are sources of authoritative GAAP for SEC registrants, but may not be included in the FASB ASC.

The FASB ASC is a major restructuring of accounting and reporting standards designed to simplify user access to all authoritative GAAP by providing the authoritative literature in a topically organized structure. The FASB ASC disassembles and reassembles thousands of nongovernmental accounting pronouncements to organize them under approximately 90 topics and include all accounting standards issued by a standard letter. FASB ASC also includes relevant portions of authoritative content issued by the SEC, as well as selected SEC staff interpretations and administrative guidance issued by the SEC. However, as mentioned, FASB ASC is not the official source of SEC guidance and does not contain the entire universe of SEC rules, regulations, interpretive releases, and staff guidance. Moreover, the FASB ASC does not include governmental accounting standards, and is not intended to change GAAP or any requirements of the SEC.

In addition to the specific guidance in the various FASB promulgations, financial statements are subject to overall guidance and principles, known as the "Fundamental Principles":

- *Realization.* Under this basic principle, economic events are accounted for only when the business has been a party to one side of a bona fide transaction. For example, if a parcel of land has appreciated in value, the gain cannot be recognized until the land has been sold. *See* FASB Statement of Financial Accounting Concepts (SFAC) No. 5.

- *Conservatism.* This principle directs that when a business is exposed to uncertainties and risks that are material, measurement and disclosure should be approached with a high degree of caution and in a prudent manner, until evidence develops that there is a significant reduction or elimination of the uncertainty. See FASB SFAC No. 2.
- *Revenue recognition.* This principle states that revenue is recognized when everything that is necessary to earn the revenue has been completed. See FASB SFAC No. 5.
- *Matching.* This requires that the revenues of any accounting period be matched with the expenses of that same period that were incurred to generate the revenues. See FASB SFAC No. 6.
- *Separate entity assumption.* This principle provides that the business is an entity that is separate and distinct from its owners. Accordingly, the finances of the firm are not to be commingled with the finances of the owners. See FASB SFAC No. 6.
- *Full disclosure.* This mandates that all of the information about the business entity that is needed by the users of its financial statements be disclosed in understandable form.
- *Consistency.* This requires that the accounting procedures applied during a given accounting period be the same procedures that were applied in previous periods, unless any changes are within generally accepted accounting principles and are properly disclosed to the users. See FASB SFAC No. 2.
- *Going concern.* The principle of "going concern" assumes that an entity will continue to operate in the near future, which is generally understood to mean more than the next 12 months, so long as it generates or obtains sufficient resources to operate.

American Institute of Certified Public Accountants

The American Institute of Certified Public Accountants (AICPA) is the national, professional organization for all certified public accountants in the United States. Its stated mission is to provide its members with the resources, information, and leadership that enable them to provide valuable services in the highest professional manner to benefit the public, as well as their employers and clients. Although individual CPAs are licensed by the individual states, the governing body for CPA exams and standards is the AICPA. Although each state can have its own requirements for licensing, the AICPA's Uniform CPA Exam is a nationally standard test. The AICPA sets professional standards for CPAs and monitors and enforces those standards.

Part of the AICPA is its Accounting Standards Team. The objectives of the Accounting Standards Team are

- To develop industry-specific guidance regarding financial accounting and reporting matters. As an example, there is specific guidance developed for GAAP application in the construction industry, set forth in an Industry Guide published by the AICPA.

- To provide guidance to members of the AICPA on financial accounting or reporting issues not otherwise covered in authoritative literature.
- To influence the form and content of pronouncements of the FASB, the Governmental Accounting Standards Board (GASB), International Accounting Standards Board (IASB), and other bodies that have authority over financial accounting or reporting standards.

Standards Other than GAAP

There are some situations where the normal application of GAAP does not apply. The alternative standards that may apply in such situations are referred to as Other Comprehensive Bases of Accounting (OCBOA). OCBOA includes income-tax basis and the cash basis of accounting that is commonly used for smaller or less sophisticated entities. OCBOA usually refers to

- A statutory basis of accounting (for example, a basis of accounting that insurance companies are required to use under the rules of a state insurance commission);
- Income-tax-basis financial statements;
- Cash-basis and modified-cash-basis financial statements; and
- Financial statements prepared using definitive criteria having substantial support in accounting literature that the preparer applies to all material items appearing in the statements (such as the price-level basis of accounting).

In situations where GAAP-basis financial statements are not necessary because of the lack of any loan covenants, regulatory requirements, or similar circumstances applicable to the entity preparing the financial statements, an OCBOA-based statement may be used. In the construction industry, the nature of construction projects and the complexities surrounding issues such as estimates to complete and matching of revenue make the use of OCBOA virtually nonexistent, except perhaps for the smallest of contractors.

Auditing Standards

AICPA members who perform auditing and other related professional services are required to comply with Statements on Auditing Standards (SASs) promulgated by the AICPA Auditing Standards Board (ASB). These standards constitute what are known as generally accepted auditing standards (GAAS). In the past, the ASB's auditing standards have applied to audits of *all* entities. As a result of the Sarbanes-Oxley Act of 2002, however, auditing and related professional practice standards to be used in the performance of and reporting on audits of the financial statements of public companies are now established by the Public Company Accounting Oversight Board (PCAOB). Audits of nonpublic companies remain governed by GAAS as issued by the ASB.

Public accounting firms registered with the PCAOB are required to adhere to all PCAOB standards in the audits of "issuers," a term defined by the Sarbanes-Oxley Act, and other entities when prescribed by the rules of the SEC (collectively referred to here as "issuers"). Those entities not subject to the Sarbanes-Oxley Act or the rules of the SEC ("nonissuers") must conduct their preparation and issuance of audit reports in accordance with standards promulgated by the ASB.

Generally Accepted Auditing Standards

GAAS consists of 10 auditing standards: three general standards, three standards for field work, and four standards of reporting, along with interpretations. They were developed by the AICPA in 1947 and have undergone minor changes since then.

General Standards

1. The auditor must have adequate technical training and proficiency to perform the audit.
2. The auditor must maintain independence in mental attitude in all matters related to the audit.
3. The auditor must use due professional care during the performance of the audit and the preparation of the report.

Standards of Field Work

1. The auditor must adequately plan the work and must properly supervise any assistants.
2. The auditor must obtain a sufficient understanding of the entity and its environment, including its internal controls, to assess the risk of material misstatement of the financial statements whether due to error or fraud, and to design the nature, timing, and extent of further audit procedures.
3. The auditor must obtain sufficient appropriate audit evidence by performing audit procedures to afford a reasonable basis for an opinion regarding the financial statements under audit.

Standards of Reporting

1. The auditor must state in the auditor's report whether the financial statements are in accordance with GAAP.
2. The auditor must identify in the auditor's report those circumstances in which such principles have not been consistently observed in the current period in relation to the preceding period.
3. When the auditor determines that informative disclosures are not reasonably adequate, the auditor must so state in the auditor's report.

4. The auditor must either express an opinion regarding the financial statements, taken as a whole, or state that such an opinion cannot be expressed in the auditor's report. When the auditor cannot express an overall opinion, the auditor should state the reasons therefore in the auditor's report. In all cases where the auditor's name is associated with the financial statements, the auditor should clearly indicate the character of the auditor's work, if any, and the degree of responsibility the auditor is taking in the auditor's report.

Types of Audits

The use of the term "audit" is often used by non-accounting professionals to refer generally to a number of different services performed by accountants and expectations on the part of their clients. To the accounting profession, however, the term "audit" has a much more precise definition. In fact, there are a number of different types of audits, and the following is a description of the services provided and intended uses of such different types of audits.

Financial Statement Audit

A *financial audit*, or more accurately, an *audit of financial statements*, is the application of testing and other procedures relating to the financial statements of a company or other legal entity (including governments), resulting in the publication of an independent opinion on whether or not those financial statements present fairly, in all material respects, the financial position and the results of operations and cash flow of a company. Financial statement audits are typically performed by independent CPA firms, due to the specialized financial reporting knowledge required to perform these audits. The financial audit is one of many assurance or attestation functions provided by accounting firms, whereby the firm provides an independent opinion based on published information. Only by having an audit performed by an independent firm of certified public accountants can one be assured that the entity performing the audit is held accountable to all of the rules and regulations described above. Many organizations separately employ or engage internal auditors, who do not attest to financial reports but focus mainly on the internal controls of the organization. External auditors may choose to place limited reliance on the work of internal auditors.

The financial statement audit is designed to reduce the possibility of a material misstatement. A misstatement is defined as false or missing information, whether caused by fraud (including deliberate misstatement) or error. "Material" is very broadly defined as something large enough or important enough to cause third parties (e.g., stockholders, banks, sureties) to alter their decisions. The assessment of what is material is a matter of professional judgment. Auditors can obtain guidance regarding the conduct of financial statement audits from Auditing Standards No. 107, Audit Risk and Materiality in Conducting an Audit.

Fraud Audit

A fraud audit is a customized set of procedures and tests specifically designed to investigate the suspicion of fraudulent activity. Unlike a financial statement audit, which is designed to assure readers that the financial statements presented are free of material misstatements, a fraud audit is designed to uncover specific fraudulent activity and to identify the fraudster or perpetrator of the fraud. Fraud audits are commonly performed by CPAs specializing in forensic accounting.

Internal Audit

A company that wishes to measure compliance with its internal policies and procedures may perform an internal audit. Internal auditors are not responsible for the execution of company activities; instead, they advise management and the board of directors (or similar oversight body) as to how to better execute their responsibilities. In view of their broad scope of involvement in reviewing the business activities of the company, internal auditors often have a variety of higher educational and professional backgrounds. Internal auditors sometimes report directly to the audit committee of the company's board of directors.

Internal auditing activity is primarily directed at evaluating and improving the company's internal controls. An internal control is broadly defined as a process, put into effect by an entity's board of directors, management, and other personnel, that is designed to provide reasonable assurance regarding the achievement of objectives in the following internal control categories:

- Effectiveness and efficiency of operations
- Reliability of financial reporting
- Compliance with laws and regulations

Management is responsible for the internal controls of the entity. Managers establish policies and processes to help the organization achieve specific objectives in each of these categories. Internal auditors then perform audits to (1) evaluate whether those policies and processes are designed and operating effectively, and (2) provide recommendations for improvement.

Based on a risk assessment of the organization, a combination of the internal auditors, management, and oversight boards generally determines where to focus internal auditing efforts. Internal auditing activity is generally conducted as one or more discrete projects.

Government Audit

The generally accepted government auditing standards (GAGAS), commonly referred to as the "Yellow Book," are produced in the United States by the Government Accountability Office (GAO).

The GAGAS apply to both financial and performance audits of government agencies. Five general standards are included:

- Independence
- Due Care
- Continuing Professional Education
- Supervision
- Quality Control

The Yellow Book includes standards to guide all audits of governmental units, without regard to the level of the unit. The standards are considered broad statements of auditors' responsibilities. The introduction to the Yellow Book states its purpose as providing "standards for audits of government organizations, programs, activities, and functions, and of government assistance received by contractors, nonprofit organizations, and other nongovernment organizations."

Government audits are often a combination of financial and performance audits. For example, auditors conduct audits of government contracts and grants with private-sector organizations, as well as of government and not-for-profit organizations where both financial and performance objectives must be audited. Performance audit objectives vary widely and include assessments of program effectiveness, economy efficiency, internal controls, compliance, and prospective analysis.

The GAGAS are classified as general, field, or reporting standards. The GAGAS incorporate the generally accepted auditing standards as promulgated by the Auditing Standards Board of the AICPA. However, there are some additional standards that relate to the accountability of government units for compliance with laws and regulations. There are also more extensive reporting requirements related to such accountability.

Contract or Project Audit

"Project audit" is a common term in the construction industry but has no specific meaning in the accounting profession. In a general sense it refers to a review of the accumulated costs on a given construction project. The services generally included are a review of the specific costs for labor, materials, equipment, and subcontractors on the project as measured against a given standard such as the contract, sales tax laws, Federal Acquisition Regulations (FAR), a joint venture agreement, or similar standard. When initiating a project audit, careful consideration should be given to the requested services, the standards to be applied, and the use of the information once complete.

Operational Audit

An operational audit is an evaluation made of management's performance and its conformity with policies, procedures, and budgets. The organization and its operations are analyzed, including the structure, controls, procedures, and processes. The objective is to assess the effectiveness and efficiency of a division, activity, or operation of the entity in meeting company goals. Recommendations to improve performance are also made. The primary user of operational audits is the firm's management. Operational audits can be performed by either external auditors or internal auditors. For each review, management receives a report that indicates how well the activities are performed and procedures are followed, suggests improvements, and provides conclusions from the work performed.

Basic Financial Statements

The term "financial statements" has varied meanings depending upon the circumstances of their creation and the level of information to be provided. The two most basic financial statements are the *income statement* and *balance sheet*. But a full set of financial statements in the construction industry would commonly include an income statement, balance sheet, cash flow statement, notes to the financial statements, and the auditors' opinion. Commonly, although they are not required, construction industry financial statements also include supplementary statements, which typically include a detailed statement of earnings by contract and a detail of general and administrative costs. As such, a request for "financial statements" needs to specify the individual statements requested. It is the review of these various statements and their comparison with similar statements for prior years that enables a knowledgeable reader to gain insight into the successes and challenges of a given construction-business entity.

It should be noted further that there are occasionally different titles used for these basic components of financial statements and certain variations in the data presented. This can be entirely acceptable so long as they are consistent from one year to the next. The following discussion uses the most common titles, and the concepts in any event remain similar from one company to the next.

Balance Sheet

The balance sheet is a statement of what the company (or other business entity) owns (its assets) and owes (its liabilities), and the excess or deficit in comparing those two values (the *owners' equity* or the *company's net worth*). Unlike other financial statements that include transactions over a period of time, the balance sheet indicates amounts at a specific point in time. Typical captions and amounts shown on the balance sheet are:

- *Current Assets* includes items such as cash and cash equivalents, short-term investments, and current accounts receivable inventory that are considered cash or readily converted to cash and so likely provide immediate purchasing power.

- *Fixed Assets* includes items such as land, buildings, and equipment that are owned by the company for its use in the operations of the business.
- *Current Liabilities* includes items such as accounts payable and accrued payroll that will consume cash in the immediate future.[1]
- *Long-Term Liabilities* includes items such as notes payable and other noncurrent payables that are obligations of the company, but are not expected to be paid within one year.
- *Owner's or Shareholders' Equity* includes items such as common stock and retained (i.e., cumulative) earnings of the company. This section of the balance sheet represents the total amount that has been invested in the company by its owners—both directly and through its earnings history.[2]

Two special accounts that are important in understanding a construction company's balance sheet are *Billings in Excess of Cost and Estimated Revenues* and *Costs and Estimated Earnings in Excess of Billings*. These accounts reflect how much a company has billed in its contracts ahead of its costs incurred (a liability, based on the premise that this excess will need to be eliminated as each contract progresses toward completion), or how much the company has incurred in costs ahead of its actual contract billings (an asset, based on the premise that billings on each contract will eventually catch up to costs incurred), respectively. These two accounts are addressed in more detail in Chapter 2.

Figure 1 is a sample balance sheet for a healthy small construction company, Example Construction.

Figure 1
Balance Sheet for Example Construction, Inc.

Example Construction, Inc.

Balance Sheets
December 31, 20X1 and 20X0

Assets	20X1	20X0
Current Assets		
Cash and cash equivalents	$ 492,700	$ 435,300
Accounts receivable (notes 1 and 3)	1,393,000	1,223,600
Costs and estimated earnings in excess of billings on uncompleted contracts (note 4)	732,600	741,800
Prepaid expenses	89,900	53,900
Total Current Assets	2,708,200	2,454,600
Fixed Assets, net	290,000	269,800
Total Assets	$ 2,418,200	$ 2,184,800

Liabilities and Shareholders' Equity	20X1	20X0
Current Liabilities		
Accounts payable .... $	904,900	$ 821,200
Accrued salaries and wages........................	138,300	155,100
Accrued and other liabilities	169,400	91,750
Billings in excess of costs and estimated earnings on		
uncompleted contracts (note 4).....................	34,500	43,700
Total Current Liabilities.........................	1,247,100	1,111,750
Long-term debt, less current maturities (note 6)	245,000	241,000
Total Liabilities.....................................	1,492,100	1,352,750
Shareholder's Equity		
Common Stock—$10 par value, 50,000 authorized shares,		
23,500 shares issued and outstanding shares............. $	235,000	$ 235,000
Additional paid-in capital.........................	65,000	65,000
Retained earnings	627,000	532,050
Total Shareholders' Equity........................... $	927,000	$ 832,050
Total Liabilities and Shareholders' Equity .... $	2,419,100	$ 2,184,800

Income Statement

The income statement is a report for a given accounting period (usually a fiscal year) that indicates the revenue earned by the business entity, the expenses incurred for that same period, and the resulting net income available to be distributed or retained by the company as appropriate. The income statement is generally presented in three main sections, the titles of which can vary somewhat from one company to another:

- *Revenue from Operations* represents the gross receipts of the company before any deductions for expenses. For a construction contractor, this amount is generally the amount of contract billings during the year, after adjustments for billing ahead or behind the actual progress on the firm's various contracts that are in progress as of the end of the accounting period. The percentage-of-completion analysis for individual contracts can be complicated, as is discussed further in Chapter 3.
- *Cost of Operations* represents the direct cost of producing the Revenue from Operations. In the construction industry, this cost generally includes the labor, material, equipment, and subcontractor costs that are directly attributable to a specific contract and are incurred at the job site. Depending on the company, there are instances where companies will treat some expenses as direct project costs for financial reporting purposes (such as roving superintendents who are not assigned to any one project, certain equipment ownership administrative expenses, and particular insurance costs and related administrative expenses) that other

entities may treat as general and administrative costs (G&A) and report elsewhere. As mentioned previously, the key to this reporting is consistency, maintaining the same accounting treatment from year to year, and thereby making comparative analysis and ratio calculations meaningful.

- *G&A Expenses* represents the expenses that are incurred by the company but are not reasonably assignable to a specific contract. G&A expenses are usually incurred either at the home office or at regional, divisional, or branch offices. They typically include the salaries of the company executives, as well as those of the accounting, human resources, marketing/business development, and information technology functions. These expenses are normally considered fixed—at least over a short time-frame—in that they do not increase or decrease based on the firm's overall volume of contract revenues. Over time, they will increase, often in a step fashion, if the company's revenues increase.

Figure 2 shows a very basic income statement for Example Construction, which illustrates that the company is growing from year to year:

Figure 2
Income Statement for Example Construction, Inc.

Example Construction, Inc.
Statements of Income
Years ending December 31, 20X1 and 20X0

	20X1	20X0
Contract revenues earned . . . . $	9,487,000	$ 8,123,400
Cost of revenues earned	8,458,500	7,392,300
Gross Profit	1,028,500	731,100
General and administrative expenses	848,300	643,100
Interest expenses	26,500	23,000
Net Income . . . . $	153,700	$ 65,000

Statement of Cash Flows

The statement of cash flows is an insightful report that demonstrates the actual sources and uses of cash by the company over the accounting period being addressed in the financial statements, and thereby indicates its liquidity and ability to meet its cash needs. This statement is required to be included in audited financial statements. The cash flow statement has four common elements:

- *Cash flows from operating activities.* This is the net income for the accounting period, adjusted by any increases or decreases in accounts receivable and accounts payable that altered the company's cash position. For example, if a company has earned net income on an accrual basis, but increased its accounts receivable by the same amount (meaning its billings were not being paid as promptly as in the prior period), the increase in cash flows from operations from year to year would be zero, despite the increased net income. Depreciation charged as an expense on the income statement, reducing the company's net income to reflect the reduced value of its fixed assets as a year of their useful life had been consumed, appears on the cash flow statement as an increase in cash because this depreciation is a noncash expense.

- *Cash flows from investing activities.* This is the change in investment and fixed asset balances over the accounting period and how they affected the cash available to the company. For example, if a company sold equipment during the year, the proceeds would add to the cash available to the company, and those proceeds would show as a positive source of cash on this statement (but as a reduction in fixed assets on the balance sheet). Purchases of additional fixed assets, by contrast, appear as a negative since they consume available cash.
- *Cash flows from financing activities.* This section of the report shows the new borrowings and/or retirement of debt of the company, as well as the owner's equity transactions. A positive subtotal for these sections indicates that the company has increased its debt; a negative amount indicates it has, on balance, reduced or retired debt or paid dividends. The payment of a dividend reduces the owner's equity in the company and appears as a negative amount, since it consumes cash.
- *Net Increase (Decrease) in Cash.* This is the net amount of the operating, investing, and financial cash flows, and represents the actual increase or decrease in the company's cash balances for the period.

The Statement of Cash Flows for Example Construction is shown in Figure 3.

Figure 3
Statement of Cash Flows for Example Construction, Inc.

Example Construction, Inc.
Statement of Cash Flow
December 31, 20X1 and 20X0

	20X1	20X0
Cash flow from operating activities:		
Net Income	$ 153,700	$ 65,000
Adjustments to reconcile net income to net cash provided by operating activities		
Depreciation	54,800	50,300
Decrease in billings in excess of costs on uncompleted contracts	(9,200)	(16,300)

	20X1	20X0
(Increase) decrease in costs in excess of billings on uncompleted contracts	9,200	(49,100)
(Increase) decrease in prepaid expenses	(36,000)	16,500
Increase in accounts payable	83,700	24,600
(Decrease) increase in accrued salaries and wages	(153,100)	24,300
(Decrease) increase in accrued and other liabilities	77,650	(39,400)
Net cash provided by operating activities	$ 180,750	$ 75,900
Cash flows from investing activities:		
(Purchase) sale of property and equipment	(75,000)	153,915
Net cash used in investing activities	$ (75,000)	$ 153,915
Cash flows from financing activities:		
Proceeds from issuance of long-term debt	44,000	68,000
Principal payments on long-term debt	(33,600)	(15,500)
Cash dividends paid	(58,750)	(58,750)
Net cash used in financing activities	$ (48,350)	$ (6,250)
Net increase (decrease) in cash and cash equivalents	57,400	223,565
Cash and cash equivalents at beginning of year	435,300	211,735
Cash and cash equivalents at end of year	$ 492,700	$ 435,300

Notes to Financial Statements

In general, a set of explanatory Notes to Financial Statements is required for audited financial statements. The notes are used to further explain, add clarity, or describe the various activities and balances contained within the other portions of the company's financial statements. There is no limit to the number of notes, and they should be carefully studied, as the notes generally explain key areas that significantly assist in understanding the basic financial statements. The *AICPA Audit and Accounting Guide—Construction Contractors* recommends that notes covering significant accounting policies, revised estimates, backlog on existing contracts, and receivables should be included within the Notes to Financial Statements of a construction contractor. The following is a partial list of notes that are commonly seen in the audited financial statements of a construction contractor:

- *Company.* This note normally contains general information about the company, its form of organization, location, and so on.
- *Summary of Significant Accounting Policies.* This note should list the significant accounting concepts used in preparing the financial statements of the company, and detailed explanations of certain accounts. The following are topics that may be covered within this note:
    - *Basis of Presentation.* Should contain a statement concerning adherence to GAAP and any departures and rationale for the departures from GAAP.

- *Use of Estimates.* Should contain a statement acknowledging that certain balances contained in the financial statements are based on management estimates, and may significantly differ from actual results.
- *Method of Reporting Affiliated Entities.* This note should contain information about the method used to integrate the finances of affiliated entities (e.g., subsidiaries and other companies under some form of common ownership or control) into the financial statements.
- *Operating Cycle.* This note should disclose whether the timing of one operating cycle (i.e., the average length of the firm's construction contracts) is longer than one year; if so, the range of contract durations for the contracts undertaken by the company should be disclosed.
- *Revenue Recognition.* This note should disclose whether the percentage-of-completion or the completed-contract method is used for revenue recognition purposes (covered in Chapter 2), and the types of contracts performed by the company.
- *Method of Reporting Joint Venture Investments.* This note should contain information about the method used to integrate the finances of joint ventures (one-time agreements to jointly undertake a contract with an unrelated firm) into the financial statements.
- *Contract Costs/Deferred Costs.* Should contain information concerning the values of unapproved change orders or claims that are included within the total contract costs.
- *Deferred Revenue.* If the company receives payments in advance of performing the services that will generate the revenue (such as an advance payment at the outset of a construction contract), this note would contain information as to how the company handles such advance payments for reporting purposes.
- *Income Taxes.* This note should provide an explanation of the company operations and earnings that are subject to income taxes imposed by various federal, state, and local jurisdictions. This note should detail the effect of income taxes on the financial statements.
- *Earnings per Share.* Should provide an explanation of how the values reported for earnings per share are determined.
- *Revised Estimates.* As noted above, the use of estimates is an element addressed in the Summary of Significant Accounting Policies note. However, estimates are frequently revised, and if these revised estimates affect the current or future accounting periods negatively, then the Revised Estimates note should be contained within the financial statements and noted separately in this note.
- *Backlog on Existing Contracts.* This note should discuss the future expected value of contracts that the company believes to have little chance of cancellation.
- *Receivables.* The note on this topic should discuss the source, components, and further comments, if necessary, regarding the accounts receivable of the company.

- *Acquisitions.* If applicable, this note should contain explanations of other business entities acquired or sold by the company.
- *Property and Equipment.* This note should identify the categories of the company's fixed assets and the corresponding reported values for each category.
- *Intangible Assets.* If applicable, this note will contain information about the amounts reported pertaining to nonmonetary assets, such as intellectual property, goodwill recognized from business acquisitions, and competitive advantages.
- *Accounts Payable and Accrued Expenses.* The note on this topic should discuss the treatment of the Accounts Payable and Accrued Expenses of the company, and provide further comments on them where necessary.
- *Notes Payable.* This note should contain further details of notes payable, including identification of the current and noncurrent obligations that are within this amount.
- *Stockholder's Equity.* This note should discuss details of any stock-related activities approved by the board of directors, such as stock splits or stock dividends.
- *Commitments and Contingencies.* This note should contain information about pending litigation, as well as any off-balance sheet arrangements.
- *Business Segment Information.* If applicable, this note should contain details as to how individual segments of the company's business performed financially.
- *Subsequent Events.* When applicable, this note details any significant events that occurred after the date of the balance sheet that could influence any third-party user of the financial statements.

Supplemental Schedules to Financial Statements

Supplemental schedules to the financial statements may also be provided as part of the audited financial statements. Supplemental schedules are used to further detail the activities of the contractor on individual projects, and allow for further analysis of the company's performance on its critical projects. Two common supplemental schedules for construction contractors are a detail of the firm's G&A expenses and a contract-by-contract detailed schedule of revenues, costs, and gross profit.

The detail of contract revenues, costs, and gross profit can be used to review the performance of a given contract performed by the company. It contains contract-specific data from the inception of the contract to the end of the reporting period, as well as the data specific to the year being reported. Samples of these supplemental schedules are attached as Appendix A and Appendix B.

Project Accounting and Revenue Recognition

Two of the issues that distinguish construction company financial statements from most other businesses are that the revenue cycle (typical contract duration) often exceeds one year, and the projected net revenue from each contract is subject to an estimate of the final cost to complete the contract. Unlike a retail company that buys and sells goods on an ongoing basis and has a relatively short revenue cycle from purchase to sale, construction contractors enter into contracts that frequently span multiple years. Further, the final profit to be recognized on any given contract is not known until the work has been completed. The established methods for contract accounting are therefore unique and are addressed in the AICPA's Construction Contractors Audit Guide and FASB Accounting Standards Codification Topics 910 and 605, formerly prescribed in Statement of Position (SOP) 81-1. These issues unique to the construction industry are discussed in more detail in Chapter 2.

Conclusion

This chapter serves as an introduction to the complexities of financial accounting for construction contractors, reporting for internal and external purposes, and the various types of audits utilized to insure proper financial reporting. Proper financial reporting for internal purposes greatly aids management in making sound decisions. Proper financial reporting for external purposes assures investors and credit grantors (such as banks and bonding companies) that their money is being used wisely. The combination of sound reporting for both purposes is essential to the success of any company.

Notes

1. The greater the excess of current assets over current liabilities, the more "liquid" a company is. This excess is a measure of the company's ability to handle short-term cash requirements. This comparison is generally expressed as current assets/current liabilities or the current ratio.

2. In general, the ratio of equity to the liabilities of a company is an indicator of the long-term financial strength of the firm. Bonding companies, among others, pay attention to this debt/equity ratio. These and other ratios and factors considered by bonding companies are discussed further in Chapter 3.

APPENDIX I–A

Supplemental Schedule of Contract Revenues, Costs, and Earnings

Contract Number	Total Contract Revenues	Total Contract Estimated Gross Profit	Revenues Earned	Total Costs Incurred	Cost of Revenues	Gross Profit (Loss)
1908	$ 6,750,220	$ 877,000	$ 5,890,500	$ 5,244,500	$ 5,143,900	$ 746,600
2130	1,471,800	127,100	1,250,400	1,139,800	1,139,800	110,600
2852	451,800	(130,100)	108,600	238,700	238,700	(130,100)
2009	11,125,000	847,900	7,337,900	7,045,500	6,721,100	616,800
1985	3,650,100	497,000	2,395,200	2,061,300	2,061,300	333,900
Small Contracts	51,300	8,400	49,800	41,700	41,700	8,100
	$ 23,500,220	$ 2,227,300	$ 17,032,400	$ 15,771,500	$ 15,346,500	$ 1,685,900

From Inception to December 31, 20X1

Appendix 1–A

From Inception to December 31, 20X1		At December 31, 20X1		For the year ended December 31, 20X1		
Billed to Date	Estimated Costs to Complete	Costs and Estimated Earnings in Excess of Billings	Billings in Excess of Costs and Estimated Earnings	Revenues Earned	Cost of Revenues	Gross Profit (Loss)
$ 5,976,000	$ 628,720	$ 15,100	$ —	$ 5,664,200	$ 4,984,500	$ 679,700
1,195,800	204,900	54,600	—	962,800	899,000	63,800
98,100	343,200	10,500	—	98,600	191,500	(92,900)
7,808,000	3,231,600	—	145,700	6,981,900	6,469,900	512,000
2,491,500	1,091,800	—	96,300	2,395,200	2,061,300	333,900
49,800	1,200	—	—	39,000	30,700	8,300
$ 17,619,200	$ 5,501,420	$ 80,200	$ 242,000	$ 16,141,700	$ 14,636,900	$ 1,504,800

Source: 2008 AICPA Audit and Accounting Guide—Construction Contractors, p. 220.

APPENDIX I–B

Supplemental Schedule of Contracts

Example Construction, Inc.
Supplemental Schedule of Contracts
December 31, 20X1

Contract		Total Contract		From Inception to December 31, 20X1			
Number	Type	Revenues	Estimated Gross Profit	Revenues Earned	Total Costs Incurred	Cost of Revenues	Gross Profits (Loss)
1908	B	$ 6,750,220	$ 877,000	$ 5,890,500	$ 5,244,500	$ 5,143,900	$ 746,600
2130	A	1,471,800	127,100	1,250,400	1,139,800	1,139,800	110,600
2852	B	451,800	(130,100)	108,600	238,700	238,700	(130,100)
2009	B	11,125,000	847,900	7,337,900	7,045,500	6,721,100	616,800
1985	B	3,650,100	497,000	2,395,200	2,061,300	2,061,300	333,900
Small Contracts		51,300	8,400	49,800	41,700	41,700	8,100
		$ 23,500,220	$ 2,227,300	$ 17,032,400	$ 15,771,500	$ 15,346,500	$ 1,685,900

Contract Types

A—Fixed Price

B—Cost-Plus-Fee

Appendix 1–B

	From Inception to December 31, 20X1		At December 31, 20X1		For the year ended December 31, 20X1		
Billed to Date		Estimated Costs Complete	Costs and Estimated Earnings in Excess of Billings	Billings in Excess of Costs and Estimated Earnings	Revenues Earned	Cost of Revenues	Gross Profit (Loss)
$ 5,976,000		$ 628,720	$ 15,100	$ —	$ 5,664,200	$ 4,984,500	$ 679,700
1,195,800		204,900	54,600	—	962,800	899,000	63,800
98,100		343,200	10,500	—	98,600	191,500	(92,900)
7,808,000		3,231,600	—	145,700	6,981,900	6,469,900	512,000
2,491,500		1,091,800	—	96,300	2,395,200	2,061,300	333,900
49,800		1,200	—	—	39,000	30,700	8,300
$ 17,619,200		$ 5,501,420	$ 80,200	$ 242,000	$ 16,141,700	$ 14,636,900	$ 1,504,800

CHAPTER 2

Revenue Recognition and Other Construction Accounting Issues

JEFFREY B. CHARKOW
WILLIAM D. GUERNIER

Introduction

The previous chapter discussed the basics of financial accounting and generally accepted accounting principles (GAAP). This chapter primarily addresses accounting for revenue on long-term construction contracts. Such contracts span more than one accounting period and are typical in the construction, defense, and computer software industries. With respect to revenue recognition, the completed-contract and percentage-of-completion methods are the two basic accounting policies prescribed by GAAP governing long-term contracts. There are pitfalls and issues that attorneys may face in evaluating a contractor's financial statements based on the percentage-of-completion method, which will be discussed below. Chapter 3 will cover some of the other reporting issues relating to construction accounting, including reference to some of the supplemental schedules that are common in the industry and/or required by sureties as part of the bond underwriting process.

GAAP for Construction Contractors

GAAP applies to financial reporting by all types of entities and industries, including the construction industry. In 1981, the American Institute of Certified Public Accountants (AICPA) issued Statement of Position (SOP) 81-1, Accounting for Performance of Construction-Type and Certain Production-Type Contracts. Until July of 2009, SOP 81-1 was the main source of guidance for GAAP in the construction industry. In July of 2009, the AICPA issued the Accounting Standards Codification (ASC), which codifies all previous sources of GAAP. In doing so, the provisions of SOP 81-1 have been codified in the

ASC in Section 605-35,[1] which provides guidance when evaluating accounting issues in the construction industry.

The guidance included in the ASC is also included in the AICPA's Audit and Accounting Guide—Construction Contractors, dated May 1, 2009 (Construction Audit Guide). This guide provides background on the construction industry (Chapter 1); discusses GAAP for construction contractors (Chapters 2–6), including cross references to the appropriate sections of the ASC; and provides guidance for the financial statement audits of construction contractors (Chapters 6–12).

Revenue Realization, the Matching Principle, and Conservatism

Under GAAP, the realization of revenue is appropriate when "products (goods or services), merchandise, or other assets are *exchanged* for cash or claims to cash."[2] In a "widget" business, the exchange concept is simple. The widget is delivered in exchange for either cash or an obligation to pay. The transactions are of a short duration, and most are completed within a single accounting period (a company's accounting period is usually a year).

On a construction project, the exchange is more complex. Transactions, that is, the performance of the contract, often extend for more than a year. The contractor receives progress payments that often do not match the contractor's progress in completing the work, and the "exchange" is likely not complete until the contractor has met all of the terms of the contract. These terms may include final or substantial completion of the work, completion of punch list items, delivery of as-built drawings, and any number of other contractual requirements.

The matching principle is closely related to the revenue realization principle. Under the matching principle, costs incurred in a period should be matched against the revenue generated in the same period. Even though costs may be incurred in a different pattern than cash payments from the customer (such as progress payments), the total revenue under the contract should be recorded proportionally with the costs as they are incurred.

Finally, conservatism is one of the most fundamental principles of GAAP. Conservatism in the case of long-term contracts requires that losses be recognized as soon as it is apparent that a loss *may* occur, even if only a small amount of the costs has been incurred. These three fundamental principles of GAAP influence accounting for construction contracts under both the completed-contract and percentage-of-completion methods of accounting.

To deal with these three, as well as other, accounting principles, GAAP for construction contractors prescribes two accounting methods for construction contracts: completed contract and percentage-of-completion. Both of these methods are explained below, but most contractors use the percentage-of-completion method, under which revenue is recognized in each accounting period based on some measure of the physical progress of the work.

Completed-Contract Method

The completed-contract method is fairly straightforward. Contract revenue, costs, and profit are all reported on the income statement upon project completion.

Example

XYZ Construction Company has a $90 million contract to construct a bridge and roadway at an estimated cost of $80 million. The work will be spread over three years (accounting periods). Costs, billings, and other data are shown in Figure 1.

Figure 1
Cost and Billing Data for XYZ Construction

	Year 1	Year 2	Year 3	Total
Approved Contract Price	$ 90,000,000	$ 90,000,000	$ 90,000,000	$ 90,000,000
Progress Billings	$ 18,000,000	$ 50,000,000	$ 22,000,000	$ 90,000,000
Cash Collected	15,000,000	35,000,000	40,000,000	90,000,000
Costs	$ 20,000,000	$ 40,000,000	$ 20,000,000	$ 80,000,000
Costs To Date	20,000,000	60,000,000	80,000,000	
Estimated Costs At Completion	$ 80,000,000	$ 80,000,000	—	

Under the completed-contract method, revenue and expense are not reported until the contract is completed in Year 3. Using this method, billings and receivables in each of the three years would be recorded on the balance sheet of XYZ Construction, as shown in Figure 2.

Figure 2
Partial Balance Sheet for XYZ Construction (Completed-Contract Method)

	Year 1	Year 2	Year 3
Selected Income Statement Accounts			
Revenue	$ —	$ —	$ 90,000,000
Costs of construction	—	—	(80,000,000)
Gross Profit	—	—	10,000,000

Figure 2 continued on page 26–

—Continued from page 25

	Year 1	Year 2	Year 3
Selected Balance Sheet Accounts			
Assets			
Construction in process . . . . (*Costs incurred*)	20,000,000	60,000,000	—
Less Billings . . . . (*Cumulative billings*)	(18,000,000)	(68,000,000)	—
Costs in excess of billings . . . .(*if positive*)	$ 2,000,000	$ —	
Liabilities			
Billings in excess of costs . . . . (*if negative*)	$ —	$ (8,000,000)	—

The accounts "Costs in excess of billings" (an asset account) and "Billings in excess of costs" (a liability account) are the differences between actual billings and costs incurred on the project. To the extent the contractor has billed less than its costs, the contractor has an asset for the amount it will eventually bill. To the extent the contractor has billed more than the costs incurred, as in Year 2, it creates a liability. The liability, however, will be reduced as the contractor incurs more costs. These accounts are often referred to as the "underbilling" and "overbilling" accounts.

Loss Contracts Under the Completed-Contract Method

Under the completed-contract method, the estimated costs at completion are not necessary to calculate profit because no profit is recognized until the contract is completed and the actual costs are known. However, under the principle of conservatism, GAAP requires that losses be recognized in full when they can be reasonably estimated. Continuing with our example, assume that in Year 2 XYZ Construction determines that a substantial amount of roadway was left out of its bid. Consequently, the contractor estimates that the project will cost an unexpected additional $15 million to complete. The contract that was projecting a profit of $10 million is now estimated to lose $5 million. GAAP requires the contractor to report this entire loss in Year 2 when it was identified. The financial statements in our example are shown in Figure 3.

Figure 3
Statements for XYZ Construction
(Completed-Contract Method, Recognizing Loss)

	Year 1	Year 2	Year 3	Total
Approved Contract Price	$ 90,000,000	$ 90,000,000	$ 90,000,000	$ 90,000,000
Progress Billings	$ 18,000,000	$ 50,000,000	$ 22,000,000	$ 90,000,000
Cash Collected	15,000,000	35,000,000	40,000,000	90,000,000

	Year 1	Year 2	Year 3	Total
Costs	$ 20,000,000	$ 40,000,000	$ 35,000,000	$ 95,000,000
Costs To Date	20,000,000	60,000,000	80,000,000	
Estimated Costs At Completion	$ 80,000,000	$ 95,000,000	—	

	Year 1	Year 2	Year 3	Total
Selected Income Statement Accounts				
Revenue	$ —	$ —	$ 90,000,000	$ 90,000,000
Costs of construction	—	—	(90,000,000)	(90,000,000)
Provision for loss on contract	—	**(5,000,000)**	—	(5,000,000)
Total Costs	—	(5,000,000)	(90,000,000)	(95,000,000)
Gross Profit **(Loss)**	$ —	$ **(5,000,000)**	$ —	$ (5,000,000)
Selected Balance Sheet Accounts				
Assets				
Accounts Receivable (Billings to date- Cash collected to date)	$ 3,000,000	$ 15,000,000		
Construction in process (Costs to date)	20,000,000	60,000,000	—	
Less: Billings (Progress billings to date)	(18,000,000)	(68,000,000)	—	
Less: Reserve for loss	—	**(5,000,000)**	—	
Costs in excess of billings (if positive)	$ 2,000,000	$ —	$ —	—
Liabilities				
Billings in excess of costs (if negative)	$ —	$ **(13,000,000)**	$ —	—

When Can a Contractor Use the Completed-Contract Method?

GAAP severely restricts a contractor's use of the completed-contract method. Indeed, there are only a few limited scenarios where the completed-contract method is appropriate.

The completed-contract method can be used when the results are not materially[3] different from the results that would be obtained under the percentage-of-completion method.[4] Additionally, the completed-contract method can be used when a contractor *cannot* provide "reasonably reliable estimates."[5] However, in completed-contract accounting, an estimated cost at completion (EAC) is still necessary to prove that the contract is not a loss contract (requiring immediate recognition of the loss).

GAAP also permits the use of the completed-contract method for a single contract or a group of contracts where reasonably dependable estimates are not possible or where "inherent hazards make estimates doubtful." Such a situation could occur on a project in a remote location, in war-time situations, or other unique circumstances.[6]

Percentage-of-Completion Method

The percentage-of-completion method is the most commonly used method of accounting for long-term contracts in the construction industry. It requires a determination of costs, revenue, and measurement of progress on the project in each accounting period. The chart shown in Figure 4 expands the earlier example of XYZ Construction, and illustrates some of the key components of percentage-of-completion accounting.

Figure 4
Cost and Billing Data for XYZ Construction
(Percentage-of-Completion Method)

	Year 1	Year 2	Year 3
Cumulative Information			
Contract Price:			
Original Contract Price	$ 90,000,000	$ 90,000,000	$ 90,000,000
Approved Change Orders To Date	—	2,000,000	8,000,000
Approved Contract Price	$ 90,000,000	$ 92,000,000	$ 98,000,000
Unpriced Change Orders/Claims	$ 2,000,000	$ 5,000,000	$ —
Estimated Costs At Completion (EAC)			
Labor	$ 35,000,000	$ 40,000,000	$ 40,000,000
All Other	45,000,000	50,000,000	50,000,000
	$ 80,000,000	$ 90,000,000	$ 90,000,000
Estimated Final Profit *(Approved Contract Price Less EAC)*	$ 10,000,000	$ 2,000,000	$ 8,000,000
Annual Information			
Progress Billings	$ 18,000,000	$ 50,000,000	$ 30,000,000
Cash Collected	15,000,000	35,000,000	40,000,000
Costs:			
Labor	$ 5,000,000	$ 20,200,000	$ 14,800,000
All Other	15,000,000	30,000,000	5,000,000
Total Costs in Period	$ 20,000,000	$ 50,200,000	$ 19,800,000
Total Costs To Date	$ 20,000,000	$ 70,200,000	$ 90,000,000
Percent Complete Information			
Percent Complete (Labor Cost)	14%	63%	100%
Percent Complete (Total Cost)	25%	78%	100%

As can be seen, the example has been expanded to include the existence of Unpriced Change Orders and Claims in Years 1 and 2, and additions to the contract price by approved change orders in Years 2 and 3. In addition, as a result of the changes and other revisions to the estimated, the costs estimated at completion (EAC) for both labor and other costs increase between Year 1 and Year 2.

Determining Costs

Incurred Contract Costs

Determining contract costs is the most basic part of contract accounting. However, it is not as simple as one might think, and many issues arise. Percentage-of-completion accounting, like completed-contract accounting, requires an accurate record of incurred contract costs. Under the completed-contract method, costs are "inventoried" until the contract is complete and then matched against revenue. In contrast, the percentage-of-completion method matches costs against revenue over the performance period of the contract in each accounting period. The focus becomes one of determining which costs are considered contract costs in the calculations.

Paragraph 2.13 of the Construction Audit Guide summarizes the appropriate accounting for contract costs. Costs that may be treated as contract costs include all "direct costs" such as material, labor, and subcontract costs as well as "indirect costs" such as indirect labor, supervision, tools, equipment, insurance, and other costs that can be identified or allocated to a contract on a "systematic and rational basis." Costs that are not charged to contracts are referred to in different ways on a contractor's financial statements, but are commonly referred to as general and administrative (G&A) expenses. These costs, as well as other costs that are not treated as direct costs, are "period costs" charged to the period in which they are incurred.

Paragraph 2.13 of the Construction Audit Guide also notes that the allocation of costs is a matter of judgment. As such, accounting for these period costs can vary dramatically among different contractors. There is typically little difference between contractors in recording the most fundamental direct costs such as trade labor, material, and subcontract costs. In the area of indirect costs, however, practices often diverge. Some contractors charge project executives as direct costs to specific contracts based on the time they spend on the projects. Others allocate project executives as indirect costs among several contracts on the basis of costs incurred on each project. Finally, some contractors account for project executives as "period costs" in the G&A expense section of the income statement.

GAAP allows for the variation in the allocation of indirect costs so long as the allocation is performed systematically, rationally, and consistently across all contracts and periods.

Estimated Cost-to-Complete

Contract accounting under either the completed-contract or percentage-of-completion method requires the contractor to establish its anticipated contract margin at completion. This is accomplished by determining the incurred costs to date plus the estimated costs to complete (ETC). Together, these provide the EAC costs. In percentage-of-completion accounting, the EAC is fundamental to the determination of the revenue recognized in each fiscal accounting period. Under GAAP, as the EAC changes from period to period, the impact of the change in revenue is accounted for on a cumulative basis in the period that the change occurs. Therefore, a change in EAC may have an enormous impact on the gross profit recognized in any particular accounting period. In the XYZ Construction example, in Year 2 the EAC increased to $90 million (an increase of $10 million), with a $2 million increase in the contract price because pending change order requests had been approved. So the accounting for the contract in Year 2 would be as shown in Figure 5.

Figure 5
XYZ Construction at Year 2 (Percentage-of-Completion Method)

		Year 1	Year 2	Total
Approved Contract Price		$ 90,000,000	$ 92,000,000	
Cost Estimate At Completion		$ (80,000,000)	$ (90,000,000)	
Estimated Final Profit		$ 10,000,000	$ 2,000,000	
Percent Complete (Total Cost)	*(Costs incurred to date/EAC)*	25%	78%	
Cumulative Gross Profit Earned	*(Estimated Final Profit × Percent Complete)*	$ 2,500,000	$ 1,560,000	
Selected Income Statement Accounts				
Revenue	*(Approved Contract Price × Percent Complete, less Previously Recognized)*	$ 22,500,000	$ 49,260,000	$ 71,760,000
Costs of construction		(20,000,000)	(50,200,000)	(70,200,000)
Gross Profit		$ 2,500,000	$ (940,000)	$ 1,560,000

Under this scenario, the contract is still profitable as of the end of Year 2, with a final gross profit projected of $2 million, and cumulative profit to be recognized through Year 2 of $1,560,000. However, since $2.5 million in profit was already recognized in Year 1, Year 2 requires the recognition of a loss of $940,000 ($2,500,000 − $1,560,000). This variability in income reporting wreaks havoc on reported earnings, especially for public companies that seek predictable, steady results.

The ETC is a critical component of the EAC, and therefore a critical component of construction contract accounting. The ETC is typically prepared by project personnel with project management and engineering experience, with input from accountants in the review process. The accounting guidance for estimating the costs to complete focuses on the following process to arrive at the EAC:

- The use of a systematic approach that correlates with the accounting system and the actual costs recorded;
- The identification of quantities and prices of all significant elements of costs;
- Consideration of the effects of wage and price escalations;
- Incorporation of periodic updates as new information is obtained; and
- Incorporation of periodic comparisons of actual costs to estimated costs.[7]

Determining Revenue

In order to determine contract revenue, the final contract price must also be determined in each accounting period. The components of the final contract price are the original contract price, the executed and/or approved change orders, and the estimated amount of unpriced (or unapproved) change orders and claims. Contract terms regarding liquidated damages or early completion bonuses may also be relevant.

The original contract price and approved change orders are easily determined. These revenue components represent a legal agreement between the contractor and the owner as to the contract price. When executed, change orders are added to the contract price for purposes of recognizing revenue for that period.

The difficult components to evaluate are unpriced change orders and claims. These can run the gamut, ranging as follows:

- The contractor and the owner (or general contractor or customer in the case of a subcontractor) have agreed on both the scope and the price, but the formally approved change order is not yet executed.
- The owner has requested a change in scope, the work is under way or completed, but the parties have not yet agreed to the price.
- Same as the above, but the owner affirmatively disputes the price as proposed by the contractor.
- Same as above, but the owner disputes the scope, that is, disputes that the issue constitutes a change.
- The dispute between the contractor and the owner has risen to the level of a legal dispute and is being pursued under the disputes provision of the contract, generally referred to as a "claim."

GAAP provides that the first two scenarios above are accounted for as "Unpriced Change Orders," and the last three are accounted for as "Claims." Each of these is discussed below. As will be seen, accounting guidance for both unpriced change orders and claims draws heavily on the conservatism principle.

Unpriced Change Orders

Commonly, the contractor submits change-order requests seeking additional compensation from the owner. The outstanding change-order requests identify the additional or changed work to be performed (or that has already been performed), but the contract has not yet been modified by a change order. These situations include circumstances in which the owner has directed the contractor to perform the work, with payment to be made on the basis of time and materials or later commercial negotiations. In accordance with the conservatism principle, to the extent that the work has been performed before the change order is executed, the costs associated with the change order request should be recorded as they are incurred.

GAAP provides that revenue on the change order requests may be recognized if it is *probable* that the change order will be approved and paid. Factors to consider in making this determination include whether the owner (or customer) has provided written approval of the scope of the change order, whether the costs are identifiable and reasonable, and the contractor's experience in getting paid for change order requests for similar issues on the project.

Claims

For accounting purposes, "claims" include any change order requests that are disputed by the owner. Claims may include charges for straightforward changes in scope, along with requested price adjustments for delays, disruptions, interferences, or acceleration. Revenue may be recognized for claims up to the amount of the costs incurred for the associated change order requests, if it is *probable* that the claim will result in additional revenue under the contract and the amount can be reasonably estimated. However, in order to recognize any such revenue, claims must also pass the following more stringent tests, as outlined in ASC 605-35-25-31:

1. The contract or other evidence provides a legal basis for the claim; or a legal opinion has been obtained, stating that under the circumstances there is a reasonable basis to support the claim.
2. Additional costs are caused by circumstances that were unforeseen at the contract date and are not the result of deficiencies in the contractor's performance.
3. Costs associated with the claim are identifiable or otherwise determinable and are reasonable in view of the work performed.
4. The evidence supporting the claim is objective and verifiable, not based on management's "feel" for the situation or on unsupported representations.

When the above tests are met, revenue from the claim may be recognized only to the extent that associated costs have been incurred.[8] The above tests are subjective determinations and usually the topic of significant discussions between the auditor and top management. This topic is discussed in more detail in Chapter 4, including counsel's role in providing legal representations in support of claims recognition.

Recognition of revenue for pending claims requires significant judgment, input from legal counsel, and sometimes advice from technical experts. GAAP also permits a contractor to take a more conservative approach, wherein claim revenue is reported only when the claim is resolved, that is, becomes an approved change order. Some contractors use this method since it removes the subjective elements of the revenue recognition process as it relates to claims, and is, by definition, more objective and certain.[9]

Unpriced Change Orders and Claims Accounting—An Example
In the XYZ Construction example, assume that in Year 2 there are $5 million of change order requests that have not yet been resolved. The work involved in the change requests is complete and the additional costs of the changed work totaled $4 million, leaving $1 million of gross profit if the amount of the change requests is eventually approved. To illustrate the accounting for these change requests, assume the following three scenarios.

Scenario 1: The contractor and the owner have resolved changes of this nature in the past, the owner has not indicated any dispute as to either the scope or proposed price of the changed work, and the contractor is therefore confident that recovery of the full amount of these change order requests is probable. The full $5 million estimated value of the change order requests is therefore recorded, increasing the contract price to $97 million.

Scenario 2: The owner has authorized the changed work but has indicated some dispute as to the price of the work. The contractor has had its outside accounting firm review the pricing of the change orders requests, and this review has confirmed that the costs included in the change order requests are reasonable. In this scenario, $4 million in revenue is recognized, and the contract price is increased by $4 million (the actual costs of the changes).

Scenario 3: The owner disputes that the changes qualify as a change in scope and contends that additional costs incurred by the contractor were actually caused by the contractor's mismanagement of its subcontractors. The contractor has retained counsel who has filed a demand for arbitration under the disputes clause of the contract. The contractor has no assurance that its claim will be recovered. Accordingly, the incurred costs of $4 million are recognized and no value is included in the contract price for the pending claim. This causes the estimated final contract profit to be reduced, resulting in a loss reported in the current period.

The accounting for these three scenarios is illustrated in Figure 6.

Figure 6
XYZ Construction Claims Scenarios, Year 2

		Year 1	Year 2 Scenarios		
			Scenario 1	Scenario 2	Scenario 3
Original Contract Price Plus Approved Change Orders		$ 90,000,000	$ 92,000,000	$ 92,000,000	$ 92,000,000
Value of Unpriced Change Orders/Claims		—	5,000,000	4,000,000	—
Contract Price		$ 90,000,000	$ 97,000,000	$ 96,000,000	$ 92,000,000
Cost Estimate At Completion (EAC)		(80,000,000)	$ (90,000,000)	$ (90,000,000)	$ (90,000,000)
Estimated Final Contract Profit		$ 10,000,000	$ 7,000,000	$ 6,000,000	$ 2,000,000
Percent Complete (Total Cost)	*(Costs incurred to date/EAC)*	25%	78%	78%	78%
Cumulative Gross Profit Earned	*(Estimated Final Profit × Percent Complete)*	$ 2,500,000	$ 5,460,000	$ 4,680,000	$ 1,560,000
Selected Income Statement Accounts					
Revenue	*(Approved Contract Price × Percent Complete, less Previously Recognized)*	$ 22,500,000	$ 53,160,000	$ 52,380,000	$ 49,260,000
Costs of construction	[G]	(20,000,000)	(50,200,000)	(50,200,000)	(50,200,000)
Gross Profit		$ 2,500,000	$ 2,960,000	$ 2,180,000	$ (940,000)

This treatment of unpriced change orders and claims well illustrates the overarching conservatism principle of GAAP, also referred to as the principle of prudence. This principle is described as an

> [a]ccounting concept that requires recording (recognizing) the expenses and liabilities as soon as possible, but the revenues only when they are realized or assured.[10]

Under this principle, unless the contractor can demonstrate that recovery is probable, the revenue that is recognized from unpriced change orders and claims is restricted until they are resolved via signed change orders or other final resolution.

Measuring Progress

In order to accurately match contract revenue with expenses in the percentage-of-completion method, a contractor's progress in completing the work must be measured at the end of each accounting period. This measure should reflect a measure of the physical progress of the work. The Construction Audit Guide describes both *input* and *output* methods for measuring progress in more detail.[11] These methods are summarized next.

Input Method of Measurement

As the name implies, the input method of measurement is based on comparing an input-to-date, such as total costs incurred, labor hours expended, labor dollars incurred, or units of material installed, to the estimated final amount of that input. Each of these input measures can and usually do provide slightly different results.

For example, using the XYZ Construction example, the labor dollar input measure of percentage completion results in a different measure of progress in both Year 1 and Year 2 than the total cost measure. Using the labor dollar input, the project is 14 percent complete at the end of Year 1 and 63 percent complete at the end of Year 2. By contrast, using total costs as the measure, the project is 25 percent complete at the end of Year 1 and 78 percent complete at the end of Year 2. Although the total income recognized over the life of the contract is the same under both methods, the amount of revenue and profit recognized in each year differs significantly because of this different measurement of physical progress.

Criticisms of the input measures method include the following:

- To the extent that costs are used as an input measure, the measure assumes that all costs incurred contribute to the physical completion of the project. This may not be the case where substantial commodity-type material is purchased up front and stored on site, but not installed until a later date. In addition, this approach gives equal weight to widely differing activities such as engineering, procurement, and direct labor. Therefore, the dollar amount expended may not reflect the physical progress of the work.
- The measure based on expended labor hours requires the inclusion of subcontractor labor hours if their hours are significant. Reliable information from subcontractors is frequently difficult to obtain.
- The measure based on labor dollars expended suffers from the same problem, with the additional flaw that different labor rates, overtime pay, and other rate differentials between the contractor and the various subcontractors may further skew the results.

Output Methods of Measurement

Output methods of measurement measure progress based on the results achieved. Output measures may include, for example, cubic yards of concrete installed, cubic yards of excavation, or linear feet of roadway complete to various stages. Although a favorable method, it is particularly difficult to apply to building construction due to the multiple and diverse elements of work, such as foundations, walls, mechanical systems, interior finishes, and roofing. For this reason, output measures work best for contracts that have a relatively homogeneous output that can be measured objectively, such as road paving and excavation contracts.

Which Measure to Use?

There is no definitive answer in the accounting guidance as to the preferred method to be used for measuring progress of the work. In some cases, contractors may use a blend of the methods, for example, labor hours for their work and units installed for subcontractor work. The Construction Audit Guide states that the method

> should be reviewed and confirmed periodically by alternative measures that involve observation and inspection. For example, the results provided by the measure used to determine the extent of progress may be compared to the results of calculations based on physical observations by engineers, architects, or similarly qualified personnel. . . .[12]

Contractors' methods vary widely on measuring progress. At the simplest level, a contractor may simply perform a manual progress estimate at the end of the year for financial accounting purposes. More sophisticated contractors have systems that integrate accounting, progress measurement, and forecasting. Labor hours are reported by detailed cost code and units installed are reported for the period. The system then forecasts the EAC and the progress against that EAC. Management adjustments to the EAC and progress estimate are then made for known anomalies, such as acknowledging that the remaining units to be installed will be on higher floors.

The key to measuring progress is to select the measure that most closely matches the peculiarities of the particular contractor's business operations and to consistently follow that same approach, unless there is a compelling reason to change. Problems arise when companies change the applicable measure from year to year. Doing so subjects the contractor to assertions that the measurement selection is being used to manipulate earnings to achieve a desired target bottom line.

Other Information in the Construction Audit Guide

As mentioned previously, the Construction Audit Guide includes the codification of GAAP under the AICPA's ASC. It also provides deeper context, including SEC requirements and the impact of the Sarbanes-Oxley Act. The Construction Audit Guide also includes complete examples of financial statements and disclosures under various scenarios.

Of particular importance in the Construction Audit Guide is Chapter 8, Controls in the Construction Industry. This chapter describes "best practices" for internal control procedures over all aspects of the construction function, including

- Estimating and bidding
- Job site accounting and controls
- Project administration and contract evaluation

- Billing procedures
- Construction equipment
- Accounting for costs and revenue

Miscellaneous Issues for Attorneys

Given the need for estimates, and the inherent subjectivity and variability involved in long-term contract accounting, discovery regarding the accounting treatment of distressed projects is often a subject that arises in litigation. Some of these issues are addressed in more detail elsewhere, but some commonly seen areas where this issue arises are purchase price disputes relating to acquisitions and financial statement disclosures regarding pending litigation.

Purchase Price Disputes

The acquisition of a construction company includes the purchase of the estimated value of the construction contracts in process. Given the estimates that are involved in long-term contract accounting, this can be a fertile area for later dispute. If these estimates prove to be wrong, the buyer will sometimes pursue the seller for overstating the value of the contracts purchased. Disputes often occur over the following issues:

- Unrealistic estimated costs to complete
- Costs recorded on the wrong projects
- Unrecorded claims from subcontractors
- Unfounded change order request where revenue was recognized
- Unrecorded liabilities for back charges, advance payments, and other costs
- Failure of the new business owner to properly manage completion of the contracts

Financial Statement Disclosure of Litigation Strategy

In the case of material affirmative claims by a contractor, GAAP requires certain disclosures in the financial statements; for example, a disclosure is required if a claim amount reported on an income statement is far less than the amount being sought in litigation. In the hands of the opposing party, this could be damaging to the prospects of recovery on the claim. The opposing party may seek to characterize the lower amount of revenue recognition as an admission that the claim's value is much less than asserted in court. As is evident from the prior discussion on revenue recognition under GAAP, however, the conservatism principle drives this result, no matter how strongly the company's management may believe in the validity of its claim.

In the case of claims against a contractor, or an owner, an accrued liability may be recorded on the books if it is material. The conservatism principle often results in a recorded liability greater than management's position in the dispute. Even though this information may be aggregated and not disclosed with respect to a specific contract or matter, an opposing party may serve discovery requests for more detailed information. The disclosures may be portrayed as an admission of liability or quantum on the claims.

Accounting Disclosure Disputes

Taking a hindsight view, shareholders, regulators, banks, and bonding companies sometimes challenge the contractor's judgment in its accounting for long-term contracts. These areas of dispute include

- Recognition of revenue for claims and unpriced change orders that prove to be significantly different from the final amount once the claim or change order request is resolved.
- Use of estimates-to-complete that were overoptimistic or unrealistic, resulting in later losses on contracts.
- Use of an inaccurate percentage complete for a particular project, and resulting unbilled revenue reflected on the balance sheet, that was very aggressive and not reflective of the progress (and related revenue) that should have been recorded for the accounting period.

If the contract subsequently runs into problems and turns out not to be profitable, the booking of the revenue and profit in prior accounting periods may in severe cases be viewed as evidence of fraudulent accounting, as opposed to merely a questionable estimating practice. The best way to avoid allegations of this nature is to institute and consistently follow a conservative approach to accounting for long-term construction contracts. Additionally, carefully documenting the facts as they are known as of each accounting period is essential in defending management's judgment from a subsequent challenge.

Conclusion

In the construction industry, one of the most critical financial reporting issues relates to the process of accounting for long-term contracts. This process is complicated and requires the exercise of judgment on the part of the accountant with respect to contractors' estimates of both revenues and costs. The various components of the calculations of income statement and balance sheet amounts require input from non-accounting personnel, much of which requires significant judgment. The assessment must, however, observe the fundamental tenets of GAAP, including revenue realization, consistency between periods, conservatism, and the matching of revenues earned with expenses incurred.

Notes

1. The ASC is not an authoritative pronouncement; rather, it is the AICPA's consolidation and interpretation of the basic pronouncements of the various ruling bodies of financial accounting. These ruling bodies have changed over time but include the Accounting Principles Board (APB) (1959 through 1973) and the Financial Accounting Standards Board (FASB) (1973 through present). The APB was the ruling body of the AICPA, while the FASB is an independent body that is currently accepted as the authoritative voice of financial accounting. In addition, the Securities and Exchange Commission (SEC) has legal authority to establish accounting standards for public companies. The SEC generally defers this responsibility to the FASB, but in some cases, has issued pronouncements that effectively create or change GAAP.

2. Accounting Standards Codification [hereinafter ASC] 605-25-1.

3. "The concept of materiality recognizes that some matters, either individually or in the aggregate, are important for fair presentation of financial statements in conformity with generally accepted accounting principles, while *other matters are not important*...." AICPA Statement on Auditing Standard No. 47 ¶ 3 (emphasis added).

4. ASC 605-35-35-92.

5. ASC 605-35-35-94.

6. *Id.*

7. *See* ASC 605-35-25-44; also included in AICPA Audit and Accounting Guide—Construction Contractors (May 1, 2009) [hereinafter Construction Audit Guide] ¶ 2.17.

8. As a practical matter, it is difficult to implement this guidance because it is not always possible to determine when the costs related to the change request or claim have been incurred. For example, if a contractor has a change order request changing a pipe dimension from 2" to 4", the additional cost of the larger pipe can be easily quantified. However, it is difficult for the contractor to segregate labor costs when the additional labor to install that larger pipe is incurred. In practice, if it is determined that recovery for a change order request is probable, the anticipated costs to perform the additional or changed work, excluding markup, is added to the anticipated final contract price.

9. Contractors who utilize this method occasionally have to defend it as being too conservative. In other words, their auditors may suggest that a portion of this revenue should be reflected in the current accounting period.

10. Business Dictionary.com, Prudence Concept, http://www.businessdictionary.com/definition/prudence-concept.html.

11. Construction Audit Guide ¶ 2.09.

12. Construction Audit Guide ¶ 2.10.

CHAPTER 3

What Sureties and Owners Look for in Contractors' Financial Statements

JAY BERNSTEIN
JEFFREY E. FUCHS*

Introduction

For both sureties and owners, a contractor's financial statements serve as an essential source of information that, when properly assessed and analyzed, can play a vital role in minimizing risks and reducing—if not avoiding—potential losses. This chapter discusses the importance of financial statements for sureties and owners, and explains what the data extracted from financial statements tells sureties and owners about the financial health of the contractors with which they do business. It also addresses other factors, including a contractor's character, that are of importance to a surety as part of its evaluation.

Surety and Owner Concerns Regarding Contractor Finances

The use of financial statements by owners varies by owner, contractor, and project. On federal government contracts, the determination of a bidder's responsibility includes the requirement that the bidder "have adequate financial resources to perform the contract, or the ability to obtain them" (Federal Acquisition Regulation (FAR) 9.104-1(a)). Financial statements are often used to make this determination, and solicitations may require bidders to submit financial statements in order to be considered for an award. For example, Section III of General Services Administration Form 527, "Contractor's Qualifications and Financial Information," requires disclosure of the contractor's assets, liabilities, and net worth, which—in lieu of completing a Section III form—a contractor may satisfy by submitting "prepared financial statements with notes."

---

* The authors wish to express special appreciation to Kathleen Horgan and Jeanette Woodcock for their accounting expertise and tireless efforts in assisting with this chapter.

Similarly, private owners seeking to evaluate contractor qualifications may elect to require the completion of American Institute of Architects (AIA) Document A305, "Contractor's Qualification Statement." Under Section 5 of A305, the prospective contractor must attach a financial statement that shows current assets, net fixed assets, other assets, current liabilities, and other liabilities. According to Section 5.1.1 of A305, it is preferable to include the most recent audited financial statement, and Section 5.1.2 requires the name and address of the certified public accountant (CPA) preparing the financial report and the date of the audit.

Like owners, sureties rely upon financial statements to assess a contractor's financial capabilities. Appreciation of the significance of financial statements to a surety requires a basic understanding of surety bonds and the role they play in the construction process.

The surety bond is a tripartite agreement, in which each party has obligations to the other two parties. The obligee (typically the owner or general contractor) is obligated to the surety to fulfill the conditions set forth in the bond for making a claim, and to the principal (typically the contractor or subcontractor) to satisfy its obligations under the underlying contract. The surety is obligated to investigate any claims by the obligee; provide the principal the opportunity to assert any defenses; and pay legitimate claims. Finally, the principal is obligated to indemnify the surety for losses, and to comply with its underlying contractual obligations to the obligee.

In the context of construction projects, the two major categories of bonds are payment and performance bonds. Almost all federal, state, and local government projects require surety bonding, and many private project owners require bonds. The ability of the contractor to obtain surety bonds is an important component of its ability to obtain work.

Payment bonds protect entities and individuals, such as subcontractors and suppliers, who supply labor and/or material on public projects, which cannot be subject to mechanic's liens. The Miller Act (40 U.S.C. § 270a) requires payment bonds on federal public works projects, and its state counterparts, sometimes referred to as "Little Miller Acts," require payment bonds for the benefit of suppliers of labor, materials, and equipment on state and local contracts. Payment bonds are often required on private projects as well.

The performance bond assures the bond's beneficiary that the surety will satisfy the performance obligations of the underlying contract in the event the principal defaults.

Surety bonds are similar to insurance policies in that under both arrangements, the obligee is entitled to be made whole for its loss. However, unlike an insurance policy, where the insurance company assumes the risk of loss, under a surety bond the surety retains rights to recover its losses from the principal. The right of indemnity is recognized by common law, and is further reinforced by the general indemnity agreement that sureties typically require contractors to execute as a condition of issuing a bond. In most instances, the general indemnity agreement contains broad language obligating the indemnitors to make the surety whole for any and all losses and expenses incurred by the surety arising from issuance of bonds to the principal. In order to obtain financial assurance that they will be able to recover their losses, sureties typically require that the general indemnity agreement be executed by the corporate entity that is being bonded, and, depending on the quality of the corporation's credit, by the corporation's senior executives (and often their spouses) individually. Thus, as opposed to insurance, in which the insurer assumes the risk of loss in return for receipt of the insurance premium, surety bonds are more akin to instruments of credit where the surety guarantees the performance of the principal. Monies advanced by the surety are expected to be reimbursed at some point by the principal, including legal fees and other expenses arising out of the surety arrangement.

Surety bonds are issued through surety bond producers, also known as agents and brokers, who are knowledgeable about the surety and construction industries. Surety bond producers usually work in agencies that specialize in surety bonds or in insurance agencies that have a subspecialty in surety bonds.

Contractors must qualify for a surety bond. Like a bank that lends money to a borrower, surety companies will only bond contractors who are deemed credit worthy. Bond producers and bonding companies will investigate the financial history of a contractor, the character of its management team, and the capacity of its resources in determining whether to issue a bond. The premium is considered, in most major respects, a fee for performing the prequalification examination, guaranteeing the contractor's performance, and for other underwriting activities. As such, the surety bond is underwritten with the expectation that the contractor has the financial capacity and construction experience to pay its subcontractors and to complete the project.

At the initial stages of the underwriting process, financial statements for the preceding two to four years (in order to spot trends) are required by the surety as part of its threshold determination as to whether or not to provide bonding to the contractor and, if approved, the amount of bonding capacity. As the underwriting process continues, and in order to confirm the status of that relationship, the prudent surety will require updated financial statements on a regular basis, often including quarterly unaudited contract status reports. Claims on the bond or other evidence that the contractor is in financial distress will prompt increased vigilance on the part of the surety in its review of the financial statements submitted by the contractor.

The Three Cs

Set forth below are the processes and steps that sureties take in evaluating a contractor to see if the contractor is an acceptable candidate for underwriting bonds for upcoming bids. Many of the issues discussed for the surety underwriting process are equally relevant to owners. Although an owner may require a bond for a given project, and the bond gives the owner a certain amount of comfort in terms of ensuring completion of the project, that is not the end of an owner's evaluation in the selection process. Many owners also rely heavily on the character component of a contractor, including past experiences. For contracts that are not bonded, many of the evaluation steps outlined below are performed by the owner or its designee, depending on the size of the contract and the owner's past experiences with the contractor in question. In addition, on an individual project, an owner may opt to separately evaluate some of the major subcontractors in a fashion similar to that described for the prime contractor.

While each surety company has its own guidelines and criteria, important considerations for any bonding company are the "three Cs"—capital, capacity, and character.

Capital means the contractor's financial strength, and typically includes an analysis of detailed financial statements for the past several years, schedules of completed projects and contracts in progress, cost records reflecting the financial status of projects, and credit reports.

Capacity encompasses the contractor's ability and skill as indicated by its past performance and experience, as well as whether the contractor's total volume of work is appropriate to the company's size and resources. Relevant information will include resumes of key personnel, the contractor's track record, and the contractor's long and short-term goals.

Character means the contractor's reputation in the business community for fair and honest dealing. Letters of recommendation from project owners may be requested and reviewed as part of this determination.

Assessing the Contractor's Capital

The surety uses the financial information provided by the contractor and its CPA to prepare reports and schedules that document its prequalification examination of the contractor and substantiate the decision whether to recommend bonding the contractor for the project. The surety looks at comparative data for two to four years and factors in the level of CPA assurance, giving more credibility to audited statements, less to reviewed statements, and even less to compiled financial information. The surety then calculates key ratios and performs an analytical review of the financial information, including comparisons to industry trends. Upon concluding its review of the income statement and balance sheet, and calculating the various ratios described above, the surety reviews the contractor's statement of cash flow, which accumulates and summarizes the total cash flow generated by the contractor over a specified period of time from all sources, including business operations, investments, and loans. The contractor should maintain a positive cash flow from operations ("operating cash flow"), as well as a positive cash flow from operations minus cash flow from investments ("free cash flow").

Assessing the Contractor's Capacity

Financial statements are not only relevant to determining the contractor's financial strength, but also shed light on the contractor's ability and skill as reflected in the company's past performance and experience. Financial statement information that is relevant to the contractor's capacity includes information regarding work in progress, job cost reporting, equipment availability and compatibility, personnel and management team, work history, business plans, and bank lines of credit.

Work in Progress

Sureties closely examine the current project workload as set forth in the contractor's work in progress (WIP) schedule, and review past performance relating to project deadlines and job planning by the contractor. As described next, the surety will carefully review the WIP schedule for information on backlog, under- and overbillings, and profit trends.

Backlog

Sureties may view a heavy backlog of jobs as an indication that the contractor's resources are overtaxed such that the contractor may not be capable of taking on additional work. If the contractor has little backlog, the surety may be concerned that the contractor cannot meet fixed overhead expenses during down times. The amount of appropriate backlog will depend on the type, size, and duration of construction projects performed by the contractor. For example, contractors with smaller projects that turn around quickly will ideally have more backlog than a contractor who typically performs very large jobs with extended durations.

Under- and Overbillings

Underbillings (often reflected as an asset on the balance sheet as "costs in excess of billings") may indicate that the contractor is financing the project for the owner; or that change orders have not been agreed upon by the owner but the costs are being incurred by the contractor; or that contract costs exceed the contractor's project estimate, resulting in reduced profits. Conversely, overbillings (captioned in the liability section of the balance sheet as "billings in excess of earned revenue") may reflect front-loaded billings, which increase cash, but create a liability on the balance sheet.[1] Overbillings create risk in situations where the amounts collected in advance of earnings have been spent for other uses at the time they are needed for completion, thereby requiring the contractor to seek cash from sources outside the contract in order to complete the work.

Profit Trends

A review of the contractor's WIP schedules for successive periods will indicate the extent to which gross profits have been steadily maintained by the contractor, which in turn indicates the quality of the contractor's estimates and the ability of the contractor to perform in accordance with its estimates.

Job Cost Reporting

Reviewing the contractor's current and historical job cost reporting is imperative to obtain assurance that the contractor has the experience to complete the bonded project. The reporting should be accurate and timely, and should include all the information about the job that the surety will need in order to make a determination. Items to be included in the contractor's job cost reports are listed in Figure 1.

Figure 1
Contract or Job Cost Reporting Requirements

- Job description—include original and estimated completion date(s) and indicate if project is bonded
- Contract price—original contract plus change orders
- Estimated direct costs
- Projected gross profit and gross profit percentage
- Billings to date
- Underbillings: Costs and earned gross profit in excess of billings
- Overbillings: Billings in excess of costs and earned gross profit
- Percentage complete
- Revenue earned
- Direct costs
- Earned projected gross profit

Equipment[2]

The surety closely examines whether the contractor has the necessary machinery and equipment to successfully perform the project, and will look at the age of the equipment and the compatibility of the contractor's equipment to the project. The surety will also confirm the contactor's ability to procure backup or alternate machinery and equipment in case of equipment failure.

Personnel and Management Team

In order to determine if there is sufficient expertise and resources available to perform the necessary tasks involved in the project, the surety reviews the personnel available to the contractor to perform the project. Of particular interest will be any indicators of whether the contractor is appropriately staffed to handle the current workload in addition to the bonded contract project. This will indicate whether the contractor is efficiently organized, has determined the personnel needed for the project, and has effectively established lines of management and communication that are appropriate for the work involved. The contractor should also be structured in a manner that incorporates the procedures, processes, and checks and balances necessary to effectively report the financial and operational information required to fulfill its obligations.

In addition to reviewing the organizational chart, the surety may review the resumes of key employees and managers to assess the capabilities and expertise of the personnel involved in the project. Also relevant to the surety are the contractor's plans for dealing with the loss of certain personnel, which may include the use of back-up personnel and cross-training. For upper-level management and owners, the surety may require and review "key man" insurance policies to determine that plans are in place to avoid disruption of business.

Work History

The surety will examine not only historical financial information, but also the performance track record of the contractor and the company's history. This will include the length of time the contractor has been in business, the geographical location of the work performed, and the type of projects undertaken. The surety will also seek assurance that the contractor has the appropriate government licenses and permits to perform the project.

Business Plan

The contractor should have a well-thought-out and detailed business plan. The surety will compare the business plan to the company's actual business experience to see if the contractor is adhering to the plan. The surety will also determine if the project to be bonded is in line with the contractor's business objective. A well-thought-out, strategic, and thorough business plan also gives the surety an understanding of the contractor's overall business and organization.

Bank Line of Credit

Maintaining a good banking relationship and having the availability to access additional funds to supplement working capital is an important part of the surety's prequalification of the contractor. If the contractor has sufficient unused lines of credit, the surety is assured that the contractor can sustain its operations as circumstances warrant.

Assessing the Contractor's Character

The third "C" considered by both sureties and owners is the character and integrity of the contractor. The surety will perform an in-depth study of the contractor's reputation, will analyze the character of the company's owner(s), and will evaluate the integrity and reliability of the management team. Recently, there has been special emphasis by sureties on the reliability of financial management to ensure timely and truthful reporting. Confidence in a contractor's financial reporting has become almost as important to sureties as its technical expertise and construction capacity, and in order to establish that confidence, it is essential for the contractor to develop a good business relationship with the surety and create a solid basis of trust. The surety will also determine the contractor's character by assessing its integrity, obtaining recommendations and references, and consulting credit and governmental reports.

Integrity Perceived During the "Meet and Greet"

One of the most important parts of the surety's prequalification evaluation process is meeting with the contractor in order to develop a business relationship. Depending on the surety, there may be several meetings with the contractor's owners, key operational personnel, and financial management team. During these meetings, the surety begins making subjective decisions regarding the contractor's character. It is imperative that the contractor be prepared and organized for meetings with the surety during the underwriting process. It is also important that the contractor quickly inform the surety of any anomalies that may arise during the process and be prepared to adequately explain any inconsistencies or problems that would concern the surety. The contractor should disclose any adverse information directly to the surety (accompanied with any necessary explanations, justifications, or qualifications), rather than allowing the surety to discover such information on its own. During the initial evaluation, and throughout the entire relationship with the surety, it is critical for the contractor to provide timely and accurate information, to be responsive to all surety requests, and to proactively manage the surety relationship by continuing to meet directly with the surety and updating all pertinent information.

Letters of Recommendation and References

The surety may gather information and obtain verification of the contractor's character from outside sources. The contractor should have a list of appropriate references to furnish the surety. The contractor should be prepared for the surety to contact third parties such as project owners for whom the contractor has previously worked; subcontractors, suppliers, and vendors with whom the contractor has a business relationship; and other outside professional service providers such as attorneys, CPAs, engineers, and architects.

Third-Party Reports

The surety may consult many available third-party and governmental reporting agencies such as Dun & Bradstreet reports, Uniform Commercial Code filings, and other public report documents. The contractor should be prepared to answer any questions or address any bad reports that may arise from commonly used reporting services. It is also important for the contractor to be current on all licenses, permits, governmental filings, and taxes. Again, the contractor is advised to immediately communicate to the surety any problems relating to third-party reports or governmental filings as well as its plan for resolving the problems, as opposed to withholding the information and allowing the surety to independently discover the problem.

Financial Statement Documents and Supplementary Schedules

As discussed more fully in Chapter 2, contractors' financial statements typically include a report from an independent CPA describing whether an independent audit was conducted or if a lower level of service was provided. Depending on the level of service, the statements are referred to as *audited*, *reviewed*, or *compiled* statements. Basically, an audited financial statement provides the highest level of assurance by a CPA; the company's financial statements are examined, internal controls are reviewed, and a determination or opinion is made as to whether the financial information is fairly stated and in accordance with generally accepted accounting principles (GAAP). A reviewed financial statement is the next level of assurance, and consists primarily of inquiries of management and analytical procedures in order to express limited assurance that the financial statement conforms to GAAP. Under a compilation, the CPA basically presents management's financial information and statements in an appropriate format, but does not express an opinion or any other form of assurance.

Most sureties require, at a minimum, reviewed financial statements; depending upon the contractor, sureties will often insist upon annual audited financial statements. Compiled and internally prepared financials are typically acceptable to a surety only during interim reporting periods.

The major components of the financial statement are discussed in Chapter 2. In addition to the basic financial statement, sureties generally require supplementary schedules of completed contracts and contracts in process, including contract amount, cost to date, estimated cost at completion, and projected profit or loss. Schedules of general and administrative expenses may also be required.

Sureties will examine all components of the contractor's audited or reviewed financial statement, including the supplementary schedules and footnotes. There are some parts considered especially important to the surety during the bonding prequalification. An optional GAAP disclosure that can be very informative to, and may be required by, the surety is information on contract backlog (the value of unearned revenue from contracts on hand), contract completion dates, and commitments on new work. This information will assist the surety in determining the contractor's workload in comparison to its workforce or resources for additional work. It may also indicate that the contractor has too little work and will not be able to cover its fixed overhead costs. Disclosure of backlog information typically includes a reconciliation of contract revenue for the year, which includes unearned contract revenue at the beginning of the year, plus new contracts and contract changes, less contract revenue realized during the year, to yield unearned contract revenue at year end. The surety may also request letters of intent and significant outstanding bids. Typically, backlog disclosures focus on revenue measurements and may also include estimates for costs to complete, gross profit, and measurement of time to perform, sometimes referred to as "burn rate."

In addition, the surety may also review the financial statements and disclosures for information such as general and administrative (G&A) costs, related party transactions, and asset purchase/lease commitments. GAAP requires disclosure of all these items, but sureties may request more detail. G&A costs will be examined by the surety to ensure they are controlled and not excessive, yet sufficient to sustain the contractor's business. Related-party transactions by definition are not at arm's length, and GAAP requires disclosure of all related-party activities. The surety will not only scrutinize these exchanges but may disallow related-party transactions in critical ratio calculations, as discussed later in this chapter. Similar to the surety's review of G&A costs, it is important that the surety determine if the contractor has sufficient fixed assets to support the bonded project and ongoing business without being financially overburdened with equipment debt and lease obligations.

Supplemental schedules are typically included with audited financial statements submitted to bonding companies. Such schedules virtually always include a detailed list of contracts completed during the year, and in process at year end. The schedule of contracts completed and in process is integral to the surety's analysis of job profit trends, and should include such information as owner/job description, estimated completion date, bond information, contract amount, estimated costs at completion, costs incurred to date, percentage complete, and underbillings or overbillings.[3] Other supplemental schedules may include aged accounts receivable and payable schedules; a schedule of direct costs, summarizing the categories of expenses directly related to generating revenue; and a schedule of G&A costs, detailing indirect expenses incurred as a result of being in business and not directly associated with generating revenues.

While supplemental schedules are not a required part of basic financial statements, the surety will normally specify the supplemental information that it wants as part of the financial statement package on which the CPA is reporting.[4] More specifically, in addition to the basic financial statement package, the surety may require certain other schedules, information, and nonfinancial data. The requirements will vary among sureties, but a checklist of possible items that may be requested by the surety during the prequalification process is presented in Figure 2.

Figure 2
Additional Schedules and Information for the Surety

- Contract earnings showing income from contracts completed and in progress for the period(s) reported
- Completed contracts with revenue and cost for the period(s) reported
- Contracts in progress as of the reporting date(s)
- Backlog information
- Inventory listing, which should include job site locations and basis for valuation
- Significant overbilling and underbilling with appropriate explanations

- Schedule of completed contracts showing revenue, costs, gross profit, and percentages for the last three to five years
- Description of the company, which might include
  - History
  - Description of related or affiliated companies
  - Key project descriptions including contract amounts, dates of completion, and job descriptions
- Business plan, including
  - Cash flow projections
  - Forecasts of fixed asset purchases
  - Financing requirements
  - Plan to accomplish business goals
  - Succession plan including resumes of key personnel
  - Recent financial budgets and forecasts
- Appraisals of fixed assets, real estate owned, and other assets
- Recent tax return filings
- Articles of incorporation
- Other significant agreements, which may include
  - Leases
  - Stock buy-sell agreements
  - Employment contracts
  - Deferred compensation agreements and other pension plan documents
  - Noncompete agreements
- Claims experience over the past three years or more, including amounts collected
- Description of litigation or lawsuits in progress
- Insurance coverage, including life insurance policies on key personnel and copies of surety bonds on any recent projects
- References (with name and address), including from
  - Bank(s) and bank officer(s)
  - Attorney(s)
  - Insurance agent(s)
  - Engineers and architects
  - Suppliers and subcontractors

Financial Tests, Measures, and Ratios Derived from the Contractor's Financial Information

As part of the bond prequalification process, the surety will perform an analysis of the contractor's key ratios and financial indicators in order to analyze the financial strengths and weaknesses of the contractor, and assess and confirm the contractor's solvency. (See Exhibit 3-1, Financial Analysis Ratios Used by Sureties.)

Exhibit 3-1
FINANCIAL ANALYSIS RATIOS USED BY SURETIES

Liquidity Ratios

Measures the contractor's ability to pay maturing obligations

$$\text{Quick Ratio} = \frac{\text{Cash} + \text{Cash Equivalents} + \text{Accounts Receivable}}{\text{Current Liabilities}}$$

$$\text{Current Ratio} = \frac{\text{Current Assets (including noncash items)}}{\text{Current Liabilities}}$$

$$\text{Net Working Capital} = \text{Current Assets} - \text{Current Liabilities}$$

$$\text{Net Worth} = \text{Total Assets} - \text{Total Liabilities}$$

Leverage Ratios

Measures the extent to which the contractor has financed its operations using debt, investments, or reinvestment of profits

$$\text{Debt to Equity} = \frac{\text{Total Debt}}{\text{Total Equity}}$$

$$\text{Debt Coverage Ratio} = \frac{\text{Income before Interest and Depreciation}}{\text{Principal and Interest Charges on Debt}}$$

$$\text{Times Interest Earned} = \frac{\text{Earnings before Interest and Taxes}}{\text{Interest Charges}}$$

Profitability Ratios

Measures the degree of the contractor's operations for a period of time

$$\text{Return on Investment or Return on Equity} = \frac{\text{Net Income}}{\text{Average Equity}}$$

$$\text{Gross Profit or Margin as a Percent of Sales} = \frac{\text{Gross Profit or Margin}}{\text{Sales}}$$

$$\text{Net Income as a Percent of Sales} = \frac{\text{Net Income}}{\text{Sales}}$$

$$\text{Return on Assets} = \frac{\text{Net Income}}{\text{Average Total Assets}}$$

$$\text{Underbillings to Net Worth} = \frac{\text{Underbillings}}{\text{Equity}}$$

Activity Ratios

Measures how effectively the contractor is utilizing its available assets

$$\text{Days Payable Outstanding} = \frac{\text{Payables}}{\text{Cost of Sales (COS) per Day (= COS for Period/Number of Days in Period)}}$$

$$\text{Days Receivable Outstanding} = \frac{\text{Accounts Receivable}}{\text{Credit Sales per Day (= Sales on Credit for Period/Number of Days in Period)}}$$

$$\text{Inventory Turnover} = \frac{\text{Cost of Sales}}{\text{Average Inventory Balance}}$$

$$\text{Sales to Assets} = \frac{\text{Total Sales}}{\text{Total Assets}}$$

Perhaps most important are the *liquidity ratios*, which measure the contractor's ability to pay maturing obligations. These ratios assess the current liquidity of the company, and are an indicator of whether the company can pay all liabilities currently due without selling any inventory. Calculation of the liquidity ratios can take several forms:

- *Quick ratio.* The quick or net quick ratio is calculated by computing the ratio of liquid current assets[5] (this normally includes cash, cash equivalents, and accounts receivable but excludes inventory, prepaid assets, and other noncash current assets) divided by current liabilities. Sureties generally require a net quick ratio in excess of 1:1.
- *Current ratio.* The current ratio calculation is similar to the net quick ratio, but includes inventory and other noncash items in current assets. This is an important indicator of whether the contractor is able to meet immediate obligations. Again, a ratio of 1:1 or greater indicates positive net working capital.
- *Net working capital.* Net working capital is the excess of total current assets to total current liabilities. It is used in conjunction with the net quick and current ratios to measure the dollar amount of the contractor's working capital.

- *Net worth.* Net worth is simply the net book value of the company, that is, total assets minus total liabilities. Stated another way, it is the sum of the owners' investment in the company (paid in capital), plus or minus the company's cumulative earnings or losses. Net worth is an important measure of a company's viability and credit worthiness because it demonstrates the owner's net investment in the company in comparison to the total assets and liabilities.

As part of the calculation of all of the above ratios, sureties commonly make various adjustments to the current assets reported in the financial statement in order to refine their analysis. Some of these adjustments might include the following:

- *Accounts receivable.* The surety will examine the collectability of the contractor's receivables and will disallow or discount for
  - Receivables aged over 90 days, which indicate to the surety that the amount may be in dispute or the funds may not be collectible;
  - Underbillings, which may not be considered currently collectible, and are prone to be discounted as the job extends and winds down;
  - Retainage, which the surety may regard as a noncurrent asset, or as an item likely to be discounted or offset as the job is closed out; and
  - Related-party receivables, which will normally be disallowed as a current asset because the funds are internal.
- *Marketable securities.* Construction contractors having surplus cash may invest the excess in various types of marketable securities. Accounting for securities can be complicated, but generally, temporary investments in marketable securities are recorded on financial statements at fair value. The footnotes to the financial statements should disclose any significant assumptions made or methods used in determining fair value, as well as the amount of any unrealized gains and losses. The surety will look at the market to determine the current value. Although marketable securities can be considered to be liquid, the surety may regard them as long-term investments and therefore opt to exclude them in their entirety.
- *Prepaid assets.* Since prepaid assets are not liquid and normally cannot be converted to cash, they are excluded from the net quick ratio calculation.
- *Other assets.* Intangibles such as goodwill are not considered to become available as cash, and are excluded. Loans receivable will be separately evaluated, and may also be excluded depending on their liquidity.

Other ratios used by the surety, detailed in Exhibit 3-1 and described next, are compared to ratios typical for the contractor's industry, which are available in such industry sources as the Almanac of Business and Industrial Financial Ratios. Typically, the surety will want the contractor's ratios to be within a reasonable range of the industry average.

- *Leverage ratios* measure the extent to which the contractor has financed its operations using debt, investments, or reinvestment of profits. This is extremely important to the surety in determining credit worthiness.

The surety will prefer that a contractor maintain a debt-to-net worth ratio of 2:1 or less, and no more than a 3:1 ratio of total debt to equity. Leverage ratios also include the "debt coverage ratio," which indicates whether the contractor has adequate operating income to cover the interest payments on its debt.

- *Profitability ratios* determine the contractor's "net profit margin," calculated as net income divided by net sales, with the result expressed as a percentage. As with leverage ratios, the net profit margin is compared with the net profit margin for the contractor's industry, and according to sureties should be within 25 percent to 30 percent of the industry average.
- *Activity ratios* measure how effectively the contractor is utilizing its available assets by focusing on the length of time in which payables and receivables are outstanding, and the length of time the contractor's inventory turns over.

Sample Analysis of a Contractor's Financial Statements

The surety takes the financial information provided by the contractor and its CPA, and prepares reports and schedules to document its prequalification examination and to substantiate the decision whether to recommend bonding the contractor for the project. The surety will look at comparative data for two to four years, and will factor in the level of CPA assurance, giving more credibility to audited statements, less to reviewed statements, and even less to compiled financial information. The surety will then calculate key ratios and perform an analytical review of the financial information, including comparisons to industry trends. Exhibit 3-2 is an example of the reports and ratio analysis a surety would compile from sample financial statements.

Exhibit 3-2
Example: Surety Ratio Report

Example Construction Contactor
Surety Ratio Report
for the years ended December 31

	2009 (Audited)	2008 (Review)	2007 (Review)	2006 (Compilation)
KEY RATIOS				
Net Quick (Current Assets without A/R > 90 Days, Retainage and Prepaids less Current Liabilities)	1,474,000	1,161,000	771,000	1,676,000
Net Worth (Total Assets less Total Liabilities)	2,751,000	2,362,000	1,936,000	2,189,000

Exhibit 3-2 (continued)–

	2009 (Audited)	2008 (Review)	2007 (Review)	2006 (Compilation)
KEY RATIOS				
Net Income	389,000	426,000	(253,000)	(9,000)
LIQUIDITY				
Quick Ratio (adjusted for A/R > 90, Days Retainage and Prepaids)	1.73	1.72	1.54	3.66
Current Ratio	1.99	1.99	1.89	4.03
Bank Line of Credit Used	0	0	0	0
Bank Line of Credit Unused	1,200,000	1,200,000	1,200,000	900,000
LEVERAGE				
Debt to Equity	86%	84%	94%	29%
Debt Cover Ratio	16%	21%	−14%	−1%
PROFITABLITY				
Return on Investment	15%	20%	−12%	0%
Gross Profit as a % of Sales	18%	19%	17%	18%
Net Income as a % of Sales	3%	5%	−5%	0%
Return on Assets	8%	11%	−8%	−1%
ACTIVITY				
Days Payable Outstanding	28.96	43.28	61.01	12.57
Days Receivable Outstanding	68.05	85.18	82.86	34.65
Sales to Assets	2.36	2.17	1.43	2.87

As shown in Exhibit 3-2, the surety would determine the contractor's financial position by analyzing the net quick ratio and current ratio. Both of these ratios are in excess of 1, indicating that the contractor has good net working capital. The net quick and net worth calculations show that the contractor can more than cover its liabilities and has a stable equity base. The debt to equity ratios are less than the typical surety's benchmark of 2:1. The profitability and activity ratios above show that the contractor is expanding business; the surety would compare these results to industry averages to determine if they are appropriate. These analyses, along with the surety's investigation of the contractor's capacity and character, are important factors in the prequalification process and in maintaining an ongoing bonding relationship between the surety and contractor.

Conclusion

Whether seeking to obtain or maintain surety credit, or to be adjudged a responsible bidder, contractors should expect their financial statements to be scrutinized and analyzed. When properly assembled and presented, the financial statement is one of the few independent sources of information available for a surety to determine whether a contractor has the capital and capacity that render it worthy of bonding, and for an owner to confirm that the contractor satisfies required standards of bidder responsibility. That being the case, it is essential for contractors to ensure that their financial records contain the necessary information, and satisfy the financial benchmarks and criteria, expected by sureties and owners. In addition to conducting a thorough analysis of a contactor's financial statements and ratios, sureties and owners will also rely heavily on their assessment of the contractor's character in completing the underwriting and/or contractor bid acceptance process.

Notes

1. For financial reporting purposes, revenue is generally recognized by the *percentage-of-completion* method computed on the *cost incurred to total estimated cost at completion* method. As a result, billings, which are computed according to contract terms on an item-by-item basis, will generally differ from earned revenue, which is computed on the basis of the estimated cost for the entire contract.

2. Equipment is generally a much more significant investment for heavy construction and site development (earth moving) contractors than for building contractors, which frequently subcontract out equipment-intensive requirements.

3. Over- and underbillings are referred to as billings in excess of earned revenue (overbillings) and costs in excess of earned revenue (underbillings) in financial statements.

4. The basic financial statements required by GAAP are the balance sheet, income statement, statement of cash flows, and statement of changes in owner's equity.

5. Construction contractors' balance sheets are often presented on an unclassified basis where assets and liabilities are listed in order of liquidity or maturity, but without a distinction between current and noncurrent balances. This is because contractors frequently have long-term contracts that extend beyond one year. In these situations, a bonding company will typically make its own determination of current assets and liabilities based upon the information provided.

CHAPTER 4

Booking of Claims for Financial Reporting Purposes

KEVIN D. DENNIS
SCOTT D. GRAY
THOMAS R. LYNCH
ROBERT J. SYMON

Introduction

Construction claims come in all shapes and sizes. Claims may arise from issues such as extra work, changed conditions, price escalation, acceleration, disruption, delay, or owner interference, and may include various types of damages such as additional direct labor and material costs, subcontractor costs, lost productive labor costs, jobsite overhead, unabsorbed or extended home office overhead, or lost profits, among others. Claims may be based on a single disputed issue and represent a comparatively small amount of the total contract value; or claims may concern a much larger issue, such as a cardinal change that results in damages significantly exceeding the original contract value. Given the variety and complexity of construction claims, combined with the uncertainty of recovery, it is often difficult for the construction contractor and its accounting and legal advisors to determine when, where, and how a claim should be booked for financial reporting purposes. In other words, how do you know whether, and to what extent, a client can recognize a claim as revenue and where that revenue should be disclosed in the financial statements?

The next section of this chapter summarizes the relevant accounting guidance on booking construction contract revenue and construction claims as provided by generally accepted accounting principles (GAAP).[1] These standards deal with the nuances and complexities of construction accounting and provide a framework for determining how to handle the recognition of revenue and financial statement disclosures required when booking claims. Specifically for the issues presented here, the American Institute of Certified

Public Accountants (AICPA) Audit and Accounting Guide—Construction Contractors is the most comprehensive compilation of relevant guidance, particularly Statement of Position (SOP) 81-1 contained within the guide.

This chapter then summarizes the applicable case law addressing the proper recognition of claims revenue, and the potential liability that lawyers and accountants may face for their representations or the representations of their clients relating to the recognition or value of claims revenue. As will be evident, while GAAP provides guidance on the proper methods for booking claims revenue, these standards leave a considerable gray area as to what is and is not proper in terms of accounting for revenue for which entitlement and amount is not yet certain.

GAAP Requirements for Booking Revenue and Claims on Long-Term Construction Contracts

General Requirements for Recognizing Revenue on Long-Term Construction Contracts

The first step in properly recognizing revenue on long-term construction contracts[2] is to select a method for measuring progress and to apply that method consistently across all similarly structured contracts of the business entity. AICPA SOP 81-1, Accounting for Performance of Construction-Type and Certain Production-Type Contracts, and Accounting Research Bulletin (ARB) No. 45 provide the relevant accounting guidance on selecting an appropriate method for measuring progress on a project and accounting for the corresponding revenue generated for that progress. SOP 81-1 and ARB No. 45 recommend use of the percentage-of-completion method of accounting, in which a pro rata portion of the estimated final profit on a contract is recognized in each period based on an appropriate measure of the completion of the project.

SOP 81-1 states in relevant part:

> 44. In practice, a number of methods are used to measure the extent of progress toward completion. They include the cost-to-cost method, variations of the cost-to-cost method, efforts-expended method, the units-of-delivery method and the units-of-work performed method. Those practices are intended to conform to ARB No. 45, paragraph 4. Some of the measures are sometimes made and certified by engineers and architects, but management should review and understand the procedures used by those professionals.
>
> 45. Some methods used in practice measure progress toward completion in terms of costs, some in terms of units of work, and some in terms of values added (the contract value of the total work performed to date). All three of these measures of progress are

acceptable in appropriate circumstances. The division concluded that other methods that achieve the objective of measuring extent of progress toward completion in terms of costs, units, or value added are also acceptable in appropriate circumstances. However, the method or methods selected should be applied consistently to all contracts having similar circumstances. The method or methods of measuring extent of progress toward completion should be disclosed in the notes to the financial statements. Examples of circumstances not appropriate to some methods are given within the discussion of input and output measures.

Similarly, ARB No. 45, paragraph 4, referenced in SOP 81-1, states as follows:

The percentage-of-completion method recognizes income as work on a contract progresses. The committee recommends that the recognized income be that percentage of estimated total income, either:

a. that incurred costs to date bear to estimated total costs after giving effect to estimates of costs to complete based on most recent information, or

b. that may be indicated by such other measure of progress toward completion as may be appropriate having due regard to work performed.

Costs as here used might exclude, especially during the early stages of a contract, all or a portion of the cost of such items as materials and subcontracts if it appears that such an exclusion would result in a more meaningful periodic allocation of income.

Regardless of which one of the above-described methods a company chooses to measure percentage-of-completion on a project and recognize revenue, the actual implementation of that method will be complex. Accounting for construction contracts on a percentage-of-completion basis requires that a contractor have the capability to accurately estimate a project's final cost and final profit and to recognize the appropriate amount of that profit in each accounting period. To the extent that these estimates change in subsequent periods, the impact of the change is recorded in that subsequent period. Thus, the GAAP standards for recognizing revenue, by their terms, call for a large amount of discretion. GAAP also implicitly calls for the accountant or lawyer to rely on the work product of others, including the contractor's personnel who prepare the estimates, when making decisions about how income should be recognized or whether a company's accounting practices are reasonable. In that case, the accountant or lawyer may seek specialized expertise (e.g., from engineers, construction managers, or architects) to examine the reasonableness of the estimates or data supporting the estimates. Regardless of the accounting method selected, it is also important to remember, as stated in SOP

81-1 (.45), that GAAP requires that financial statements contain an explicit disclosure of the method used to measure progress on projects. The importance of disclosing fundamental changes in accounting treatment of claims revenue is the subject of one of the cases discussed later in this chapter.

While there is a large amount of discretion involved in implementing the percentage-of-completion method for recognizing revenue, GAAP does provide some clear guidelines on what is not proper. The most important example of a prohibited method of measuring percentage-of-completion is the use of cash payments, such as for the achievement of certain events (i.e., milestone payments) or for mobilization (to either start a project or a new work item). In many instances, these payments do not reflect the actual percentage of work completed. GAAP requires that the measurement of percentage-of-completion be based on the progress of the work and *not* on payments received pursuant to a payment schedule. SOP 81-1 (.6) states:

> 6. In practice, methods are sometimes found that allocate contract costs and revenues to accounting periods on (a) the basis of cash receipts and payment or (b) the basis of contract billings and costs incurred. Those practices are not generally accepted methods of accounting for financial reporting purposes. However, those methods are appropriate for other purposes, such as the measurement of income for income tax purposes, for which the timing of cash transactions is a controlling factor. Recording the amounts billed or billable on a contract during a period as contract revenue of the period, and the costs incurred on the contract as expenses of the period, is not acceptable for financial reporting purposes because the amounts billed or billable on a contract during a period are determined by contract terms and do not necessarily measure performance on a contract. Only by coincidence might those unacceptable methods produce results that approximate the results of the generally accepted method of accounting for contracts that are appropriate in the circumstances.

Thus, an accountant should not rely on the timing of payments as a measure of the percentage-of-completion for a particular project.

GAAP Guidelines for Recognizing Revenue on Change Orders or Claims

A unique aspect of the construction industry that adds substantial complexity to the revenue recognition process is the right of the owner (or higher-tier contractor) to direct changes to the work, and the related issue of accounting for unpriced or disputed change orders or claims. Construction contracts in the United States typically give the project owner the right to direct changes to the work, in exchange for providing equitable compensation for the effect of the change on the project cost and time of performance. This generally includes the right to direct the contractor to proceed with the changed work in instances in which the scope of the change has not been defined or agreed between the parties and/or in which the equitable price or schedule adjustment has not been negotiated and agreed upon.

"Constructive changes" present a similar problem. Constructive changes generally represent instances in which there is a dispute over whether a particular aspect of the work is included within the original contract or reflects a change from what is required by the contract. Typically, construction contracts also require that the contractor continue performing the work pending resolution of the dispute regarding the existence of such constructive changes.

This ability of the owner to order the implementation of a change (formal or constructive) before a final agreement on price often results in "unpriced change orders," "unpriced claims," or disputed claims at the end of an accounting period. Such unpriced change orders and claims require that the contractor periodically prepare an appropriate estimate of the final agreed price or cost for these changes. Thus, accounting for change orders and claims that have not been approved as to entitlement or quantified as to price adds significantly to the complexity and uncertainty of the accounting for contracts in the construction industry.

As it relates to the specific issue of the recognition of revenue from claims or unapproved change orders, the basic guidance is again provided in SOP 81-1.[3] With respect to accounting for changes to the original contract price, SOP 81-1 discusses four scenarios. These scenarios and the relevant accounting treatment are as follows:

- *Approved change orders* occur where both scope and price are agreed. In this case, both change order revenues and projected change order costs should be reflected in the percentage-of-completion calculation.[4]
- *Unpriced change orders* occur where the extra work to be performed is defined, but the adjustment to the contract price is to be negotiated later.[5] In this case, if the recovery of an increase in contract price is "probable . . . [the costs] should be treated as costs of contract performance in the period in which they are incurred, and contract revenue should be recognized to the extent of costs incurred."[6] Revenue in excess of estimated costs can be recorded when "realization is assured beyond a reasonable doubt . . . such as circumstances in which an entity's historical experience provides such assurance."[7]
- *Claims* are defined and discussed in SOP 81-1 (.65) as follows:

65. Claims are amounts in excess of the agreed contract price (or amounts not included in the original contract price) that a contractor seeks to collect from customers or others for customer-caused delays, errors in specifications and designs, contract terminations, change orders in dispute or unapproved as to both scope and price, or other causes of unanticipated additional costs.

Recognition of amounts of additional contract revenue relating to claims is appropriate only if it is probable that the claim will result in additional contract revenue and if the amount can be reliably estimated. These two requirements are satisfied by the existence of all the following conditions:

   a. The contract or other evidence provides a legal basis for the claim; or a legal opinion has been obtained, stating that under the circumstances there is a reasonable basis to support the claim.
   b. Additional costs are caused by circumstances that were unforeseen at the contract date and are not the result of deficiencies in the contractor's performance.
   c. Costs associated with the claim are identifiable or otherwise determinable and are reasonable in view of the work performed.
   d. The evidence supporting the claim is objective and verifiable, not based on management's "feel" for the situation or on unsupported representations.

   > If the foregoing requirements are met, revenue from a claim should be recorded only to the extent that contract costs relating to the claim have been incurred. The amounts recorded, if material, should be disclosed in the notes to the financial statements. Costs attributable to claims should be treated as costs of contract performance as incurred.

- *Unapproved change orders* occur where change orders are in dispute or are unapproved in regard to both scope and price, and should be evaluated as claims.[8]

In light of the guidance described above, some key issues to address when considering the reasonableness of decisions to recognize revenue for change orders and claims include:

- Does the contractor have reasonable procedures and internal controls in place to collect reliable accounting information from its various subsidiaries and/or affiliates?
- Have company personnel at appropriate levels (e.g., project manager of project in question; controller or general manager of a subsidiary or affiliate) provided certification or representations supporting the change orders or claims in question?
- Does the contractor have established procedures for developing change orders or claims for changed work that is consistent with the way change orders are written and presented in the construction industry? If so, have the subject change orders or claims been prepared in compliance with those procedures?

- Are the change orders or claims in question based upon significant factual evidence that the specific amounts claimed are due?
- Do the types of costs claimed logically flow from the types of changes or impacts that are alleged to have occurred?
- Are the submitted costs calculated using recognized methodologies and adequately supported by underlying documentation?
- Is there some form of acknowledgment on the part of the contractor's customer that there are amounts due, and a basis for entitlement, for the change orders or claims in question?
- Has contractor's counsel provided its opinion as to the legal basis for the claims and the potential for recovery?

Paying attention to these issues and complying with the guidance set forth in SOP 81-1 are the keys to ensuring that a contractor is properly accounting for claims revenue in accordance with GAAP.

Liabilities Associated with Attorney Opinion Letters Related to Claims

The case law on attorney liability for statements made to third parties regarding their client's claims generally holds that compliance with GAAP provides a "safe harbor" for statements made in claim opinion letters. In other words, the best way to avoid exposure to liability for opinion letter statements is to ensure that the claim meets the four factors set forth in SOP 81-1(.65) above for GAAP compliance. Furthermore, lawyers and accountants will generally not be held liable for any misrepresentations in an opinion letter unless it can be proven that they knowingly assisted in creating the misrepresentation or were recklessly negligent.[9] The case law indicates that compliance with GAAP will insulate lawyers against any argument that they were "recklessly negligent" in making a misstatement regarding the value of a claim.[10]

As explained above, GAAP compliance with respect to construction claims requires that (1) it is probable that the claim will result in additional contract revenue; and (2) the amount of the claim can be reliably estimated. As previously noted, SOP 81-1 (.65) then sets forth the four factors above for ensuring a claim complies with GAAP.

The lawyer should be careful to ensure that each of these four criteria are met, either through his own study of the claim or through written confirmation from the client, before writing any opinion letter regarding the client's claim. If the claim does not meet these criteria, the lawyer should insist that the claim value be amended to meet GAAP before any opinion letter is rendered.

After the lawyer is satisfied that the claim complies with GAAP, he should also ensure that the letter, in some form, expresses the contingent nature of the claim. In other words, the letter should make clear the lawyer is not guaranteeing recovery in the amount of the claim. Statements or opinions that treat a claim as certain revenue, without disclosing the contingent nature of the claim, may also expose a lawyer to liability.[11]

Finally, if the lawyer encounters any "red flags" while evaluating the validity of the claim, such as, for example, a lack of reasonable procedures and internal controls by the client for collecting reliable accounting information, evidence that outside parties have questioned the accounting practices of the client, or an inability by the client to support the value of the claim, then the lawyer should refuse to render the letter. Ignoring red flags or suspicious events such as those described above are the primary evidence of the type of "reckless negligence" that is the standard applied when seeking to hold a lawyer liable for an opinion letter.[12]

Liability of Lawyers and Accountants for Statements Made in the Scope of Client Representation

In the aftermath of widely publicized accounting scandals involving Enron, Refco, and other large companies, a legal debate has emerged regarding the extent to which secondary actors such as lawyers and accountants should be held liable for negligent or intentional misrepresentations relating to various types of accounting fraud and other accounting-related misrepresentations. The extent to which lawyers and accountants practicing in the construction industry can be held liable for their client's improper reporting of revenue for unapproved claims is one strand in this larger debate over secondary actor liability. In general, lawyer and accountant liability for statements made in connection with booking of claims can be divided into two categories: "primary liability" and "aiding and abetting liability." Primary liability is the term used when the lawyer or accountant is the alleged wrongdoer. Aiding and abetting, or "secondary" liability, on the other hand, describes a scenario in which the injured party seeks to hold the lawyer or accountant liable for assisting the wrongdoing of the primary violator, usually the client corporation or its officers. The scope and nature of both primary and aiding and abetting liability are discussed below.

Regardless of whether the theory of liability is primary or secondary, the seminal cases in this area suggest that compliance with GAAP, including specifically SOP 81-1 (.65), may provide a "safe harbor" to lawyers and accountants from liability relating to statements made to third parties regarding their clients' treatment of unrealized claims revenue.[13] For example, in *Securities & Exchange Commission v. Morris*, the court applied SOP 81-1 (.65) to determine whether a chief financial officer was negligent in reporting claims as income on publicly filed financial documents.[14] Accordingly, it can be logically inferred that compliance with GAAP will in most cases insulate the professional advisor. Furthermore, lawyers and accountants will generally not be held liable for misrepresentations relating to claims recognition unless it can be proven that they knowingly assisted in creating the misrepresentation or were recklessly negligent.

Primary Liability

The most high-profile litigation relating to lawyer and accountant primary liability for alleged fraud or negligent misrepresentations in connection with accounting practices has arisen in the context of federal securities laws. A substantial number of recent cases have also addressed lawyer and accountant primary liability in the context of state common law tort suits. The legal concepts governing primary liability of lawyers and accountants under federal law and state law are often similar and overlapping. However, the underlying basis for liability in the state context (common law liability theories) and the federal context (statute-based liability) are fundamentally different. For this reason, lawyer and accountant primary liability under state and federal law are discussed separately.

Primary Liability Under Federal Securities Law

For primary liability to attach under federal securities laws, the alleged misrepresentation by the lawyer or accountant must have been made in connection with the purchase or sale of a publicly traded security.[15] Additionally, the alleged misstatement must have been publicly disseminated so as to influence investor behavior.[16] The Supreme Court has stated that in order to establish primary liability under federal securities laws, a plaintiff must show (1) a material misrepresentation or omission by the accountant or attorney; (2) *scienter* (i.e., knowledge); (3) a connection between the misrepresentation or omission and the purchase or sale of a security; (4) reliance upon the misrepresentation or omission; (5) economic loss; and (6) loss causation.[17]

The federal circuit courts have grappled with the question of what constitutes the making of a "material misrepresentation or omission" under this standard.[18] The Second, Tenth, and Eleventh Circuits have adopted a bright-line test that requires the secondary actor, that is, the lawyer or accountant, to publish or sign the alleged material misstatement.[19] In other words, in order to be liable for an alleged fraudulent misrepresentation under this bright-line test, it must be apparent to the world that the lawyer or accountant was the person making the statement, and not the client. Other federal courts, including the Ninth Circuit, have adopted a more flexible standard known as the "substantial participation" test.[20] Under this test, a secondary actor can be charged with primary liability if he or she substantially participates in the preparation of materially false or misleading statements. So under this standard, the lawyer or accountant need not sign the statement to be held liable for an alleged fraud. Rather, the lawyer or accountant's participation in the preparation of the alleged material misrepresentation, for example by drafting a fraudulent statement to be disseminated under the name of the client, can lead to liability for the lawyer or accountant provided the other elements for primary liability, including the knowledge/*scienter* requirement, are proven.[21] The substantial participation test has been criticized because it is difficult to distinguish from the substantive test for aiding and abetting liability, as discussed below.

Despite the subtle differences in various judicial pronouncements regarding the test for primary liability, practical guidance in this area can be extracted from a trilogy of federal district court cases that deal with primary liability in the context of recognizing claims or unapproved change orders as revenue under SOP 81-1. Of particular importance are two decisions from the Southern District of Texas concerning allegations that Halliburton's chief financial officer committed fraud and was negligent in approving certain Securities and Exchange Commission (SEC) filings of Halliburton, without disclosing in the filings that Halliburton had changed its accounting practices to allow for recognition of unapproved claims as revenue.[22] The SEC brought claims against Halliburton's CFO under both "primary" and "aiding and abetting" liability theories on the ground that he had "reviewed, edited and signed" the financial reports filed with the SEC.[23]

Specifically, the SEC alleged in *Morris* that from 1993 until the first quarter of 1998, Halliburton had recognized claims for additional compensation during the period such claims were resolved, but that in the second quarter of 1998, Halliburton "began recognizing as revenue claims for additional contract compensation arising from cost overruns that Halliburton had not resolved with its customers."[24] As a result of this accounting change, losses from cost overruns on several Halliburton contracts were "reduced or eliminated" for purposes of the company's financial statements.[25] Although the SEC did not allege that Halliburton had violated any accounting principles by changing its accounting treatment of unapproved claims, the SEC alleged instead that the failure to disclose the accounting change over six reporting periods made the periodic reports and other public statements issued during those periods materially misleading.[26]

While the court refused to dismiss the SEC's primary liability counts at the motion to dismiss stage,[27] the court later dismissed those counts at the request of the SEC. In affirming the SEC's voluntary dismissal of its claims against Morris, the court felt compelled to issue a written decision exonerating Morris. Indeed, the court relied on SOP 81-1 (.65) and stated that "[a]ccounting principles allow recognition of unapproved claims for additional compensation if and when it is probable that the claims will be paid and the amounts can be reliably estimated."[28] The court further found that Halliburton's "decision to recognize the unapproved claim revenue under SOP 81-1 (.65) was based on the conclusion that it was probable that the claims would be paid and the amounts could be reliably estimated."[29] As such, Halliburton's accounting practices were deemed proper as a matter of law.

With respect to the SEC's argument that Halliburton's CFO was negligent in failing to disclose a material accounting change, the court noted that the key question was "whether it was reasonable to conclude that the risk of nonpayment of the unapproved claims for additional compensation, considered with the other aspects of the company's financial condition, was not material and did not have to be disclosed,"[30] and that "negligence in this context requires the absence of a reasonable basis."[31] The SEC argued that the failure to disclose the accounting change was material because the lack of disclosure made it difficult to meaningfully compare periodic income reports from years preceding the accounting change to periodic reports produced after the accounting change. [32] In rejecting this argument, the *Morris* court pointed to the fact that Halliburton did not accrue any significant amounts of unapproved claim revenue prior to its accounting change in 1998, and that the periodic reports produced prior to the accounting change would not have been materially different *even if* Halliburton had used the new accounting treatment in the earlier reports.[33] Therefore, the court reasoned, even if Halliburton had been recognizing unapproved claims as revenue in previous reports, the previous reports would have been materially the same and comparison between the new and old reports would have been difficult regardless of disclosure of the accounting change. [34] The *Morris* court also relied on the extensive "materiality" review conducted by Halliburton accountants and its outside accounting firm, as well as the large amount of income Halliburton reported as a whole, in determining that the accounting change was not material.[35] Although the propriety of Halliburton's use of SOP 81-1(.65) with respect to unapproved claims was not directly at issue in *Morris*, the court's decision supports the notion that it is proper to recognize unapproved claims as revenue "if it is probable that the claim will result in additional contract revenue and if the amount can be reliably estimated."

Another federal district court case, *In re Raytheon Securities Litigation*, helps to define to what extent it is proper to recognize unapproved claims as income under SOP 81-1(.65). [36] In *Raytheon*, multiple plaintiffs brought a private class action suit against Raytheon, some of its corporate officers, and its outside accounting firm PricewaterhouseCoopers (PwC) for allegedly violating federal securities laws by overstating unapproved claim revenue from government contracts in violation of GAAP.[37] Internal company documents showed Raytheon stood to lose over $433 million under certain government contracts but, due to recognition of certain unapproved claims as revenue, those losses were significantly reduced in Raytheon's public reports.[38] The court denied Raytheon's motion to dismiss because (1) internal documents showed that the actual losses on the government contracts would be greater than Raytheon had reported; (2) historical data showed that Raytheon had collected only 20 percent to 30 percent of its claimed amounts on similar unapproved claims, but was recognizing a much greater percentage of recovery as revenue in its public reports; and (3) information about the contracts at issue showed that recovery to the extent recognized by Raytheon in its public reports "was a long shot."[39]

In holding that plaintiffs had stated a claim sufficient to survive a motion to dismiss, the court rebuked the Raytheon defendants' argument that since "GAAP require a fair degree of leeway" and "a large measure of judgment and guesswork," the plaintiffs could not show the requisite degree of *scienter* based upon Raytheon's alleged violation of GAAP alone.[40] To the contrary, the court found that although GAAP "tolerates a range of reasonable treatments . . . an application of GAAP that strays beyond the boundaries of reasonableness will provide evidence from which *scienter* can be inferred." The court relied on a First Circuit case for the proposition that "violations of GAAP standards . . . could provide evidence of scienter."[41]

While *Raytheon* stands for the principle that knowing violations of GAAP can lead to liability under federal securities laws, the case also provides a level of protection for secondary actors such as lawyers and accountants. In dismissing the complaint against PwC on PwC's motion to dismiss, the court found it relevant that PwC was not aware of the internal Raytheon documents that allegedly showed that Raytheon's accounting treatment of the unapproved claims violated GAAP.[42] The court also found that the complaint did not contain any allegations that PwC was confronted with red flags such as (1) PwC knowledge that Raytheon's own internal audit controls were "skimpy or nonexistent"; (2) "that PwC butted heads with Raytheon over the company's accounting practices"; or (3) that "Raytheon's accounting practices were ever called into question by any inside or outside source in a manner that would give a reasonable auditor pause."[43] Based on the failure to allege facts from which the requisite level of *scienter* could be inferred against PwC, the court dismissed the claim against PwC.[44] Thus, *Raytheon* upheld the principle that secondary actors, like their client counterparts, must know or have reason to know of an alleged fraud in order to be held liable for a client's accounting violations.

A third decision dealing specifically with recognition of unapproved claims revenue, *Fuechtman v. Mastec, Inc.*,[45] refused to dismiss a suit that alleged that the corporation and its officers "intentionally recognized millions of dollars worth of revenue from change orders they knew would never be paid."[46] The decision stands for the commonsense principle that an individual or corporation can be held liable under federal securities laws by participating in a scheme to improperly recognize unapproved claims as revenue, with knowledge that such claims will not be recovered. *Fuechtman* is consistent with *Morris* and *Raytheon* in holding that determining whether knowing violations of GAAP actually occurred is not a matter to be determined on a motion to dismiss.[47]

In short, secondary actors such as lawyers and accountants can avoid legal liability and damages for accounting misstatements made by clients as long as the client's application of GAAP appears reasonable and the lawyer or accountant is not aware of any red flags that would lead one to believe that a violation of GAAP has occurred or that the recognition of revenue under SOP 81-1 (.65) was improper. Otherwise, lawyers and accountants do face potential liability.

Primary Liability Under State Law

There are no known state-law court decisions that deal with the issue of lawyer or accountant liability for the treatment of unapproved claims under GAAP. However, a multitude of state law opinions have held that a lawyer can be liable for fraud or negligent misrepresentation claims based on statements made by the lawyer in an opinion letter.[48] Other state courts have held generally that a lawyer cannot be held liable to a nonclient for actions taken in the scope of representing a client.[49] These opinions rely, to varying degrees, on public policy concerns that imposing lawyer liability for actions taken within the scope of a client representation could have a "chilling effect" on the effectiveness of legal representation.

"Secondary" or "Aiding and Abetting" Liability

The federal securities laws permit the SEC to pursue individuals for "aiding and abetting" securities law violations.[50] This cause of action is not available to private plaintiffs, however.[51] *Restatement (Second) of Torts* § 876 also recognizes a cause of action for aiding and abetting certain common-law torts, but this potential theory of liability has not been relied upon by any court in the context of the treatment of unapproved claims under GAAP.[52]

The only known case dealing with aiding and abetting liability in connection with the treatment of unapproved claims under GAAP is the *Morris* case described earlier.[53] The court there considered whether Morris knowingly aided and abetted Halliburton's violations of federal securities laws. The applicable test for establishing aider and abettor liability under federal securities laws was stated as follows:

> To establish aider and abettor liability for securities violations, the plaintiff must show that: (1) a primary violator committed a securities violation; (2) the alleged aider and abettor had a general awareness of his role in the violation; (3) the aider and abettor knowingly rendered substantial assistance in furtherance of it.[54]

In granting Morris' motion to dismiss the SEC's aiding and abetting count, the court focused on the second and third elements of this aider and abettor liability test, pertaining to the level of awareness of wrongdoing held by the secondary actor. In this regard, the court stated that:

> A plaintiff can state a claim for aiding and abetting securities fraud by showing "severe" or "extreme" recklessness, but that requires allegations that the alleged aider and abettor encountered "red flags" or "suspicious events creating reasons for doubt" that should have alerted him to the improper conduct of the primary violators.[55]

The court further added that "the degree of knowledge required should depend on how ordinary the assisting activity is in the business involved. . . . If the evidence shows no more than transactions constituting the daily grist of the mill, we would be loathe to find [aiding and abetting] liability without clear proof of intent to violate the securities laws."[56] Based on this, and the finding that the SEC's allegations only involved day-to-day business activities of Morris and failed to point to any red flags or suspicious events, the court dismissed the SEC's aiding and abetting claim with prejudice.[57]

The *Morris* decision provides lawyers and accountants with a measure of confidence that, absent awareness of a fraudulent scheme or misrepresentation, and knowing participation in the scheme, aiding and abetting liability will not attach to actions undertaken for a client.

Conclusion

Many of the cases discussed in this chapter use compliance with GAAP, and in particular SOP 81-1(.65), as the metric for imposing liability where improper recognition of claims revenue is alleged, regardless of whether the theory is primary or secondary liability. Additionally, where a lawyer is merely a secondary actor, he may have greater protection from liability for statements made in relation to recognition of claims revenue. Where a party is a secondary actor, liability will likely not attach unless the plaintiff can show that the secondary actor exhibited "severe" or "extreme" recklessness with respect to the recognition of revenue. Lastly, as demonstrated by *Fuechtman v. Mastec*, making knowingly false statements relating to claims revenue will often lead to liability based on common-law fraud or federal securities laws.

Notes

1. Generally accepted accounting principles (GAAP) encompass the conventions, rules, and procedures necessary to define accepted accounting practice at a particular time. The standard of generally accepted accounting principles includes not only broad guidelines of general application, but also detailed practices and procedures.

2. Long-term construction contracts are those contracts that span more than one accounting period (generally defined as a calendar or fiscal year). AICPA Audit and Accounting Guide—Construction Contractors § 1.09 (March 1, 2008).

3. SOP 81-1 states that "additional guidance on the application of generally accepted accounting principles is needed. This statement of position provides that guidance." In providing this guidance, SOP 81-1 references APB Statement 4, ARB No. 43, ARB No. 45, FASB Statement No. 5, and APB Opinion No. 20, among others.

4. SOP 81-1 para. 61.

5. *Id.*

6. *Id.* para. 62 b.

7. *Id.*

8. *Id.* para. 63.

9. Sec. & Exch. Comm. v. Morris, 2005 WL 2000665, at *9–10 (S.D. Tex. Aug. 18, 2005) (granting motion to dismiss claim for aiding and abetting securities fraud based on alleged noncompliance with GAAP and stating that "[a] plaintiff can state a claim for aiding and abetting securities fraud by showing 'severe' or 'extreme' recklessness, but that requires allegations that the alleged aider and abettor 'encountered red flags' or 'suspicious events creating reasons for doubt' that should have alerted him to the improper conduct of the primary violators").

10. *Id.*
11. *Id.*
12. *Id.*
13. Sec. & Exch. Comm. v. Morris, 2007 WL 614210, at *9–10; *See also In re* Raytheon Sec. Litig., 157 F. Supp. 2d 131, 148 (D. Mass. 2001) (denying defendant's motion to dismiss claim that accountants had committed securities fraud by making false statements in improperly recognizing construction claims revenue under GAAP and stating that "GAAP are intended to provide a reliable degree of predictability, and an application of GAAP that strays beyond the boundaries of reasonableness will provide evidence from which *scienter* can be inferred").
14. *Morris*, 2007 WL 614210, at *9–10.
15. Stoneridge Inv. Partners, LLC v. Scientific-Atlanta, 128 S. Ct. 761, 768 (2008).
16. *Id.* at 769.
17. *Id.* at 768.
18. Elizabeth Cosenza, *Rethinking Attorney Liability Under Rule 10b-5 in Light of the Supreme Court's Decisions in Telltabs and Stoneridge*, 165 GEO. MASON L. REV. 1, 17 (2008).
19. *See* Ziemba v. Cascade Int'l, Inc., 256 F.3d 1194, 1205 (11th Cir. 2001); Wright v. Ernst & Young LLP, 152 F.3d 169, 175 (2d Cir. 1998); Anixter v. Home-Stake Prod. Co., 77 F.3d 1215, 1226–27 (10th Cir. 1996).
20. *E.g., In re* Software Toolworks, Inc. Sec. Litig. v. Painewebber, 50 F.3d 615, 628 n.3 (9th Cir. 1994); S.E.C. v. Durgarian, 477 F. Supp. 2d 342, 352–53 (D. Mass. 2007); Employers Ins. of Wassau v. Musick, Peeler & Garrett, 871 F. Supp. 381, 388–89 (S.D. Cal. 1994) (citing *In re* ZZZZ Best Sec. Litig., 864 F. Supp. 960, 970 (C.D. Cal. 1994)).
21. *In re* ZZZZ Best Sec. Litig., 864 F. Supp. at 970.
22. *Morris*, 2007 WL 614210, at *1.
23. Sec. &. Exch. Comm. v. Morris, No. Civ. A. H-04-3096, 2005 WL 2000665, at *1 (S.D. Tex. Aug. 18, 2005).
24. *Id.* at *1.
25. *Id.* at *2.
26. *Id.* at *1.
27. *Id.* at *13.
28. *Morris*, 2007 WL 614210, at *2.
29. *Id.* at *3.
30. *Id.*
31. *Id.*
32. *Id.* at *4.
33. *Id.*
34. *Id.*
35. *Id.*
36. *In re* Raytheon Sec. Litig., 157 F. Supp. 2d 131 (D. Mass. 2001).
37. *Id.* at 136.
38. *Id.* at 138–39.
39. *Id.* at 156.
40. *Id.* at 147–48.

41. *Id.* at 147 (citing Greebel v. FTP Software, Inc., 194 F.3d 185, 203 (1st Cir. 1999)).

42. *In re Raytheon Sec. Litig.*, 157 F. Supp. 2d at 156.

43. *Id.* at 155.

44. *Id.* at 156.

45. Fuechtman v. Mastec, Inc., 390 F. Supp. 2d 1265, 1268 (S.D. Fla. 2005).

46. *Id.* at 1266.

47. *Id.* at 1268.

48. Credit Union Cent. Falls v. Groff, 966 A.2d 1262, 1272 (R.I. 2009); Greycas, Inc. v. Proud, 826 F.2d 1560, 1565 (7th Cir.1987), *cert. denied*, 108 S. Ct. 775 (1988) (attorney who supplied opinion letter to lender in furtherance of client/borrower's loan application liable for misrepresentations); Century 21 Deep S. Props, Ltd. v. Corson, 612 So. 2d 359, 374 (Miss. 1992) (modifying the requirements of legal malpractice actions based on an attorney's negligence in performing title work by abolishing the requirement of attorney-client relationship and extending liability to foreseeable third parties who detrimentally rely); Petrillo v. Bachenberg, 655 A.2d 1354, 1357–60 (1995) (surveying abandonment of privity requirement in favor of liability for attorneys who induce reliance by nonclients); Chem-Age Ind., Inc. v. Glover, 652 N.W.2d 756, 770 (S.D. 2002) (applying § 51 of the Restatement); McCamish, Martin, Brown & Loeffler v. F.E. Appling Interests, 991 S.W.2d 787, 791 (Tex. 1999) (discussing liability when attorney invites a nonclient's reliance). *See also* RESTATEMENT (THIRD) OF THE LAW GOVERNING LAWYERS § 51(2)(a)(b), at 356–57 (2000) (recognizing a duty of care to nonclients when the attorney (1) "invites the non-client to rely on the lawyer's opinion or provision of other legal services, and the non-client so relies," and (2) "the non-client is not, under applicable tort law, too remote from the lawyer to be entitled to protection"); RESTATEMENT (THIRD) OF THE LAW GOVERNING LAWYERS § 95 illus. 1, at 21–22 (2000) (attorney's duty of care where borrower client retains attorney to provide an opinion letter to lender verifying good title in order to secure loan for client).

49. *See* Eugene J. Schiltz, *Civil Liability for Aiding and Abetting: Should Lawyers Be "Privileged" to Assist Their Clients' Wrongdoing?*, 29 PACE L. REV. 75 (2008) (citing Alpert v. Crain, Caton & James, P.C., 178 S.W.3d 398, 405–06 (Tex. App. 2005); Reynolds v. Schrock, 142 P.3d 1062 (Or. 2006); Dixon Fin. Servs, Ltd. v. Greenberg, 2008 WL 746548 (Tex. App. 2008); Durham v. Guest, 171 P.3d 756 (N.M. Ct. App. 2007), *cert. granted*, 172 P.3d 1286 (N.M. 2007)).

50. Cent. Bank of Denver, N.A. v. First Interstate Bank of Denver, N.A., 511 U.S. 164, 171 (1994).

51. *Id.*

52. *See* Schiltz, *supra* note 49 (collecting cases).

53. *Morris*, 2005 WL 200665, at *7–11.

54. *Id.* at *7.

55. *Id.* at *9 (citing cases).

56. *Id.* at *8–9 (citing Woodward v. Metro Bank of Dallas, 522 F.2d 84, 94 (5th Cir. 1975)).

57. *Id.* at *11.

CHAPTER 5

Navigating a Construction Contract Audit: Standards, Rights, and Obligations

JOHN A. BECKA
SHANNON J. BRIGLIA
COLIN A. DAIGLE

Introduction

Whether the owner is a public entity such as a federal, state, or local government agency or a publicly held or private company, project owners share a singular purpose when conducting project audits: to gain assurance that they are paying a fair price for the agreed-upon product. Collectively, project audits are driven by demands to manage cost, ensure compliance with regulations and contracts, enhance transparency on governance programs, satisfy lenders, and avoid or resolve disputes. Government regulations or contract requirements set the parameters for parties' expectations in an audit, including defining how and when audits are conducted and how audit findings are typically resolved. By developing an understanding of the audit process, parties to a construction contract will not only be prepared to meet these obligations, but will understand the standards governing the audit, increasing the quality of the audit process.

This chapter will first address audits conducted in the context of public contracts. Federal government contract audits are typically performed under the auspices of, or with reference to, the standards established by the Defense Contract Audit Agency (DCAA).[1] The two key guides for understanding DCAA audits are the Federal Acquisition Regulation (FAR), especially the cost principles found at Part 31.2 (discussed in more depth in Chapter 8), and the DCAA Contract Audit Manual (DCAM).[2] Even for nonfederal public audits, state and local agencies often model contract terms or regulations based on the FAR, including Part 31 cost principles, and look to the DCAA audit programs and procedures for guidance. Audits conducted under contracts where the owner is a private entity are typically subject only to the terms and conditions set forth in the contract, or as established by practice in the industry.

The second portion of this chapter addresses private contract audits, typically performed to assess compliance with the contract terms that govern cost and performance. Unlike a DCAA audit where the FAR and DCAM provide direction, private sector audits are governed by contract language that stipulates allowable or reimbursable costs. Contracts may also state the scope and frequency of an audit and define the responsibilities of the owner, contractor, architect, and auditor. The type of contract, such as guaranteed maximum price or lump sum, will also focus the areas of an audit, including how an auditor will plan a review to identify and address areas where the risk of improper billings can be greatest. While there are several widely used standard-form contracts used in construction, each contract in the private sector is potentially unique, thereby affecting the standards, the focus, and the frequency of audits from one project to the next. These topics and others, together with a discussion of commonly evaluated cost components, are analyzed and summarized.

Public Sector Audits

Introduction

Most public contracts, including contracts with federal, state, or local governments and including professional services contracts, are subject to audits. The largest and most widely recognized audit agency for federal contracts is the DCAA, and the procedures and standards of this agency are discussed below.

FAR 52.215-2, the Audit and Records clause, gives the government the right to examine and audit a contractor's records. The clause sets forth the limits of such an audit:

52.215-2 Audit and Records—Negotiation.

As prescribed in 15.209(b), insert the following clause:

AUDIT AND RECORDS—NEGOTIATION (MAR 2009)

(a) As used in this clause, "records" includes books, documents, accounting procedures and practices, and other data, regardless of type and regardless of whether such items are in written form, in the form of computer data, or in any other form.

(b) *Examination of costs.* If this is a cost-reimbursement, incentive, time-and-materials, labor-hour, or price redeterminable contract, or any combination of these, the Contractor shall maintain and the Contracting officer, or an authorized representative of the Contracting officer, shall have the right to examine and audit all records and other evidence sufficient to reflect properly all costs claimed to have been incurred or anticipated to be incurred directly or indirectly in performance of this contract. This right of examination shall include inspection at all reasonable times of the Contractor's plans, or parts of them, engaged in performing the contract.

(c) *Cost or pricing data.* If the Contractor has been required to submit cost or pricing data in connection with any pricing action relating to this contract, the Contracting officer, or an authorized representative of the Contracting officer, in order to evaluate the accuracy, completeness, and currency of the cost or pricing data, shall have the right to examine and audit all of the Contractor's records, including computations and projections, related to—

(1) The proposal for the contract, subcontract, or modification;
(2) The discussions conducted on the proposal(s), including those related to negotiating;
(3) Pricing of the contract, subcontract, or modification; or
(4) Performance of the contract, subcontract, or modification.

Audits are performed during the negotiation and administration phases of a contract, and are also normally undertaken as part of the review of large change orders, requests for equitable adjustments (REAs) and claims, or as a final condition of consummating a settlement of a dispute that has been negotiated in advance of the audit. As the phrase implies, a prenegotiation audit serves as a pricing aid to the government, and assists the agency in arriving at a negotiated contract price. An audit of incurred costs assists the contracting officer in determining the allowability of claimed costs, including annual overhead rates and costs, while an audit of cost or pricing data (i.e., a defective pricing audit) has the objective of determining whether the data was submitted in accordance with statutory standards, and was current, accurate, and complete when submitted. Audits are also performed by DCAA to determine compliance with the rules and regulations codified as the Cost Accounting Standards (CAS).[3]

Since many of the audits discussed above are conducted after costs have been incurred, it is important that the contractor's records comply with the FAR requirements. A contractor must maintain records that will document amounts billed under its contracts, and, if in a cost-reimbursable environment, must have a job cost system in place so that costs for individual contracts are segregated and reconciled. Record retention requirements for contractors are established at FAR subpart 4.7. The retention period is generally three years after final payment has been received for the contract. However, some records are required to be kept for up to four years from the end of the contractor's fiscal year in which an entry is made charging or allocating a cost to a government contract or subcontract.[4]

When performing an audit, the auditor will evaluate whether the cost incurred, proposed, or claimed is "reasonable." Reasonableness is defined at FAR 31.201-3:

> (a) A cost is reasonable if, in its nature and amount, it does not exceed that which would be incurred by a prudent person in the conduct of competitive business. Reasonableness of specific costs must be examined with particular care in connection with firms or their separate divisions that may not be subject to effective competitive restraints. No presumption of reasonableness shall be attached to the incurrence of costs by a contractor. If an initial review of the facts results in a challenge of a specific cost by the contracting officer or the contracting officer's representative, the burden of proof shall be upon the contractor to establish that such cost is reasonable.
>
> (b) What is reasonable depends upon a variety of considerations and circumstances, including—
>
> > (1) Whether it is the type of cost generally recognized as ordinary and necessary for the conduct of the contractor's business or the contract performance;
> > (2) Generally accepted sound business practices, arm's-length bargaining, and federal and state laws and regulations;
> > (3) The contractor's responsibilities to the Government, other customers, the owners of the business, employees, and the public at large; and
> > (4) Any significant deviations from the contractor's established practices.

Determination that a cost is unreasonable is a somewhat subjective process and conclusion. As a result, disputes often arise in the context of such determinations, with contractors taking the position that it is not DCAA's role to second-guess business decisions or judgments made by the contractor. These disputes often focus on compensation levels and plans.

With respect to other types of audits and responsibilities, DCAA auditors who uncover illegality, fraud, or waste during the course of an audit are required to report such findings to the Inspector General for further action.[5] The primary goal of a DCAA compliance audit is to ensure that the federal government is procuring products and services without overpaying for them. DCAA is responsible for performing audits of all Department of Defense (DoD) contracts that are subject to audit, and those of many other civilian agencies.

The DCAA has developed a series of policies and procedures by which the operations of a company undergoing an audit are gauged. To be compliant with DCAA, a company must have documented policies and procedures that are strictly followed; employ a documented labor charging system; utilize prescribed accounting and billing system properties; and train its employees to comply with the established compliance requirements.[6] Obviously, the size of a contractor is a determining factor in how detailed these written procedures are, but all contractors must consistently follow acceptable cost accounting charging and allocation processes, regardless of the level of detail of their written procedures. Labor costs and overhead rates are typically the focus of a DCAA compliance audit.[7] Costs must be allocated and accumulated separately by cost category, such as direct versus indirect costs, and per contract.[8] "Indirect costs (such as the costs of accounting, billing and payroll, human resources (HR) and benefits personnel) must be consistently documented and allocated across the direct cost items."[9] Indirect cost rates are typically audited annually on cost-justified contracts (meaning those where the costs incurred must be supported, which includes all cost-reimbursable contracts) whose duration spans more than one year.

According to the DCAA's publications, the major areas of emphasis in a DCAA audit include the following:

> (1) internal control systems, (2) management policies, (3) accuracy and reasonableness of cost representations, (4) adequacy and reliability of records and accounting systems, (5) financial capability, and (6) contractor compliance with contractual provisions having accounting or financial significance. . . ."[10]

Audits usually occur during the proposal phase on negotiated firm-fixed-price contracts and following the incurred cost phase for flexibly priced contracts, such as cost reimbursement or time and materials contracts.[11] Although the primary method of contracting in the construction industry has been in the form of competitively bid, firm-fixed-price contracts, other methods are also utilized, and cost data is now often shared at the time of bid and negotiation of a government contract. Further, even if the original contract is not subject to audit in terms of how the price was developed, change orders typically require cost justification; therefore, the issue of audits and DCAA audits arises for most contractors, even under a competitively bid, firm-fixed-price contract.

DCAA historically has had a cooperative attitude toward helping contractors with compliance, allowing contractors to continue with a contract even after an audit detects minor deficiencies in their systems if the contractor pledges to work toward resolving the deficiencies prior to the next audit.[12] As explained below, however, this cooperative approach may be changing, with the launch in December 2008 of a new Audit Guidance Memorandum by DCAA that appears to severely restrict the operation of and options available to auditors.

What Is the DCAA?

The Defense Contract Audit Agency was formed on January 8, 1965, as the culmination of a process initiated in 1939 to promote and achieve uniformity and consistency in audit functions and rulings for the various branches of the military. As of the end of 2009, the DCAA consists of approximately 4,000 people located at more than 300 field audit offices throughout the United States, Europe, and the Pacific. The DCAA provides standardized contract audit services for the DoD, as well as accounting and financial advisory services regarding contracts and subcontracts to all DoD components responsible for procurement and contract administration. These services are provided in connection with negotiation, administration, and settlement of contracts and subcontracts. DCAA also provides contract audit services to other government agencies.[13]

DCAA consists of six major organizational components: a headquarters located in Fort Belvoir, Virginia, and five regions. The five regional offices manage more than 300 field audit offices and suboffices located throughout the United States and overseas. DCAA may also establish a resident office at a contractor's location when the amount of audit workload justifies the assignment of a permanent staff of auditors and support staff. A DCAA liaison office may be established at a DoD procurement or contract administration office to provide effective communication and coordination among procurement, contract administration, and contract audit elements.

When Does DCAA Conduct Audits?

DCAA may conduct audits when requested by an agency or department of the DoD or another government agency through a cross-servicing arrangement. There are a variety of reasons why DCAA is requested to conduct an audit. Examples of situations where DCAA is asked to perform an audit include the following:

- Review of a contractor's or subcontractor's initial price proposal submitted in response to a request for proposal or request for quotation for all types of negotiated contracts[14]
- Price proposals resulting from contract change orders
- Price proposals resulting from a claim alleging government-caused delay
- Price proposals resulting from an equitable adjustment claim submitted by a contractor under the disputes clause of the contract
- Forward pricing rate agreements to establish indirect rates for proposal purposes
- Incurred cost submissions to establish final indirect cost rates
- Postaward audits to determine if cost and pricing data were defective
- Disclosure statement adequacy and compliance with cost accounting standards
- Operational reviews of a contractor's accounting system, internal control system, compensation system, and procurement system

DCAA Audit Procedures

General procedures for how DCAA conducts audits are detailed in the DCAA Contract Audit Manual (DCAM 7640.1)[15] referred to as the DCAM.[16] The DCAM is updated and reprinted twice a year and operates as the field manual for all auditors. Although it is not a regulation, and therefore does not have the force and effect of law, the DCAM not only provides guidance to auditors but also provides a roadmap to contractors as to how DCAA will view particular issues and treat the allowability of certain costs. In addition to the DCAM, the DCAA may issue Audit Guidance Memoranda[17] and Audit Guidance Programs[18] to clarify or implement specific policies and procedures. The DCAM provides specific guidance as to how DCAA should conduct the audit, including detailed protocols for the entrance, interim, and exit conferences that are typically held.

DCAA follows generally accepted government auditing standards (GAGAS) issued by the Comptroller General of the United States. GAGAS were developed to provide guidelines to help government auditors maintain competence, integrity, objectivity, and independence in their work. GAGAS incorporate and comply with the auditing standards and procedures of the American Institute of Certified Public Accountants (AICPA).[19] In addition to the GAGAS, DCAM, and Audit Guidance Memoranda, the auditors at DCAA also regularly refer to the FAR, particularly Part 31, as the primary regulation applicable to most federal agencies in their acquisition of supplies and services. The FAR, together with agency supplements to the FAR, such as the DoD Federal Acquisition Regulation Supplement, the CAS,[20] and specific contractual provisions, create the framework within which the audit will be conducted.

An audit commences with an entrance conference between the DCAA auditor and the contractor's representative. At the entrance conference, the DCAA auditor will explain the purpose of the audit, how long the audit is expected to last, and the types of documents the auditor would like to review. The parties will normally discuss and agree upon a person in the contractor's organization who will be the point of contact with DCAA. From the contractor's viewpoint, it is best to establish a single point of contact for DCAA to ensure that full compliance is achieved with a minimum of confusion or delay. DCAM guidance for data requests states, "Complex, detailed, and time consuming procedures, such as requiring all data requests be written and/or funneled through a single individual only, are an obstruction to efficient audit operations."[21] However, it is recommended that contractors attempt to get requests in writing and establish a reasonable period of time to respond to the request for data. Contractors are advised to keep copies of any documents given to the auditors for future reference.

During the course of the audit, interim meetings may be agreed to by the auditor and the contractor. In the case of a cost proposal, the meetings should provide the auditor with the opportunity to discuss items in the proposal so that a complete and accurate understanding of the data is obtained by the auditor. Interim meetings will also allow for the auditor to inform the contractor of any problems encountered in obtaining or interpreting requested data. If an operational audit is being conducted, any problems found by the auditor can be discussed and initial findings may be disclosed at an interim meeting, and corrective measures implemented thereafter.

When the audit has been completed, the DCAA auditor should hold an exit conference with the contractor. For a cost-proposal audit, the auditor should provide the contractor with a summary of the factual audit results. The contractor should be given the opportunity to respond to the auditor's findings. In some audits, such as postaward audits, the contractor may be given a draft of the audit report and provided an opportunity to make comments that will be included in the final report. For an operational audit, the contractor will be provided with the auditor's recommendations and given the opportunity to prepare a written response to be included in the audit report. DCAA will not normally supply a copy of its final report to the contractor, especially in a REA or claim situation, but the contractor can request such a report through the contracting officer. Draft audit reports, except those dealing with negotiation of forecasted costs or those dealing with costs potentially under litigation, can be provided to the contractor for review and comment.[22] For reports with forecasted costs, the auditor should discuss any factual differences, unsupported items, cost or pricing data inadequacies, and incidences of CAS/FAR noncompliance and obtain the contractor's response for inclusion in the final audit report.[23]

Audit of REAs and Claims

The DCAA is frequently called upon to audit REAs and delay and disruption claims. Because there is a $650,000[24] threshold for obtaining cost and pricing data, including modifications to sealed bids or negotiated contracts, proposals for REA and delay claims exceeding the $650,000 threshold are subject to DCAA audit. Audits of REAs and delay claims are governed by FAR 52.215-2, the Audit and Records clause previously quoted, which gives the government the right to examine and audit a contractor's records.

REA and claims are most often submitted pursuant to the changes clause of the contract, found at FAR 52.243. The DCAA focus for a REA or claim audit is on quantum—the damages claimed—rather than entitlement, as entitlement is a legal issue. Courts routinely find that the results of a DCAA audit are not government admissions of responsibility for the damages, but are simply verification that the contractor has accurately stated incurred costs in compliance with applicable accounting principles and has provided sufficient supporting documentation for such costs.[25] An REA seeking increased costs as the result of changes caused by government action may be computed by specifically segregating the increased costs or by using the total cost method or modified total cost method.[26] The DCAA preference is to specifically segregate the increased costs in the contractor's accounting system. This is not always possible, however, in impact and delay claims.[27]

Delay claims result from the contractor claiming that the government caused a delay in contract performance and therefore the contractor's costs were increased.[28] Here again, the auditor focus will be on quantum. Some of the cost elements the auditor will review include the following:

- Changes in labor rates or material costs resulting from the labor being performed in a later period.
- Acceleration costs relating to a contractor's attempt to recover time because the government did not relax the contract completion date for compensable and excusable delays.
- Extended job site overhead, usually calculated as a rate per day.
- Costs at the contract site relating to equipment that was idle during the delay period.
- Unabsorbed overhead resulting from the shift in direct costs from one accounting period to another. DCAA will in all likelihood recommend using the Eichleay formula[29] to calculate such costs, and assess the underlying conditions for the use of the Eichleay formula.

The Role of the DCAA Auditor in the Procurement Process

In the realm of federal contracting, the contracting officer is charged with the responsibility of making final determinations regarding the allowability of costs, whether incurred for the performance of the base contract or requested in a change order or claim.[30] The contracting officer may request audit services[31] to assist in this determination, in which case the DCAA auditor acts in an advisory capacity to the contracting officer.[32] The contracting officer is not bound by the DCAA audit report but must consider the report and the concerns of the auditor.[33]

Where the contracting officer and auditor disagree on any points raised in the audit report, DoD policies provide for internal review and resolution of disputes with DCAA to achieve a unified resolution of an audit report.[34] Among other things, the DoD policy requires detailed documentation of the disagreement, efforts made to resolve the disagreement between the contracting officer and auditor, and an escalating series of discussions between DoD and DCAA officials in an attempt to resolve the disagreement. DoD's policy was issued in accordance with Office of Management and Budget Circular No. A-50, "Audit Followup," which prescribes policies and procedures for executive agencies to establish follow-up systems to ensure prompt and proper resolution and implementation of findings and recommendations in federal audit reports.[35] Secretaries of the Military Departments and Directors of the Defense agencies are required by DoD Directive 7640.2 to maintain adequate follow-up systems and establish procedures to monitor and ensure the proper, timely resolution, and disposition of contract audit reports.[36] Also, the directive requires the Office of the Inspector General, DoD, to monitor and evaluate contract audit follow-up systems and program performance within DoD. Recently, DoD issued a Memorandum for resolving contract audit recommendations in the context of proposal audits, implementing a similar process as is used for incurred costs audits.[37] This Memorandum also authorizes revisions to the Defense Federal Acquisition Regulation Supplement to include the policy of internal resolution of disagreements between DCAA and DoD regarding proposal audits.

Consequences of Noncompliance: Exercise of Auditor Discretion

Until recently, auditors exercised fairly wide discretion in the discharge of auditor duties and interpretation and application of GAGAS. This discretion allowed considerable flexibility in the audit process, and fostered a sense of cooperation between contractors and DCAA. Prior to December 2008, if during the course of an audit it appeared that a significant deficiency or combination of deficiencies "(1) adversely affected contractor's ability to initiate, authorize, record, process or report . . . costs . . ., (2) resulted in at least a reasonable possibility that unallowable costs will be charged to the Government, and (3) the potential unallowable cost was not clearly immaterial,"[38] then the auditor was required to report that a significant deficiency or material weakness with the contractor's accounting system existed. This two-step exercise required the auditor to first determine whether the deficiencies resulted in, or could result in, unallowable costs being charged to the government and then to assess whether the unallowable costs were material, before reporting the deficiency as a significant deficiency or a material weakness. The auditor was also permitted to render partial inadequate opinions, with an opportunity for the contractor to cure the deficiency.

This two-step exercise of professional judgment, which allowed for significant exercise of auditor discretion, was revised in December 2008, following a General Accounting Office inquiry into alleged failures of DCAA to comply with GAGAS in the audits of 14 large contractors. At that time, DCAA issued revised audit guidance containing the simple instruction that auditors *must* report *any* internal control deficiency as a significant deficiency or material weakness, and they *must* opine that the contractor system under review is inadequate.[39] This new policy is widely seen as changing the rules of the game from cooperative partnering to adversarial positioning. Auditors are no longer able to report partial inadequacies or allow contractors to cure the deficiency prior to DCAA reporting it upstream. The auditor's report of the contractor's failure to accomplish any applicable control objective renders the system inadequate and makes it more likely that the contracting officer will take immediate action such as disapproving the system (effectively terminating the contract) and pursuing suspension of a percentage of progress payments or payments reimbursing incurred costs.[40] Contrary to prior guidance and practice, this approach "severely restricts the discretion of DCAA field auditors to exercise judgment in making determinations as to the significance of internal control deficiencies and recommendations as to the adequacy of contractor systems."[41]

The other major change in the 2008 revisions included revising the access to records policy to permit the government to suspend payment for a failure to timely provide access "upon request" to records and personnel necessary to conduct the audit. This new guidance is at odds with the FAR's Audit and Records clause, which has always required contractors to provide requested records within "reasonable times," and appears to exceed available statutory authority to the extent that DCAA attempts to enforce a right to have access to specific personnel.[42] Thus, it remains to be seen whether the FAR or this new DCAA audit guidance will be modified to achieve consistency between them.

Reduction of Payment Request via Notice of Intent to Disallow

Where an audit reveals costs or cost systems containing a significant deficiency or material weakness that are not in compliance with the contract terms, the auditor will report the deficiency or weakness to the contracting officer, who may issue a Notice of Intent to Disallow Costs under FAR 52.242-1, resulting in the nonpayment of the disallowed costs. The notice is required to be preceded by "reasonable efforts," through discussions with the contractor, to "reach a satisfactory settlement."[43] A notice to disallow may also be issued as to costs already incurred. This notice is not considered a final decision under the Disputes clause of the contract, and a contractor is entitled to pursue a claim under the Disputes clause as to any disallowed costs.[44]

Suspension of Payment

An opinion by an auditor of a significant deficiency or material weakness could also result in the total suspension of payment by the government.[45] Similar to the provisions for reduction of payments, FAR 52.242-1 and the DCAM set forth procedures requiring reasonable efforts to reach a resolution prior to implementation of suspension.

Interest and Penalties for Unallowable Costs

Most government contracts contain the standard FAR interest clause,[46] allowing the government to recover interest from the time of demand for repayment[47] of disallowed costs, as a penalty for invoicing for disallowable costs. In addition, the government may collect statutory penalties for submission of unallowable costs for certain types of contracts covered by the statute.[48] Statutory penalties can be up to two times the amount of the disallowed cost allocated to covered contracts for which a proposal for settlement of indirect costs has been submitted, plus interest to compensate the United States for the use of any funds that the contractor has been paid in excess of the amount to which the contractor was entitled. These penalties are assessable if the head of the agency determines that a cost submitted by a contractor in its proposal for settlement is expressly unallowable under a cost principle.

Liability for Fraudulent Claims for Payment

Contractors and architectural/engineering firms who knowingly submit claims for payment of unallowable costs, whether in the form of a request for reimbursement, payment requisition, claim submission, or settlement, are subject to liability for damages, and for civil and criminal penalties under the False Claims Act.[49] The civil penalties for knowingly submitting, or causing another person or entity to submit, false claims for payment of government funds is liability for up to three times the damages the government sustains by reason of that submission, plus penalties of $5,000 to $10,000 per false claim. The criminal penalty for knowingly and falsely submitting a claim for unallowable costs is up to five years in prison and fines of up to a maximum of $1 million.[50]

Private Sector Audits

Introduction

Owner audits in the private sector are typically customized by project and contract type, allowing owners to validate that they were billed pursuant to the terms of the contract and that the stipulated scope of work was delivered. The universe of private sector owners is rather broad. There are developers who are contracting for "one-off" projects with a contractor; universities with ongoing capital expansion and improvement programs; large corporations building or improving new plants or offices; and a variety of other owners building individual projects around the globe. Inherent in the construction function is that the contractor manages and maintains records detailing the cost of construction. Owners seldom receive, as part of the ongoing contract administration and requisitioning process, the same detailed cost information that contractors contemporaneously track, so the owner's audit rights provide the access needed to review these details.

Beyond basic cost verification and compliance with contractual terms, owners may employ audit processes to validate, track, and record project cost for financial accounting as part of corporate governance. Considering that most owner entities are subject to financial statement audits, a capital construction project can represent a material cost to the organization. Therefore, the project may be subject to internal audits and other reviews, just like any other division of the business where money is spent or invested. Owners may also use contractual audit rights to facilitate a cost-segregation study as part of an entity's tax planning. While Internal Revenue Service[51] scrutiny for cost segregation can include a detailed review of building costs that are supported with drawings and specifications, owner audits can facilitate the assessment and documentation requirements.

Audits may also be performed periodically during construction as part of dispute avoidance and early resolution practices, where the owner not only enhances transparency and accountability for those performing the project, but also develops a more detailed project record. By reviewing and obtaining detailed documentation contemporaneously during construction, the owner is better prepared to assess, resolve, or refute issues regarding cost, schedule, scope, and quality. For certain projects, owners may also use an audit function in support of fraud prevention, starting by creating an "audit mindset" among project participants that are subject to this review. Regardless of the reason, project audits are fundamentally grounded in the provisions of the contract, such as those regarding price, changes, and the audit function itself.

Comparison of Private and Public Sector Audits

Unlike DCAA audits, which are governed by established, uniform regulations and standards, the terms and conditions of commercial contracts are often unique and can differ greatly from one project to another, depending on the individualized needs of a particular owner for transparency and accountability. While an audit is focused on verifying costs, advisors to owners, contractors, and other stakeholders should understand that there can be a disparate range of what can be included in an audit. Customization of private sector audits can occur in relation to the scope of what costs are included, how often an audit is performed, and the recovery or mitigation remedies available to both owners and contractors. Accordingly, the needs of the owner and the capability and resources of the contractor must be considered in drafting fair and balanced terms.

Private sector audits share a common goal with the DCAA audit process—ensuring that the owner is not paying more than it should for the cost of a project. In achieving this goal, private sector audits share the following similarities with the DCAA audit process:

- Audit entrance meetings and close out meetings are conducted, with the potential of additional, interim meetings dictated by the circumstances.
- Exceptions noted by the auditor are communicated to the contractor, allowing for a response.
- Contract provisions frame the findings of the audit.
- Audits may be focused on change orders and claims.
- Audits will consider the contractor's job cost accounting, time-tracking systems, experience of the contractor's staff, and internal controls.
- Findings of contractually excluded costs ("disallowed" in government contract parlance) can result in adjustments to the payments to the contractor.

Types of Commercial Audits

A private owner has considerable flexibility in deciding what type of audit rights to include in its commercial contract, such as incurred cost audits, contract performance audits, change order audits, contract close-out audits, and claim audits.

Incurred cost audits are commonly performed in connection with guaranteed maximum price (GMP) and cost-plus contracts without a GMP, where the costs incurred and invoiced for reimbursement are reviewed to determine if the costs conform to the contractually defined "Cost of the Work."[52] Generally, absent any contract provisions to the contrary, the costs of performing the work that the contractor incurs on-site are included in the cost of the work, while most off-site costs such as home office costs are excluded. In certain contracts, the costs that are excluded are assumed to be included in the contractor's fee.

Contract performance audits focus on the contractor's cost-efficient execution of its duties to the owner and project team. While there are numerous performance requirements written into a contract, these audits are typically focused on the contractor's responsibilities to manage cost, schedule, scope, quality, and contingency. A contract performance audit may include verifying that the contractor is (1) properly updating project schedules and properly documenting the project; (2) ensuring that subcontractors are competitively selected and are being currently paid; and (3) obtaining lien releases.

Authority for the owner to *audit change orders* is frequently provided for. For firm-fixed-price or lump sum contracts, change orders (and, in many circumstances, the actual costs of allowance items) are likely the primary items subject to an audit, as costs for the base work were negotiated in one price and are excluded from audit review. Change orders present a greater risk for overcharges to owners. Unlike base contract work, which is typically competitively bid and procured before the work begins, leading to a certain confidence in the accuracy of the price for a defined scope, the circumstances under which a change order arises, including the immediate nature of the work and the uncertainty of the scope, may result in artificial cost inflation or unnecessary costs. The right to audit change orders provides an incentive for the contractor to accurately price change orders and gives peace of mind to owners, who have recourse to conduct an audit where indications of inflated costs, improper pricing, or duplication of base scope may be present.

Close-out audits may be performed prior to or in support of the project's completion and may be a contractual hurdle to release of retainage. These reviews may involve an in-depth review of incurred costs for cost-plus or GMP contracts; a performance-type review for lump sum contracts, such as an inspection of quantities and materials installed; or a review of punch list items and estimated cost to complete for any contract. One example of an audit being a contractual prerequisite to the release of retainage is the language of the American Institute of Architects (AIA) A201–2007 General Conditions, which stipulates that retainage is released after the architect's determination of "substantial completion." Prior versions of this form contract required achievement of final completion for the full release of retention. From an audit standpoint, the contract language defines the measures of completion necessary to issue final payment to the contractor, including provisions regarding the release of retention. Accordingly, owners may use the audit function to attain a greater level of assurance that the project is as complete as the contractor states, especially given that commercial owners typically intend new buildings to generate or support revenues once finished.

Claim audits can be performed to facilitate settlement between owners and contractors, or as part of a litigation proceeding. In the latter situation, an auditor's access to the contractor may be somewhat more limited and/or delayed than the access available prior to the initiation of litigation. Regardless of the circumstances, the audit will focus on the goal of verifying the amounts claimed by a contractor, including verification of allowable costs, proper pricing of change orders, and the absence of cost duplication.

Contractual Provisions Addressing Audit Rights and Accounting Records

The scope of owner audits in the commercial sector is controlled by contract language. Often "Owner Audit Rights" provisions are included in the contract or, in some contract forms, included in a section of the contract dealing with "Accounting Records." Both provisions are important, as the former provides for the process while the latter elaborates on the subject matter. For example, the AIA form General Conditions stipulates in its "Accounting Records" clause that

> The Owner and the Owner's auditors shall, during regular business hours and upon reasonable notice, be afforded access to, and shall be permitted to audit and copy, the Contractor's records and accounts, including complete documentation supporting accounting entries, books, correspondence, instructions, drawings, receipts, subcontracts, Subcontractor's proposals, purchase orders, vouchers, memoranda and other data relating to this Contract.[53]

In the absence of such express contractual language, audit rights may be implied by law or enforced in a court proceeding where one party asserts fraud and seeks an accounting. Contracts frequently stipulate how long the contractor must maintain its accounting records for the project. For example, the Engineers Joint Contract Documents Committee (EJCDC) form contracts require that the "Contractor shall preserve all such documents for a period of three years after the final payment by Owner."[54] The AIA A102–2007 form agreement also requires that the contractor maintain project records, including accounting records, for a period of three years following final payment.[55]

Audit rights granted to owners quite often extend to subcontracts, thereby allowing an owner the ability to verify the costs directly with the various trades and suppliers. A "flow down" provision is frequently employed to ensure that the owner has the right to audit subcontractor records. The language employed in A102–2007 is explicit: "If the Subcontract is awarded on a cost-plus a fee basis, the Contractor shall provide in the Subcontract for the

Owner to receive the same audit rights with regard to the Subcontractor as the Owner receives with regard to the Contractor...."[56]

Audit Rights Clauses—Implications for Contractors

In addition to defining the audit process and documentation, contract clauses may also address the practices and controls contractors must follow in accounting for the cost of the work. These clauses serve to protect owners by strengthening an owner's right to require that contractors meet a standard or employ practices that can help owners corroborate the integrity of the costs. At the same time, these clauses address business practices of contractors that are applied to all its projects. While these stipulations are reasonable from an accounting perspective, contractors should be mindful of the implications should deficiencies be noted.

The AIA form contract allows the audit to consider the contractor's controls: "The accounting and control systems shall be satisfactory to the Owner."[57] It should be noted that an audit of a contractor's project and financial controls for the purpose of expressing an opinion that they are adequate can be costly, time consuming, and far in excess either of an owner's budget for audit expense or a contractor's reasonable expectation. Audits can, however, address controls on a more limited basis through a review of a contractor's policies and procedures, judgmental sampling and tracing of costs through a contractor's systems, discussions with the contractor's management and accounting personnel, or inquiries to a contractor's financial statement auditors.

Another point of contention that commonly crops up in the audit context relates to the frequent, but vague, reference to "generally accepted accounting *practices*." The EJCDC family of contract documents employs this amorphous standard to define the limit of an audit, as follows: "Whenever the Cost of the Work for any purpose is to be determined pursuant to Paragraphs [*Costs Included*] and [*Costs Excluded*], Contractor will establish and maintain records thereof in accordance with generally accepted accounting practices...."[58] It should be noted that "generally accepted accounting *practices*" are not the same as generally accepted accounting *principles* (GAAP). There is no established standard for "generally accepted accounting *practices*," and what may be deemed generally accepted in one situation may differ from another. However, this language may result in an owner expectation that the contractor conforms to an accepted industry standard. It is important for all parties involved in the audit to understand the distinction, and for the contractor to clarify any concerns should it employ any accounting practices that are not GAAP but that the contractor finds to be generally accepted accounting practices. For this (and other practical) reasons, an owner should ensure that the audit team selected to perform any audits of contractors has the requisite construction industry experience so that issues are not unnecessarily created due to a lack of familiarity with industry accounting practices.

Finally, contractors should consider that some owners may modify audit rights to allow greater access to a contractor's business, provide enhancements to the owner's right to recover costs due to deficiencies noted in an audit, or even recover audit fees themselves should financial exceptions exceed a certain amount. Thus, careful review of audit clauses is imperative. Moreover, once an audit is initiated, the contractor may consider inquiring as to whether the auditor has a contingent fee agreement, under which the auditor is compensated based on a percentage of the costs recovered. Although use of contingent audit contracts has sparked debate among advisors to both owners and contractors, and clearly can raise questions about the auditor's motivation, the practice exists and should be considered in the event an audit is conducted.

Informational Requests by Auditors

The success of an owner audit is predicated on the auditor's ability to work with project stakeholders and obtain sufficient documentation to corroborate the costs or performance of a project. The auditor will familiarize himself with the project and contract documents, and will review payment applications and meeting minutes obtained directly from the owner. After an auditor develops a preliminary understanding of the project and its status, the focus turns to the contractor.

As with the DCAA audit approach discussed above, auditors typically begin the audit process with an introductory meeting or conference call, which is usually followed by a detailed written request directed to the contractor for access to relevant employees and/or documentation to support costs. Auditors will maintain their own workpapers and document trail regarding these requests and the information obtained in response to them. It is in the contractor's interest to memorialize its responses so that it may later demonstrate compliance with the request, if required.

Generally, auditors will evaluate the normal commercial practices the contractor employs to conduct its business as they relate to how contractors manage and record the cost of a project. This can include an overall query about job cost accounting, including processes and procedures for tracking labor, material, equipment, subcontracts, overhead, change orders, and contingency costs. Auditors will consider the type of accounting software, internal controls, and experience of the contractor's project cost and financial accounting teams in reaching their conclusions. Auditors will also evaluate the contractor's overall record keeping from both an organizational and retention standpoint to ascertain the reliability and accuracy of the contractor's financial information.

Examples of contractor employees whom an auditor may want to interview include project managers, accountants, insurance and compliance officers, and chief financial officers. Project managers and accountants provide information about direct costs and the cost-tracking processes, while compliance officers and chief financial officers are generally more knowledgeable about self insurance rates, previous audits conducted on other projects, home office overhead cost pools and overhead rate development, and cost presentation on the contractor's financial statements. Auditors may also seek access to the contractor's legal counsel to clarify questions relating to procurement arrangements or other contracts the contractor cites as having a bearing on costs billed to the owner. It is also not uncommon for the contractor's executive management to become involved in the audit on its own initiative, to assess the progress of the audit, or to ensure a timely and efficient process.

Unique contracts may require development of project-specific requests, but standard audit requests for documentation include the following:

- Contracts, subcontracts, and purchase orders
- Payroll reports, labor-manpower reports, time sheets, third-party invoices, labor agreements, and benefits calculations
- An identification of the location and title of any employee charging directly to the project
- Details on self insurance charges or insurance company audits on purchased insurance plans
- An identification of any related parties whose costs are charged to the project
- Any postaward agreements as to stipulated labor, burden, equipment, insurance, or other cost rates
- Details as to the development of internal equipment rates, if not contractually stipulated
- Third-party invoices for subcontractors, material suppliers, and rented equipment, among others
- Proof of payment for project costs through cancelled checks, wire remittances, and bank statements
- Job cost chart of accounts and job cost reports with detail and summation of contractor's costs for labor, equipment, and materials

In the case of audits of change orders and claims, an auditor may require information from the contractor about costs that are not specifically attributed to the owner's project. For example, to validate home office overhead costs, an auditor may request information about corporate general and administrative costs, including the cost of officers' salaries, or a contractor's total contract revenues in a period (where allocations are performed on this basis). For lost-productivity costs, an auditor may require the contractor's original estimate or historic labor cost and production results from other projects.

As part of reviewing the documentation produced by the contractor, auditors evaluate whether the audit evidence qualifies as "contemporaneous documentation," which includes information that was generated and documented at the time an event took place or the cost was incurred, or whether the documentation was created later. Contractors need to maintain processes that provide acceptable documentation to support costs; when this information does not exist and a contractor simply tabulates its own costs, such costs will likely become a target in an owner audit.

Audit Frequency

The frequency of an audit program is based on the needs of the project, with more frequent audits employed to supplement an owner's project team assessments, or for projects that owners perceive to be at greater risk. Examples of why the owner may designate a project as high risk include the following:

- Construction in remote locations
- Use of unfamiliar contractors
- A contract with significant allowance items
- Contract provisions calling for savings flowing to the owner for subcontractor buy-outs
- Construction during periods of cost escalation, such as following a devastating hurricane season where reconstruction drives up costs
- Building during periods of economic downturn, where the need both for owners to manage costs and for contractors to maximize revenues are heightened

On a typical project, the owner may decide to limit audits to select change orders or to perform the review of incurred cost only at the conclusion of construction operations. Conversely, some owners, especially when embarking on a larger program of capital expenditures, may audit early in the process, with the goals of identifying issues before they become larger and creating an atmosphere of audit and oversight, so that the contractor plans and progresses the job and its administration accordingly. As audits represent a cost not just to the owner but to the contractor, based on the resources they must make available, successful audit programs are structured to be reasonable.

Audit frequency and scope may also be adjusted based on the owner's needs, such as where regular reviews focused in specific areas are done to facilitate loan draws or contractor payment application reviews, so that the audit findings can immediately be factored into the assessment of a payment requisition. AIA A102–2007 provides for an audit of progress payment requests, with the immediate right to adjust the next payment if discrepancies are identified. Article 12.1.7.6 of this AIA form contract directs: "Subtract the shortfall, if any, indicated by the Contractor in the documentation required by Section 12.1.4 to substantiate prior Applications for Payment, or resulting from errors subsequently discovered by the Owner's auditors in such documentation."[59]

Job Cost Systems and Accounting

Project audits often focus on the review of the contractor's project cost accounting information. Generally, the contractor's job cost accounting system will record the project's direct cost of construction and its general conditions costs (field overhead/indirect costs). Data from the contractor's job cost system is often directly incorporated into the contractor's financial accounting system, which is used to generate financial statements. When the contractor's financial statements are audited, the fact that the job cost system is part of an audited financial process can help the project auditor substantiate and gain comfort with the costs that have been billed to the owner.

Project cost accounting methods can vary from one contractor to another, and from one type of accounting software to another. However, a common goal is to account for the cost of the work for the specific project, segmented by scope. Project accounting can be customized for a particular project, to align with the scope of work defined in the contract. Project cost accounting systems, which can include a commercial software package capable of multiple functions or a combination of software and contractor-developed tools such as spreadsheets, should provide project budgets, adjustments for change orders, actual costs incurred, and estimates to complete.

The cost-tracking structure for a project is delineated by groupings such as phases, accounts, or subaccounts, depending on project need. This structure is commonly referred to as a Work Breakdown Structure (WBS). A WBS will likely include line items for labor, material, subcontract, and equipment costs. The WBS structure utilized by contractors normally follows the 16 divisions established by the Construction Specifications Institute (01 General Conditions, 02 Site Construction, 03 Concrete, etc.). Within each phase, additional subgroups are used, adding a greater level of specificity to track the cost of the work being done. The total cost of the contractor's work can be summarized generally when all project costs are combined with the general and administrative costs incurred by the home office and that are allocable to the contract. Home office costs are almost always included within the contractor's fee and not directly stated in the contractor's payment applications. Home office costs may also be excluded from job cost reports, or simply applied to job costs using the prevailing percentage markup.

Auditor's Role versus the Architect's Responsibilities

An important function of the project architect is to review progress completion and certify applications for payment. Many contract forms, such as AIA A102–2007, place the burden for determining the amount of a progress or final payment on the architect: "Based on the Architect's evaluations of the Contractor's Applications for Payment, the Architect will review and certify the amounts due the Contractor and will issue Certificates for Payment in such amounts."[60] The owner may withhold payments to the contractor based on the review of payment certifications performed by the architect.

As important as this role is, the architect's review of a payment request is not the equivalent of an audit. In fact, AIA standard form agreements are careful to limit the architect's responsibilities in this respect:

> In taking action on the Contractor's Applications for Payment, the Architect shall be entitled to rely on the accuracy and completeness of the information furnished by the Contractor and shall not be deemed to represent that the Architect has made a detailed examination, audit

or arithmetic verification of the documentation submitted . . . ; that the Architect has made exhaustive or continuous on-site inspections; or that the Architect has made examinations to ascertain how or for what purposes the Contractor has used amounts previously paid on account of the Contract. Such examinations, audits and verifications, if required by the Owner, will be performed by the Owner's auditors acting in the sole interest of the Owner.[61]

Agreements between owners and architects for professional services also typically clarify responsibility for owner audits: "The Owner shall furnish all legal, insurance, and accounting services, including auditing services, that may be reasonably necessary at any time for the Project to meet the Owner's needs and interests."[62]

Given the importance of the contractor payment process, and considering the scope of an architect's review in certifying payments, owners can employ audits to support these processes and to investigate issues. As discussed above, the scope of these audits can entail more than cost verification, including an assessment of the contractor, subcontractor, or vendor's performance and compliance with the contract.

Construction Project Auditors

Auditing a construction contract entails different skills from auditing an owner's financial statements. While similarities exist between the methodologies and techniques employed to verify cost,[63] the construction contract auditor's purpose is not to develop an opinion about the accuracy of historic financial information prepared by a management team for the benefit of third parties. Rather, the auditor is verifying contract compliance and accuracy of costs, often in real-time, for an owner's management team. In many cases, the owner intends to rely upon the results of the audit to pay a requisition, change order, or claim.

Project auditors must be skilled in evaluating contractors' job cost systems, calculating contractor markups, delineating project cost types such as direct and indirect, and understanding how time-related costs are incurred. Specialized knowledge of project cost accounting, contract assessments, and audit techniques not only benefits the owner, but serves the interests of the contractor, as the auditor can serve as translator to the owner to provide assurance that the contractor has managed the project appropriately, or to isolate and remediate suspected problem areas with the contractor. In some cases, where contractors and subcontractors have deficiencies in accounting and record keeping, the auditor can assist with techniques and alternative methods to validate cost. The skill of the auditor can also have a direct effect in avoiding payment interruptions and minimizing conflicts over disputed costs. This is why (sometimes to the confusion of the contractor), an audit team might not rely on the results of an audit that has recently been performed by another audit team on a different project. Even though some of the issues being reviewed are similar, it is important for the contractor to understand the varied levels of experience, quality, and scope of auditors, which can result in very different approaches to the audit process. Conversely, to the extent that other audit work has been performed on the contractor's indirect cost records and rates, and an audit team has access to that auditor and its back-up and approach, reliance on that prior work should be considered in performing an efficient audit and avoid "re-inventing the wheel."

A project audit can support the audit of the owner's financial statement, particularly where the results of a major project audit may have a substantial impact on the financial statement.[64] For owners conducting large capital projects where financial statement auditors are likely to review the project, the scope and depth of a project audit along with the qualifications of the project audit team should be carefully evaluated to maximize the benefits of both processes. In this situation, the owner should endeavor to include the outside audit firm, or the firm engaged to review the overall system of internal controls, in reviewing and approving the audit steps being taken by the construction project audit team so that it can rely on such work as part of the year-end financial audit.

Audits can be performed by the owner's staff or through external consultants. In some cases, it may be a combination of the two. Owners will consider a variety of factors in selecting an audit team, including the following:

- Audit cost
- Availability and technical skills of internal staff versus external consultants
- Benefits to the financial statement audit
- Contract type, price, and the size of the scope of work subject to review
- Problems on past projects (delays, cost overruns, defaults, disputes, etc.)
- Familiarity with the contractor
- Scrutiny by investors, lenders, and the public, among others

When staffing an audit team using internal personnel, owners may include employees from financial divisions such as internal audit or accounting. Some organizations have experienced personnel dedicated to internal audit functions who can assist with project auditing, or owners may engage staff from their capital project management or facilities management divisions, who may also be engaged in some form of project oversight already. It is also not uncommon for owner personnel from procurement divisions to participate in the audit function, especially where large, specialized, or long-lead-time equipment is purchased and installed.

Owner audits conducted by outside parties are typically performed by accountants or consultants with project cost and contract audit specialization.

Cost engineers, quantity surveyors, other construction management professionals, and attorneys may become involved if the circumstances warrant.

Auditing the "Reasonable"

As with the requirements under federal contracts, audits in the commercial sector frequently involve a determination of "reasonable" costs. What is reasonable is not defined in any of the commonly used industry contracts, allowing the parties to determine what is reasonable based upon the particular circumstances. AIA forms, in particular A201–2007 General Conditions, A102–2007, and A103–2007 for cost-plus type contracts, contain numerous examples of costs that are specifically required to be reasonable, including the following:

- For owner termination for convenience, the contractor is due "reasonable overhead and profit on the Work not executed."[65]
- Owner backcharges related to a contractor's default includes "the reasonable cost of correcting such deficiencies."[66]
- Withholding payment to a contractor when there is "reasonable evidence that the Work cannot be completed for the unpaid balance of the Contract Sum."[67]
- Failure to pay by the owner followed by suspension of work by the contractor, where the contractor may be due its "reasonable costs of shut-down, delay and start-up, plus interest."[68]
- Materials costs "in excess of those actually installed to allow for reasonable waste and spoilage."[69]
- Miscellaneous costs, including "reasonable petty cash expenses of the site office."[70]
- "That portion of the reasonable expenses of the Contractor's supervisory or administrative personnel incurred while traveling in discharge of duties connected with the Work."[71]

While some of these costs are unlikely to amount to material sums, an owner audit can be planned so that the owner will understand and document the contractor's accounting practices and performance in managing costs, which may avoid conflict later in the project. For example, in the case of an owner backcharge following termination and reprocurement from another contractor, a comparison of the terminated contractor's cost for similar work with the cost incurred by the replacement contractor can support the reasonableness of the owner's backcharge, and possibly avoid a dispute over the value of the backcharge amount.

High-Risk Areas Subject to Contract Audit

As a matter of audit planning, preliminary identification of high-risk or problematic areas in preparation for an audit is a best practice. To assess these risks, auditors consider project elements such as contract type and the audit provisions that establish the scope of review, the definition of costs, and the owner and contractor teams involved.

Labor Costs

A contractor's labor cost represents a significant portion of total project cost and therefore bears heightened scrutiny. An audit of labor cost can include a review of time sheets, job cost reports, payroll reports, and insurance and union agreements, among other areas. Auditors will test labor cost to verify that the amounts charged to the project match what was paid to the employees and other providers of labor-related costs. Contractors should be prepared to demonstrate that the rates used to bill the project reflect the current costs actually being incurred. This includes validation that markups are applied correctly and appropriately based on the employee's trade and level (apprentice, journeyman, foreman, etc.). Some contracts may provide fully loaded labor rates directly in the agreement, by trade and level, while others may define what is allowable as labor cost. While labor rates drive a larger portion of total labor cost, labor markups are the more common risk area. AIA A102–2007 defines allowable labor markups as "[c]osts paid or incurred by the Contractor for taxes, insurance, contributions, assessments and benefits required by law or collective bargaining agreements and, for personnel not covered by such agreements, customary benefits such as sick leave, medical and health benefits, holidays, vacations and pensions, provided such costs are based on wages and salaries included in the Cost of the Work."[72] Auditors will evaluate whether these costs are billed pursuant to applicable agreements and also verify if these amounts are charged elsewhere to the owner, such as by direct billing. For example, an exception is likely to be noted for two weeks of vacation time billed directly to the project for an employee who only worked one month on the job.

Incentive Compensation—Bonuses

Contracts that allow direct billing to the owner for incentive compensation for employees generate an additional high-risk area in an audit. Incentive compensation can include "[b]onuses, profit sharing, incentive compensation and any other discretionary payments paid to anyone hired by the Contractor or paid to any Subcontractor or vendor, with the Owner's prior approval."[73] Beyond a review to ensure these amounts are not included in hourly markups or the overhead charged in change orders, these costs can become open to interpretation as to what is reasonable if the owner and contractor are not clear about what specifically can be included in the cost of the work. Primary considerations include the amount of the bonus, the information provided to the owner when approving it, whether the owner actually did approve it, and whether the merit payment reflected performance that benefited the project. For example, a retirement bonus charged to the project for 30 years of work by a superintendant is likely to become an audit exception, since most of a bonus for long service plainly did not relate to the current project. Incentive compensation and profit sharing may also be accounted for by contractors as a corporate expense, included in the contractor's fee.

Off-Site Labor

Off-site labor for tasks such as fabrication, manufacturing, preassembly, or staging is not uncommon in construction. The AIA form contract classifies "[w]ages and salaries of the Contractor's supervisory or administrative personnel engaged at factories, workshops or on the road, in expediting the production or transportation of materials or equipment required for the Work, but only for that portion of their time required for the Work"[74] as a cost of the work. Labor performed off site typically presents oversight challenges for the owner and its architect or other representatives. Accordingly, an audit will consider the contractor's ability to demonstrate discrete time tracking by task and project, time descriptions, the contractor's own supervision and approval of the work, and the accounting and management controls implemented in recording these costs, among other factors. Charges for home office personnel are often specifically prohibited by the terms of the contract.

Costs Subject to Prior Owner Approval

Another area of audit risk is costs that, by contract, can be reimbursed only with the prior consent of the owner. The risk consideration is the owner's approval. A standard clause allowing preapproved costs in AIA A102–2007 reads:

> Where any cost is subject to the Owner's prior approval, the Contractor shall obtain this approval prior to incurring the cost. The parties shall endeavor to identify any such costs prior to executing this Agreement.[75]

To validate costs in this category, auditors look for proof of the owner's approval, including details regarding whether the approval was for a one-time instance of the cost or for the balance of the project. Contracts may not require this approval to be in writing; however, it is in both the owner's and contractor's interest to memorialize these agreements for any cost of the job that is material in amount. This provision can often apply to employees working off site, or to new supervisory staff assigned to the project.

Equipment Costs

Equipment costs are another area of high risk in an audit, especially when change orders or claims are presented for extra equipment usage or cost escalation. Depending on the circumstances, equipment costs for added usage are often tied to increased manpower, and an audit may consider this correlation. Third-party equipment rentals can provide a less involved audit process[76] while contractor-owned equipment can raise a variety of questions. For example, the auditor may consider whether the contractor is overstating its actual costs by using an internal rental rate that includes the recovery of costs such as annual insurance or certifications, in order to assess whether the increased usage charge recovers more cost than was actually incurred. For this reason, contracts that anticipate the use of contractor-owned equipment often contain provisions outlining exactly how equipment will be reimbursed (e.g., 60 percent of published Blue Book rates or specific rates for each piece of equipment that are stipulated in the contract).

Miscellaneous Costs

Miscellaneous costs are scrutinized during an audit, often resulting in a finding that insufficient audit evidence is available to corroborate the purpose, actual amount, and benefit to the owner's project. Further, miscellaneous costs must be evaluated to verify that the amount is not duplicated in a markup or fee. Examples of miscellaneous costs identified in AIA A201–2007 include the following:

- "Self-insurance for either full or partial amounts of the coverages required by the Contract Documents. . . ."[77]
- "Fees of laboratories for tests required by the Contract Documents, except those related to defective or nonconforming Work. . . ."[78]
- "Costs for electronic equipment and software, directly related to the Work. . . ."[79]
- "[E]xpenses incurred in accordance with the Contractor's standard written personnel policy for relocation and temporary living allowances of the Contractor's personnel required for the Work."[80]
- "That portion of the reasonable expenses of the Contractor's supervisory or administrative personnel incurred while traveling in discharge of duties connected with the Work."[81]

Related Parties

If the contractor utilizes a related party to perform portions of the work, the auditor must examine whether unallowable, excessive, or duplicated costs are being charged. The AIA contract forms require prior owner approval for the use of a related party by the contractor[82] and define a related party as

> a parent, subsidiary, affiliate or other entity having common ownership or management with the Contractor; any entity in which any stockholder in, or management employee of, the Contractor owns any interest in excess of 10 percent in the aggregate; or any person or entity which has the right to control the business or affairs of the Contractor. The term "related party" includes any member of the immediate family of any person identified above.[83]

The rationale for caution and preapproval of the use of related parties is obvious. An auditor must evaluate whether the contractor's interest in the performance of its affiliate has compromised its obligation to mitigate costs charged to the owner, or whether the use of a related party involves shared resources, such as general and administrative personnel or offices, resulting in duplicative billing of these costs.

Subcontractors

Subcontractor defaults are a risk to any project and owners elect to become more involved in subcontract oversight, often by monitoring payments to subcontractors. Typical contract language to facilitate this oversight reads: "The Owner has the right to request written evidence from the Contractor that the Contractor has properly paid Subcontractors and material and equipment suppliers amounts paid by the Owner to the Contractor for subcontracted Work."[84] The owner's invocation of this right either before or during an audit is permissible and should be anticipated.

Contract Allowances

Contract allowances frequently require an audit to ensure that the excess over the allowance being claimed by the contractor reflects the full allowance amount included in the lump sum. An audit of an allowance can be complicated where the owner has selected the vendors or agreed to prices during construction.[85] This type of owner involvement can foster disputes regarding the allowance. In some cases where contracts permit, audits can be performed to investigate the contractor's assertion of different pricing for an allowance.

Discounts, Rebates, and Refunds

Discounts, rebates, and refunds can often be a focal point in an owner audit where the actual cost of the work can be reduced through these types of cost recoveries obtained by the contractor. Most contracts give the owner the benefit of trade discounts, rebates, refunds, and amounts received from sales of surplus materials and equipment.[86] Certain projects also receive tax-exempt status for some or all direct costs or, in some cases, tax exemptions limited to the cost of materials. The contractor may also receive cash discounts for early payments to subcontractors or vendors based on purchase order terms or other agreements. Audits are typically designed to ascertain if these discounts are being obtained by the contractor, and if so, whether appropriate credits are given to the owner. Sometimes, quantity discounts are treated as annual miscellaneous income in the contractor's financial statements, and the job charges for materials are shown at the gross amount before discount. Requests for copies of purchase agreements from these vendors will typically identify any such arrangements.

Conclusion

Construction contract audits can be invasive, lengthy, and costly, but they can also be extremely revealing, and thus serve an important function in the industry. The somewhat adversarial nature of the process ensures that the primary purpose of audits is achieved: the assurance that the owner of the project pays a fair price for what it receives. In the face of either regulatory requirements or contractual directives, contractors have a strong incentive to thoroughly and contemporaneously record, control, and maintain their cost records and to report them accurately to the project owner in exchange for project payments or additional compensation. Whether governed by the FAR and DCAM or the terms of a commercial contract, the obligations of the contractor to comply with an audit and demonstrate its "reasonable" costs are clear. Similarly, the consequences of noncompliance can be harsh, including the disallowance of claims, reduction of payment requests, penalties and fines, and, in extreme circumstances, actions for fraud or breach of contract. Understanding the rights, standards, and obligations inherent in the audit function will have a direct and positive impact on the bottom line.

Notes

1. 41 U.S.C. § 422(k) authorizes the government to audit contractors' records to determine compliance with cost accounting standards and practices. Although there are other government audit agencies, the DCAA is by far the largest and most widely recognized and utilized audit agency.

2. The DCAA Contract Audit Manual, discussed in more detail below, is available at http://www.dcaa.mil/cam.htm, Chapter 0: Introduction to the DCAA Contract Audit Manual. See Appendix A, DCAA Contract Audit Manual (CAM): DCAAM 7640.1 for the DCAM table of contents.

3. The 19 Standards and Administration regulations of the Cost Accounting Standards are found at Federal Acquisition Regulation 30.000–607 and 48 C.F.R. ch. 99 (the FAR Appendix), and are applicable to a subset of federal government contractors based on individual and cumulative contract amounts awarded during cost accounting periods. A more thorough discussion of CAS is included in Chapter 8.

4. See FAR 4.700 for specific requirements.

5. DCAM 4-702.

6. Curt Finch, *DCAA—What Is It? How Can You Comply?*, 8(11) PM WORLD TODAY (Nov. 2006), *available at* http://www.pmforum.org.

7. DCAA Pamphlet No. 7641.90, *Information for Contractors*, § 1-501 (Jan. 2005).

8. *Id.* at § 1-101.

9. *Id.*

10. *Id.* at § 1-501.

11. *Id.* at § 1-501.b.

12. Rich Wilkinson & Jim Rogers, *Survival of the Fittest—What You Need to Know About the New DCAA Rules* 2008 (Deltek White Paper) http://www.deltek.com/learning-tools/default.asp.

13. DCAA History, http://www.dcaa.mil/.

14. DCAA audits of proposals are not the equivalent of a contracting officer's responsibility determination but may later serve as evidence of financial ability in a bid protest. *Ala. Aircraft Indus., Inc.—Birmingham v. United States*, 83 Fed. Cl. 666, 685 (2008) (although not the

equivalent of a responsibility determination, which includes, among other factors, the presence of adequate financial resources to support an undertaking, DCAA audit findings are relevant in a bid protest as evidence of the awardee's ability to perform).

15. DCAA Contract Audit Manual, ch. 4, sect. 300. See DCAM Table of Contents, Appendix A. The DCAM is available online at http://www.dcaa.mil under DCAA Publications, or can be purchased from the Superintendent of Documents, U.S. Gov't Printing Office, Wash., D.C. 20402 (GPO Catalog No. D-1.46/2:7640.1/1283).

16. *Id.* at 1-201.1.b.

17. The Audit Guidance Memoranda are is available at http://www.dcaa.mil. *See* Appendix B, Audit Guidance and Audit Management Guidance Memorandums for Regional Directors (MRDs).

18. *See* Appendix C, Directory of Audit Programs (AP) and Other Audit Guidance (OAG) Documents.

19. DCAA pamphlet no. 7641.90, at § 1-301.d.

20. Pub. L. No. 100-679. Regulations implementing CAS include 48 C.F.R. pt. 9903 and FAR Part 30. There are many exemptions to CAS, including sealed bid contracts, negotiated contracts, subcontracts in excess of $650,000, and contracts with small businesses (48 C.F.R. § 9903.201-1(b)). *See* Chapter 8 for a more complete discussion of CAS.

21. DCAM 4-302.1(b)(2).

22. DCAM 10-212.2(a).

23. DCAM 10-212.2(c).

24. FAR 15.403-4.

25. *Orlosky, Inc. v. United States*, 68 Fed. Cl. 296, 317 (2005) (citing cases); *Tecom, Inc. v. United States*, 66 Fed. Cl. 736, 774 (2005) (an audit will bear on the credibility of any attempt by the government to question the accuracy of a contractor's claim, but it does not concede or admit liability); *Flink/Vulcan v. United States*, 63 Fed. Cl. 292 310 (2004) (same); *R.P. Richards Const. Co. v. United States*, 51 Fed. Cl. 116, 125 (2001) (audit findings not an admission of liability).

26. Different methodologies for calculating damage claims are covered in Chapter 9.

27. *See* Chapter 9 for a more complete discussion of delay and impact claims.

28. *Id.*

29. *See id.* for discussion of the Eichleay formula.

30. Only the contracting officer is authorized to execute, administer, and terminate contracts. This authority includes the ability to execute modifications on behalf of the government. FAR 43.102(a) & (b).

31. FAR 42.102. The contracting officer may also delegate some of his authority to others. FAR 42.302.

32. *United States v. Westinghouse Elec. Co.*, 788 F.2d 164, 168 (1986) (auditors advise contracting officers in the process of negotiating contracts); *Cuneo v. Schlesinger*, 484 F.2d 1086 (D.C. 1973); *Newport News Shipbuilding & Drydock Co. v. Reed*, 655 F. Supp. 1408 (E.D. Va. 1987) (referencing advisory capacity of auditors).

33. Tex. Instruments Inc., 89-BCA ¶ 21,489 (ASBCA 1988) (review of senior acquisition officer is necessary where contracting officer disagrees with DCAA audit recommendation, but contracting officer still has authority to make an independent decision after receipt of the senior acquisition officer's review and recommendation); *but see* Black River L.P., 97-2 BCA ¶ 29,077 (ASBCA 1997) (mentioning *in dicta* that contracting officer cannot issue final decision until supported by DCAA finding).

34. Dep't of Def. Instruction No. 7640.2 (Aug. 22, 2008), applicable to DCAA audits, *available at* http://www.dtic.mil/whs/directives/corres/pdf/764002p.pdf. *See* Dep't of Def. Directive No. 7650.3 (Oct. 18, 2006) (providing similar policy and process for disputes

arising concerning GAO audit reports), *available at* http://www.dtic.mil/whs/directives/corres/pdf/765003p.pdf.

35. Dep't of Def. Instruction No. 7640.02, Encl. 3 ¶ 3.a, provides for disposition within 12 months of report issuance.

36. These obligations include a semiannual reporting obligation, currently performed via a Web-based Contract Audit Follow-Up (CAFU) system. Audits are tracked by the DoD Inspector General to determine the amount of questioned costs (funds) that are at risk of loss or have been sustained. Ultimately, the information is reported to Congress.

37. Memorandum from Office of the Under Sec'y of Def., Resolving Contract Audit Recommendations (Dec. 4, 2009), *available at* http://www.acq.osd.mil/dpap/policy/policyvault/USA006857-09-DPAP.pdf and Appendix D of this chapter.

38. DCAA MRD 08-PAS-011(R) (Mar. 3, 2008), superseded by MRD 08-PAS-043(R).

39. MRD 08-PAS-043(R).

40. Nicole Owren-Wiest, *Revised DCAA Audit Guidance Demands Greater Contractor Responsiveness* (Winter 2009), http://www.wileyrein.com/publication.cfm?publication_id=14187.

41. Sheppard Mullin, *New DCAA Guidelines Severely Restrict Auditor Authority to Exercise Judgment in Audit of Internal Controls*, Gov't Contracts Blog (Jan. 12, 2009), http://www.governmentcontractslawblog.com/2009/01/articles/audits/.

42. See Owren-Wiest, *supra* note 40, at 1

43. FAR 42.801(a) and CAM 6-902.

44. FAR 42.803(b)(3).

45. DCAA, Audit Guidance on Significant Deficiencies/Material Weaknesses and Audit Opinions on Internal Control Systems, Audit Guidance Memo 08-PAS-043(R) (Dec. 19, 2008), *available at* http://www.dcaa.mil/.

46. FAR 32.617(a) requires that FAR 52.232-17 be included in most contracts.

47. FAR 52.232-17.

48. See 10 U.S.C. § 2324(a).

49. 31 U.S.C. § 3729 (civil penalties) and 18 U.S.C.§ 287 (criminal penalties).

50. See Chapter 11 for an expanded discussion of the False Claims Act. See *False Claims in Construction Contracts* (C. Sink & K. Pages, eds., Am. Bar Ass'n Forum on the Construction Industry 2007), for a complete treatment of the False Claims Act and the state False Claims Act Statutes.

51. Internal Revenue Serv., Cost Segregation Audit Techniques Guide (rev. Mar. 2008), *available at* http://www.IRS.gov.

52. Two commonly used commercial contracts, The American Institute of Architects' [hereinafter AIA] A102-2007 (cost plus a fee with a guaranteed maximum price) and A103-2007 (cost plus a fee without a guaranteed maximum price), contain detailed definitions for what costs are included in or excluded from the cost of the work.

53. AIA Document A102–2007, Standard Form of Agreement Between Owner and Contractor Where the Basis of Payment is the Cost of the Work Plus a Fee with a Guaranteed Maximum Price, art. 11.

54. Eng'rs Joint Contract Documents Comm. [hereinafter EJCDC] C-525–2007, Suggested Form of Agreement Between Owner and Contractor for Construction Contract (Cost Plus), art. 13.01.

55. AIA Document A102–2007, art. 11.

56. *Id*. art. 10.3.

57. *Id*. art. 11.

58. EJCDC C700-2007, Standard General Conditions of the Contract, art. 11.01.D.

59. AIA Document A102–2007, art. 12.1.7.6

60. AIA Document A201–2007, art. 4.2.5.
61. AIA Document A102–2007, art. 12.1.9.
62. AIA Document B101–2007, art. 5.8.
63. Audit techniques such as invoice reviews, tracing payment, and judgmental sampling may be employed in both financial statement and project audits.
64. The financial statement auditor can consider the results of a project audit as part of a financial statement review. However, the extent to which the findings of a project audit are relied upon is at the financial statement auditor's discretion.
65. AIA Document A201–2007, art. 14.4.3.
66. *Id.* art. 2.4.
67. *Id.* art. 9.5.1.4.
68. *Id.* art. 9.7.
69. AIA Document A102–2007, art. 7.4.2.
70. AIA Document A103–2007, art. 7.5.4.
71. *Id.* art. 7.6.10.
72. AIA Document A102–2007, art. 7.2.4.
73. *Id.* art. 7.2.5.
74. *Id.* art. 7.2.3.
75. *Id.* art. 7.1.2.
76. Third-party equipment costs should be substantiated by appropriate vendor invoices that detail, among other items, dates of use, time in use, location used, rates and rate composition, and overtime charges.
77. AIA Document A201–2007, art. 7.6.1.
78. *Id.* art. 7.6.4
79. *Id.* art. 7.6.6.
80. *Id.* art. 7.6.9.
81. *Id.* art. 7.6.10.
82. AIA Document A-102–2007, art. 7.8.2.
83. *Id.* art. 7.8.1.
84. AIA Document A201–2007, art. 9.6.4.
85. ConsensusDOCS No. 205 (Rev. 2009), Standard Short Form Agreement Between Owner and Contractor (Where the Contract Price is a Lump Sum), art. 11.
86. AIA Document A201–2007, art. 9.1.

APPENDIX 5-A

DCAA Contract Audit Manual (CAM) DCAAM 7640.1

This manual is available to the public on an indefinite subscription basis from the Superintendent of Documents, U.S. Government Printing Office (GPO), Order Processing Code: 5852, phone (202) 512-1800 or fax (202) 512-2250.

All inquiries for additional information should be directed to the local DCAA field audit office, the address and telephone number of which can be found in the Audit Office Locator.[1] The contractor's business location where the accounting records are maintained should be used for determining the appropriate DCAA office. If assistance is needed in determining the cognizant DCAA office, contractors may call DCAA Headquarters at (703) 767-3274.

User comments/suggestions are welcome; refer to Section 0-007 of the CAM.

Current audit guidance not yet incorporated into the CAM can be found on the audit guidance page.[2]

Contents	
Chapter	**Title**
Foreword	DCAA Contract Audit Manual (July 2007)
Chapter 0	Introduction to the DCAA Contract Audit Manual (Nov 30, 2009)
Chapter 1	Introduction to Contract Audit (Jun 30, 2009)
Chapter 2	Auditing Standards (Jun 30, 2009)
Chapter 3	Audit Planning (Apr 22, 2009)
Chapter 4	General Audit Requirements (Jun 29, 2009)
Chapter 5	Audit of Policies, Procedures, and Internal Controls Relative to Accounting and Management Systems (Jun 30, 2009)
Chapter 6	Incurred Costs Audit Procedures (Nov 2, 2009)

Chapter	Title
Chapter 7	Selected Areas of Cost (Sep 23, 2009)
Chapter 8	Cost Accounting Standards (Nov 9, 2009)
Chapter 9	Audit of Cost Estimates and Price Proposals (Oct 22, 2009)
Chapter 10	Preparation and Distribution of Audit Reports (Oct 22, 2009)
Chapter 11	Audit of Contractor Compliance with Contract Financial Management Requirements (Aug 6, 2008)
Chapter 12	Auditing Contract Termination, Delay/Disruption, and Other Price Adjustment Proposals or Claims (Dec 31, 2008)
Chapter 13	Audits at Educational Institutions, Nonprofit Organizations, and Federally Funded Research and Development Centers (FFRDCs) (Feb 28, 2008)
Chapter 14	Other Contract Audit Assignments (Nov 9, 2009)
Chapter 15	Other DCAA Functions (Dec 31, 2008)
Appendix A	Contract Cost Principles and Procedures (Mar 11, 2008)
Appendix B	Statistical Sampling Techniques (Mar 6, 2009)
Appendix C	Reserved
Appendix D	Technical Specialist Assistance (Jun 30, 2009)
Appendix E	Graphic and Computational Analysis Techniques (Jun 30, 2009)
Appendix F	Reserved
Appendix G	Reserved
Appendix H	Reserved
Appendix I	Work Sampling (May 19, 2009)
Topical Index	Topical Index (Nov 3, 2009)

Notes

1. http://apps.dtic.mil/wobin/WebObjects/DCAAzipcode.
2. http://www.dcaa.mil/openguidance.htm.

APPENDIX 5-B

Audit Guidance and Audit Management Guidance Memorandums for Regional Directors (MRDs)[1]

Open as of October 31, 2009
The memorandums listed are in Adobe's PDF format unless otherwise noted.

Date	MRD Number	Subject	CAM Ref	5-Digit Activity Code
10/22/2009	09-PAS-021(R)	Audit Guidance on the Status of Contractor Systems of Internal Controls as Documented in the Contractor Organization and Systems and Scope of Audit Sections of Audit Reports	10-210.7, 10-306	NA
8/24/2009	09-PSP-016(R)	Audit Guidance on Review of Dependent Health Benefits Costs	NA	NA
8/3/2009	09-PAS-015(R)	Audit Guidance on Evaluation of Final Vouchers	10-900 and Various Others	15400
7/23/2009	09-PAS-014(R)	Audit Guidance on Federal Acquisition Regulation (FAR) Revisions Related to Contractor Code of Business Ethics and Conduct	5-306, 5-311.3, 5-907g	11070
7/13/2009	09-PAC-013(R)	Audit Guidance on Accounting for Employee Stock Ownership Plan (ESOP) Costs as a Result of Revisions to CAS 415, Accounting for the Cost of Deferred Compensation	NA	19412, 19415

Date	MRD Number	Subject	CAM Ref	5-Digit Activity Code
7/2/2009	09-PAS-012(R)	Audit Alert on Link to DoDIG Fraud Handbook	NA	NA
6/30/2009	09-PSP-011(R)	Audit Guidance on Performing Audits of Subcontract Forward Pricing Proposals	9-104, 9-106, 10-304.8	NA
6/17/2009	09-PAC-010(R)	Audit Alert on Issuing Audit Reports When a CAS Noncompliance is Found During Normal Audit Functions	NA	NA
6/15/2009	09-PPD-009(R)	Audit Alert on the Use of the Incurred Cost Electronically (ICE) Model	NA	NA
6/1/2009	09-PAC-008(R)	Audit Guidance on the Executive Compensation Cap for Contractor Fiscal Years 2009 and Beyond	6-414.8	NA
6/1/2009	09-PAC-007(R)	Audit Alert on Reviewing Projected Pension Costs	NA	NA
4/15/2009	09-PPD-006(R)	Audit Guidance on Approving and Rescinding Contractor's Authorization to Participate in the Direct Bill Program for Major Contractors	6-1007	11010, 11015
4/9/2009	09-PSP-005(R)	Audit Alert on Performing Audits of Part(s) of a Proposal	NA	NA
3/13/2009	09-PAS-004(R)	Audit Guidance on Reporting Significant/Sensitive Unsatisfactory Conditions Related to Actions of Government Officials	4-803, 4-804	NA
3/3/2009	09-OO-010(R)	Audit Management Guidance—Reporting Suspected Contractor Fraud and Other Contractor Irregularities	Figure 4-7-2	NA
1/30/2009	09-PAS-003(R)	Audit Guidance on Working Paper Documentation of Judgmental Selections	4-403	NA
1/22/2009	09-PPD-002(R)	Audit Guidance on Performance of Earned Value Management Systems (EVMS) Audits	11-202.2, 11-202.8, 11-203.5	17770

APPENDIX 5-B: AUDIT GUIDANCE AND AUDIT MANAGEMENT   111

Date	MRD Number	Subject	CAM Ref	5-Digit Activity Code
12/22/2008	08-PPD-044(R)	Audit Guidance on Reconciling Billed Costs to Contractor's Accounting Records when Reviewing Interim Public Vouchers	NA	NA
12/19/2008	08-PAS-043(R)	Audit Guidance on Significant Deficiencies/Material Weaknesses and Audit Opinions on Internal Control Systems	10-408.2	NA
12/19/2008	08-PAS-042(R)	Audit Guidance on Denial of Access to Records Due to Contractor Delays	1-504.3, 10-304.8	NA
12/19/2008	08-PAS-041(R)	Audit Guidance on Limited Scope Audit Reports on Internal Controls	3-300, 5-110, 10-408.2, 10-413	OAG
12/19/2008	08-PPD-040(R)	Audit Guidance on Discontinuance of the MOCAS Priority Audit Initiative	NA	NA
11/25/2008	08-PPD-038(R)	Audit Guidance on Discontinuance of the DCAA T&M Initiative	NA	NA
11/10/2008	08-OAL-073(R)	Audit Guidance Revision to DCAA's Role in Source Selection Evaluation Boards (SSEB) and Providing Financial Liaison Advisory Services	15-305.10	NA
11/3/2008	08-PPD-037(R)	Audit Guidance on Assessing Compensation Reasonableness through Benchmarking	5-808.8c(2)	NA
10/20/2008	08-PPD-036(R)	Audit Alert on Current Economic Conditions and Financial Condition Risk Assessments	NA	NA
10/9/2008	08-PPD-035(R)	Audit Alert on Assessing Compensation Reasonableness When a Contractor Uses Compensation Consultants to Determine Executive Compensation	NA	NA

APPENDIX 5-B: AUDIT GUIDANCE AND AUDIT MANAGEMENT

Date	MRD Number	Subject	CAM Ref	5-Digit Activity Code
10/8/2008	08-PPD-034(R)	Audit Guidance for Annual Testing of Contractor Eligibility for Direct Bill Program	6-1000	11015
10/3/2008	08-PAS-032(R)	Audit Guidance on Release of Contractor Proprietary Information to Third-Party Service Providers	1-507	NA
10/2/2008	08-PPD-031(R)	Audit Management Guidance on DCAA Training Related to OMB Circular A-133 Audits	NA	NA
9/24/2008	08-PSP-030(R)	Audit Guidance on Agreed-Upon Procedures (AUP) Engagements	10-1000, 14-1000	17900, 28000
9/12/2008	08-PAS-028(R)	Audit Guidance on In-Process Integrated Product Teams (IPTs) Assignments and Other Teaming Arrangements Involving the Contractor	NA	NA
8/11/2008	08-PAS-026(R)	Audit Guidance on DCAA Audit Services Performed in Support of Integrated Product Teams (IPTs)	NA	NA
8/5/2008	08-PAS-024(R)	Audit Guidance Discontinuing DCAA Participation in Integrated Product Teams (IPTs)	NA	NA
8/1/2008	08-PAS-023(R)	Audit Alert on Working Paper Documentation	NA	NA
7/31/2008	08-PAS-022(R)	Audit Alert on Handling Disagreements on Audit Findings	NA	NA
7/28/2008	08-OTS-049(R)	Effecting Cost Suspensions and Disallowance on Cost Reimbursement Contracts for Direct Bill Authorized Contractors Using Wide Area Workflow	6-1007.7	NA
6/19/2008	08-PPD-020(R)	Audit Guidance on Audits of Contractor Cost Data Reports (CCDRs)	11-408	NA
6/19/2008	08-PSP-019(R)	Audit Alert on Performance of Postaward (Defective Pricing) Audits	NA	NA

APPENDIX 5-B: AUDIT GUIDANCE AND AUDIT MANAGEMENT 113

Date	MRD Number	Subject	CAM Ref	5-Digit Activity Code
5/19/2008	08-PPD-018(R)	Audit Guidance on the Executive Compensation Cap for Contractor Fiscal Years 2008 and Beyond	6-414.8	NA
4/24/2008	08-PAS-015(R)	Audit Alert—Lobbying Costs Related to Legislative Earmarks	NA	NA
4/24/2008	08-PPD-014(R)	Audit Guidance on DoD Commercial Time-and-Materials (T&M) and Labor-Hour (LH) Contracts	6-1000	17740, 17910
3/4/2008	08-PAC-010(R)	Audit Guidance on the Application of FAR 31.205-6(p), Limitation on Allowability of Compensation for Certain Contractor Personnel	6-414.9	NA
3/3/2008	08-PAS-011(R)	Audit Guidance on Reporting Internal Control Deficiencies	5-109, 5-110, 5-1200, 10-408.2	NA
2/5/2008	08-PAS-003(R)	Audit Guidance on the July 2007 Revision to Generally Accepted Government Auditing Standards (Yellow Book)	2-203.1, 2-303, 4-301, 10-212.2, 10-407	10501, 10502, 10503
12/6/2007	07-OTS-065(R)	Suspension and Disallowance of Costs on Cost Reimbursement Contracts on Contractor Interim Billings Submitted Using the Wide Area Workflow (WAWF)—Receipts and Acceptance System	NA	NA
11/26/2007	07-PPD-038(R)	Audit Alert on Reporting Questioned Costs on Time-and-Materials (T&M) and Labor Hour (LH) Contracts	NA	NA
11/21/2007	07-PAC-037(R)	Audit Alert on the Application of Non-DoD Agency FAR Supplements to DCAA Audits	NA	NA
10/16/2007	07-PPD-035(R)	Audit Guidance on Cost and Software Data Reporting (CSDR) Manual (DoD 5000.04-M-1)	11-400	17870

APPENDIX 5-B: AUDIT GUIDANCE AND AUDIT MANAGEMENT

Date	MRD Number	Subject	CAM Ref	5-Digit Activity Code
10/10/2007	07-PAS-034(R)	Audit Guidance on Documentation for Cancelled Assignments	4-403f(3), 2-303a	NA
10/05/2007	07-PPD-033(R)	Audit Alert on the Adequacy of Contractor's Final Indirect Cost Rate Proposals	NA	NA
09/07/2007	07-PPD-031(R)	Audit Guidance Alert on the Use of DCAA Form 1 to Suspend or Disapprove Costs on Cost Reimbursement Contracts	6-900	NA
09/05/2007	07-PSP-030(R)	Audit Guidance on Supporting Contracting Officer's Cost Realism Analysis	Various Chapters in 9 & 10	27000
08/31/2007	07-PAC-029(R)	Audit Alert on Insurance Industry Settlement Agreements and Potential Credits Due on Government Contracts	NA	NA
08/23/2007	07-PPD-027(R)	Audit Guidance on the Inclusion of Washington Area Office in the Multi-Segment Contract Responsibility Matrix	5-103.2a(1)	NA
08/15/2007	07-PPD-026(R)	Audit Guidance and Related Audit Program Changes for OMB Circular A-133 Audits	13-704	10110
07/31/2007	07-PPD-023(R)	Audit Guidance on Time-and-Materials (T&M) and Labor Hours (LH) Contracts	3-2S1, 5-1100, 6-204	10100
07/26/2007	07-PAC-021(R)	Audit Alert on Contractor Responsibility for Maintaining Pension Data Records	NA	NA
07/18/2007	07-PPD-020(R)	Audit Guidance on Nonmajor Incurred Cost Audit Program	6-105	10100
07/11/2007	07-PPD-018(R)	Audit Guidance on the Use of Electronic Document Access (EDA)	3-202	NA
05/01/2007	07-PAC-013(R)	Audit Guidance on the Impact of the Pension Protection Act of 2006	9-703.8b, 7-606, 8-412b	19412

APPENDIX 5-B: AUDIT GUIDANCE AND AUDIT MANAGEMENT

Date	MRD Number	Subject	CAM Ref	5-Digit Activity Code
04/25/2007	07-OTS-022(R)	Audit Guidance Memorandum: Direct Submission of Interim Public Vouchers—Special Requirements Related to Wide Area Work Flow (WAWF)	6-1007.1	NA
04/13/2007	07-OTS-019(R)	Audit Guidance Memorandum: Updated Criteria for Large File Size Review	4-407(d)(2)	NA
04/11/2007	07-PPD-011(R)	Audit Guidance on Reporting the Results of Desk Reviews of Low-Risk Incurred Cost Submissions	6-104.5(8), 10-506	10100
01/23/2007	07-PPD-004(R)	Revisions to Audit Guidance and Audit Programs on Financial Condition Risk Assessments and Financial Capability Audits	NA	NA
01/18/2007	07-PAC-002(R)	Audit Alert on the Evaluation of Directly Associated Unallowable Costs	NA	NA
10/12/2006	06-PAC-037(R)	Transmittal of Director, Defense Procurement and Acquisition Policy (DPAP) Interim Guidance on the Impact of the Pension Protection Act of 2006 on Forward Pricing	NA	NA
08/28/2006	06-OWD-039(R)	Audit Management Guidance on Capturing Audits of Corporate and Intermediate Home Offices, Including Shared Services, in DMIS/Reimbursables	NA	NA
08/15/2006	06-PAC-028(R)	Audit Guidance on Revised FAR 31.205-11 Limiting the Allowable Depreciation Costs for Assets Reacquired Subsequent to a Sale-and-Leasebck Transaction	7-207, 7-4XX	10100, 21000, 23000, 27000, 28000
07/07/2006	06-PAC-023(R)	Audit Guidance on Compensation Costs Arising from Stock Options	7-2123, 8-415	NA
12/29/2005	05-PPD-076(R)	Audit Guidance on Recovery Audits	NA	NA

APPENDIX 5-B: AUDIT GUIDANCE AND AUDIT MANAGEMENT

Date	MRD Number	Subject	CAM Ref	5-Digit Activity Code
12/19/2005	05-PAC-074(R)	Audit Guidance on Revision to FAR 31.205-35, Relocation Costs	7-1004.5	NA
11/22/2005	05-OWD-062(R)	FY 2006 Audit Management Guidance for Iraq Reconstruction	NA	10180
08/25/2005	05-PAC-055(R)	Audit Guidance on Including Inactive Employees in the Calculation of CAS 413.50(c)(12) Pension Segment Closing Adjustments	8-413.3	19413
06/06/2005	05-PAC-041(R)	Audit Guidance on Revised FAR Part 30, Cost Accounting Standards Administration, and Related Contract Clause and Solicitation Provisions	NA	NA
04/12/2005	05-OWD-019(R)	Deactivation of Activity Code 19400	NA	19400
01/21/2005	05-PPD-010(R)	Audit Guidance for Financial Condition Risk Assessments and Financial Capability Audits Requested under the Utility Privatization Initiative	14.310	NA
11/08/2004	04-PPD-061(R)	Audit Guidance on Wide Area Workflow (WAWR) Implementation	6-1000	11010, 11015, 15400, 41500
10/28/2004	04-PQA-059(R)	Audit Guidance on Draft Report Referencing	4-403	NA
08/11/2004	04-PSP-045(R)	Director, Defense Procurement and Acquisition Policy (DPAP) Guidance on Contract Pricing and Cost Accounting-Compliance with DFARS 252.211-7003, Item Identification and Valuation	7-2125 New	NA
7/27/2004	04-PAC-041(R)	Audit Guidance on Impact of Medicare Prescription Drug, Improvement and Modernization Act of 2003 on Contractor Postretirement Benefit (PRB) Costs	7-609.2	10100, 10110, 10160, 10170, 19416, 21000, 23000, 25000, 27000, 28000

APPENDIX 5-B: AUDIT GUIDANCE AND AUDIT MANAGEMENT

Date	MRD Number	Subject	CAM Ref	5-Digit Activity Code
07/13/2004	04-PAC-040(R)	DCMA/DCAA Joint Guidance Implementing the Teledyne Decision on CAS 413.50(c)(12) Segment Closing Adjustments	8-413.3	19413
05/11/2004	04-PPD-028(R)	Revised Audit Guidance on Audits of Contractor Prepared Reconciliations	14-911	17330
04/12/2004	04-PPD-023(R)	Audit Guidance on Compensation Costs for Contractor Employees Located in Foreign Countries and Performing Work under Iraq Reconstruction Contracts	5-808	13020, 10100, 10110, 10160, 10170, 21000, 23000, 25000, 27000, 28000, 42000, 42097, 42098, 42099
04/09/2004	04-PAC-022(R)	Audit Guidance on Review of Orders under GSA Schedule Contracts	NA	10100, 10110, 10160, 10170, 21000
05/16/2002	02-PAC-040(R)	Transmittal of DDP Guidance on Changes in Cost Accounting Practice	NA	19100

Notes

Last updated December 4, 2009
1. Available at http://www.dcaa.mil/openguidance.htm.

APPENDIX 5-C

Directory of Audit Programs (AP) and Other Audit Guidance (OAG) Documents[1]

The Standard Audit Programs listed are in Adobe's PDF format.

Activity Code	Doc Type	Version No. and Date		Program Description	URL
10100	AP	4.4	Oct 2009	Audit Program for Incurred Costs—Concurrent Auditing Major & Non-Major	http://www.dcaa.mil/sap/10100_AP_Concurrent_Auditing_Major_and_Nonmajor.pdf
10100	OAG	2.4	Jan 2006	Concurrent Audit of Incurred Costs—Audit Areas Matrixed to the MAARs	http://www.dcaa.mil/sap/Concurrent_Auditing_Appendix.pdf
10100	AP	3.0	Apr 2007	Audit Program for Nonmajor Desk Review	http://www.dcaa.mil/sap/10100_AP_Nonmajor_Desk_Review.pdf
10100	AP	9.0	Jul 2007	Audit Program for Incurred Costs—Nonmajor Post Year End Audit	http://www.dcaa.mil/sap/10100_AP_Nonmajor_Post_Year_End_Auditing.pdf
10100	AP	8.7	Nov 2007	Audit Program for Incurred Costs—Major Post Year End Audit	http://www.dcaa.mil/sap/10100_AP_Major_Post_Year_End_Auditing.pdf
10100	OAG	1.1	Oct 2003	Risk Assessment Checklist ADVU15	http://www.dcaa.mil/sap/31-a-2_RiskAssessmentChecklistADVU15.pdf
10100	AP	1.0	Jan 2007	Audit Program for Incurred Costs—Corporate Shell	http://www.dcaa.mil/sap/10100_AP_Corporate_Shell.pdf

APPENDIX 5-C: DIRECTORY OF AUDIT PROGRAMS

Activity Code	Doc Type	Version No. and Date		Program Description	URL
10110	AP	3.2	Nov 2009	A-133 Audit	http://www.dcaa.mil/sap/10110_AP_A-133_Audits.pdf
10160	AP	5.4	Oct 2009	Audit Program for Consultant and Professional Service Costs	http://www.dcaa.mil/sap/10160_AP_Consultant_Services.pdf
10160	AP	2.2	Oct 2006	Incurred Costs (Individual Packages)—Other	http://www.dcaa.mil/sap/10160_AP_Other.pdf
10180	AP	1.1	Oct 2006	Iraq Direct Cost Testing	http://www.dcaa.mil/sap/10180_AP_NA.pdf
10310	AP	3.4	Apr 2008	Audit Program for Non-Major Contractors Labor Floorchecks	http://www.dcaa.mil/sap/10310_AP_NA.pdf
10320	AP	1.2	Oct 2006	Audit Program for MAAR 13—Purchase Existence and Consumption	http://www.dcaa.mil/sap/10320_AP_NA.pdf
10501	AP	3.1	Nov 2009	Operations Audit—Management Systems	http://www.dcaa.mil/sap/10501_AP_NA.pdf
10502	AP	3.1	Nov 2009	Operations Audit—Labor Elements	http://www.dcaa.mil/sap/10502_AP_NA.pdf
10503	AP	3.1	Nov 2009	Operations Audit—Materials and Other Cost	http://www.dcaa.mil/sap/10503_AP_NA.pdf
11010	AP	10.9	Nov 2009	Audit Program for Billing System and Related Internal Controls	http://www.dcaa.mil/sap/11010_AP_NA.pdf
11010	OAG	4.2	Aug 2006	Internal Control Matrix—Billing System Controls	http://www.dcaa.mil/sap/BILL-Internal_Control_Matrix.pdf
11015	AP	7.0	Oct 2008	Audit Program for Annual Testing of Contractor Eligibility for Direct Bill Program	http://www.dcaa.mil/sap/11015_AP_NA.pdf
11020	AP	5.6	Nov 2009	Audit Program for Budget and Planning System and Related Internal Controls	http://www.dcaa.mil/sap/11020_AP_NA.pdf

APPENDIX 5-C: DIRECTORY OF AUDIT PROGRAMS

Activity Code	Doc Type	Version No. and Date		Program Description	URL
11020	OAG	3.3	Sep 2007	Internal Control Matrix for Audit of Budget and Planning System Controls	http://www.dcaa.mil/sap/ BDGT-Internal_Control_Matrix .pdf
11070	AP	7.1	Nov 2009	Audit Program for Control Environment and Overall Accounting Controls	http://www.dcaa.mil/ sap/11070_AP_NA.pdf
11070	OAG	5.0	Jul 2009	Internal Control Matrix for Control Environment and Overall Accounting Controls	http://www.dcaa.mil/sap/ ACTG-Internal_Control _Matrix.pdf
11510	OAG	4.2	Sep 2007	Internal Control Matrix for IT System General Internal Controls	http://www.dcaa.mil/sap/ ITG-Internal_Control_Matrix .pdf
11510	AP	5.7	Nov 2009	Audit Program for EDP General Controls	http://www.dcaa.mil/ sap/11510_AP_NA.pdf
12030	AP	7.5	Nov 2009	Audit Program for Purchasing Controls	http://www.dcaa.mil/ sap/12030_AP_NA.pdf
12030	OAG	4.2	Oct 2006	Internal Control Matrix for CPSR/Purchasing System Audit	http://www.dcaa.mil/sap/ PURC-Internal_Control_Matrix .pdf
12500	OAG	4.1	Jun 2006	Internal Control Matrix for Material Management and Accounting System (MMAS)	http://www.dcaa.mil/sap/ MMAS-Internal_Control _Matrix.pdf
12500	AP	9.4	Nov 2009	Audit Program for Material Management and Accounting Systems (MMAS) Controls	http://www.dcaa.mil/ sap/12500_AP_NA.pdf
13010	AP	9.4	Nov 2009	Audit Program for Accounting and Control of Labor Cost	http://www.dcaa.mil/ sap/13010_AP_NA.pdf
13010	OAG	4.2	Jun 2006	Internal Control Matrix for Accounting and Control of Labor Cost	http://www.dcaa.mil/sap/ LABR-Internal_Control_Matrix .pdf
13020	AP	7.4	Nov 2009	Audit Program for Compensation Controls	http://www.dcaa.mil/ sap/13020_AP_NA.pdf

APPENDIX 5-C: DIRECTORY OF AUDIT PROGRAMS

Activity Code	Doc Type	Version No. and Date		Program Description	URL
13020	OAG	4.2	Sep 2007	Internal Control Matrix for Compensation System Audit	http://www.dcaa.mil/sap/COMP-Internal_Control_Matrix.pdf
13500	AP	4.4	Nov 2009	Audit Program for Major Contractors Labor Floorchecks/Interviews	http://www.dcaa.mil/sap/13500_AP_NA.pdf
14980	OAG	4.1	Jun 2006	Internal Control Matrix—Audit Program for Indirect and Other Direct Cost Controls	http://www.dcaa.mil/sap/INDR-Internal_Control_Matrix.pdf
14980	AP	6.7	Nov 2009	Audit Program for Indirect and Other Direct Cost Controls	http://www.dcaa.mil/sap/14980_AP_NA.pdf
15400	AP	3.1	Oct 2009	Evaluation of Final Vouchers	http://www.dcaa.mil/sap/15400_AP_NA.pdf
15600	AP	3.2	May 2007	Audit Program for Review of the Quarterly Limitation On Payments (QLOP) Statement	http://www.dcaa.mil/sap/15600_AP_NA.pdf
17100	AP	4.5	Nov 2009	Audit Program for Termination, Cost Contracts	http://www.dcaa.mil/sap/17100_AP_Cost_Contracts.pdf
17100	AP	4.5	Nov 2009	Audit Program for Termination, Fixed Inventory Basis	http://www.dcaa.mil/sap/17100_AP_Fixed_Inventory_Basis.pdf
17100	AP	4.6	Nov 2009	Audit Program for Termination, Total Cost Basis	http://www.dcaa.mil/sap/17100_AP_Fixed_Total_Cost_Basis.pdf
17200	AP	6.2	Oct 2006	Audit Program for Claim Audit, Delay—Disruption	http://www.dcaa.mil/sap/17200_AP_Delay-Disruption.pdf
17200	AP	4.3	Mar 2008	Audit Program for Claim Audit, Other	http://www.dcaa.mil/sap/17200_AP_Other.pdf
17310	AP	2.4	May 2008	Audit of Contract Overpayments	http://www.dcaa.mil/sap/17310_AP_NA.pdf
17330	AP	1.3	Nov 2009	Audit Program for Reconciliation of Contracts	http://www.dcaa.mil/sap/17330_AP_NA.pdf

APPENDIX 5-C: DIRECTORY OF AUDIT PROGRAMS

Activity Code	Doc Type	Version No. and Date		Program Description	URL
17390	AP	2.4	May 2008	Contractor Compliance with Billing Instructions	http://www.dcaa.mil/sap/17390_AP_Contractor_Compliance_with_Contract_Billing_Inst.pdf
17500	AP	5.7	Nov 2008	Audit Program for Progress Payments Based on Cost Incurred	http://www.dcaa.mil/sap/17500_AP_Cost.pdf
17500	AP	4.5	Nov 2009	Audit Program for Flexible Progress Payment Proposals	http://www.dcaa.mil/sap/17500_AP_Flexible.pdf
17500	AP	4.6	Nov 2008	Audit Program for Progress Payments Based on Percentage or Stage of Completion	http://www.dcaa.mil/sap/17500_AP_Percentage_of_Completion.pdf
17600	AP	6.2	May 2008	DFAS Financial Capability Audit	http://www.dcaa.mil/sap/17600_AP_DFAS_Requested_Financial_Capability_Audit.pdf
17600	AP	8.2	May 2008	Audit Program for Financial Capability Audits	http://www.dcaa.mil/sap/17600_AP_Financial_Capability_Audit.pdf
17610	AP	3.2	Nov 2008	Audit Program for Modified Financial Condition Risk Assessment	http://www.dcaa.mil/sap/17610_AP_Modified_Financial_Condition_Risk_Assessment.pdf
17740	AP	1.1	Nov 2009	Post Award Accounting System Audit at Contractors with DoD Commercial Time-and-Materials (T&M) or Labor-Hour (LH) Contracts	http://www.dcaa.mil/sap/17740_AP_Post_Award_Acct_Sys_DoD_Commercial.pdf
17740	AP	4.6	Jun 2009	Post Contract Award Accounting System Audit at Nonmajor Contractors	http://www.dcaa.mil/sap/17740_AP_Post_Contract_Award_Acct_Sys.pdf
17740	AP	5.5	Jun 2009	Preaward Survey of Prospective Contractor Accounting System	http://www.dcaa.mil/sap/17740_AP_Pre_Award_Accounting_System.pdf

APPENDIX 5-C: DIRECTORY OF AUDIT PROGRAMS

Activity Code	Doc Type	Version No. and Date		Program Description	URL
17750	AP	4.7	Nov 2009	EVMS, System and Report Surveillance	http://www.dcaa.mil/sap/17750_AP_EVM_System_and_Report_Surveillance.pdf
17760	AP	3.6	Nov 2009	EVMS, Report Surveillance	http://www.dcaa.mil/sap/17760_AP_EVM_Report_Surveillance.pdf
17770	AP	3.5	Sep 2008	Audit Program for EVM System Compliance	http://www.dcaa.mil/sap/17770_AP_EVM_System_Compliance.pdf
17850	AP	4.1	Nov 2006	CPRs, C/SSRs, and CFSRs	http://www.dcaa.mil/sap/17850_AP_CPR_CSSR_CFSR.pdf
17860	AP	2.1	Nov 2006	Other Program Management System Effort	http://www.dcaa.mil/sap/17860_AP_Other_Program_Management_System_Effort.pdf
17870	AP	3.3	Nov 2009	CCDR	http://www.dcaa.mil/sap/17870_AP_CCDR.pdf
17900	AP	2.1	Nov 2006	Agreed Upon Procedures, Other Than Price Proposals	http://www.dcaa.mil/sap/17900_AP_Agreed_Upon_Procedures_-_Other_Than_Price_Proposal.pdf
17900	AP	2.1	Nov 2006	Other	http://www.dcaa.mil/sap/17900_AP_Other.pdf
17900	AP	1.1	Nov 2006	Iraq Initial Direct Cost Testing	http://www.dcaa.mil/sap/17900_AP_Iraq_Initial_Direct_Cost_Testing.pdf
17900	AP	4.1	Jun 2009	Defense Security Cooperation Agency (DSCA)	http://www.dcaa.mil/sap/17900_AP_Iraq_Initial_Direct_Cost_Testing.pdf
17910	AP	1.1	Nov 2009	Contract Audit Closing Statements for DoD Commercial Time-and-Materials (T&M)/Labor-Hour (LH) Contracts	http://www.dcaa.mil/sap/17910_AP_CACS_DOD_COMMERCIAL_TM_AND_LH.pdf
19100	AP	2.4	Oct 2009	Audit Program for Adequacy of Initial Disclosure Statement	http://www.dcaa.mil/sap/19100_AP_Adequacy_Audit_of_Initial_Disclosure_Statement.pdf

APPENDIX 5-C: DIRECTORY OF AUDIT PROGRAMS

Activity Code	Doc Type	Version No. and Date		Program Description	URL
19100	AP	3.4	Oct 2009	Audit Program for Compliance of Initial Disclosure Statement	http://www.dcaa.mil/sap/19100_AP_Compliance_of_Initial_Disclosure_Statement.pdf
19100	AP	3.5	Oct 2009	Audit Program for Revised Disclosure Statement Adequacy and Compliance	http://www.dcaa.mil/sap/19100_AP_Concurrent_Adequacy_and_Compliance_Revised_DS.pdf
19200	AP	2.2	Nov 2006	Audit Program for Reporting Noncompliance with Disclosed or Established Practices, CAS or FAR	http://www.dcaa.mil/sap/19200_AP_Noncompliance.pdf
19403	AP	6.8	Nov 2009	Audit Program for Cost Accounting Standard No. 403, Allocation of Home Office Expenses to Segments	http://www.dcaa.mil/sap/19403_AP_NA.pdf
19404	AP	5.7	Nov 2009	Audit Program for Cost Accounting Standard No. 404, Capitalization of Tangible Assets	http://www.dcaa.mil/sap/19404_AP_NA.pdf
19407	AP	5.6	Nov 2009	Audit Program for Cost Accounting Standard No. 407, Use of Standard Costs For Direct Material and Direct Labor	http://www.dcaa.mil/sap/19407_AP_NA.pdf
19408	AP	5.7	Nov 2009	Audit Program for Cost Accounting Standard 408	http://www.dcaa.mil/sap/19408_AP_NA.pdf
19409	AP	5.7	Nov 2009	Audit Program for Cost Accounting Standard 409	http://www.dcaa.mil/sap/19409_AP_NA.pdf
19410	AP	6.6	Nov 2009	Audit Program for Cost Accounting Standard No. 410, Allocation of Business Unit General and Administrative Expenses to Final Cost Objectives	http://www.dcaa.mil/sap/19410_AP_Compliance.pdf

APPENDIX 5-C: DIRECTORY OF AUDIT PROGRAMS

Activity Code	Doc Type	Version No. and Date		Program Description	URL
19410	AP	1.1	Nov 2009	Audit Program for Cost Accounting Standard No. 410, Allocation of Business Unit General and Administrative Expenses to Final Cost Objectives for Offsite Locations	http://www.dcaa.mil/sap/19410_AP_Offsite_Locations.pdf
19411	AP	5.7	Nov 2009	Audit Program for Cost Accounting Standard No. 411, Accounting for Acquisition Costs of Material	http://www.dcaa.mil/sap/19411_AP_NA.pdf
19412	AP	3.0	Aug 2009	Audit Program for Incurred Pension Cost and CAS 412 and 413 Compliance	http://www.dcaa.mil/sap/19412_AP_NA.pdf
19413	AP	2.7	Nov 2009	Joint Review Program for Segment Closing Adjustments	http://www.dcaa.mil/sap/19413_AP_NA.pdf
19414	AP	5.6	Nov 2009	Audit Program for Cost Accounting Standard No. 414, Cost of Money as an Element of the Cost of Facilities Capital	http://www.dcaa.mil/sap/19414_AP_NA.pdf
19415	AP	6.1	Nov 2009	Audit Program for Cost Accounting Standard No. 415, Accounting for the Cost of Deferred Compensation	http://www.dcaa.mil/sap/19415_AP_NA.pdf
19416	AP	2.8	Nov 2009	Audit Program for Incurred Insurance Costs and CAS 416 and FAR Compliance	http://www.dcaa.mil/sap/19416_AP_Incurred_Insurance_Cost_and_CAS_416_FAR_Compliance.pdf
19416	OAG	N/A	N/A	JNTCIPRINS—Insurance Summary Schedule	http://www.dcaa.mil/sap/JNTCIPRINS-Insurance_Summary_Schedule.pdf

APPENDIX 5-C: DIRECTORY OF AUDIT PROGRAMS

Activity Code	Doc Type	Version No. and Date		Program Description	URL
19417	AP	5.7	Nov 2009	Audit Program for Cost Accounting Standard No. 417, Cost of Money as an Element of the Cost of Capital Assets Under Construction	http://www.dcaa.mil/sap/19417_AP_NA.pdf
19418	AP	5.6	Nov 2009	Audit Program for Cost Accounting Standard No. 418, Allocation of Direct and Indirect Costs	http://www.dcaa.mil/sap/19418_AP_NA.pdf
19420	AP	5.7	Nov 2009	Audit Program for Cost Accounting Standard No. 420, Accounting for Independent Research and Development Costs and Bid and Proposal Costs	http://www.dcaa.mil/sap/19420_AP_NA.pdf
19500	AP	4.4	Oct 2009	Audit Program for CAS Impact Proposal Evaluations	http://www.dcaa.mil/sap/19500_AP_NA.pdf
21000	AP	5.5	Jun 2009	Audit Program for Price Proposal Over $10 Million	http://www.dcaa.mil/sap/21000_AP_Over_$10_Million.pdf
21000	AP	6.3	Nov 2009	Audit Program for Price Proposal Under $10 Million	http://www.dcaa.mil/sap/21000_AP_Under_$10_Million.pdf
23000	AP	4.10	Nov 2009	Audit Program for Audit of Forward Pricing Rate Agreement	http://www.dcaa.mil/sap/23000_AP_NA.pdf
24010	AP	8.4	Nov 2009	Audit Program for Estimating System Controls	http://www.dcaa.mil/sap/24010_AP_NA.pdf
24010	OAG	3.2	Jun 2006	Internal Control Matrix—Audit Program for Estimating System Controls	http://www.dcaa.mil/sap/ESTG-Internal_Control_Matrix.pdf
27000	AP	5.5	Oct 2009	Audit Program for Cost Element Review	http://www.dcaa.mil/sap/27000_AP_NA.pdf

Activity Code	Doc Type	Version No. and Date		Program Description	URL
27000	AP	1.1	Dec 2007	Audit Program for Evaluation of Cost Realism in Price Proposals	http://www.dcaa.mil/sap/27000_AP_Cost_Realism.pdf
28000	AP	5.0	Jun 2007	Audit Program for Application of Agreed-Upon Procedures	http://www.dcaa.mil/sap/28000_AP_Agreed_Upon_Procedures.pdf
28500	AP	2.3	Jun 2009	Program for Application of Agreed-Upon Procedures—Single Process Initiative (SPI) Cost-Benefit Analysis	http://www.dcaa.mil/sap/28500_AP_Single_Process_Initiative.pdf
42000	AP	6.3	Nov 2009	Audit Program for Post Award Audits	http://www.dcaa.mil/sap/42000_AP_NA.pdf

Notes

Last modified: December 3, 2009

1. Available at http://www.dcaa.mil/standardguidance.htm.

APPENDIX 5-D

Department of Defense Policy for Resolving Contract Disagreements

OFFICE OF THE UNDER SECRETARY OF DEFENSE
3000 DEFENSE PENTAGON
WASHINGTON, DC 20301-3000

ACQUISITION,
TECHNOLOGY
AND LOGISTICS

DEC 4 2009

MEMORANDUM FOR COMMANDER, U.S SPECIAL OPERATIONS
    COMMAND (ATTN: ACQUISITION EXECUTIVE)
  COMMANDER, U.S. TRANSPORTATION
    COMMAND (ATTN: ACQUISITION EXECUTIVE)
  ASSISTANT SECRETARY OF THE ARMY
    (ACQUISITION, LOGISTICS AND TECHNOLOGY)
  ASSISTANT SECRETARY OF THE NAVY
    ASN, (RESEARCH, DEVELOPMENT AND
    ACQUISITION)
  ASSISTANT SECRETARY OF THE AIR FORCE
    (ACQUISITION)
  DIRECTORS, DEFENSE AGENCIES
  DIRECTORS, DOD FIELD ACTIVITIES

SUBJECT: Resolving Contract Audit Recommendations

    The Department fully supports contracting officers making informed decisions within the scope of their authority utilizing the advice of specialists in audit, law, engineering, etc., as the case may be, to ensure that our contracts fulfill the requirements of our warfighters while obtaining the best business deal for the taxpayers.

    This memorandum sets forth DoD's policy for resolving disagreements when the contracting officer does not include significant audit report recommendations (excluding unsupported costs) from the Defense Contract Audit Agency (DCAA) in establishing his/her pre-negotiation objective. For the purposes of this memorandum, a significant disagreement is when the contracting officer in the pre-negotiation objective plans to sustain less than 75 percent of the total recommended questioned costs in a DCAA audit report on a contactor proposal valued at $10 million or more.

    It is essential that contracting officers attempt to resolve significant issues brought to their attention by DCAA audit reports. When significant disagreements occur, the contracting officer shall discuss the basis of the disagreement with the auditor prior to negotiations. The contracting officer shall document that discussion, and the basis for disagreement in the pre-negotiation objective (or pre-business clearance) and in a written communication to the auditor prior to commencing negotiations, e.g., an email confirming the discussion or a copy of the applicable portion of pre-negotiation objective. Approval of the pre-negotiation objective confirms that the discussion with DCAA and the basis for disagreement is adequately documented and supported. Once the negotiation objective is approved, the contracting officer may proceed with negotiations.

    If after the discussion between the contracting officer and the auditor, the auditor does not agree with the contracting officer, DCAA's management may request that the

DoD Component's management review the contracting officer's decision. DCAA's request for the Component's higher-level review shall occur within three business days after receiving the contracting officer's written communication.

If the differences cannot ultimately be resolved at the Component's highest management level, the Director, DCAA, may contact me to discuss the disagreement. If the DCAA Director believes that I have not adequately addressed the matter, the disagreement may finally be elevated to the Under Secretaries for Defense, Acquisition, Technology, Logistics and Comptroller.

Each DoD Component shall implement procedures for this policy. The procedures will provide DCAA's Senior Executives access to refer significant disagreements for higher-level review to a Component Senior Executive (i.e., SES) or General Officer within the contracting officer's chain of command, prior to reaching my office for review. The component procedures shall also provide that the contracting officer will document the disposition of the higher-level review of disagreements in a memorandum for the contract file.

Notwithstanding the above, the DCAA Director may contact me on any disagreement with audit recommendations which he believes requires my attention, (e.g., precedent setting or of high interest to the Department).

The Military Services, the Defense Contract Management Agency, and the Defense Logistics Agency, will coordinate with Headquarters DCAA on the Components' procedures and provide DCAA with a copy of the final procedures within 60 days of this memorandum. The purpose of this coordination is to provide both parties an understanding of the persons or positions in each organization who will be involved in the higher-level review process. The remaining DoD Components will provide their proposed procedures to my point of contact below within 60 days. My office will coordinate those proposed procedures with DCAA Headquarters.

It is neither expected nor necessary that the contracting officer and the contract auditor agree on every issue. They have different, yet complementary, roles in the process. It is expected that the auditor and contracting officer will work together, recognizing that it is the contracting officer's ultimate responsibility to determine fair and reasonable contract values.

A Defense Acquisition Regulation (DAR) Council Case will be established within the next 30 days to revise the Defense Federal Acquisition Regulations Supplement (DFARS) or its companion document, Procedures, Guidance, and Information (PGI), to incorporate this policy memorandum. The point of contact for this action is Mr. Clyde Wray at 703-602-8387 or clyde.wray@osd.mil.

Shay D. Assad
Director, Defense Procurement
and Acquisition Policy

CHAPTER 6

Types of Financial Reports and Opinions Issued by CPAs and Applicable Professional Standards

PAUL M. JAMES
STEPHEN B. SHAPIRO
ANITA M. SHECKELLS
CLAUDIA R. WOLTER
WILEY R. WRIGHT, III

Introduction

Construction lawyers frequently encounter financial statements and other types of accounting reports in counseling clients, and in assisting clients with project administration, pricing, change order issues, claim management, and dispute resolution. These reports take numerous forms, include varying information, and carry with them differing levels of reliability. The distinctions among the various types of reports commonly encountered are very important, particularly if the report was generated by a certified public accountant (CPA).[1]

This chapter reviews the basic methods of financial reporting offered by CPAs, identifies key distinctions among the reports, and provides general information about the content and general reliability of such reports. This chapter also discusses the professional standards that CPAs rely upon in creating financial reports and providing expert consulting services.[2]

Financial Statement Reporting and Applicable Standards

Financial Statements

Financial statements are the most common form of accounting reports and are recognizable to most people in the business world. In simple terms, financial statements are reports that provide an overview of a business entity's financial condition and position. There are four basic types of financial statements:

- A *balance sheet* is a report that provides information regarding an entity's assets, liabilities, and equity at a given point in time. Balance sheets are sometimes referred to as a "statement of financial position" or a "statement of financial condition."
- An *income statement* is a report that provides information regarding an entity's income, expenses, and profits during a defined time period. An income statement can also be referred to as a "profit and loss statement" or a "P&L."
- A *statement of stockholder's equity* (may also be a "statement of equity" for a noncorporate entity) explains changes in an entity's equity during a defined reporting period.
- A *statement of cash flows* provides information regarding an entity's cash flow activities during a defined time period, particularly its operating, investing, and financing activities.

Financial statements are often complex and may be based on assumptions and estimates that influence the statements. These assumptions and estimates are typically summarized in a set of disclosures (commonly referred to as notes) that are included in the financial statements. Because notes describe material items, they are an integral component of financial statements. Notes are a required part of the financial statements except for compilations, in which they may be omitted if the compilation report identifies the omission.

Audit, Review, and Compilation Engagements

Although accounting reports and financial statements can take many forms, there are three basic levels of financial reporting provided by CPAs: audited, reviewed, and compiled financial statements. Each type of engagement involves different levels of CPA services and different procedures with varying levels of assurance. The highest level of assurance is placed on audit reports, followed by review reports, and finally compilation reports, which offer no assurance. In fact, a compilation report specifically states that the CPA has "not audited or reviewed the accompanying financial statements and, accordingly, does not express an opinion or any other form of assurance on them."[3]

The level of assurance a company obtains regarding its financial statements is often dictated by third parties such as banks, sureties, regulatory agencies, and investors. Companies generally obtain audits because a third party relying on the financial statements requires an audit. The company may be able to obtain better rates for financing or bonding if its financial statements are accompanied by a higher level of assurance.

One of the most important attributes relied on by those using audit and review reports is that such reports have been prepared independently and are therefore free from undue influence. Although not required to be independent when performing compilation procedures, the CPA typically is, nevertheless. As with any profession, CPAs are bound to a code of professional conduct[4] to help support the public's reliance on financial reports. The American Institute of Certified Public Accountants (AICPA) Code of Conduct provides a set of rules governing the relationships between the CPA and his clients. The purpose of these rules is to maintain the CPA's independence from the client and to eliminate conflicts of interests between CPA and client.

A CPA must be independent to issue an audit or a review report. Independence may be affected by a relationship or relationships between the CPA and the business entity. Threats to independence include a financial self-interest in the entity, a family interest, management participation, self-review of the CPA's non-audit work within the context of an audit engagement, an adverse interest such as a litigation threat, and undue influence by management.

Audited Financial Statements

An audit is an examination of historical financial statements performed in accordance with generally accepted auditing standards (GAAS) in effect at the time the audit is performed. GAAS are standards issued by the American Institute of Certified Public Accountants (AICPA) Auditing Standards Board. There are 10 auditing standards, augmented by Statements on Auditing Standards that interpret the GAAS. Furthermore, under certain circumstances, regulatory authorities may have additional requirements applicable to business entities under their jurisdiction, and CPAs must also consider these requirements when performing their audits.

Auditing Standards[5]

The 10 auditing standards are as follows.

General Standards:

1. The auditor must have adequate technical training and proficiency to perform the audit.
2. The auditor must maintain independence in mental attitude in all matters relating to the audit.
3. The auditor must exercise due professional care in the performance of the audit and the preparation of the report.

Standards of Field Work:

4. The auditor must adequately plan the work and must properly supervise any assistants.
5. The auditor must obtain a sufficient understanding of the entity and its environment, including its internal controls, to assess the risk of

material misstatement of the financial statements whether due to error or fraud, and to design the nature, timing, and extent of further audit procedures.
6. The auditor must obtain sufficient appropriate audit evidence by performing audit procedures to afford a reasonable basis for an opinion regarding the financial statements under audit.

Standards of Reporting:

7. The auditor must state in the auditor's report whether the financial statements are presented in accordance with generally accepted accounting principles (GAAP).
8. The auditor must identify in the auditor's report those circumstances in which such principles have not been consistently observed in the current period in relation to the preceding period.
9. When the auditor determines that information disclosures are not reasonably adequate, the auditor must so state in the auditor's report.
10. The auditor must either express an opinion regarding the financial statements, taken as a whole, or state that an opinion cannot be expressed in the auditor's report. When the auditor cannot express an overall opinion, the auditor should state the reasons therefore in the auditor's report. In all cases where an auditor's name is associated with financial statements, the auditor's report should clearly indicate the character of the auditor's work, and the degree of responsibility the auditor is taking.

Report Types

A CPA issues several types of reports with respect to audited financial statements, based on the level of review and verification that the CPA performs and the CPA's ability to verify the information presented. As detailed below, these reports are significantly different. It is important to understand these differences and their relevance when reviewing or relying on an audited financial statement.

Unqualified Reports and Opinions

An unqualified opinion represents that the financial statements present fairly, in all material respects, the financial position, results of operations, and cash flows of the business entity in conformity with GAAP. There are circumstances that may require the CPA to add an explanatory paragraph or additional language to the audit report without affecting the CPA's unqualified opinion. Circumstances requiring explanatory language or information include

- When the auditor's opinion is based in part on the report of another auditor.
- When substantial doubt exists as to the entity's ability to continue as a going concern.

- When supplementary information is reported, such as schedules detailing work-in-process, accounts-receivable aging, costs of revenues, or operating expenses.

An unqualified opinion can be easily identified based on the language in the report. The following language illustrates a standard audit report representing an unqualified opinion:

> We have audited the accompanying balance sheet of XYZ Company as of December 31, 20XX, and the related statements of income, stockholders' equity, and cash flows for the year then ended. These financial statements are the responsibility of the Company's management. Our responsibility is to express an opinion on these financial statements based on our audit.
>
> We conducted our audit in accordance with auditing standards generally accepted in the United States of America. Those standards require that we plan and perform the audit to obtain reasonable assurance about whether the financial statements are free of material misstatement. An audit includes examining, on a test basis, evidence supporting the amounts and disclosures in the financial statements. An audit also includes assessing the accounting principles used and significant estimates made by management, as well as evaluating the overall financial statement presentation. We believe that our audit provides a reasonable basis for our opinion.
>
> In our opinion, the financial statements referred to above present fairly, in all material respects, the financial position of XYZ Company as of December 31, 20XX, and the results of its operations and its cash flows for the year then ended in conformity with accounting principles generally accepted in the United States of America.

An unqualified opinion represents the highest level of assurance CPAs provide with respect to financial statements, indicating there are no material departures from GAAP or other material issues that require disclosure.

Qualified Opinion
A qualified opinion states that, except for the effects of the matter(s) to which the qualification relates, the financial statement presents fairly, in all material respects, the financial position, results of operations, and cash flows of the entity in conformity with GAAP. For example, a CPA may provide a qualified opinion when the CPA determines that there is not sufficient or appropriate audit evidence to provide an unqualified opinion, or there is a departure from GAAP. A CPA may also provide a qualified opinion when restrictions are placed on the scope of the audit that preclude the CPA from expressing

an unqualified opinion, but are not so great that the CPA feels it is necessary to disclaim an opinion as described below. This latter type of qualified report might occur, for example, when the CPA is not in a position to observe a material physical inventory count, or cannot examine certain records or documentation that have been destroyed in a natural disaster.

The CPA is required to identify the factors leading to a qualified audit opinion by including specific disclaimers or qualifying statements in his report. It is important to identify and understand these qualifications before relying on a qualified audit report. The following is typical language found in a qualified audit report due to a departure from GAAP (added language emphasized):

> We have audited the accompanying balance sheet of XYZ Company as of December 31, 20XX, and the related statements of income, stockholders' equity, and cash flows for the year then ended. These financial statements are the responsibility of the Company's management. Our responsibility is to express an opinion on these financial statements based on our audit.
>
> We conducted our audit in accordance with auditing standards generally accepted in the United States of America. Those standards require that we plan and perform the audit to obtain reasonable assurance about whether the financial statements are free of material misstatement. An audit also includes assessing the accounting principles used and significant estimates made by management, as well as evaluating the overall financial statement presentation. We believe that our audit provides a reasonable basis for our opinion.
>
> *As described in Note X to the financial statements, land and buildings are stated at appraised value in the accompanying balance sheet. In our opinion, such assets should be stated at acquisition cost, net of depreciation, to conform with accounting principles generally accepted in the United States of America. If the financial statements were corrected for the departure from generally accepted accounting principles, fixed assets, net of depreciation, and retained earnings would be decreased by $XXX,XXX as of December 31, 20XX, and net income would be decreased by $XX,XXX for the year then ended.*
>
> In our opinion, *except for the effects of valuing the land and buildings at appraised value as explained in the preceding paragraph,* the financial statements referred to above present fairly, in all material respects, the financial position of XYZ Company as of December 31, 20XX, and the results of its operations and cash flows for the year then ended in conformity with accounting principles generally accepted in the United States of America.

Adverse Reports and Opinions

An adverse opinion report states that the financial statements do not present fairly the financial position, results of operations, or cash flows of the business entity being audited in conformity with GAAP. CPAs issue adverse opinions when the CPA concludes that an entity's financial statements are misrepresented, misstated, or fail to accurately reflect the entity's financial performance and health. The CPA must determine that the extent of the misstatement is sufficiently severe, or the misstatement is sufficiently material, to require the CPA to express an adverse opinion.

Circumstances that could lead to an adverse opinion include financial statements that omit material activities and key financial information related to wholly owned subsidiaries of the audited entity that should be consolidated into the financial statements of the audited entity. An example of language indicating an adverse opinion in such circumstances is as follows:

> As described in Note X to the financial statements, the Company's financial statements do not include the accounts of LMN Company and 123 Company that are wholly owned subsidiaries of the Company. In our opinion, accounting principles generally accepted in the United States of America require that the Company's financial statements include the accounts of LMN Company and 123 Company.
>
> In our opinion, because of the matters discussed in the preceding paragraph, the financial statements referred to above do not present fairly, in conformity with accounting principles generally accepted in the United States of America, the financial position of XYZ Company, Inc. as of December 31, 20XX, or the results of its operations or its cash flows for the year then ended.

Adverse opinions are rare, because the entity will generally seek to amend its financial statements to correct severe departures from GAAP before the report is issued. An adverse opinion can have a significant adverse influence on any pending business transaction. Lawyers who encounter an adverse opinion should appropriately investigate the circumstances underlying that opinion, and take whatever steps may be required under the circumstances before relying on the information presented in such a report.

There may be circumstances when a qualified or adverse opinion still provides useful information for the construction lawyer, such as when the nature of the issue resulting in the adverse opinion or disclaimer is unrelated to the presentation of income and expenses associated with the particular contract of interest.

Disclaimer of Opinion

A disclaimer of opinion report states that the CPA does not express an opinion on the financial statements. The CPA may decline to express an opinion whenever the CPA is unable to form an opinion as to the fairness of the presentation of the financial statements in conformity with GAAP. The CPA should provide all of the substantive reasons for such a disclaimer. A disclaimer of an opinion is appropriate when the CPA has not performed an audit sufficient in scope to enable the CPA to form an opinion concerning the financial statements. This situation can occur, for example, when the CPA is unable to confirm the existence of accounts receivable, or cannot perform alternative procedures to gain confidence with regard to accounts receivable balances in the underlying financial statements.

The following is a typical example of language associated with a disclaimer of opinion:

> We were engaged to audit the accompanying balance sheet of XYZ Company as of December 31, 20XX, and the related statements of income, stockholders' equity, and cash flows for the year then ended. These financial statements are the responsibility of the management of the Company.
>
> *Pursuant to the Company's request, we did not confirm accounts receivable totaling $XXX,XXX at December 31, 20XX, by direct correspondence with customers of the Company. We were unable to satisfy ourselves about the accounts receivable balance through other auditing procedures.*
>
> *Since accounts receivable as of December 31, 20XX, materially affect the determination of financial position, results of operations and cash flows, the scope of our work was not sufficient to enable us to express, and we do not express, an opinion on the financial statements referred to in the first paragraph.*

Reviewed Financial Statements

The second major category of CPA reports is reviewed financial statements. The professional standards applicable to the CPA's work for a review report are the Statements on Standards for Accounting and Review Services (SSARS), issued by the AICPA. A review engagement typically includes applying analytical procedures to financial data, including developing expectations and comparisons to expectations; making inquiries of management and other personnel as deemed appropriate; obtaining representations from management for all periods covered by the review report; and performing all of the procedures for a report on compiled financial statements, which are discussed in greater detail below.

A review is often required by third parties, and provides a minimum level of assurance that the CPA is not aware of any material modifications necessary for the statements to be in accordance with GAAP. When issuing a review, the CPA states that he is not expressing an opinion regarding the fair presentation of the financial statements in accordance with GAAP.

The following is an illustration of language appearing in a review report on financial statements prepared in accordance with GAAP:

> We have reviewed the accompanying balance sheet of XYZ Company as of December 31, 20XX, and the related statements of income, stockholders' equity, and cash flows for the year then ended, in accordance with Statements on Standards for Accounting and Review Services issued by the American Institute of Certified Public Accountants. All information included in these financial statements is the representation of the management (owners) of XYZ Company.
>
> A review consists principally of inquiries of company personnel and analytical procedures applied to financial data. It is substantially less in scope than an audit in accordance with generally accepted auditing standards, the objective of which is the expression of an opinion regarding the financial statements taken as a whole. Accordingly, we do not express such an opinion.
>
> Based on our review, we are not aware of any material modifications that should be made to the accompanying financial statements in order for them to be in conformity with generally accepted accounting principles.
>
> A review is used in circumstances where the users of the financial statements, such as a lender for a small contractor, do not require the contractor to incur the expense of an audit and are satisfied with the reduced level of assurance given by the CPA in a review.

Compiled Financial Statements

The third major category of CPA reports is compiled financial statements, also referred to as compilations. Compilations are reports in which the CPA presents information in the form of a financial statement that is merely the representation of the client's management, and not an expression of any assurance by the CPA. When performing a compilation, the CPA is not required to make inquiries or perform other procedures to verify, corroborate, or review the information supplied by the business entity. SSARS are the professional standards used by a CPA in preparing compilations.

The types of financial statements typically seen in the form of compilations include

- Historical financial statements
- Personal financial statements

- Prospective financial statements
- Pro forma financial statements
- Management-use-only financial statements
- Specified elements or accounts of financial statements

The following illustrates the language found in a compilation report on financial statements issued in accordance with GAAP:

We have compiled the accompanying balance sheet of XYZ Company as of December 31, 20XX, and the related statements of income, stockholders' equity, and cash flows for the year then ended, in accordance with Statements on Standards for Accounting and Review Services issued by the American Institute of Certified Public Accountants.

A compilation is limited to presenting in the form of financial statements information that is the representation of management (owners). We have not audited or reviewed the accompanying financial statements and, accordingly, do not express an opinion or any other form of assurance on them.

The professional standards do not require that the CPA be independent to perform a compilation. However, if the CPA is not independent, he must state so in the report, but is not allowed to provide the reason for the lack of independence. The AICPA's Accounting and Review Services Committee is considering revising this requirement to allow the CPA to disclose the reason for his lack of independence.

Under SSARS 8, the CPA is allowed to compile management-use-only financial statements without issuing a compilation report. In order to do this, the financial statements must, in fact, be only for internal management use and must not be reasonably expected to be used by a third party. Management must provide a representation in writing to the CPA that the use of the financial statements will be limited to members of management and that the statements will not be distributed to third parties. There are both pros and cons of issuing management-use-only financial statements. Some CPAs believe the application of SSARS 8 provides a more cost-effective way of providing financial statements to clients who do not intend to distribute such statements to third parties. Other CPAs believe that history has shown that such statements frequently end up in the hands of third-party users in any event, and thus that SSARS 8 should rarely be applied. If it appears SSARS 8 could be applicable, the CPA and the contractor should carefully discuss the intended use of the statements and whether SSARS 8 is or is not an appropriate option.

Compilations are often required by third parties in order to obtain financial statements for an entity that are something other than internally prepared financial statements. In many cases, banks and bonding companies will accept compilations for purposes of interim financial statements. A compilation states that it is limited to presenting, in the form of financial statements, information that is in fact the representation of management. Although CPAs are not required to perform procedures to gain any comfort level regarding the underlying data, third parties generally have more confidence in a financial statement compiled by a CPA than they do with internally prepared financial statements.

Table Comparison: Audit, Review, Compilation

The distinguishing characteristics of the various forms of accounting reports related to financial statements (audits, reviews, and compilations) are listed in Table 1.

Going-Concern Issues

In all three types of CPA reports—audits, reviews, and compilations—the CPA must consider whether the business being examined constitutes a "going concern," that is, whether the business entity is able to continue operations. Generally, for financial reporting purposes, an entity's ability to continue as a going concern for a reasonable time period is assumed, unless significant information is presented to the contrary. Doubt regarding an entity's ability to continue as a going concern arises when the entity

- Encounters negative trends in key financial indicators;
- Defaults on debt, restructures debt, or seeks new sources of financing;
- Encounters external forces, which give rise to uncertainty such as loss of business line or key customers, loss of key employees, or pending or threatened litigation; or
- Encounters internal forces such as noneconomic long-term commitments or labor stoppages.

When performing audits, reviews, or compilations, the CPA must consider management's plans to mitigate the cause for any such uncertainty and the likely impact of those plans on the future operations of the company. Plans that may mitigate the above factors include plans to dispose of assets, borrow additional funds, restructure debt, reduce or delay expenditures, obtain a capital infusion, or delay capital payouts.

The CPA must address the issue of potential inability to continue as a going concern in the same manner as other uncertainties. A disclosure in the notes to the applicable financial statements should be added addressing the uncertainty. The disclosure should provide the reasons for the uncertainty and set forth management's plans to address the going-concern issues. Even if the CPA determines that a substantial doubt regarding the ability to continue as a going concern is alleviated by mitigating factors, the CPA should still consider the need for a going-concern disclosure in the notes to the financial statements.

The CPA's responsibility for addressing an entity's ability to continue as a going concern varies depending on the level of reporting provided. For compilations and reviews, the report need not be modified, even if there is substantial doubt about the entity's ability to continue as a going concern, so long as a note is added to the financial statements.

Table 1
Comparison of Compilation, Review, and Audit Engagements*, *

	Compilation Engagement†	Review Engagement‡	Audit Engagement
1. Level of assurance	No assurance as to GAAP	Limited assurance as to GAAP	Statements are fairly presented in accordance with GAAP
2. Entities covered	Non-issuer only	Non-issuer only	Issuer or non-issuer
3. Knowledge of client's Industry	Knowledge of the accounting principles and practices of the industry and general understanding of the client's business	Knowledge same as compilation *plus* an increased understanding of the client's business	Extensive knowledge of the economy, the relevant industry, and the client's business [SAS No. 108 (AU 311)]
4. Inquiry procedures required	Inquiries not required unless information supplied by the client is questionable	Inquiry and analytical procedures required *plus* additional procedures if the information appears questionable	Inquiry, analytical procedures [SAS No. 56 (AU 329)], and other audit procedures
5. GAAP disclosures omitted	Substantially all disclosures required by GAAP may be omitted, without restriction on use [Exception, see SSARS No. 3 (AR 300)]	Disclosures required by GAAP must be included or report must be modified to include the disclosures	Inadequate disclosure requires qualified or adverse opinion
6. Known departures from GAAP measurements	Disclosure required in modified compilation report [Exception, see SSARS No. 3 (AR 300)]	Disclosure required in modified review report	Departure from GAAP requires qualified or adverse opinion
7. Accountant's independence	Accountant does not have to be independent	Lack of independence precludes issuing review report	Non-issuer—compilation report [SSARS No. 1 (AR 100)] if not independent
8. Obtain an understanding of internal control and risk	Not required	Not required	Required by SAS No. 109 (AU 319)

	Compilation Engagement[†]	**Review Engagement**[‡]	**Audit Engagement**
9. Engagement letter	Recommended	Recommended	Required. [SAS No. 108 (AU 310) requires the accountant to obtain an understanding with the client regarding the audit services to be performed and to document that understanding through a written communication with the client.]
10. Representation letter	No mention	Required	Required by SAS No. 85 (AU 333)

* Adapted from Dan. M. Guy, Disclosure Needs in Financial Reporting for Closely Held Businesses, 1978 Accounting Research Convocation, Univ. of Ala., and PPC's GUIDE TO COMPILATION AND REVIEW ENGAGEMENTS. John R. Clay, Dan M Guy, et al; Thirty-first Edition- Copyright 2009 Thomson Reuters/PPC; reprinted with permission. To order, please call (800) 431-9025, option1.
** This table does not cover engagements relating to personal financial statements, prospective financial information, or reviews of financial statements of public companies. In addition, this table does not cover financial statements prepared on a comprehensive basis of accounting other than GAAP.
† Items 1–10 apply to all compiled financial statements expected to be used by a third party, as well as compiled management-use-only financial statements submitted to the client with a SSARS No. 1 report. Items 5 and 6 do not apply to compiled management-use-only financial statements in which the accountant chooses the communication alternative of an engagement letter in lieu of a SSARS No. 1 report. In addition, Item 9, the engagement letter, is *required*, not *recommended*, for compiled management-use-only financial statements in which a SSARS No. 1 report is not issued.
‡ Excludes interim reviews of issuers. *See* SAS No. 100 (AU 722). (Section 623 discusses situations when a SSARS review report may be applicable to issuers.) "Issuer" refers to an issuer of publicly held securities.

In the context of an audit engagement, by contrast, the CPA must modify the report if there is substantial doubt about the entity's ability to continue as a going concern. An example of an explanatory paragraph on this issue that would be included in the audit report is as follows:

> The accompanying financial statements have been prepared assuming that the Company will continue as a going concern. As discussed in Note X to the financial statements, the Company [describe events

giving rise to uncertainty, such as "has suffered three consecutive years with net operating losses"], which raises substantial doubt about its ability to continue as a going concern. Management's plans in regard to these matters are also described in Note X. The financial statements do not include any adjustments that might result from the outcome of this uncertainty.

If a construction contractor's financial statements include a note stating there is substantial doubt about its ability to continue as a going concern, the contractor will most likely have difficulty obtaining financing or bonding, and the contractor's vendors may well require advance payment for goods and services. Even if the note indicates mitigating factors with respect to the substantial doubt, the company's creditors, surety, and vendors are all on notice that the company is experiencing financial difficulties and that they should be cautious when undertaking further business with the contractor.

Special Report Engagements

In addition to audits, reviews, and compilations, CPAs also issue special reports. Special reports include, but are not limited to,

- Reports on specified elements, accounts, or items of a financial statement;
- Reports on compliance with contractual agreements or regulatory requirements related to financial statements;
- Reports on financial presentations to comply with contractual agreements or regulatory provisions;
- Reports on financial information presented in prescribed forms or schedules that require a prescribed form;
- Reports on unaudited financial statements (in association with financial statements); and
- Reports on incomplete financial information.

Two examples of special reports are agreed-upon procedures reports and application of accounting principles reports. These types of reports are covered by different professional standards than those for audits, reviews, and compilations. The principal differences between these special reports and reports issued for audits, reviews, and compilations relate to the subject matter covered and the intended use of the report. With respect to agreed-upon procedures and application of accounting principles reports, the CPA expresses an opinion on information that is less than that contained in a complete set of financial statements. The CPA's opinions concerning this information are expressed after performing specific agreed-upon procedures with respect to the subject matter of the special report. The party presenting the information to the CPA (i.e., the business entity) is responsible for determining the sufficiency of the procedures. As a result, the dissemination of special reports is restricted to that specific party or parties. By contrast, in an audit, review, or compilation report, there are no restrictions on the report's dissemination to third parties.

An agreed-upon procedures report will contain language similar to the following:

Independent Accountant's Report on Applying Agreed-Upon Procedures

We have performed the procedures enumerated below, which were agreed to by management of XYZ, Inc., solely to assist you in evaluating the accompanying Statement of Contract Costs of XYZ, Inc. for the year ended December 31, 20XX. XYZ, Inc.'s management is responsible for the statement of contract costs. This agreed-upon procedures engagement was conducted in accordance with attestation standards established by the American Institute of Certified Public Accountants. The sufficiency of these procedures is solely the responsibility of those parties specified in the report. Consequently, we make no representation regarding the sufficiency of the procedures described below either for the purpose for which this report has been requested or for any other purpose.

[Discussion of procedures and findings]

We were not engaged to and did not conduct an examination, the objective of which would be the expression of an opinion on the accompanying Statement of Contract Costs of XYZ, Inc. Accordingly, we do not express such an opinion. Had we performed additional procedures, other matters might have come to our attention that would have been reported to you.

This report is intended solely for the information and use of the management of XYZ, Inc., and is not intended to be and should not be used by anyone other than the management of XYZ, Inc.

The language that would typically be contained in an application of accounting principles report is as follows:

Application of Accounting Principles

We have been engaged to report on the appropriate application of accounting principles generally accepted in [country] to the specific transaction described below. This report is being issued to XYZ

Company for assistance in evaluating accounting principles for the described specific transaction. Our engagement has been conducted in accordance with standards established by the American Institute of Certified Public Accountants.

[Description of Transaction]

The facts, circumstances, and assumptions relevant to the specific transaction as provided to us by the management of XYZ Company are as follows:

[Appropriate Accounting Principles]

[Discussion of generally accepted accounting principles]

Concluding Comments

The ultimate responsibility for the decision on the appropriate application of accounting principles generally accepted in [country] for an actual transaction rests with the preparers of financial statements, who should consult with their continuing accountant. Our judgment on the appropriate application of accounting principles generally accepted in [country] for the described specific transaction is based solely on the facts provided to us as described above. Should these facts and circumstances differ, our conclusion may change.

Restricted Use

This report is intended solely for the information and use of the Board of Directors and management of XYZ Company and is not intended to be and should not be used by anyone other than these specified parties.

These two types of special reports may be useful in circumstances where a business (such as a construction contractor) needs an opinion from a CPA concerning certain information that is less in scope than that contained in a complete set of financial statements. For example, in an agreed-upon procedures report, the CPA may express an opinion concerning the revenue and costs of a specific contract based on the application of analytical procedures that are agreed to between the CPA and business or contractor. This information could include the entire contract revenue and costs or specific elements derived from it, such as a computation of a daily general condition rate or the costs related to a particular change order. As the example language indicates, an application of accounting principles report may be utilized to indicate how the financial statement information of the entity would be affected by the application of specific accounting principles, other than GAAP, that are in use in a specific foreign location.

Further information about these types of special reports may be found in the AICPA attestation standards.

Consulting and Expert Services

Consulting and expert services cover a wide variety of services that may be performed by a CPA or accountant who has particular technical or industry specific expertise. When a CPA performs these services, he is obligated to comply with the AICPA professional standards[6] discussed below. If using the CPA designation in connection with his report or communications regarding these services, the CPA may be required to be licensed, depending upon the state in which the services are provided. The appropriate state's licensing body determines whether or not a CPA is required to be licensed in order to perform these services.

Consulting Services

Consulting services, historically referred to as management advisory services, business advisory services, or management services, include a wide range of expertise involving specific technical disciplines and specific industry knowledge. When performing consulting services, CPAs are obligated to follow the general standards of the profession contained in Rule 201 of the AICPA Code of Professional Conduct. These general standards are

- *Professional competence.* Undertake only those professional services that the member or the member's firm can reasonably expect to be completed with professional competence.
- *Due professional care.* Exercise due professional care in the performance of professional services.
- *Planning and supervision.* Adequately plan and supervise the performance of professional services.
- *Sufficient relevant data.* Obtain sufficient relevant data to afford a reasonable basis for conclusions or recommendations in relation to any professional services provided.

In addition to these general standards set forth in Rule 201 of the AICPA Code of Professional Conduct, CPAs are also obligated to follow the additional general standards of the Statement on Standards for Consulting Services, as established in Rule 202 of the AICPA Code of Professional Conduct. These additional standards are

- *Client interest.* Serve the client interest by seeking to accomplish the objectives established by the understanding with the client while maintaining integrity and objectivity.
- *Understanding with client.* Establish with the client a written or oral understanding about the responsibilities of the parties and the nature, scope, and limitations of services to be performed, and modify the

understanding if circumstances require a significant change during the engagement.
- *Communication with client.* Inform the client of (1) conflicts of interest that may occur pursuant to interpretations of Rule 102 of the Code of Professional Conduct (regarding integrity and objectivity), (2) significant reservations concerning the scope or benefits of the engagement, and (3) significant engagement findings or events.

Consulting services performed by CPAs that are not covered by these general standards may nevertheless be subject to other AICPA Technical Standards, such as Statements on Auditing Standards, Statements on Attestation Standards, and Statements on Standards for Accounting and Review Services, according to the nature of the services. Engagements for tax return preparation, tax planning or advice, tax representation, personal financial planning, and bookkeeping services are subject to specific standards as well. Ethical and other standards also apply to services involving the preparation of written reports, and to the provision of oral advice on the application of accounting principles to specified transactions or events, either complete or proposed, and associated reporting.

Consulting services include the following general categories. Each of the general categories of consulting services is covered by the general professional standards identified above.

Consultations
In a consultation, the CPA's function is to advise a business or its counsel in a short time frame, based mostly, if not entirely, on existing personal knowledge about the client, the circumstances of the situation presented, the technical matters involved, any information provided by the client, and the mutual intent of the parties. Examples of consultations include reviewing and commenting on a client-prepared business plan and suggesting computer software for further client investigation.

Advisory Services
In providing advisory services, the CPA's function is to develop findings, conclusions, and recommendations for client consideration and decision making. Examples of advisory services include operational review and improvement studies, analyses of accounting systems, assistance with strategic planning, and defining requirements for information systems.

Implementation Services
When providing implementation services, the CPA's function is to put an action plan into effect. An action plan contains the specific steps or procedures for accomplishing an objective, such as the installation of a computerized system. Client personnel and resources may be pooled with the CPA's to accomplish the implementation objectives. The CPA is responsible to the client

for the conduct and management of his engagement activities. Examples of implementation services include providing computer system installation and support, executing steps to improve productivity, and assisting with accomplishing or implementing organizational mergers.

Transaction Services

Transaction services are services related to a specific client transaction or transactions, generally with a third party. Examples of transaction services include insolvency services, valuation services, preparation of information for obtaining financing, analysis of a potential merger or acquisition, and litigation-related services.

Staff and Other Support Services

Staff and other support services involve providing appropriate staff and related support to perform tasks specified by the client. The CPA's staff is directed by the client as circumstances require. Examples of staff and other support services include data processing, facilities management, computer programming, bankruptcy trusteeship, and comptrollership activities.

Product Services

Product services involve providing the client with a specified product and associated professional services to support the installation, use, or maintenance of that product. Examples of product services include the sale and delivery of packaged training programs, sale and implementation of computer software, and sale and installation of systems development methodologies.

Expert Witness and Consulting Expert Services

There are several differences between an accountant's audit-type report and related services (often referred to as "attest" reports and services) and an expert witness report. One of the most important differences is the level of evidence (as that term is used by CPAs) that is required to support the CPA's opinions. For an audit, the professional standards require that the CPA obtain sufficient audit evidence to support an opinion. In order to obtain sufficient audit evidence, the CPA must perform specific procedures as prescribed by generally accepted auditing standards.

In contrast, for an expert witness or consulting expert report, the applicable professional standards require that the CPA obtain sufficient relevant data to support his opinions and conclusions. The determination of what is sufficiently relevant is more subjective than in the audit context. Further, specific procedures for obtaining the required sufficient relevant data are not prescribed in the consulting service standards, as they are in the auditing standards. Unlike in an audit engagement, the CPA in a consulting engagement may rely on his own experience with respect to the industry involved or the issue in dispute in reaching an opinion. Given the higher degree of latitude afforded the CPA in an expert witness engagement, it is important to thoroughly explore the bases for the CPA's opinion.

The topics addressed in accountant expert witness reports routinely encountered in construction and government contract construction disputes include the following:

- Financial modeling used to determine the value of a business or a contract
- Cash-flow analyses
- Lost profits calculations
- Valuing contract losses
- Computing time-related escalation costs
- Computing labor efficiency costs
- Computing overhead costs
- Computing material, equipment, and job site costs
- Comparing planned versus actual costs
- Determining whether costs are allowable under the Federal Acquisition Regulation, the Cost Accounting Standards, or other cost standards
- Various productivity models
- Fraud and false claims act violations
- Cost allocation issues
- GAAP
- Overlapping requirements of applicable standards
- Asset valuation
- Various earnings and income analyses

While there are no specific reporting standards imposed by the AICPA that the CPA must adhere to when providing expert services, there are report requirements for expert witnesses in civil litigation and other formal proceedings in certain circumstances, depending upon the jurisdiction in which the matter is pending. The applicable rules and standards governing testifying and nontestifying experts vary from state to state and may be subject to local rules, court rules, as well as the individual practices of presiding judges. The Federal Rules of Civil Procedure (FRCP) provide useful general guidance in this area, and are the focus for discussion here. Most federal courts also have local rules, and some federal judges develop even further detailed requirements. The CPA engaged as an expert must work closely with counsel to develop any work product, including disclosures and reports, in accordance with all the applicable rules and procedures.

Discovery of Testifying and Nontestifying Experts[7]

FRCP 26 governs expert discovery. This rule has specific "automatic disclosure" requirements for information concerning a testifying expert's background, opinions, and the work product that forms the basis for his opinion.

These disclosure rules are important considerations in determining how to use CPA experts in litigation.

Automatic Disclosure

Under FRCP 26(a)(2)(A), a party must disclose the identity of any witness that it may use at trial as an expert. Additionally, the party must produce a written report, prepared and signed by the witness "if the witness is one retained or specially employed to provide expert testimony in the case or one whose duties as the party's employee regularly involve giving expert testimony."[8] This report must include the complete opinion of the witness, identify any data or other information considered by the expert in forming the opinion, provide information about the expert's qualifications, list the cases in which the witness has testified as an expert at trial or at a deposition in the past four years, and include a statement of the compensation to be paid to the expert.[9] Unless a different date is authorized by the court, expert disclosures must be made at least 90 days before trial or within 30 days of the opposing party's expert disclosure, if the expert testimony is intended to be used to contradict that evidence.[10]

Scope of Discovery

Under FRCP 26(b)(4)(A), the opposing party is entitled to depose any person who has been identified as an expert for trial. Ordinarily, the opposing party cannot utilize interrogatories or conduct a deposition to learn facts or opinions of an expert hired either in anticipation of litigation or to prepare for trial who is not going to be called as a witness. Exceptional circumstances must be shown to obtain discovery from nontestifying litigation consultants.

There is often significant risk of designating a formerly nontestifying or consulting expert as a testifying expert, as opposing parties may seek through discovery all work product created by or received by the expert during his engagement as a consulting expert. Given the broad automatic disclosure rules discussed above, careful consideration must be given to using testifying experts, particularly a CPA who has been a valuable resource for trial counsel in preparing or responding to financial elements of a construction dispute.

Admissibility of Evidence

Whether an expert's testimony will be admissible at trial is governed by Rule 702 of the Federal Rules of Evidence. Rule 702 states:

> If scientific, technical, or other specialized knowledge will assist the trier of fact to understand the evidence or to determine a fact in issue, a witness qualified as an expert by knowledge, skill, experience, training, or education, may testify thereto in the form of an opinion or otherwise, if (1) the testimony is based on sufficient facts or data, (2) the testimony is the product of reliable principles and methods and (3) the witness has applied the principles and methods reliably to the facts.

Applying Rule 702, the U.S. Supreme Court has outlined the federal standard for admissibility of expert testimony. In *Daubert v. Merrell Dow Pharmaceuticals, Inc.*, the Supreme Court held that the trial judge must "ensure that any and all scientific testimony or evidence admitted is not only relevant, but reliable."[11] In other words, the judge has a responsibility to act as the "gatekeeper" for allowing expert evidence. Judges may consider a variety of factors in determining admissibility of expert testimony, such as testing, peer review, error rates, and acceptability in the scientific community.[12] This is a flexible standard of review, subject to judicial discretion.

The Supreme Court extended the application of the *Daubert* principles to nonscientific and other technical forms of expert testimony in *Kumho Tire Company v. Carmichael*.[13] The Supreme Court held there that "where such [expert] testimony's factual basis, data, principles, methods or their application are called sufficiently into question . . . the trial judge must determine whether the testimony has a reliable basis in the knowledge and experience of the relevant discipline."[14] The Court also noted that "the judge must have considerable leeway in deciding in a particular case how to go about determining whether particular expert testimony is reliable."[15] The trial judge accordingly has broad discretion in admitting or rejecting expert testimony and evidence. For the expert testimony of a CPA to be admissible at trial, the judge will consider the reliability and relevancy of that testimony on a case-by-case basis, and counsel must be prepared to demonstrate the applicability of the CPA's industry experience, expertise, and analysis to the dispute in question.

Privilege Applied to Consulting Experts

Where prevailing state law does not recognize an accountant-client privilege, accountants or financial advisors hired to assist attorneys may nevertheless qualify for protection under the attorney-client privilege. Rule 503 of the Federal Rules of Evidence, which governs attorney-client privilege, provides that

> a client has privilege to refuse to disclose and to prevent another person from disclosing confidential communications made for the purpose of facilitating the rendition of professional legal services to the client, (1) between himself or his representative and his lawyer or his lawyer's representative, or (2) between his lawyer and the lawyer's representative, or (3) between representatives of the client or between the client and a representative of the client, or (5) between lawyers representing the client.[16]

Generally, a CPA hired as a nontestifying consultant by an attorney to assist the attorney in analysis of a client's financial information will qualify as a "lawyer's representative" and will therefore be covered by attorney-client privilege. In *United States v. Kovel*, the court recognized that the attorney-client privilege extended to communications from an attorney's client to an accountant hired by the attorney to assist the attorney in understanding the client's financial information.[17] But, the court also explained, "what is vital to the privilege is that the communications be made *in confidence* for the purpose of obtaining *legal* advice *from the lawyer*."[18] So if the accountant is providing services or advice at the request of the attorney or to assist the attorney in the rendering of legal advice, the communications would likely be privileged. Under the *Kovel* doctrine, "to sustain a privilege an accountant must be 'necessary, or at least highly useful for the lawyer which the privilege is designed to permit.'"[19]

The attorney-client privilege has also been extended to situations where an accountant is hired by an attorney to assist in giving the client tax advice,[20] and to an accountant who prepared a statement of the client's net worth at the request of the attorney.[21] However, there is no comprehensive attorney-accountant-client privilege, and the ability to protect a CPA's work product from disclosure based on this privilege will be considered on a case-by-case basis.

Attorney-client privilege only applies to communications between attorney and client. However, attorney work product, although not technically privileged, is protected from discovery in appropriate circumstances.[22] Attorney work product includes "interviews, statements, memoranda, correspondence, briefs, and mental impressions" prepared by the attorney in the course of his legal duties in preparation for litigation. Such work product is protected from discovery absent a showing of necessity.[23] All documents prepared *by* the attorney or *for* the attorney are accordingly not discoverable, barring a substantial need by the opposing party, so long as the documents were prepared in anticipation of litigation or in preparation for trial.[24] In appropriate circumstances, the protections afforded to attorney work product may also be available to work prepared by a nonattorney who is the agent of a party or the party's attorney. Therefore, reports or analyses prepared by a CPA at the request of counsel can be protected from discovery. However, applicable local rules and procedures should be consulted before directing a CPA to create any written record of his work product that could be subject to disclosure in litigation.

Conclusion

When dealing with reports created by CPAs, it is important to understand the basic differences in report types and the applicable standards and levels of assurance that apply, which vary with each type of report. Generally, CPAs are deeply involved in reviewing and reporting upon the financial data that may become relevant in any commercial dispute, including construction industry matters. Construction practitioners therefore need a basic appreciation of the fundamental rules that apply to CPA practice.

In addition, CPAs also often play an important role in the creation of specialized reports and in the provision of customized consulting and expert services where the formalized rules of conduct and assurance procedures play a far more distant role. The CPA can, therefore, be a valuable expert and a significant asset to counsel in representing clients in construction industry matters and disputes. Counsel must give due consideration to the applicable discovery and disclosure standards that apply to a CPA's work as an expert witness. Counsel must also be keenly aware of the distinction between privilege-protected consulting experts and testifying experts in the jurisdictions in which they practice.

Notes

1. As used in this chapter, "CPA" may refer to a public accounting firm or to an individual accountant.
2. It is important to note that professional standards applicable to CPAs are complex and require specific training to fully understand. Therefore, we recommend that you consult with a qualified professional in evaluating any financial report.
3. AICPA's Statement on Standards for Accounting and Review Services No. 1.
4. *See* AICPA Code of Prof'l Conduct, www.aicpa.org/About/code/index.html.
5. The auditing standards are available on the AICPA Web site, www.aicpa.org.
6. AICPA Statement on Standards for Consulting Services No. 1.
7. This section discusses the rules and standards as generally applied in federal courts. Local federal court and state court rules should be consulted prior to engaging CPAs as testifying experts or nontestifying consultants.
8. Fed. R. Civ. P. 26(a)(2)(B).
9. *Id.*
10. Fed. R. Civ. P. 26(a)(2)(C).
11. 509 U.S. 579, 589 (1993).
12. *Id.* at 593–94.
13. Kumho Tire Co. v. Carmichael, 526 U.S. 137, 149 (1999).
14. *Id.* at
15. *Id.* at 152.
16. Fed. R. Evid. 503(b).
17. United States v. Kovel, 296 F.2d 918 (1961).
18. *Id.* at 922. (emphasis in original).
19. Cavallaro v. United States, 284 F.3d 236, 247–48 (2002) (quoting *Kovel*, 296 F.2d at 922).
20. United States v. Cote, 456 F. 142, 144 (8th Cir. 1972).
21. United States v. Judson, 322 F.2d 460, 462 (9th Cir. 1963).
22. Fed. R. Civ. P. 26(b)(3).
23. Hickman v. Taylor, 329 U.S. 495, 511 (1947).
24. Charles Alan Wright & Arthur R. Miller, Federal Practice and Procedure § 2024, at 359 (2d ed. 1994).

CHAPTER 7

Contract Types and Accounting Issues Related to Changes in Price and Cost Reimbursement

MICHAEL R. BENES
JEFFREY G. GILMORE
DOUGLAS A. TRUEHEART

Introduction

In both the public and private sectors, stakeholders employ a broad spectrum of contracting approaches—from firm-fixed-price to unlimited cost reimbursement. The various contract types, reduced to their essence, represent different methods of allocating and balancing, between the parties, risks of cost overruns or profit.

In the public sector, the choice of contract type is often regulated.[1] Aside from laws protecting workers and consumers, which are beyond the scope of this book,[2] the choice of contract type by private parties is not regulated and is negotiated between the contracting parties. The first part of this chapter will concentrate on contract types and related economic risk allocation measures that are typically employed in the private sector.

Under any contract type, however, it will eventually become necessary for the parties to determine the cost of some or all of the work. The need to determine cost under a cost-reimbursement contract is self-evident. But even under firm-fixed-price contracts, the parties will almost invariably need to determine the cost of some element of the work in order to determine the proper price for changes in the work. The second part of this chapter will explore accounting issues involved in determining the cost of the work and related contract provisions.

Since many of the contract types employed in the private sector include terms that are similar to those employed by governments, especially the federal government, this chapter will periodically refer to regulations that do not directly apply to private contracts, but which are illustrative and helpful in understanding the parties' obligations.

Contract Types, Forms, and Performance Issues Related to Costs

Firm-Fixed-Price Contracts

A predictable price is generally an objective of all buyers of construction goods and services. A lump-sum or fixed-price[3] arrangement is a desirable approach for an owner wishing to minimize the risk of unexpected variations in price.[4] A fixed price for goods and services can usually be implemented if the project design is complete and all requirements are clearly spelled out in the project specifications. By accepting a fixed price, the contractor is incentivized to control costs and efficiently deploy its labor, material, and equipment resources in order to maximize its profits. The opportunity to enhance profitability comes with the contractor's assumption of risks related to cost overruns. Generally, cost overruns must be borne by the contractor unless the contract contains remedy-granting terms allowing an adjustment in the contract amount for events and other circumstances beyond the contractor's control that directly cause the particular cost overrun.[5] One major risk for the contractor under a fixed-price contract is that the market price for labor and materials will change.[6]

Economic Price Adjustment

Under some circumstances, the owner may have difficulty finding a contractor willing to accept the risk of market fluctuations for particular commodities at a reasonable price. In such circumstances the parties may employ a fixed price with economic price adjustment arrangement. Economic price adjustment terms provide a mechanism for price adjustment for changes in certain equipment and material prices identified by the parties in their initial agreement.[7]

Typically, the specific equipment and materials subject to adjustment are identified, together with a designation of the formula and applicable price indices to be used in calculating any price adjustments. The most widely used indices are maintained by the Bureau of Labor Statistics (BLS) and its Producer Price Index (PPI), which measures the changes in output prices for construction materials and labor. Each of the indices created by PPI is classified under a PPI-specific North American Industry Classification System (NAICS) code. Each index appears in tables available in periodic PPI reports that are available online through the BLS Web site.[8] There are PPI codes for over 10,000 individual products and groups of products released each month for virtually every industry in the mining and manufacturing sectors of the U.S. economy, including items such as concrete, rebar, steel, precast concrete pipe, asphalt, and fuel. Because BLS publishes only price indexes, not actual or average prices, the parties must adopt a formula for using the index to calculate the escalation in prices.[9] BLS provides the following guidelines for developing escalation clauses:

- Establish the base selling price subject to escalation
- Select an appropriate index or indexes
- Clearly identify the selected index and cite an appropriate source
- Specify whether seasonally adjusted indexes or unadjusted indexes are to be used

- State the frequency of price adjustment
- Provide for missing or discontinued data
- Specify that calculations of price adjustments shall always use the latest version of the PPI data published as of the date specified for such calculations; this requires that contracting parties explicitly agree on the date the price adjustment calculations are to be made
- Avoid locking indexes used for escalation into any particular reference base period
- Define the mechanics of price adjustment[10]

As noted in the BLS guidance, "escalation clauses sometimes contain *a floor, a ceiling*, or both, to limit the total price adjustment during the life of the contract. If the upper or lower limit is reached, the parties may renegotiate prices for the duration of the contract. Some contracts specify that no price adjustments are to be made until a minimum change in the selected index has taken place. Contracts may also provide that an escalation is to apply in both an upward and downward direction or in one direction only."[11]

Cost-Reimbursement Contracts

If the parties are unable to sufficiently define the scope of work to be performed by the contractor to allow a reasonably reliable estimate of costs, or if qualified contractors are simply unwilling to accept the risk of variations in estimated costs (particularly on large-scale multiyear projects), more flexible pricing arrangements will often be adopted, based on the cost of the work plus fee, unit prices,[12] or other variations that allow the contractor to be paid for elements of work that cannot be precisely determined or reduced to a fixed price.[13]

A cost-reimbursement contract can still include mechanisms to control the cost. The most commonly employed approach is the guaranteed maximum price (GMP) contract, which sets an upper limit on the price to be paid to the contractor. The GMP is usually subject to adjustment if the scope of work changes or other defined circumstances occur.[14] The GMP can be coupled with incentives to control overall costs, such as the sharing of cost savings with the contractor.

The contract type that involves the greatest cost risk for the owner is a cost-plus-percentage fee arrangement, under which the owner agrees to pay for allowable costs[15] incurred (as defined by the contract) together with a specified percentage mark-up for profit and overhead. The cost-plus arrangement relieves the contractor of virtually all economic risks associated with fluctuations in costs, productivity, and poorly defined scope. As noted in *Urban Data Systems, Inc. v. United States*,[16] the owner faces a unique dilemma under a cost-plus arrangement:

> As in any cost-plus-a-percentage-of-cost contract, there still remains an incentive to the contractor "to pay liberally for reimbursable items because higher costs mean a higher fee to him, his profit being

determined by a percentage of cost." *Muschany v. United States*, 324 U.S. 49, 62, 65 S.Ct. 442, 449, 89 L.Ed. 744 (1945). The key is that the contractor is penalized for efficient and economical performance and rewarded for noneconomical performance.[17]

The anomalous incentive for the contractor to increase its fee by increasing costs can be reduced or eliminated either by capping the fee or fixing it based upon estimated rather than actual costs.

Under any form of cost-reimbursement contract, the owner must implement procedures for careful oversight of contractor performance and rigorous arrangements for review and monitoring of cost accounting records, timely periodic cost reports, and verification of incurred costs, including well-defined audit rights in order to help manage the risk of unwarranted cost growth. For its part, the contractor must maintain adequate records and controls to ensure that it can demonstrate and justify the costs it incurs and can notify the owner, as necessary, when costs are incurred for unanticipated circumstances that may entitle the contractor to adjustment in any cost or price limits stated in the contract.

The contract should define the reimbursable costs that will be allowed. The federal government has promulgated a comprehensive set of regulations governing the costs that will be paid under its cost-reimbursement contracts in Chapter 31 of the Federal Acquisition Regulation (FAR), commonly known as the Cost Principles. These provisions may be used as a reference for private contracts as well.

For instance, under the FAR a cost is reimbursable only if it is reasonable and allocable to the contract.[18] A cost is "reasonable" if in its nature and amount it does not exceed that which would be incurred by a prudent person in the conduct of a competitive business.[19] A cost is allocable if it is incurred specifically for the contract, or benefits both the contract and other work, and can be distributed to them in a reasonable proportion to the benefits received.[20]

Such general propositions in the Cost Principles may be useful in defining reimbursable costs in private contracts. Care, however, should be taken since many of the more specific Cost Principles may not be appropriate for application in a private contract.[21]

Selected Forms for Cost-Reimbursable Contracting

Many cost-reimbursable contracting forms are widely available. Although not an exhaustive listing, the following are some of the forms in use:

- AIA Document A133-2009, Standard Form of Agreement Between Owner and Construction Manager as Constructor, where the basis of payment is the cost of the work plus a fee with a guaranteed maximum price (replaces previous AIA Document A121 CMc 2003 edition) (American Institute of Architects)

- DBIA Document No. 530-2009, Standard Form of Agreement Between Owner and Design-Builder—Cost Plus Fee with an Option for a Guaranteed Maximum Price (Design-Build Institute of America)
- AIA Document A102-2007, Standard Form of Agreement Between Owner and Contractor, where the basis of payment is the cost of the work plus a fee with a negotiated guaranteed maximum price
- EJCDC C-525-2007, Standard Form of Agreement Between Owner and Contractor for Construction Contract (Cost-Plus) (Engineers Joint Contract Documents Committee)

The above forms, like the terms mandated for federal cost-reimbursable contracting arrangements by the FAR, share the common objective of prescribing a tightly controlled and carefully monitored mechanism for payment of incurred costs, with or without a fixed fee. An excellent example of language defining reimbursable costs is provided in Article 11 of the General Conditions that are designed for use with EJCDC C-525-2007. This contract provision is reproduced in its entirety in the Appendix to this chapter.

Contractor's Duty to Notify Owner of Increased Costs Under Cost-Reimbursement Contracts

One key area of potential conflict between owners and contractors involves unexpected cost overruns and/or costs that exceed the guaranteed maximum price. Relying on language such as the following, owners often contend that the contractor or construction manager has accepted a fiduciary obligation to inform the owner about and protect it from potential cost overruns:

> The Contractor accepts the relationship of trust and confidence established by the Contract and covenants with the Owner to cooperate with the Owner, Architect, and Owner's Consultants and utilize the Construction Manager's skill, efforts, and judgment . . . in furthering the interests of the Owner; to furnish efficient business administration and supervision; to make reasonable efforts to furnish at all times an adequate supply of workers and materials; and to perform the Work in an expeditious and economical manner consistent with the interests of the Owner and as required by the Contract Documents. . . . [22]

Two frequently cited Maryland decisions address the validity of breach of fiduciary duty claims against a contractor on a cost-reimbursement contract with a guaranteed maximum price. In *Jones v. J.H. Hiser Construction Co.*,[23] the court rejected a substantial portion of the contractor's claim because the contractor failed to comply with its obligation to keep the residential owner informed of cost increases as they occurred. Although it reached a different result on the particular facts of the case, the court in *Kahle v. John McDonough Builders, Inc.*,[24] also recognized the general principle that a contractor's failure to keep the owner informed of cost increases could bar its recovery under a cost-plus contract.[25]

Audit Rights

Auditing is a necessary function for prudent administration of a cost-reimbursable contracting arrangement. Just as a typical payment application review process is critical in the evaluation of progress payment requests on a fixed-price contract, cost accounting records must be examined on a cost-plus project to determine compliance with applicable requirements and disallowance of noncompliant costs.[26] Further, since some unallowable costs will inevitably be paid, credit for and recovery of such unallowable costs must be provided for in future payment adjustments.[27] The administration of the contract must be organized to ensure access to cost accounting records and systems, and procedures for verification of claimed costs.

An example of an audit clause is Article 13 of EJCDC C-525-2007:

> Contractor shall keep such full and detailed accounts of materials incorporated and labor and equipment utilized for the Work consistent with the requirements of Paragraph 11.01.D of the General Conditions and as may be necessary for proper financial management under this Agreement. Subject to prior written notice, Owner shall be afforded reasonable access during normal business hours to all Contractor's records, books, correspondence, instructions, drawings, receipts, vouchers, memoranda, and similar data relating to the Cost of the Work and Contractor's fee. Contractor shall preserve all such documents for a period of three years after the final payment by Owner.

If detailed cost accounting and cost verification procedures are specified by the contract, it is incumbent upon the parties to adhere to those requirements. Failure to abide by the specified procedures could be construed as a waiver.[28]

Cost Accounting Issues Related to Cost-Reimbursement Contracts and Changes Under Fixed-Price Contracts

The central issue in any cost-plus or reimbursable GMP contract, as well as under fixed-price contracts when dealing with change orders or delay claims, is what is meant by "cost of the work." Generally, the term means the costs necessarily incurred by the contractor in the proper performance of the work. Determining what the cost of the work is for a construction contractor can present significant challenges, however. This section will address some of those challenges as well as contract provisions that may help ensure that the cost of the work is determined fairly between the parties.

Labor Costs

Labor costs will almost always be one of the largest cost elements on a construction project. Drafters of agreements must therefore be cognizant of the major issues that may arise in determining whether labor charges are reimbursable or nonreimbursable.

Labor costs can be associated with

- Construction workers directly employed by the contractor at the construction site
- The contractor's supervisory and administrative personnel stationed at the site
- The contractor's supervisory and administrative personnel engaged at factories, workshops, or on the road engaged in expediting the production or transportation of materials or equipment required for the specific project
- The contractor's personnel stationed at the contractor's principal office or offices who are not directly related to any specific project

The elements of labor costs generally include

- Base wages or salaries
- Overtime or shift differential premiums
- Fringe benefits such as sick leave, medical and health benefits, holidays, vacations, and pensions
- FICA, state and federal unemployment taxes, workers' compensation, and assessments required by law or collective bargaining agreements
- Bonuses, profit sharing, or other incentive compensation

The labor costs ultimately charged to a given project will be based on the nature of the work, the hours devoted to the project, and the rate at which the person performing the work is compensated. Issues can arise with respect to all three areas. Some of the issues can, and in most instances should, be addressed by specific provisions in the contract. Other issues may be governed by a more general provision in the contract, and it is always incumbent on both the owner and the contractor to ensure that the proper records are maintained to address any potential dispute.

On-Site Construction Workers

In preparing a bid for a fixed-price or GMP contract, a contractor or subcontractor will estimate the required number of hours for each job classification based on skill level. Workers having a specialized skill, such as a bricklayer, will be paid a higher hourly rate than a common laborer. The bid will be based on the projected aggregate number of hours for each job classification times the expected hourly cost for each respective job classification. The number of job classifications will be based on the complexity of the project, and the hourly costs will be based on what the contractor expects to pay a worker performing the tasks for each job classification. While a government project will normally contain extensive provisions regarding the cost of labor, a private sector contract may simply state that labor costs are those "necessarily incurred by the contractor in the proper performance of the work at rates not higher than the standard paid at the place of the project."[29]

As noted, the fixed-price or GMP is based upon an estimate of labor costs. To the extent the contractor or subcontractor incorrectly estimates the relevant factors, it is at risk. However, factors that are within the owner's control, such as design errors or changes in scope, can result in not only an increase in labor hours but also a requirement for skills that may not have been originally contemplated. Related delays may force the work into a later time period when the "standard paid" is higher.

Under a fully cost-reimbursement contract, the owner bears these increased costs regardless of cause. Under a fixed-price or GMP contract, the contractor is usually entitled to an increase in price only if the owner is responsible for the circumstances giving rise to the increase. In either case, it is essential that procedures be established by the contractor to measure the labor costs actually incurred by the contractor.

On-Site Supervision and Administrative Personnel

In developing the bid, the contractor will identify its projected needs with respect to supervisory and administrative personnel required to be on site, and the time frame when they will be needed. Disputes often arise when the projected needs increase as a result of a change in scope or duration of the work. Disputes may also arise when home office personnel, such as engineers, are temporarily assigned to the site. The issue there is whether the on-site time should be a direct charge to the project or whether the cost of the home office personnel is included in the fee or markup intended to cover home office overhead costs. To avoid disputes, it is advisable to state in the contract the maximum authorized field office staff positions that will be considered reimbursable unless subsequently changed for reasons approved by the owner by a formal change order. The contract should also address when the reimbursable labor costs may begin to be charged, which may be the contract start date or the date that the employee arrives on site, and the end date, which typically is the date the employee concludes service at the site, but in no event later than a specified number of days after substantial completion of the project. For employees temporarily assigned to the field, the contractor must be prepared to demonstrate that the associated labor costs are not being double counted—that is, once in the fee or markup to recover home office expenses and a second time as a direct project cost.

Off-Site Personnel Providing Direct Project Services

It is not unusual for a contractor to employ personnel off site who are performing services directly related to specific projects. An example would be an employee expediting the production or transportation of materials or equipment that are required for a specific project. Since such employees typically work on multiple projects during any given time period, disputes can arise as to how their compensation costs should be allocated among those specific projects. Disputes can also arise with respect to associated costs, such as rent, communication costs, and equipment usage. To avoid disputes, the contract should identify the off-site positions authorized to directly charge the project, and how those charges are to be calculated. Typically, the labor overhead costs associated with these types of employees will be recouped through a burden rate applied to the compensation element. As illustrated in connection with home office expenses below, there are multiple methods of deriving an appropriate rate. There must be agreement between the owner and the contractor at the time the contract is bid for whatever methodology is utilized.

Home Office Personnel

Virtually all contractors incur costs relating to the activities of the contractor's home or corporate office that are necessary to run the business and support the projects in the field. Such activities include development of corporate strategy, corporate-wide accounting, human resources, and sales and marketing (including bid and proposal preparation). The associated costs include the compensation of the employees engaged in these activities, plus home office rent, utilities, insurance, communications costs, and other costs of a similar nature. These activities support the company as a whole and generally cannot be directly associated with a specific project. The associated costs, however, must be recouped from the income generated by the projects.

The manner in which this is accomplished varies and should be directly addressed in the contract to avoid disputes. Some contracts provide that home office costs of this nature are recovered via a percentage markup on direct costs that may or may not be inclusive of profit. This method has a risk for the contractor. For instance, the project may incur a significant weather delay during which little direct costs (on which the markup is based) are incurred, although there is no corresponding drop in home office expense during that same period. This requires the contractor to provide for such contingencies in the markup percentage, or provide some other mechanism to recover home office overhead when the project duration varies from the original plan. As a result of such uncertainties, some contractors seek to provide that actual home office costs incurred during the time period of the project will be allocated to the project based on a formula that considers all of the contractor's projects being worked on during the period. For instance, the contract might provide that actual home office costs will be allocated to the project for a given period based on the revenues generated by the specific project as a percentage of the contractor's total revenue from all projects during that same period. This reduces the risk to the contractor but creates uncertainty for the owner, since the costs allocated to the owner's project then become dependent on the contractor's other projects. As a result, it is not uncommon for the contract to specify that home office overhead will be a fixed percentage of direct costs based on the bid, with an additional allocation based on a formula for change orders and excusable delays.

Whatever method is employed, it is important to identify the activities and the associated costs to be included in the home office overhead pool. It is not uncommon for disputes to arise in the case of employees whose activities are generally classified as part of home office overhead, but who may be called to spend an extended period at a project site performing work directly related to the project. An example would be an engineer normally involved in developing bids who may be brought to the project site to address an unexpected problem that arises on site. If the contract allows as "cost of the work" the compensation of all employees performing services on site, and the engineer's compensation is also included in the home office overhead pool, the owner could end up paying the same cost twice. It is important for the owner to ensure at the time the contract, or an affected change order, is being negotiated that the same cost is not charged twice.

When home office overhead is charged to a project based on actual costs, disputes may also arise with respect to whether the magnitude of a given cost is in line with the local prevailing rates. Executive bonuses are a good example. If key executives are also owners of the contractor, the issue is whether the bonus is part of home office overhead or, in actuality, a profit distribution to the owners of the company. In other words, what the project owner thought was included in the project fee or profit should not also be included in the home office overhead charge. Where actual overhead costs are to be allocated to a project, both the nature and the magnitude of such costs must be considered at the time the contract or change order is negotiated.

Wages and Benefits

The labor costs included in the cost of work for a given project will be the actual costs paid to employees for the time actually spent working on the project, and costs paid to others directly related to such time. The actual cost will include the base wage, overtime and shift differential premiums, fringe benefits, employment taxes, and in some cases, incentive compensation such as bonuses. Highlighted below are some of the issues that should be considered with respect to each element.

Base Wages

Disputes relating to base wages often center on whether the base is appropriate for the nature of the work being performed, and who should bear the costs of a wage increase given to an employee when the nature of the work being performed has not changed. The first issue relates to whether the workforce reflects a proper mix of skills and job classifications, as mentioned previously. Wage increases for the same work can result from a change in law, such as an increase in the minimum wage, or from a contractor having to pay a premium for a given skill in a tight labor market. The owner may dispute the increase over what was reflected in the bid, requiring the contractor to justify that the increase does not result in a rate higher than the standard rate for similar work paid in the same geographic area.

Overtime Premiums and Shift Differentials

Employment laws generally require that hourly employees be paid time and a half for all hours worked over 40 hours in a given week. Some contractors will also pay a premium, or shift differential, to employees who work hours that are considered outside of the normal workday. For instance, work on a road construction project that is performed at night to avoid creating traffic congestion may carry with it a shift differential. Issues surrounding overtime and shift differentials can be broken into three categories: (1) who is entitled to the premium; (2) the base on which the premium is calculated; and (3) whether the premium is authorized.

Who Is Entitled to the Premium?
Federal and state employment laws define who is exempt from the requirement to be paid overtime. Exempt employees include executives, managers, and certain administrative and professional employees.[30] For example, an employee is exempt under the Fair Labor Standards Act if his primary work duty is "the performance of office or non-manual work directly related to the management or general business operations of the employer or the employer's customers," and his primary duty "includes the exercise of discretion and independent judgment with respect to matters of significance."[31] Construction supervisors may be exempt or nonexempt, depending on the scope of their responsibilities.[32] The tests for who is or is not exempt are not explicit.

However, some general rules are clear. For example, exempt executives and managers are employees whose duties primarily consist of the management of the project, who customarily and regularly direct the work of two or more employees, and who have the authority to hire and fire other employees, or whose word in such decisions is given significant weight.[33] Exempt administrative employees are generally employees who perform office or nonmanual work directly related to management policies or general business operations of the employer and who customarily and regularly exercise discretion and independent judgment. Exempt professionals are generally employees whose work requires advanced knowledge that must customarily be acquired by a prolonged course of specialized instruction. Architects and engineers are examples of exempt professionals associated with a construction project.[34] Employees not falling into an exempt category are considered nonexempt employees, entitled by law to be paid overtime. Most hourly construction workers are nonexempt employees.[35]

Most nonexempt employees are paid on an hourly basis, while most exempt employees are paid a salary. Many contractors incorrectly believe that all salaried employees are exempt, or assume that they are exempt strictly on the basis of their job title. The legal definition of exempt and nonexempt, however, is based on the nature of the work actually performed and the corresponding level of responsibility. The risk to the contractor of a misclassification is an after-the-fact determination that overtime wages are owed. This determination would typically be made after the contract is completed, at a time when the contractor no longer has the ability to recoup the overtime cost from the owner.

It should also be noted that many contractors pay some or all of their exempt employees for extra hours worked, either at straight time or time and a half. This can often lead to a dispute if the policy is not made clear to the owner, who might reasonably assume that no overtime premium will be paid to exempt salaried employees.

Base on Which Premium Is Calculated
The base on which overtime is calculated is generally that portion of an employee's compensation that is dependent strictly on the number of hours worked. This would include the base hourly wage, but typically does not include fringe benefits such as health benefits, paid vacation days, holiday pay, and paid sick days. Certain benefits may not be required by law to be included in an employee's base, but the contractor's policies can have the effect of increasing the cost of each overtime hour worked. For instance, if the contractor has a defined contribution plan that includes overtime wages in the definition of compensation, the hourly contribution cost for overtime hours will be one and one half times the cost of a normal hour for a nonexempt employee.

Since overtime will almost certainly be incurred at some point during any significant construction project, it is important that the owner understand the contractor's policies as to what is included in the wage base prior to the contract being awarded. It is important that the contractor understand what is required by law to be included in the wage base in order to avoid a possible after-the-fact determination by a government agency that additional wages are owed, when it is too late to recoup reimbursement from the owner. To the extent that a contractor's policies differ from what is required by law, either with respect to employees to be paid a premium or the base on which it is calculated, it is advisable that the contractor's policy be reflected in the contract.

Even in instances where the contractor and the owner agree as to the amount of overtime premium payable to a given employee, there can still be disputes as to the amount allocable to a given project. For instance, it is possible that an employee may work on multiple projects in a given week. Under most employment laws, overtime is paid on hours in excess of 40 hours worked in a week. When an employee works days of varying lengths on multiple projects during a week, it may be very unclear as to which project should bear the overtime cost. For instance, the employee may work two eight-hour days on one owner's project and three 12-hour days on another owner's project in the same week. Arguably, the full 12 hours of overtime should be charged to the second owner's project. It is not uncommon, however, for a contractor to utilize an accounting practice where the total compensation paid to an employee for a given week is allocated to each project based on the total hours on each project. This would have the effect of inflating the charges to the first owner's project and undercharging the second owner for that week, but this effect may average out over time. Again, the owner must understand the contractor's practice to avoid being overcharged; the contractor must ensure that in the aggregate it collects its total actual costs.

Authorization

While some overtime may be reflected in the original bid, overtime costs are often the result of change orders and schedule delays. Overtime resulting from inefficiencies caused by the contractor is almost never reimbursable. Most contracts require that for any overtime to be reimbursable, authorization must be obtained from the owner prior to the overtime work being performed. This, however, is not always practical due to the time required to obtain the authorization. In such situations, the contractor should at least file the request for authorization and maintain records to demonstrate the need for the overtime, and the additional costs that would occur as a result of delay. The request should be as specific as possible with respect to the classification of the employees who will incur the overtime.

The law generally requires that a nonexempt employee be compensated for any overtime worked, whether the work has been authorized or not. The contractor should also be aware that most states' employment laws do not allow the "banking" of hours, where overtime hours are exchanged for time off in future periods.[36] *E.g.* CAL. LAB. CODE §§ 204.3 and 513.

Fringe Benefits

Like many employers, contractors generally provide fringe benefits such as medical and health benefits, sick leave, holidays, vacation, and retirement plans for their employees. Contractor practices with respect to providing such fringe benefits vary widely. Some provide no or almost no benefits directly, but instead increase their employees' cash compensation. Certain benefits, however, can be provided through a plan that provides tax advantages not only to the employee but also to the employer. For instance, premiums for employer-provided health insurance do not constitute wages subject to income tax for the employee, or wages subject to FICA for either the employee or the employer. Contractors that do offer benefits may provide them through plans they administer themselves, or through plans administered by third parties. The costs associated with a given employee may be charged directly to a given project, or may be aggregated with similar costs for all employees on the project and charged as part of a burden rate applied to all wages.

Disputes often arise in connection with whether a fringe benefit cost was actually paid. Such issues often arise in connection with benefits that start accruing the day the employee starts work, but are forfeited in total if the employee terminates employment prior to working a minimum period. For instance, a vacation policy may provide that an employee accrues a half hour of vacation time for every 10 hours worked. The contractor will likely build that cost into the employee's hourly rate from the start of employment. If the policy provides that the accrued vacation is forfeited if the employee is employed for less than a full year, the owner will have been billed for a cost that the contractor never actually paid. Other costs, such as medical insurance, are often a fixed amount not dependent on either the number of hours worked or dollar amount of base wages paid. The contractor may build the cost into an hourly rate based on the projected number of hours the employee will work. If the actual hours worked vary from the projection, the amount charged within the hourly rate will vary from the actual amount paid. To avoid overcharging, the contract could specify that fringe benefit costs will be reimbursed only to the extent the contractor can prove that the costs were actually paid. This may not always be practical, since the actual costs may not be known until much later, especially on an individual employee basis. If that problem is anticipated, it may be sensible, especially for larger contracts with numerous employees being charged to the contract, to adjust the charged fringe benefit rate downward by a percentage intended to anticipate actual cost experience.

FICA, State, and Federal Unemployment Taxes

FICA (Social Security) and federal and state unemployment taxes have annual limitations on the amount of wages that are subject to the tax. Some contractors fail to take these limitations into account, billing the owner as if these payroll taxes apply to the entirety of the employee's wages, and thereby effectively charging more than the actual costs. Some contractors will charge the owner for payroll taxes relating to a given employee as those taxes are paid, charging one rate until the wage limitation is reached and a lower rate thereafter. This practice can lead to distortions depending on when the employee worked on a particular project. Still other contractors build payroll taxes into an overall burden rate calculated based on the total annual payroll taxes compared to the employee's total projected annual wages. An overall burden rate results in an even rate charged throughout the year, but can be inaccurate if the employees are not paid the projected wages. To avoid disputes, the owner and contractor should agree during contract negotiations that the annual caps will be considered and agree on the method by which such taxes will be charged as cost of the work.

Bonuses and Other Incentive Compensation

Both the contractor and the owner can benefit from employees being incentivized to work in an efficient manner. Such incentives are often provided in the form of additional compensation paid as a bonus. It is not uncommon for issues to arise as to whether a bonus was intended to represent a reimbursable cost or whether it was intended to come from the contractor's profit or fee. Discretionary bonuses paid on completion of the project are almost always considered as a sharing of the project's profits, unless specifically provided otherwise in the contract. Accordingly, any bonus intended to represent a reimbursable cost should be addressed in the contract, providing the formula on which it will be based and requiring the contractor to demonstrate it was actually paid.

Insurance

The construction contract will typically specify both the minimum scope and limits of insurance coverages that the contractor is required to have. The scope typically includes commercial general liability insurance, workers' compensation, and automobile liability insurance, as well as professional liability insurance when professional services such as engineering and architectural services are included in the work to be provided. Disputes often arise as to what types of insurance costs are to be allocated directly to a specific project, how the allocation is to be made, and in the case of self-insurance, how the premiums are to be calculated.

General liability insurance, equipment floaters, workers' compensation insurance, and auto insurance are typically charged directly to each project, while property insurance on the home and any regional offices, fidelity bonds, and insurance of a like nature associated with the business as a whole are included in home office overhead. The contract should specify what coverages are to be considered a reimbursable cost. Often insurance costs are allocated by including them in the labor burden rate that is applied as a percentage of wages. This may or may not be the way the actual insurance premium is calculated. For instance, the premium for general liability insurance is often based on annual expected revenues of the contractor, not amounts paid for labor. If the premium has been charged to the owner based on a percentage of labor cost, at some point an adjustment must be made so the charge is indicative of revenues generated by the project rather than just labor cost.

Most contracts will require the contractor to provide a certificate of coverage to validate that the coverage is in place, and the actual premium costs will be evidenced by payments to an insurance company. Issues will often arise, however, when the contractor self-insures all or a portion of the risk, or when the insurance is obtained through an affiliate or a captive insurance company. In such instances, the owner must first be assured that the contractor has the financial ability to assume the risk. This may be accomplished by requiring the contractor to procure a bond guaranteeing payment of losses and related investigations, claims, administration, and defense expenses, where appropriate. The reason a contractor will self-insure is to reduce costs, and it is appropriate that the savings in doing so inure to the contractor's benefit. At the same time, the owner should not be charged an amount in excess of what the coverage would cost if obtained from an independent insurance company. Since premiums charged by insurance carriers consider a multitude of factors specific to a given insured, including history and condition of the insured property, the contract should make clear that the charge for self-insurance should not exceed the cost of the desired coverage if obtained from a financially sound independent insurance company, taking into consideration the contractor's history and any other factors that would be considered by the insurance company in establishing the premium.

Equipment Pricing

As the quantity of labor increases on a project, the equipment needed by the contractor on site usually correspondingly increases. Depending on the type of work being performed, the cost of equipment may exceed the cost of direct labor. For example, equipment is a higher component of cost for heavy civil construction, like road building, than for other types of construction.

Construction equipment used in performing the work is normally a reimbursable cost, part of the "cost of the work," under GMP contracts as well as other types of cost-reimbursable contracts. However, most contract provisions do not clearly define how the cost of equipment is to be determined. Even within lump-sum contracts, the cost of equipment can become a disputed item when the contractor is pricing change order work performed. The definition of recoverable equipment cost is often left for later determination. In many instances, the issue does not arise until a claim is being presented. The determination of the equipment cost in a GMP contract with a large equipment component can become contentious and involve a substantial amount.

Standard contract language related to the allowed cost of construction equipment for purposes of cost reimbursability or as part of a claim may read as follows:

> Rental charges for temporary facilities, machinery, equipment and hand tools not necessarily customarily owned by construction workers that are provided by the Contractor at the site and costs of transportation, installation, minor repairs, dismantling and removal. The total rental cost of any Contractor-owned item may not exceed the purchase price of any comparable item. Rates for Contractor-owned equipment and quantities of equipment shall be subject to the Owner's prior approval.[37]

The best practice with respect to a contract containing such a clause would be for the parties to develop an agreed-upon equipment pricing list or exhibit. What should be done early in the contracting process is not always done, however. Unfortunately, if the contract indicates equipment rates will be subject to the owner's approval and the owner's approval was never obtained, the ultimate price to be paid can become a dispute between the parties that could have been avoided.

There are various approaches to determining construction equipment costs. The primary alternative methods that are generally used in pricing equipment on reimbursable contracts are rate books, actual costs, and pricing sheets.

Rate Books

The easiest method for the contractor to use in charging equipment costs is to utilize one of the numerous construction equipment rate books. These books are straightforward to use and are often referenced in the contract as the source for pricing equipment used on the project. The major equipment rate books include the Rental Rate Blue Book (usually abbreviated as the Blue Book), which is utilized by most state transportation agencies in pricing equipment for extra work on their transportation projects.[38] The Blue Book is updated monthly and contains pricing for over 15,000 items of equipment. The rate for each piece of equipment is broken down into monthly, weekly, daily, and hourly rates. The rates are further subdivided into the ownership cost and the estimated hourly operating cost.

Although having four separate ownership rates (monthly, weekly, daily, and hourly) may seem like a nice feature, it also can create problems in pricing the equipment under cost-reimbursable contracts. Assuming the contract does not specify the rate, the contractor may utilize the hourly rate when pricing equipment. If the equipment has been used almost full time on the project for many months, the use of hourly rates will very likely overcompensate the contractor. The Blue Book rate assumes that the hourly rates are to be used for intermittent extra work, which means that the piece of equipment will not be charged continuously, while the monthly rate assumes the piece of equipment is in almost continuous use. As such, when charging the cost of equipment that is on the site for a substantial period, the monthly rate is normally the one most applicable.

Most equipment rate books also provide a methodology for adjusting the rate to account for equipment that is on standby and not operating. This adjusted rate is generally applicable when there has been a project delay and the equipment was required to remain at the site, but was not able to be utilized. In the case of the Blue Book, the calculation of the standby rate is defined in the rate book. The Blue Book also defines standard adjustments that should be made to the listed rates for regional variations, as well as for the age of the piece of equipment and the severity of the work the piece of equipment is performing.

As can be seen by this simplified explanation of the Blue Book, there can be disputes even if a contract specifies the use of Blue Book rates, or for that matter, any other equipment rate book. In addition to the Blue Book, other industry equipment rate books include the Cost Reference Guide, the Associated Equipment Distributors Rental Rates Compilation (also known as AED), the Corp of Engineers guide, and the National Electrical Contractors Association (NECA) "Tool and Equipment Rental Schedule." The NECA publication indicates that its rental rates are based upon average initial purchase price, ownership expenses, and use periods. The experience records and schedules of individual electrical contractors, as well as schedule and practices of equipment rental dealers, provide the basis for the published rates.

Actual Contractor Cost

An alternative to utilizing an equipment rate book for rental rates is to use the contractor's actual cost. Determining a contractor's actual equipment cost can be a very difficult task, however, due to the numerous methods contractors use to record and report usage of equipment, as well as the costs associated with equipment use and maintenance. As discussed below, the methodology contractors use in estimating work may shed some light on the methodology used for costing equipment and capturing equipment cost as part of the cost of the work. As with equipment rate books, actual equipment costs should be divided into two major components: ownership cost and operating cost.

Ownership Costs

Equipment ownership cost encompasses the basic cost of owning the equipment even if it is not used. If, for example, a rate is needed for equipment that is required for some reason to sit idle on a project, the rate for that equipment will be made up of at least a portion of the ownership cost component, and will not contain any of the operating cost components since the equipment is not being operated. The ownership cost of equipment comprises three major subcomponents: depreciation, indirect expenses including property tax and insurance, and cost of funds. These costs are generally considered to be incurred at the same rate no matter how much the equipment is used, and are therefore considered an expense that needs to be recovered even when equipment is on standby and not being used.

Ownership cost is largely made up of the depreciation expense for the piece of equipment. Depreciation is the methodology to expense the purchase price of the asset (the piece of equipment) over the estimated useful life of the asset. For example, if a contractor purchases a new backhoe to perform work on a project, the cost chargeable to the project is not the entire original purchase price of the backhoe. This is because at the end of the project the backhoe is still available for use on future projects; it still has useful life remaining. Depreciation is a method of charging or expensing the backhoe over its estimated useful life. As an example, if the contractor buys a $200,000 backhoe and estimates that the backhoe will be used for 10 years, and will not have any salvage value at the end of the 10 years, the straight-line depreciation amount for the backhoe is $20,000 per year. If any of these variables—purchase price, useful life, and salvage value—is changed, the annual depreciation amount would be different.

The depreciation method used in this example is straight line, meaning the asset is assumed to be consumed equally over the estimated period of its life. Other depreciation methodologies include various accelerated methods that are used mostly for income tax purposes. Over the years, the IRS has allowed various methods of accelerating depreciation into the early years of the ownership of the asset. In some cases, the contractor can fully depreciate the asset in the year the asset is purchased for tax purposes if it meets the requirements of Section 179 of the Internal Revenue Code. All accelerated methods increase the depreciation charge in the earlier years of asset ownership, on the theory that the asset depreciates more rapidly in the earlier years than in later years. This concept may not be true for most major construction equipment, however.

Depreciation expense is recorded by the contractor within its general ledger each year for all owned equipment as one expense item. The recorded expense is usually supported by a subsidiary fixed asset ledger containing specific information related to each asset, including its purchase price, the date of purchase, estimated useful life, estimated salvage value, and the depreciation method being employed. The contractor will also generally have an asset capitalization policy that will contain asset life estimates and purchase price thresholds for including the item as a capitalized asset. A piece of equipment being claimed as cost of the work on a contract should be shown on the contractor's fixed asset ledger.

The second subcomponent of ownership cost relates to what is generally termed the indirect cost of ownership, including taxes, insurance, and storage of the equipment when it is not being used on a project. Property taxes and insurance expenses are generally recorded as an expense for the entire fleet of equipment. The equipment insurance premium is generally based upon the value of the entire equipment fleet and, in some cases, contractors also purchase equipment floaters and equipment riders related to specific equipment. Property taxes are generally based upon the book value of the equipment and the physical location of the equipment. Book value as set forth on the company's financial statements may not be the same value that individual municipalities or other local jurisdictions require to be used for computing the property taxes on the contractor's equipment fleet. Some municipalities may require specific depreciation calculations that vary from those used for book depreciation.

A contractor can compute the taxes and insurance applicable to specific pieces of equipment by allocating the contractor's overall property tax and equipment insurance expense based upon the individual piece of equipment's value as compared to the total equipment fleet value. Many contractors record the property taxes on equipment as well as the equipment insurance in indirect construction general ledger accounts. Other contractors, especially smaller contractors, may record the property taxes and equipment insurance expense in the contractor's general and administrative or home office overhead accounts within the general ledger. How home office overhead is being recovered within the contract definition of "cost of the work" will determine if there are potentially duplicate costs being claimed.

The third subcomponent of actual ownership cost is the cost of funds. The cost of funds is actually imputed interest related to the company's investment in the equipment. Rate books include this as part of the ownership component of the equipment rate. Some consider cost of funds an interest charge that is generally excluded from the definition of "cost of the work." Others consider the cost of funds a return on the investment in equipment that the contractor has had to make and therefore an amount that should be recovered within the cost of equipment, as part of the cost of the work.

Unlike depreciation, property tax, and equipment insurance, which are recorded within the company's general ledger, the cost of funds is not an expense included in the general ledger. Because of this, many disputes arise as to whether any cost should be included within a contractor's equipment rates for cost of funds. If actual cost is to be used for pricing equipment, the contract needs to define how the cost of funds should be considered and computed.

Operating Costs

The second component of equipment cost is the equipment operating expense. Operating expenses include such items as fuel, oil, grease, and repairs. These expenses are incurred as the equipment is used and these items are being consumed. Some contractors charge these expenses directly to the job, while others charge them to an indirect equipment cost pool, and then allocate them to the specific projects for which the costs were incurred. Some larger contractors with large equipment fleets utilize equipment-costing software modules that allow them to track repairs and expenses to the individual piece of equipment, as well as track each item's actual operating usage for preventative maintenance purposes. For smaller contractors the operating expense is generally not charged contemporaneously to an individual piece of equipment.

In the case of major overhauls, the overhaul will generally increase the life of the asset and, therefore, the cost is capitalized. The depreciation records previously described will identify major overhauls or repairs that have been capitalized and which need to be considered in computing the actual cost of the piece of equipment.

Pricing Sheets or Lists

Some contractors maintain pricing sheets itemizing their owned equipment and stating the rates at which such equipment will be charged to a third-party renter or individual project for use of the equipment. To avoid the above-described difficulties of determining the actual cost of equipment, such pricing sheets can be used either to specify the price to be charged or as a reference to test the contractor's contentions as to the cost that should properly be charged to the job.

If such a pricing sheet used for third-party rentals does not exist, the contractor's perceived actual cost of its equipment can often be derived from the contractor's estimating and bidding system. Many contractors have developed internal bidding rates for each major piece of owned equipment, used in assembling contract bids. The job cost charge rates for these same pieces of equipment generally match the estimating/bidding rates. The most common method of charging equipment cost to jobs is by an internal rental rate. Usually an hourly rate is determined by the contractor for each piece of equipment. The first step in developing such a rate is dividing the original purchase price by the estimated years of useful life. To this annual amount, the contractor then adds an estimated cost for annual repairs, insurance, property tax, and any other ownership and operating costs. The resulting total estimated annual cost is then divided by the estimated hours that the piece of equipment will be used during the year to determine the hourly charge rate for the year. This rate per hour generally becomes the bidding rate as well as the job cost charge rate.

The most straightforward use of pricing sheets is to specify in the contract that particular pieces of equipment will be charged to the cost of the work at unit prices that are based upon rates specified in the pricing sheet, for the period that the equipment is needed at the job. In utilizing a contractor's pricing sheet in this manner, however, the owner should be cautious to make sure the project is only being charged for the cost of equipment and not double charged for indirect costs or a hidden profit. Rate sheets that are used for rental to third parties will almost invariably include such elements and should be adjusted downward to remove them. Pricing sheets that are used for the contractor's own estimating purposes, however, may not include such elements and may represent a reasonable basis for specified unit prices to include in the contract.

Even when unit prices are not established in advance, the contractor's pricing sheets may still represent a reasonable basis for the owner and contractor to agree upon as a proxy for the cost of equipment, as a reasonable way to avoid the detailed analysis of actual cost. Moreover, in a dispute, such lists can provide evidence as to the reasonable cost that should be charged to the project for equipment.

To the extent that the contractor charges equipment to individual projects based upon the same rates it uses for estimating, this provides considerable insight as to the contractor's perception of its actual cost. The equipment dollars actually charged to job cost are generally captured in a few general ledger accounts, and can be compared to the actual equipment cost on an overall fleet basis. By comparing the total dollars of equipment charged to job cost with the actual equipment fleet cost, the amount by which the contractor has over- or under-allocated its actual equipment costs can be determined. If there is a large under- or over-allocation, an adjustment may need to be made to the job-costed dollars to account for this systemic over- or under-allocation of equipment cost included within the contractor's equipment internal rates. On the other hand, if this comparison reveals that the contractor's total equipment costs are consistent with the total it charges to its projects, many owners will find this satisfactory verification that the contractor's job charge rates for equipment are generally reasonable.

The calculation of actual equipment cost is not a small undertaking, depending upon the number of pieces of equipment that are involved. It is much easier to determine the cost of equipment when the equipment is rented from an independent third party, and the prices are accordingly set by market forces. On the other hand, some contractors establish affiliated equipment-operating companies that rent the equipment to the construction entity. When the rental company has common ownership with the construction company, care should be undertaken to confirm that the rates are truly reasonable rates consistent with market prices.

The easiest way to avoid equipment rate disputes under cost-reimbursable contracts is to agree in advance on the pricing methods or equipment rental rate books or specific price sheets that will be used, as well as define how these sources will be applied. Developing a list of equipment and the project charge rate is an approach that should eliminate or at least greatly reduce equipment rate disputes between the parties.

Small Tools

Disputes occasionally arise regarding the identification and pricing of small tools charged to the cost of the work. Generally, small tools are defined by the contractor through its asset capitalization policy. If the cost of a tool is less than the contractor's capitalization policy requires for capitalization, the tool is expensed when purchased. Small tools are generally considered to be consumed in a relatively short period of time and are, therefore, not capitalized. This may mean that the cost of the tool is entered into job cost, and on some reimbursable contracts, paid for by the owner. Some contracts provide for such remaining tools to become the property of the owner at the end of the project, since the owner has paid for them. On the other hand, many owners are not interested in acquiring a collection of used tools that they are unlikely to use again and that are largely worn out and have little or no value. Some contracts, for example the EJCDC general conditions, specify that the market value of the tools at the end of the project is to be credited to the cost of the work, and the contractor retains the tools. The market value then has to be determined, however, and this may be an exercise not worth the effort.

In some contracts, small tools are defined as any item with less than a $500 purchase price. If the tool is charged to the project by the contractor on a rate basis, the contract generally provides that the contractor cannot charge more than the purchase price of the tool, as a maximum. To eliminate the accounting and the valuation issues associated with dealing with small tools in detail, some owners elect to allow the contractor to charge small tools as an added percentage within its labor rate. The contractor recovers its cost of small tools based on the labor dollars charged to the project. For each labor hour worked by craft employees, the contractor adds a set rate per hour or percentage (often 5 percent) to cover its cost of small tools.

Computer Charges

Another area that generates significant discussion and dispute is the approach utilized when charging for computer equipment and software. Some owners take the position that computers are overhead and therefore should not be charged separately to the project. Most small contractors do not account for computers separately, and do consider them overhead. However, all project sites of any size generally have at least one computer at the site, and often many. Today's superintendents may carry handheld computers to capture project progress in the field. Computers are used to monitor schedules, generate design sketches and drawings, report project progress, e-mail, submit requests for information, run building information models, and review project-based databases of the project files.

Larger contractors attempt to keep company/home office overhead as low as possible. Consistent with this, they charge projects for computer usage. Since most company employees have a computer assigned to them, the computer charge is prorated to the projects on which each employee works. A monthly rate is generally established to cover the computer, the help desk, maintenance, software, and upgrades. Most standard-form contracts do not address the charge basis for computers, often resulting in confusion as to whether this is an allowable project charge and part of cost of the work. Until standard-form contracts are revised to specify the charge basis for computers and software, the parties must take the initiative to discuss and agree as to how these items are to be charged.

Conclusion

The common objective on any construction project is to secure predictable prices for construction services. A firm-fixed-price contract is the obvious solution for an owner wishing to avoid pricing variations that exceed its budget constraints. However, many factors often prevent the parties from simply agreeing on a lump-sum price. Regardless of the reason for the particular pricing risks, some form of cost-reimbursable contract may prove to be the best option for allocating the risk of pricing that is not susceptible to a reliable estimate. Once a cost-reimbursable delivery system is chosen, the parties must develop clear contract terms defining those costs that will be reimbursed, exclusions to cost reimbursability, and a mechanism for sharing and confirming the accuracy of cost accounting data.[39]

Occasionally, some pricing elements can be fixed, subject to allowances for specific items to be paid on a cost-reimbursable basis. If a hybrid pricing arrangement is adopted, it is imperative that the drafter avoid ambiguities concerning the intended pricing terms.[40] Similarly, if a cost-reimbursable contract specifies unit prices for some items of work, the contract should clearly establish if the unit prices are fixed, or subject to adjustment based on actual costs incurred.

Extreme volatility in construction-related commodities has been a significant challenge in recent years, particularly for fixed-price and fixed-unit price arrangements.[41] Sudden spikes in the cost of materials, such as steel, have illustrated this problem and caused severe financial distress in some cases.[42] Absent special terms allowing pricing modifications for specified items based on changes in published pricing data, such as the Bureau of Labor Statistics Producer Price Index, contractors may have limited options to seek an adjustment.[43] Unless a substantial contingency is otherwise built into the pricing arrangement, or other factors make commodity pricing more predictable for a given project, material escalation provisions should be considered as an option for balancing the risk associated with unforeseen pricing volatility.

Although many standard-form contracts provide guidance for the development of terms to implement a cost-reimbursable pricing arrangement, suitable provisions must be crafted to accommodate the unique needs of each industry, project, and trade. Particular attention should be given to the troublesome labor, material, and equipment cost categories addressed in this chapter, together with any distinctive pricing issues that may arise under the circumstances of a particular project. The contract language must clearly delineate the categories of reimbursable direct costs and indirect costs allocable to the contract, and provide a mechanism for cost verification.

Notes

1. State and federal procurement requirements address pricing alternatives for government contractors. For example, under the Federal Acquisition Regulation (FAR), various pricing alternatives are addressed (*E.g.* Subpart 16.2—Fixed-Price Contracts and Subpart 16.3—Cost-Reimbursement Contracts). Similarly, state procurement codes deal with pricing options. *E.g.*, VA. CODE ANN. § 2.2-4331—Contract pricing arrangements: "Except as prohibited in this section, public contracts may be awarded on a fixed price or cost reimbursement basis, or on any other basis that is not prohibited."

2. *E.g.*, The Fair Labor Standards Act (establishes minimum wage, overtime pay, record keeping, and youth employment standards affecting full-time and part-time workers in the private sector and in federal, state, and local governments); Davis-Bacon Act (requires that each contract over $2,000 to which the United States or the District of Columbia is a party for the construction, alteration, or repair of public buildings or public works shall contain a clause setting forth the minimum wages to be paid to various classes of laborers and mechanics employed under the contract. Under the provisions of the Act, contractors or their subcontractors are to pay workers employed directly upon the site of the work no less than the locally prevailing wages and fringe benefits paid on projects of a similar character).

3. Gen. Const. v. Greater St. Thomas, 107 S.W.3d 513, 520 (Tenn. App. 2002) ("lump-sum" synonymous with "fixed-price").

4. Aniero Concrete Co. v. New York City Const. Auth., 308 F. Supp. 2d 164, 191 (S.D.N.Y. 2003) ("The fixed-price contract is more risky for the general contractor because, in order to obtain the job, the contractor must agree to a guaranteed maximum price, or 'GMP.' This requires the general contractor to enter into contracts with its subcontractors and vendors on terms that will allow the general contractor to complete the project sufficiently below the contract price to cover the general contractor's costs and overhead and turn a profit.").

5. Remedy-granting terms may include provisions dealing with changes, owner-caused delay, suspension of work, differing site conditions, and so on. Numerous changes alone do not transform a lump-sum contract into a cost-plus arrangement. *See* U.S. Fid. and Guar. Co. v. Braspetro Oil Servs. Co., 219 F. Supp. 2d 403, 480 (S.D.N.Y. 2002)

6. N. Ind. Pub. Serv. Co. v. Carbon County Coal Co., 799 F.2d 265, 278 (7th Cir. 1986); *see* P.T.& L. Constr. Co. v. New York, 578 N.Y.S.2d 921, 922 (App. Div. 1992) ("Neither general labor shortages, the unavailability of skilled operators or technical specialists nor the loss of employees on whose assistance the contractor had counted in the performance of the contract constitutes grounds for excuse of performance or modification of the contract price."); McNamara Constr. Co. v. United States, 509 F.2d 1166 (Ct. Cl. 1975) (rejecting mutual mistake of fact theory because contractor assumes risk of labor cost increases); Robert McMullan & Son, Inc., ASBCA No. 11998, 68-1 BCA ¶ 7068 ("For all such general difficulties in obtaining and retaining the required labor force, the contractor is held responsible, even though the labor shortage may be unanticipated."). In *Commercial Contractors, Inc. v. U.S. Fidelity & Guaranty Co.*, 524 F.2d 944 (5th Cir. 1975) (applying Alabama law), a masonry subcontractor lost eight workers to another subcontractor. The subcontractor argued that the resulting labor shortage rendered performance impossible, but the court rejected the argument. The Fifth Circuit held that the contractor had "assumed the risk of providing labor, and that included the risk of whether he could be competitive with other subcontractors in an overcrowded building market." *Id.* at 955.

7. *See* FAR 16.203 (Fixed-price contracts with economic price adjustment).

8. Bureau of Labor Statistics, http://www.bls.gov/ppi.

9. *See* Bethlehem Steel Corp. v. Litton Indus., Inc., 321 Pa. Super. 357, 468 A.2d 748, 759 (Pa. Super. 1983) (In the context of a ship construction contract, the court noted "the

critical importance of escalation in long-term multi-million dollar ship construction during a period of double digit inflation" but held that a court cannot fashion an escalation clause for parties who are unable to do so for themselves.); *see also* Bethlehem Steel Co. v. Turner Const. Co., 161 N.Y.S.2d 90, 2 N.Y.2d 456 (N.Y. 1957).

10. Bureau of Labor Statistics, Producer Price Indexes: Escalation Guide for Contracting Parties, (July 27, 2006), http://www.bls.gov/ppi/ppiescalation.htm.

11. *Id.*

12. Md. State Highway Admin. v. David A. Bramble, Inc., 351 Md. 226, 717 A.2d 943 (Md. 1998) (claim of ambiguity in unit price of asphalt for temporary versus permanent road work rejected); Barnard Constr. Co. v. City of Lubbock, 457 F.3d 425 (5th Cir. 2006) (where the estimated quantities are shown for classes of work and used only as a basis for estimating and comparing bids, it is understood payment shall be for the actual amount of work done and materials furnished on the project at the agreed-upon unit prices).

13. *See also* Marshall Contractors, Inc. v. Brown Univ., 692 A.2d 665 (R.I. 1997) (failure of parties to fully agree upon price and scope of design-build project before construction opens door for contractor to pursue a *quantum meruit* recovery).

14. Many courts have grappled with the nuances of cost-reimbursable pricing under a GMP contract. *See* Bouten Constr. Co. v. M & L Land Co., 877 P.2d 928, 125 Idaho 957 (Idaho App. 1994) (cost-plus contract was subject to a GMP, which was not waived as a result of changes directed by the owner even though the change order procedure was generally not followed; likewise the contractor did not lose its right to seek increases to and adjustment of the GMP either because of delay or because of its failure to strictly comply with the change order provisions in the contract due to owner's delays in producing final contract documents); Davis v. Sliney, 1988 WL 75331 (Tenn. Ct. App.) (Use of the word "estimated" in conjunction with the words "maximum cost" does not change the meaning of "estimated" or make it or the phrase ambiguous. Estimate indicates an approximation or rough calculation of the maximum cost of labor, material and other construction costs likely to be required, not an expression of a GMP.); J.E. Hathman, Inc. v. Sigma Alpha Epsilon Club, 491 S.W.2d 261, 266 (Mo. 1973) (that the word "estimated" was used in conjunction with the words "maximum cost" does not change the meaning of "estimated" or make it or the phrase ambiguous).

15. Planning Sys. Corp. v. Murrell, 374 So.2d 719, 722 (La. App. 4 Cir. 1979) (in a cost-plus contract it is implicit that the costs must be reasonable and proper).

16. 699 F.2d 1147 (Fed. Cir. 1983).

17. *Id.* at 1152.

18. FAR 31.201.2.

19. FAR 31.201-3.

20. FAR 31.201.4.

21. *E.g.*, FAR 31.205-1 (public relations and advertising costs); FAR 31.205-14 (entertainment costs); FAR 31.205-10 (cost of money); FAR 31.205-20 (interest and other financial costs); FAR 31.205-22 (lobbying and political activity costs); FAR 31.205-47 (costs related to legal and other proceedings).

22. Similar language is included in AIA Document A102-2007 (Article 3), AIA Document A111-1997 (Article 3), and AIA Document A114-2001 (Article 3).

23. 484 A.2d 302 (Md. Spec. App. 1984).

24. 582 A.2d 557 (Md. Spec. App. 1991).

25. In *Eastover Ridge, LLC v. Metric Constructors, Inc.*, 139 N.C. App. 360, 533 S.E. 2d 827 (2000), N.C. App., *rev. denied*, 546 S.E.2d 93 (N.C. App. 2000), despite similar language stating that the contractor accepts a relationship of trust and confidence, the court declined to impose the heightened duty of a fiduciary upon a contractor in connection with a cost-plus contract.

26. Disputes can arise when proprietary pricing information related to indirect costs is the subject of the audit request. *See* Orion Ref. Corp. v. Shaw Constructors, 839 So. 2d 161, 164 (La. App. 2003) (addressing conflicting contract terms and audit of both nondirect costs and reimbursable direct costs; held that owner was entitled to an audit for "any reasonable purpose" including discovery of information necessary to the pursuit of a legal claim).

27. *See* Barnett and Herenchak, Inc. v. N.J. Dep't of Transp., 648 A.2d 256, 276 N.J. Super. 465 (N.J. Super. A.D. 1994) (state did not dispute quality of services but audit demonstrated that contractor improperly billed for substantial nonbusiness expenses and for labor costs that were not actually incurred).

28. Standard Constr. Co. v. Nat'l Tea Co., 62 N.W.2d 201, 240 Minn. 422 (Minn. 1953) ("with the assent of both parties a practice was established which was inconsistent with the [cost accounting] provision of the contract, and a waiver of the right to demand compliance with that provision resulted").

29. AIA A102 art. 7.5.2 (2007).

30. *See* 29 U.S.C. § 213(a)(1).

31. 29 C.F.R. § 541.200(a).

32. *Compare* Cotton v. HFS-USA, Inc., 620 F. Supp. 2d 1342 (M.D. Fla. 2009) (supervisor with little discretion who performed a minor amount of nonexempt activities was not exempt) *with* Black v. Colaska Inc., No. C07-823JLR, 2008 WL 4681567 (W.D. Wash. 2008) (project manager with significant discretion and responsibility for job profitability was exempt).

33. Johnson v. Big Lots Stores, Inc., 604 F. Supp. 2d 903 (E.D. La. 2009).

34. Dingwall v. Friedman Fisher Assocs., P.C., 3 F. Supp. 2d 215 (N.D.N.Y. 1998); Martin v. Malcolm Pirnie, Inc., 949 F.2d 611, 614 (2d Cir.1991), *cert. denied*, Malcolm Pirnie, Inc. v. Martin, 506 U.S. 905, 113 S. Ct. 298, 121 L. Ed. 2d 222 (1992).

35. 29 C.F.R. §541.3(a); Hopkins v. Texas Mast Climbers, LLC (S.D. Tex. 2005); Baker v. Flint Eng'g & Constr. Co., 137 F. 3d 1436 (10th Cir. 1998); Baker v. Barnard Constr. Co., 146 F. 3d 1214 (10th Cir. 1998).

36. *See* Moreau v. Klevenhagen, 508 U.S. 22, 23, 113 S. Ct. 1905, 123 L. Ed. 2d 584 (1993) (Fair Labor Standards Act allows public employers to award compensatory time, instead of overtime, on a time and a half basis, as long as the affected employees agree in advance to accept compensatory time).

37. AIA A102 art. 7.5.2 (2007).

38. *See* 23 C.F.R. § 635.120.

39. See Equity Lifestyle Props. v. Fla. Mowing, 556 F.3d 1232 (11th Cir. 2009) (although described as a cost-plus arrangement, the percentage of profit was to be calculated based on the unit prices, regardless of the relationship between those unit prices and the actual costs accrued).

40. *Id.*; Hickman v. Kralicek Realty & Const. Co., 129 S.W.3d 317, 84 Ark. App. 61 (Ark. App. 2003) (contract had features of both a cost-plus contract and a fixed-price contract, but court found contract was a cost-plus contract and owner was obligated to pay all unforeseen costs over contractor's bid); Spirtas Co. v. Div. of Design and Constr., 131 S.W.3d 411 (Mo. App. 2004) (contract with a mixture of flat-fee provisions and unit pricing was ambiguous, based on deviations from projected numbers of units included in the base flat sum of the contract).

41. *See* S. Dredging Co., ENGBCA No. 5843, 92-2 BCA ¶ 24,886 (under a fixed-price contract a contractor assumes the risk of increases in the cost of materials and supplies).

42. Holder Const. Group v. Ga. Tech, 640 S.E.2d 296 (Ga. App. 2006) (contractor assumed risk of difficulties due to an increase in steel prices and the late delivery of steel materials).

43. *E.g.* Seaboard Lumber Co. v. United States, 308 F. 3d 1283 (Fed. Cir. 2002) (force majeure); Raytheon Co. v. White, 305 F. 3d 1354 (Fed. Cir. 2002) (commercial impracticability); S. Welding & Mfg. Co. v. United States, 373 F. 2d 982 (Ct. Cl. 1967) (mutual mistake); Aluminum Co. of Am. v. Essex Group, Inc. 499 F. Supp 53 (W.D. Pa. 1980) (frustration of purpose).

APPENDIX

EJCDC Article 11: Reimbursable Costs

EJCDC C-700: Standard General Conditions of the Construction Contract provides in relevant part:

Article 11—Cost of the Work; Allowances; Unit Price Work

1.01 Cost of the Work

A. *Costs Included:* The term Cost of the Work means the sum of all costs, except those excluded in Paragraph 11.01.B, necessarily incurred and paid by Contractor in the proper performance of the Work. When the value of any Work covered by a Change Order or when a Claim for an adjustment in Contract Price is determined on the basis of Cost of the Work, the costs to be reimbursed to Contractor will be only those additional or incremental costs required because of the change in the Work or because of the event giving rise to the Claim. Except as otherwise may be agreed to in writing by Owner, such costs shall be in amounts no higher than those prevailing in the locality of the Project, shall not include any of the costs itemized in Paragraph 11.01.B, and shall include only the following items:

1. Payroll costs for employees in the direct employ of Contractor in the performance of the Work under schedules of job classifications agreed upon by Owner and Contractor. Such employees shall include, without limitation, superintendents, foremen, and other personnel employed full time on the Work. Payroll costs for employees not employed full time on the Work shall be apportioned on the basis of their time spent on the Work. Payroll costs shall include, but not be limited to, salaries and wages plus the cost of fringe benefits, which shall include social security contributions, unemployment, excise, and payroll taxes, workers' compensation, health and retirement benefits, bonuses, sick leave, vacation and holiday pay applicable thereto. The expenses of performing Work outside of regular working hours, on Saturday, Sunday, or legal holidays, shall be included in the above to the extent authorized by Owner.

2. Cost of all materials and equipment furnished and incorporated in the Work, including costs of transportation and storage thereof, and Suppliers' field services required in connection

therewith. All cash discounts shall accrue to Contractor unless Owner deposits funds with Contractor with which to make payments, in which case the cash discounts shall accrue to Owner. All trade discounts, rebates and refunds and returns from sale of surplus materials and equipment shall accrue to Owner, and Contractor shall make provisions so that they may be obtained.

3. Payments made by Contractor to Subcontractors for Work performed by Subcontractors. If required by Owner, Contractor shall obtain competitive bids from subcontractors acceptable to Owner and Contractor and shall deliver such bids to Owner, who will then determine, with the advice of Engineer, which bids, if any, will be acceptable. If any subcontract provides that the Subcontractor is to be paid on the basis of Cost of the Work plus a fee, the Subcontractor's Cost of the Work and fee shall be determined in the same manner as Contractor's Cost of the Work and fee as provided in this Paragraph 11.01.

4. Costs of special consultants (including but not limited to engineers, architects, testing laboratories, surveyors, attorneys, and accountants) employed for services specifically related to the Work.

5. Supplemental costs including the following:
   a. The proportion of necessary transportation, travel, and subsistence expenses of Contractor's employees incurred in discharge of duties connected with the Work.
   b. Cost, including transportation and maintenance, of all materials, supplies, equipment, machinery, appliances, office, and temporary facilities at the Site, and hand tools not owned by the workers, which are consumed in the performance of the Work, and cost, less market value, of such items used but not consumed which remain the property of Contractor.
   c. Rentals of all construction equipment and machinery, and the parts thereof whether rented from Contractor or others in accordance with rental agreements approved by Owner with the advice of Engineer, and the costs of transportation, loading, unloading, assembly, dismantling, and removal thereof. All such costs shall be in accordance with the terms of said rental agreements. The rental of any such equipment, machinery, or parts shall cease when the use thereof is no longer necessary for the Work.
   d. Sales, consumer, use, and other similar taxes related to the Work, and for which Contractor is liable, as imposed by Laws and Regulations.
   e. Deposits lost for causes other than negligence of Contractor, any Subcontractor, or anyone directly or indirectly employed

by any of them or for whose acts any of them may be liable, and royalty payments and fees for permits and licenses.

    f. Losses and damages (and related expenses) caused by damage to the Work, not compensated by insurance or otherwise, sustained by Contractor in connection with the performance of the Work (except losses and damages within the deductible amounts of property insurance established in accordance with Paragraph 5.06.D), provided such losses and damages have resulted from causes other than the negligence of Contractor, any Subcontractor, or anyone directly or indirectly employed by any of them or for whose acts any of them may be liable. Such losses shall include settlements made with the written consent and approval of Owner. No such losses, damages, and expenses shall be included in the Cost of the Work for the purpose of determining Contractor's fee.

    g. The cost of utilities, fuel, and sanitary facilities at the Site.

    h. Minor expenses such as telegrams, long distance telephone calls, telephone service at the Site, express and courier services, and similar petty cash items in connection with the Work.

    i. The costs of premiums for all bonds and insurance Contractor is required by the Contract Documents to purchase and maintain.

B. *Costs Excluded:* The term Cost of the Work shall not include any of the following items:

1. Payroll costs and other compensation of Contractor's officers, executives, principals (of partnerships and sole proprietorships), general managers, safety managers, engineers, architects, estimators, attorneys, auditors, accountants, purchasing and contracting agents, expediters, timekeepers, clerks, and other personnel employed by Contractor, whether at the Site or in Contractor's principal or branch office for general administration of the Work and not specifically included in the agreed upon schedule of job classifications referred to in Paragraph 11.01.A.1 or specifically covered by Paragraph 11.01.A.4, all of which are to be considered administrative costs covered by the Contractor's fee.

2. Expenses of Contractor's principal and branch offices other than Contractor's office at the Site.

3. Any part of Contractor's capital expenses, including interest on Contractor's capital employed for the Work and charges against Contractor for delinquent payments.

4. Costs due to the negligence of Contractor, any Subcontractor, or anyone directly or indirectly employed by any of them or for whose acts any of them may be liable, including but not limited to, the correction of defective Work, disposal of materials or

equipment wrongly supplied, and making good any damage to property.
   5. Other overhead or general expense costs of any kind and the costs of any item not specifically and expressly included in Paragraphs 11.01.A.
C. *Contractor's Fee:* When all the Work is performed on the basis of cost-plus, Contractor's fee shall be determined as set forth in the Agreement. When the value of any Work covered by a Change Order or when a Claim for an adjustment in Contract Price is determined on the basis of Cost of the Work, Contractor's fee shall be determined as set forth in Paragraph 12.01.C.
D. *Documentation:* Whenever the Cost of the Work for any purpose is to be determined pursuant to Paragraphs 11.01.A and 11.01.B, Contractor will establish and maintain records thereof in accordance with generally accepted accounting practices and submit in a form acceptable to Engineer an itemized cost breakdown together with supporting data.

1.02 **Allowances**
A. It is understood that Contractor has included in the Contract Price all allowances so named in the Contract Documents and shall cause the Work so covered to be performed for such sums and by such persons or entities as may be acceptable to Owner and Engineer.
B. Cash Allowances:
   1. Contractor agrees that:
      a. the cash allowances include the cost to Contractor (less any applicable trade discounts) of materials and equipment required by the allowances to be delivered at the Site, and all applicable taxes; and
      b. Contractor's costs for unloading and handling on the Site, labor, installation, overhead, profit, and other expenses contemplated for the cash allowances have been included in the Contract Price and not in the allowances, and no demand for additional payment on account of any of the foregoing will be valid.
C. Contingency Allowance:
   1. Contractor agrees that a contingency allowance, if any, is for the sole use of Owner to cover unanticipated costs.
D. Prior to final payment, an appropriate Change Order will be issued as recommended by Engineer to reflect actual amounts due Contractor on account of Work covered by allowances, and the Contract Price shall be correspondingly adjusted.

1.03 Unit Price Work

A. Where the Contract Documents provide that all or part of the Work is to be Unit Price Work, initially the Contract Price will be deemed to include for all Unit Price Work an amount equal to the sum of the unit price for each separately identified item of Unit Price Work times the estimated quantity of each item as indicated in the Agreement.

B. The estimated quantities of items of Unit Price Work are not guaranteed and are solely for the purpose of comparison of Bids and determining an initial Contract Price. Determinations of the actual quantities and classifications of Unit Price Work performed by Contractor will be made by Engineer subject to the provisions of Paragraph 9.07.

C. Each unit price will be deemed to include an amount considered by Contractor to be adequate to cover Contractor's overhead and profit for each separately identified item.

D. Owner or Contractor may make a Claim for an adjustment in the Contract Price in accordance with Paragraph 10.05 if:
   1. the quantity of any item of Unit Price Work performed by Contractor differs materially and significantly from the estimated quantity of such item indicated in the Agreement; and
   2. there is no corresponding adjustment with respect to any other item of Work; and
   3. Contractor believes that Contractor is entitled to an increase in Contract Price as a result of having incurred additional expense or Owner believes that Owner is entitled to a decrease in Contract Price and the parties are unable to agree as to the amount of any such increase or decrease.

CHAPTER 8

Government Contract Cost Accounting Issues Affecting Construction Contractors

EDWIN C. GIDDINGS
MATTHEW R. KRAFFT
PATRICK A. McGEEHIN

Introduction

When performing federal government contracts, construction companies are required to comply with a comprehensive and complex set of government regulations. These regulations are contained within Title 48 of the Code of Federal Regulations (CFR). Of primary interest to government contractors are 48 CFR Chapter 1 parts 1 through 52, referred to as the Federal Acquisition Regulation (FAR), and 48 CFR parts 9900 to 9905, referred to as the Cost Accounting Standards (CAS).

The FAR's provisions cover the entire government procurement process from the submission of bids or proposals through contract close out. They address a wide range of topics including conflicts of interest, drugs in the workplace, environmental protection, Buy American requirements, small business programs, and improper business practices such as kickbacks and collusion. Of interest here, the FAR also details numerous highly technical accounting and pricing requirements bearing directly on the process by which federal government contracts are bid, and the determination of the amount and nature of costs that contractors may include in government billings.

The CAS consists of 19 highly technical cost accounting pronouncements, issued by the government's Cost Accounting Standards Board. These standards provide guidance on how costs charged to government contracts are to be measured in amount and allocated between accounting periods and among contracts. The CAS covers a wide range of cost accounting issues, including fixed asset capitalization and depreciation, inventory valuation, deferred compensation, insurance, and indirect rate calculation methodology.

Pricing and cost accounting regulations are found throughout the FAR and CAS, such as in the following provisions:

- Cost and pricing data for estimating costs as part of a bid submission (FAR Part 15)
- Methods for allocating costs to specific contracts or task orders for both bidding and actual cost charging purposes (CAS and FAR Part 31)
- Costs that are deemed "unallowable" as either direct or indirect costs for purposes of both pricing estimates or seeking reimbursement (FAR Part 31)
- Contract financing and payments (FAR Part 32)
- Construction and architect-engineer contracts (FAR Part 36)
- Standard contract provisions (FAR Part 52)

In addition to these issues, FAR Part 31 includes provisions relating to cost "reasonableness," and provides guidance for obtaining advance agreements for specific elements of cost, as well as regulations dealing specifically with costs incurred by construction companies.

In this chapter, we examine the pricing and accounting issues contained in the FAR and CAS from the perspective of construction contractors. We will discuss some of the problems unique to the construction industry that these regulations present, and offer some practical tips on how to avoid potential pitfalls.

Contracting Methods

Practically speaking, construction contracts are procured by one of two basic methods: sealed bidding and contracting by negotiation. Generally, contracts procured in response to an Invitation for Bids (IFB) are governed by FAR Part 14, Sealed Bidding, and are not subject to cost or pricing data requirements in connection with the original contract award. On the other hand, contracts procured in response to a Request for Proposal (RFP) are governed by FAR Part 15, Contracting by Negotiation, and may be subject to requirements for submission of cost or pricing data. It is important to note that fixed-price contracts may be negotiated, and if they are, they may be subject to requirements for submission of cost or pricing data. In addition, even though a contract may have been awarded through sealed bidding, any material change or modification to the contract after award will most likely be subject to negotiation and FAR Part 15 requirements for cost or pricing data.

Cost or Pricing Data and FAR Part 15, Contracting by Negotiation

When negotiating a government contract, in some instances the contractor may be required to share, or "disclose," to the government, its cost estimates, overhead allocation methodologies, and other factors forming the basis of its proposed price. This information is divided into two broad categories, "Cost or Pricing Data" and "Information Other than Cost or Pricing Data." Cost or pricing data is defined by the FAR as "all *facts* that, as of the date of agreement on price . . . reasonable buyers and sellers would reasonably expect to affect price negotiations significantly" (emphasis added). In addition to cost or pricing data, offerors are required to submit or disclose other information. Specifically, the regulations require that "any type of information that is not required to be certified . . . and is necessary to determine price reasonableness or cost realism" be disclosed.[1] Providing cost or pricing data and information other than cost or pricing data is intended to place the government and the contractor on an equal footing when negotiating contract price, in those cases where the goods or services being procured are not traded in the marketplace. In such cases, the government cannot rely on the marketplace to establish fair and reasonable prices. In other words, the government cannot necessarily "shop around" for the best deal on a nuclear power plant, an aircraft carrier, or a large design-build construction project.

FAR Part 15 applies to all negotiated contracts (contracts awarded using other than sealed bidding procedures). FAR Part 15.403, Obtaining Cost or Pricing Data, requires contractors, with certain exceptions, to disclose all proposed contract costs. Specifically, it requires, with certain exceptions, that contractors submit to the government all "cost or pricing data" upon which proposed contract prices are based. Currently, the contract size threshold for submitting cost or pricing data is $650,000.[2] Important exceptions to the requirement for cost or pricing data include

- Acquisitions below the simplified acquisition threshold
- When prices are based on adequate competition
- The acquisition of a commercial item
- Where a waiver of the requirement has been granted

The exception for adequate competition is particularly important to construction contractors. Determining whether there is adequate competition is the subject of lengthy criteria in FAR 15.403. These criteria mostly deal with situations involving two or more bidders or the expectation of two or more bidders. However, the contracting officer is permitted to determine that a price is reasonable and not obtain cost or pricing data when "[p]rice analysis clearly demonstrates that the proposed price is reasonable." As a result, while the adequate competition exception most often applies in the procurement of the original contract, this exception may also be employed for the pricing of change orders (where there are no competitors) if the contracting officer can clearly determine that the proposed price is reasonable. Regardless of the exceptions, given the large dollar size of most construction contracts, the increasing frequency of negotiated procurements, and the relatively low certification thresholds, contractors may frequently find themselves in the position of certifying cost or pricing data.

Cost or Pricing Data Certification

When cost or pricing data are required, contractors will also be required to execute and submit a Certificate of Current Cost or Pricing Data, certifying that the data provided is "current, accurate and complete" as of the date on which the price agreement is reached. If it is later determined that the cost or pricing data submitted was not current, accurate and complete, the government may assert that data upon which the price was negotiated was "defective." In that case, the negotiated contract price may be adjusted downward (subject to specific offsets, if any), and the contractor may be subject to fines and penalties. If considered sufficiently egregious, a contractor's failure to disclose may be considered reckless disregard for the truth and result in a government allegation of a false claim. 31 U.S.C. §§ 3729–3733. The actual certification language is as follows:

> This is to certify that, to the best of my knowledge and belief, the cost or pricing data (as Defined in Section 15.401 of the Federal Acquisition Regulation (FAR) and required under FAR Subsection 15.403-4) submitted, either actually or by specific identification in writing, to the contracting officer or to the contracting officer's representative in support of [THIS PROPOSAL] are accurate, complete, and current as of [THE DATE OF AGREEMENT UPON PRICE]. This certification includes the cost or pricing data supporting any advance agreements and forward pricing rate agreements between the offeror and the Government that are part of the proposal.
>
> Signature: _____

Cutoff Dates and Cost Sweeps

As can be seen from the required language of the certificate, the timing of the submission and the certificate are critical. The certificate refers to "the date of agreement upon price." Contract negotiations can take weeks or even months to conclude, during which time additional or revised cost or pricing data may become available within the contractor's organization. FAR 15.406-2-(c) requires the contracting officer and the contractor to establish cutoff dates for updating cost or pricing data. The contractor must carefully assemble any and all data that was available to it during the period of negotiation—right up to the time of agreement on price—and provide it to the government, if it is possible that the information that the contractor has in its possession could have a bearing on the price that the government is accepting. This process, often referred to as a "TINA (Truth in Negotiation Act) sweep," is critically important. Issues regarding defective pricing, which may require a contractor to prove that certain information was disclosed prior to agreement on price, can come up years after project completion, and long after the people who negotiated the contract have gone elsewhere. Cost or pricing data provided to the government, including TINA sweep sign-off sheets and supporting bid prices, should be assembled into a permanent bid file and retained until after the contract has been closed out and the applicable statute of limitations has expired.

Note that the government can charge the contractor with defective pricing (and false claims) even if a signed certificate was not submitted. Any time a contractor provides cost or pricing data to the government, the contractor must take all steps possible to verify and document that the information provided was current, accurate, and complete. Additionally, the possibility of a false claim is not limited to certified cost and pricing data, but applies to "information other than cost or pricing data" as well.

Practical Considerations

Contractors who do not maintain comprehensive job cost accounting systems may find compliance with these FAR Part 15 requirements difficult. For example, the rates charged for equipment obtained from sister divisions, which project personnel view as costs, are, in most cases, actually internal charging rates containing non-cost-based markups. Additionally, items such as related-party real property rental charges and self-insurance premium costs may well contain markups that are difficult to identify and eliminate. Similarly, related-party management fees, or charges for computer usage, training, and so on, which are normally allocated to commercial contracts at rates established by management, often contain an element of non-cost-based markup. Prior to submission and certification of cost or pricing data, it is essential that all non-cost-based markups either be identified and removed from the contract bid price or be clearly disclosed as prices containing non-cost-based markups rather than consisting only of cost.[3]

The following are some examples of situations that can lead to the government bringing defective pricing actions against a contractor. Depending on the circumstances, any of these issues could rise to the level of a false claim if intent is established or the government can prove reckless disregard:

- Providing cost information based solely upon journeyman rates while intending to use apprentices for some of the craft labor
- Including cost for equipment to be used for a project (or for extra work) that was scheduled to be repaired (and was not on site) during the subject period
- Including unallowable costs in proposed overhead rates

- Including indirect costs at levels based on past results, when it is clear that the rates will decrease based on work volume increases already known
- Duplicating costs in a daily rate and markup without disclosure and without the application of a credit
- Including costs in a daily rate that do not vary with the passage of time
- Including estimated production rates that do not take into account recent results of learning curve efficiencies
- Including costs in a proposal for materials or services at full rates, when the vendor provides discounts based on volume or other factors, without disclosure

As is evident from these examples, the key to avoiding defective pricing or false claims allegations is an understanding of the government's definition of cost or pricing data and comprehensively disclosing all facts that could be considered to be cost or pricing data and all information other than cost or pricing data that is necessary to determine price reasonableness or cost realism.

Unallowable Costs Under Government Contracts

There are certain specific categories of costs that the government has classified as "unallowable" and therefore not reimbursable. Unallowable costs may not be included in contractor estimates on negotiated contracts, within disclosed cost or pricing data in payment requisitions on cost-reimbursement contracts, or in requests for equitable adjustment (REAs) or claims based upon incurred or estimated costs. There are over 50 unallowable cost categories discussed in detail in FAR Part 31 (the Cost Principles). A listing of the individual cost elements dealt with in the Cost Principles can be found at Exhibit 8-1. Exhibit 8-2 provides a checklist of commonly incurred categories of costs, indicating which are allowable and which are considered unallowable. Although Exhibit 8-2 is a helpful summary tool to generally determine if a cost area might involve unallowable costs, it must be stressed that the discussion in the FAR is very detailed for many of these cost categories. In addition, the FAR is supplemented by decisions issued over the years by the Boards of Contract Appeals (the Armed Services Board of Contract Appeals and its civilian agency counterpart) and is also supplemented by various agency-level FAR Supplements, such as the Department of Energy Acquisition Regulations. A complete reading of FAR Part 31 provisions and associated cases is necessary to fully comprehend and assess the classification of individual contract costs as allowable or unallowable.

Exhibit 8-1
FAR Cost Principles

FAR Part 31.205, Selected Costs

31.205-1 Public relations and advertising costs.
31.205-2 [Reserved]
31.205-3 Bad debts.
31.205-4 Bonding costs.
31.205-5 [Reserved]
31.205-6 Compensation for personal services.
31.205-7 Contingencies.
31.205-8 Contributions or donations.
31.205-9 [Reserved]
31.205-10 Cost of money.
31.205-11 Depreciation.
31.205-12 Economic planning costs.
31.205-13 Employee morale, health, welfare, food service, and dormitory costs and credits.
31.205-14 Entertainment costs.
31.205-15 Fines, penalties, and mischarging costs.
31.205-16 Gains and losses on disposition or impairment of depreciable property or other capital assets.
31.205-17 Idle facilities and idle capacity costs.
31.205-18 Independent research and development and bid and proposal costs.
31.205-19 Insurance and indemnification.
31.205-20 Interest and other financial costs.
31.205-21 Labor relations costs.
31.205-22 Lobbying and political activity costs.
31.205-23 Losses on other contracts.
31.205-24 [Reserved]
31.205-25 Manufacturing and production engineering costs.
31.205-26 Material costs.
31.205-27 Organization costs.
31.205-28 Other business expenses.
31.205-29 Plant protection costs.
31.205-30 Patent costs.
31.205-31 Plant reconversion costs.
31.205-32 Precontract costs.
31.205-33 Professional and consultant service costs.
31.205-34 Recruitment costs.
31.205-35 Relocation costs.
31.205-36 Rental costs.
31.205-37 Royalties and other costs for use of patents.
31.205-38 Selling costs.
31.205-39 Service and warranty costs.
31.205-40 Special tooling and special test equipment costs.

FAR Part 31.205, Selected Costs (*continued*)

31.205-41 Taxes.
31.205-42 Termination costs.
31.205-43 Trade, business, technical and professional activity costs.
31.205-44 Training and education costs.
31.205-45 [Reserved]
31.205-46 Travel costs.
31.205-47 Costs related to legal and other proceedings.
31.205-48 Research and development costs.
31.205-49 Goodwill.
31.205-50 [Reserved]
31.205-51 Costs of alcoholic beverages.
31.205-52 Asset valuations resulting from business combinations.

Exhibit 8-2
Checklist of Allowable and Unallowable Costs

Cost Element	Allowable	Unallowable
Advertising		
Mass mailings		X
Exhibits		X
Help wanted	X	
Ads for disposal of excess materials	X	
Promotional items (imprinted key chains, T-shirts, pens, etc.)		X
Public Relations		
Press/public communications related to project activities and accomplishments	X	
General liaison related to matters of public concern	X	
Open house		X
Displays		X
Demonstrations for general public		X
Alcoholic Beverages		X
Bad Debts		X
Late Fees		X
Bonuses per Approved Plan	X	
Overtime Premium		
Direct charge personnel with government approval	X	
Direct charge personnel without government approval		X
Indirect charge personnel	X	
Fringe Benefits		
Per established plan	X	
In excess of established plan		X
Personal use of company automobiles (includes commuting)		X

Cost Element	Allowable	Unallowable
Severance		
Per established plan	X	
In excess of established plan		X
"Golden Parachute" payment		X
Contingency Reserves		X
Donations & Contributions		X
Employee Morale, Health & Welfare		
In-house publications	X	
Parties		X
Picnics		X
Award ceremonies	X	
Awards (monetary & nonmonetary)	X	
Gifts to employees (birthday, baby, etc.)		X
Snack bar costs in excess of revenue	X	
Flowers per written policy (bereavement)	X	
Flowers not per written policy		X
Entertainment		
Social activities		X
Tickets to shows, games, etc.		X
Lodging and transportation		X
Golf outings		X
Fines and Penalties		X
Traffic Tickets		X
Fund-Raising Activities		X
Investment Counsel		X
Interest		
Late fees		X
Interest on Borrowings (however represented)		X
Lobbying (in kind or cash)		
Influencing legislation		X
Influencing elections, referendums, initiatives		X
Contributions to PACs		X
Legislative liaison activities		X
Providing technical or factual data	X	
Losses on Contracts		X
Memberships, Dues, and Subscriptions		
Clubs (country, health, golf, dining etc.)		X
Business, trade or professional	X	
Technical periodicals	X	
Civic/community		X

Exhibit 8-2
Checklist of Allowable and Unallowable Costs (*continued*)

Cost Element	Allowable	Unallowable
Part-time Undergraduate or Postgraduate (work-related)		
Training materials	X	
Textbooks	X	
Fees	X	
Tuition	X	
Salary to attend classes during working hours		X
Recruitment Costs		
Employment office	X	
Help wanted	X	
Travel for interviews	X	
Relocation costs	X	
Aptitude testing	X	
Color advertisements		X
Excessive-size advertisements		X
Relocation		
Employed less than 12 months		X
Employed more than 12 months	X	
Transportation	X	
House hunting	X	
Selling expenses of former residence (current employees)	X	
Continuing maintenance costs of former residence (current employees)	X	
Costs associated with new residence		X
Loss on sale of former home		X
Mortgage payments on former home		X
Travel (Employees and Directors)		
Airfare coach class	X	
Excess airfare over standard coach		X
Excess over government per diem rates		X
Auto mileage at current GSA rate per mile	X	

Note: The classification of the costs included in this checklist as allowable and unallowable is made on a general basis. The classification of actual costs as allowable or unallowable should be made only after consideration of the specific circumstances in which they were incurred.

Many of the Cost Principles were originally drafted with manufacturing, defense, or service contractors in mind and may not seem to apply in the construction context. However, all of the Cost Principles apply to all federal government contracts, unless specifically exempted or excluded in some fashion. As such, it is necessary to make sure that all indirect cost pools, including home office overhead pools (commonly referred to as general and administrative (G&A) costs), and any direct contract charges, are "scrubbed" for unallowable costs so that government billings do not include any unallowable costs allocated as either direct or indirect costs.

FAR Provisions Specifically Relating to Construction Contracts and Advance Agreements

The bulk of the FAR Cost Principles are contained in Part 31.2, Contracts with Commercial Organizations. However, tucked away within the preceding section, innocuously labeled "Applicability," is the often overlooked, but important, Subpart 31.105, Construction and Architect-Engineer Contracts. This subpart supplements the Cost Principles applicable to all commercial organizations contained in Subpart 31.2.

In apparent recognition of the problematic nature of applying many FAR Cost Principles to construction contracts, the first guidance contained in FAR 31.105 is a statement that advance agreements, for such items as home office overhead, partners' compensation, employment of consultants, and equipment usage costs, are particularly important in construction contracts to "express the parties' understanding and avoid possible subsequent disputes or disallowances."[4]

While the advance agreement itself may be subject to FAR Part 15 disclosure requirements, the time and resources required to negotiate an advance agreement are often a small fraction of those required to establish allowable costs for these items in accordance with the FAR at a later date. As noted previously, many contractors follow the practice of charging jobs or pricing change orders using market-based billing rates for such items as payroll burdens, insurance, staff salaries, equipment, and central office support costs. Without an advance agreement establishing charge rates for these items, determining actual costs can be quite difficult. Accordingly, the use of advance agreements when possible can be very helpful and cost-effective.

Specific Cost Areas

Company-Owned Construction Equipment

Of particular concern in the pricing of construction contracts is the use of company-owned equipment. After stating the importance of advance agreements for pricing construction equipment, Part 31.105 defines construction equipment and sets forth principles for establishing allowable equipment cost when advance agreements are not obtained.

The first requirement is that actual cost data shall be used when both ownership and operating costs for each piece of equipment or groups of similar equipment can be determined from the contractor's accounting records. Use of actual cost is not discretionary if the cost data needed to determine both ownership and operating costs by individual piece or similar groups is available. Although the Cost Principles refer to *both* ownership and operating costs, the implementation of this provision over the years has led to varying results. Consequently, it is not always clear whether or not the government requires that actual cost data be available for *both* ownership and operating costs, or if the availability of actual cost for one element (e.g., depreciation and other ownership costs) requires a contractor to include the other element at actual cost.

In cases where equipment ownership and operating cost data is not available, allowable costs are determined by predetermined schedules of construction use rates, such as the Construction Equipment Ownership and Operating Expense Schedule, published by the U.S. Army Corps of Engineers (the Corps Manual), or similar industry or commercially published schedules. The Corps Manual consists of 12 volumes covering rates for different regions of the United States and foreign locations. Each volume includes lengthy listings of charge rates for different types and sizes of equipment. The contracting parties typically use these rates in pricing change orders, REAs, and claims when actual cost data is not available. However, even where the Corps rates were referenced in the contract, accepted by Defense Contract Audit Agency (DCAA) based on the contracting officer's direction, and used by the contracting parties on past change orders, a recent Court of Federal Claims decision held that each of the rates in the Corps Manual had to be recalculated if the contractor paid less for the equipment than the total equipment value estimate outlined in the Corps Manual for that type of equipment.[5] This decision seems inconsistent with the basic intent of the Corps Manual, as it raises the question as to why the Corps would bother to publish in excess of 20,000 rates in 12 volumes if a recalculation is required every time the rates are used.

The FAR requires that when predetermined equipment rates are used, all costs covered by the rate schedule shall be identified and eliminated from other direct and indirect costs charged to the contract.[6] Thus when using equipment schedules, it is important to identify the costs included within the rate schedule and ensure that the same costs are not claimed elsewhere. For example, the Corps Manual includes fuel, maintenance, and repairs within equipment operating expenses. Contractors often include these costs in jobsite general conditions instead of an equipment cost account. Care must be taken when using Corps Manual operating expense tables to remove the covered operating costs from any general conditions reimbursement calculations. As another example, the Corps Manual treats tire wear as an operating cost, whereas contractors often do not accrue tire wear but rather record tire replacement cost as part of the costs incurred at regional equipment maintenance centers, and thereby build this cost into their equipment rental rates. This can also require a reconciliation adjustment if using a Corps Manual rate for ownership but a company actual rate for operating expenses.

Additionally, the equipment costs as determined by a rate schedule may need to be added to the contractor's indirect cost allocation base costs when determining the contractor's overhead rate(s), if such overhead rates are to be applied to the equipment costs using the Corps Manual rates. Alternatively, a contractor can, as its established rate approach, adopt a methodology whereby the Corps Manual rates are not subject to an indirect cost rate markup, and make appropriate adjustments to the indirect cost base to eliminate any direct equipment costs, so as to properly address this overhead allocation issue.

Construction equipment rented from any organization under common control is subject to the rental cost principles in FAR 31.205-36(b)(3), which provides that such rental rates are allowable only to the extent they do not exceed the normal costs of ownership and maintenance, excluding interest and other unallowable costs. If the contractor's equipment rental division has an established practice of renting to unaffiliated firms in sufficient volumes to establish a true market price, then, per FAR 31.205-36(b)(3), the same rental prices charged to affiliated firms would be considered allowable. In this situation, the government considers the related-party price to have been set by the market, thereby resulting in a reasonable price. Otherwise, regardless of the reasonableness of the rates, the rates cannot exceed the cost of ownership absent an advance agreement.

As a rule, interest expense is an unallowable cost under the FAR.[7] However, facilities capital cost of money (COM), an amount determined by applying an interest rate set by the Treasury Department (see Exhibit 8-3) to the contractor's average annual book value of plant and equipment, is allowed per the provisions of CAS 414, Cost of Money as an Element of the Cost of Facilities Capital. The COM factors are also built into the Corps Manual equipment rates. Accordingly, contractors may not include the book value of their major construction equipment in their COM calculations for allocation purposes if they are also using the Corps Manual rates to recover equipment costs.

General Conditions—Field Overhead Costs

A frequent source of confusion is the treatment of general conditions or field overhead-type costs on government construction contracts. These costs typically include employment costs for superintendents, project management personnel, and field office staff, as well as site utilities and cleanup, and are allowable as either direct or indirect costs, provided the accounting practice used is in accordance with the contractor's established practices.[8] For example, if project accounting services are provided at a regional office (service center), and the

Exhibit 8-3
Prompt Pay Interest Rate History

Period	Rate	Federal Register
Jul-09–Dec-09	4.875	Vol. 74, No. 126, 07/02/09, p. 31,794
Jan-09–Jun-09	5.625	Vol. 73, No. 250, 12/30/08, pp. 79,977–78
Jul-08–Dec-08	5.125	Vol. 73, No. 127, 07/01/08, p. 37,529
Jan-08–Jun-08	4.750	Vol. 72, No. 249, 12/31/07, p. 74,408
Jul-07–Dec-07	5.750	Vol. 72, No. 125, 06/29/07, pp. 35,742–43
Jan-07–Jun-07	5.250	Vol. 71, No. 250, 12/29/06, pp. 78,513–14
Jul-06–Dec-06	5.750	Vol. 71, No. 126, 06/30/06, pp. 37,638–39
Jan-06–Jun-06	5.125	Vol. 70, No. 247, 12/27/05, p. 76,497
Jul-05–Dec-05	4.500	Vol. 70, No. 126, 07/01/05, p. 38,253
Jan-05–Jun-05	4.250	Vol. 69, No. 250, 12/30/04, pp. 78,522–23
Jul-04–Dec-04	4.500	Vol. 69, No. 124, 06/29/04, pp. 38,952–53
Jan-04–Jun-04	4.000	Vol. 68, No. 249, 12/30/03, p. 75,317
Jul-03–Dec-03	3.125	Vol. 68, No. 126, 07/01/03, p. 39,185
Jan-03–Jun-03	4.250	Vol. 67, No. 247, 12/24/02, pp. 78,566–67
Jul-02–Dec-02	5.250	Vol. 67 No. 126, 07/01/02, p. 44,264
Jan-02–Jun-02	5.500	Vol. 66 No. 249, 12/28/01, p. 67,366
Jul-01–Dec-01	5.875	Vol. 66 No. 127, 07/02/01, p. 34,990
Jan-01–Jun-01	6.375	Vol. 65 No. 250, 12/28/00, p. 82,457

contractor's practice is to include that cost in company-wide G&A expense, then the costs for project accounting cannot be charged directly to a government contract, but must instead be included in the G&A rate being charged to the government. Otherwise, these costs would be viewed as being charged twice, once as an indirect cost and again as a direct cost. Conversely, if the contractor has an established practice of charging its regional service center costs directly to contracts on an hourly rate basis, then the costs would be allowable as a direct cost, unless this treatment is specifically prohibited by the contract terms. Of course, these costs would not then be charged to any indirect cost pool and recovered a second time through application of an indirect cost rate.

An additional source of confusion regarding general conditions and field overhead is the use of the term "overhead." In government contract parlance, overhead is generally used to mean an indirect cost that is allocable to multiple cost objectives (meaning multiple contracts). In construction contracting, home office overhead (that is, G&A) generally fits this description. However, contract general conditions costs, sometimes referred to as field overhead, are in this sense not really overhead costs, since they are not allocated to multiple contracts. They are only "indirect" in the sense that they are in support of the performance of the work of the entire contract (e.g., mechanical, electric, earthwork, concrete, steel placement), as opposed to just one element of the construction work. These costs are direct costs with respect to the contract. However, such general conditions costs (if not considered to be one-time charges or time related in nature) are allocable to multiple cost objectives within the contract and, therefore, may be included as a percentage of contract direct costs in a change order or claim situation. As discussed above, due to the varying methods of viewing and attempting to recover field overhead costs, obtaining advance agreements as to the approach to be used for any markup or daily rate approaches is recommended to avoid needless disagreements.

Entertainment

With respect to entertainment costs, the FAR provides that the costs of amusement, diversions, social activities such as tickets to shows or sporting events, and costs of social, dining, and country clubs are all unallowable, regardless of whether the cost is reported as taxable income by the employee.[9]

To construction contractors, costs falling within this exclusion frequently include the entertainment account at the home office level, and certain job expenses such as tickets to sporting events, topping-out parties, holiday gatherings, company picnics, and gifts.

There is some ambiguity in the FAR on this point, since certain employee morale and welfare costs, such as wellness/fitness centers, company-sponsored sports teams, and employee food and dormitory services, are allowable. However, costs qualifying for this morale and welfare exception are limited, and caution is urged when claiming them for reimbursement.

Self-Insurance (31.205-19)

The FAR provides that the cost of purchased and self-provided insurance obtained per the requirements of a government contract, or that is necessary for the general conduct of the business, is allowable. The cost of purchased insurance is relatively straightforward and does not normally create issues, except when the contractor experiences retroactive adjustments resulting in receiving refunds or paying additional premiums. For such adjustments, the treatment must be consistent in terms of how the contractor assigns these costs to current or future periods. However, the situation with respect to self-insurance, which includes insurance obtained from "captive insurers," is significantly more complex. There are a number of specific rules relating to the allowable cost of self-insurance that often cause problems for contractors.

FAR 31.205-19(c)(1) incorporates CAS 416, Accounting for Insurance Costs, into the FAR, making it applicable to all federal contracts (including those not covered by CAS) for the purpose of determining the cost of self-insurance. CAS 416 states that actual losses experienced "should not become a part of self insurance cost." Rather, that standard requires that each period's self-insurance charge be based on the contractor's "projected average loss" and that the calculation of the projected average loss take into consideration the contractor's past loss experience and anticipated conditions. In other words, contractors must estimate the amount of allowable self-insurance costs based on forward-looking projections of past losses. This is an element of cost in the FAR that, unlike overhead and certain other costs, requires a prospective rather than retroactive application. If the contractor incurs some losses in a given year under a self-insurance program, those losses will factor into its setting of future reserves and cost assignments, but will not normally result in any retroactive adjustment of the insurance costs for prior periods.

Another important consideration is situations where purchased insurance is available (which is generally the case for construction contractors). The FAR limits the allowable cost for self-insurance and related administration expense to the cost of comparable purchased insurance.[10]

Travel

The allowable cost of travel for transportation, lodging, meals, and incidental expenses is limited by a number of specific rules. For example, the cost of airfare is limited, with certain exceptions, to the cost of standard coach fare.[11] Lodging, meals, and incidentals are limited to government per diem amounts, which are published on a city-by-city and year-by-year basis by the General Services Administration in the Federal Travel Regulations (FTRs).[12] Although there are some exceptions to the use of the FTR per diem rates, they are very limited. There are also additional restrictions on the use of private automobiles, company-owned aircraft, and so on that frequently come into play.

Legal Fees

Legal fees connected with proceedings brought by federal, state, local, or foreign governments against the contractor for failure to comply with laws or regulations are unallowable if the contractor is found to be at fault or agrees to a settlement.[13] Otherwise, legal fees are allowable to the extent that they do not exceed a percentage set by the government. The percentage may vary with the complexity of the case but cannot exceed 80 percent of the total fees incurred.

The cost of legal services required to document and price extra work under the contract and to prepare REAs is generally considered allowable as a contract administration expense. However, the costs of legal services required to "prosecute" claims are unallowable. The line between preparing an REA and prosecution of a claim is often grey. The cases hold, as a general rule, that costs incurred prior to the government's initial rejection of a proposed settlement amount prepared by a contractor—i.e., prior to the certification of a claim by the contractor under the Contract Disputes Act (CDA)—are allowable.[14] Costs incurred after certification of a CDA claim are generally considered unallowable (with a corresponding allowance at that point of CDA interest on the claim from the date of certification until paid).[15] However, this line is not always clearly drawn. The underlying purpose of incurring the cost—that is, materially furthering the negotiation process or prosecuting a claim against the government—is the principle by which allowability of REA preparation costs is determined. The government sometimes looks to a point prior to the claim certification date and takes the position that a dispute existed at that earlier date. As a result, the contracting officer may disallow REA preparation costs for periods prior to the formal claim certification date, since the effort being put forth earlier was actually, in the contracting officer's view, relating to prosecution of a claim rather than to the furtherance of the negotiation process. Issues also arise in terms of different dates for allowability of REA preparation costs for subcontractors, which might be different from those of the prime contractor under the same analysis utilized for the prime contractor.

Other legal fees that are unallowable include fees for defense of antitrust suits, corporate organization and reorganization costs, contract award protest costs, and certain costs related to disputes with other contractors, such as under teaming agreements and joint ventures.

Volume and Other Discounts

Under FAR 31.205-5, Credits, a contractor is required to credit back to the government the proper share of any discounts or credits that it receives from vendors. In the construction industry, it is common for a contractor to receive volume discounts from vendors for purchases of a wide variety of goods and services. In a commercial environment, contractors often charge the costs of these items to the job or the overhead pool at full retail, and then credit the rebate or credit to an indirect cost pool when received. This can be problematic if the contractor is representing to the federal government that the initial retail cost charge is actual cost. Further, even if the contractor's policy is to apply the credit as part of an indirect cost pool (e.g., apply it to G&A), a government auditor may nevertheless argue that the government and the contractor are not really using a cost-based approach to the establishment of a margin (G&A and profit) rate for the project, but instead using a flat negotiated or contractually stipulated overhead or profit rate. As a result, the government sometimes maintains that it is not receiving the benefit of this credit as part of the total cost of the specific cost-justified contract or change order at issue. Contractors should disclose all such discount arrangements and, if material, apply a reasonable credit to projects through their divisional overhead rates or through other equitable mechanisms. As discussed below, for contractors subject to the CAS with disclosure requirements, this treatment should be clearly outlined in the disclosure statement.

Construction and Architect-Engineer Contract Requirements (FAR Part 36)

FAR Part 36 deals exclusively with construction and architect-engineer contracts. The topics that FAR Part 36 covers include construction performance reporting, construction specifications, government estimates, liquidated damages, contract types, inspections, and notices of awards. FAR Subpart 36.5 addresses a number of construction contract clauses, including the key clauses covering differing site conditions, permits and responsibilities, use and possession prior to completion, and accident prevention.

It should be noted that FAR Part 36 contemplates fixed-price construction contracts resulting from both sealed bids and contracting by negotiation. Fixed-price contracts may be priced on a lump-sum or unit price basis, or a combination of both methods. FAR Part 36 also permits use of cost-reimbursable contracts for construction contracting in limited circumstances.

Payment Provisions

To this point, discussion has centered on the cost aspects of construction contracting with the federal government. FAR 52.232 includes the government contract clauses dealing with payments and the procedures for billing the government for work performed and costs incurred. There are 38 separate clauses in this section of the FAR dealing with payments. Two of particular interest to construction contractors are FAR 52.232-5, Payments Under Fixed-Price Construction Contracts, and FAR 52.232-27, Prompt Payment for Construction Contracts.

Progress Payments

Progress payments for fixed-price construction contracts are in many ways similar to the typical payment process under commercial construction contracts. The contract price is partially paid over time in progress payments as the work proceeds. Payments are generally made monthly, but may be more frequent. The FAR contains a list of requirements for progress payment applications, including itemization of amounts requested, subcontractor information, retainage, reimbursement for bond premiums, and final payments.

Itemization of Amounts Requested

The progress payment application must contain an itemization of amounts requested related to the various elements of work required by the contract and covered by the payment requested. On a fixed-price contract, this generally takes the form of a schedule of values, and for a building contract might include such items as mobilization, site clearing, foundation, structural steel, and bond premiums.

Subcontractor and Additional Information
In addition to the progress of each element of work, the payment application must include a listing of the amounts included for work performed by each subcontractor, the total amount of each subcontract, the amounts previously paid to each subcontractor, and additional supporting data as may be required by the contracting officer.

The additional subcontract information is of particular importance, as the progress payment application requires certification that all payments to subcontractors and suppliers from previous pay applications have been made, and that all similar amounts in the current application are intended to be paid to the subcontractor involved. Further, if the contractor discovers that amounts previously certified in a payment request fail to conform to the specifications, terms, or conditions of the contract, the contractor is required to pay interest on that amount to the government until the contractor notifies the contracting officer that the deficiency has been corrected, or until the unearned amount is applied against a subsequent progress payment.

In addition to billing for completed work, the payment application may include billing for material delivered to the site, and preparatory work performed may also be considered in determining amounts to be included in progress payments.

Retainage
The FAR provides that the contracting officer shall authorize payment in full of a progress payment application if the contracting officer finds that satisfactory progress has been made during the period covered by the application. If satisfactory progress has not been made, the contracting officer is authorized to withhold up to 10 percent of the amount of the progress payment as retainage. Also, on completion of each separate building or other division of a contract for which the price is stated separately, payment is to be made for the completed work without retention. As such, retention has become the exception instead of the rule in federal government construction contracts.

Reimbursement for Bond Premiums
The payments clause contains a unique provision at FAR 52.232-5(g), Reimbursement for Bond Premiums. This provides that the government will reimburse the contractor for the amount of bond premiums paid for performance and payment bonds after the contractor has furnished evidence of full payment to the surety. This reimbursement is made without the retention that may apply to other contract work. While seemingly straightforward, this clause was the

subject of a notable case, *Morse Diesel International, Inc. v. United States*,[16] which held that the contractor's bond premium invoices were unpaid at the time they were presented for reimbursement and were inflated, in that the broker provided a partial rebate of the premium to the contractor. Nevertheless, the timing of the payment of the bond premium and the amount of the bond premium itself had no impact on any government's liability to pay the total value of work performed, since the contract amount that was competitively awarded did not change as a result of the requisition for and payment of the bond premium. The issue was simply as to when the surety was actually paid, and what the amount of the payment was, net of the rebate back to the contractor. Because the contractor overbilled and prematurely billed the amount of the bond premium, the contractor forfeited other claims in excess of $53 million and was subject to damages and penalties for violations of various antifraud statutes.

One obvious implication of this case is that payment applications must not contain false claims (here, that payment was made when it was not). Additionally, it highlights the importance of properly accounting for rebates. Further complications may arise when affiliated companies are involved in the brokering of the bond or reinsurance of the bond premium. This all emphasizes the overall point that the potential adverse consequences dictate that a prudent contractor will err on the side of overdisclosure and conservative billing.

Final Payment

Final payment is made after completion and acceptance of all work, presentation of a properly executed voucher, and presentation of a release of all claims against the government, other than those claims specifically excepted by the contractor.[17]

Prompt Payment for Construction Contracts

The Prompt Payment for Construction Contracts clause generally provides that the due date for progress pay applications is 14 days after the designated billing office receives a proper payment request. An interest penalty is payable by the government on payments that are not made by the due date. The interest penalty does not apply to retention, or to delays due to disagreements between the government and contractor over the payment amount. Interest is paid at the same rate used for COM under FAR Part 31 and for claims under the CDA.[18] As with many FAR provisions, the prompt payment provisions included in the prime contract are provisions that are required to flow down to subcontractors as well, requiring prime contractors to pay their subcontractors promptly after receipt of payment from the government, or to pay interest if the payment is late.

Cost Accounting Standards

Background and Purpose

The Cost Accounting Standards (CAS) are a set of 19 pronouncements issued by the Cost Accounting Standards Board that outline acceptable procedures for the measurement of costs, the assignment of costs to cost accounting periods, and the allocation of costs to cost objectives. The standards were issued during the 1960s in response to widespread criticism of practices then used by government contractors to determine the amount of costs to be billed to the government. Congress intended that the CAS would require contractors to implement a uniform set of practices for the assignment of their costs to government contracts.

The CAS regulations also require that a contractor complete and file a disclosure statement that describes in detail its cost accounting and assignment practices if it meets certain coverage thresholds.

Coverage and Exemptions

The implementing regulations provide exemptions for certain contracts from the CAS. For example, contracts with small businesses and sealed-bid contracts are exempt. Especially important to construction contractors, negotiated firm-fixed-price contracts or subcontracts awarded on the basis of adequate competition without submission of cost or pricing data are exempt. For other contracts, the regulations establish size thresholds for "CAS coverage." To be subject to CAS coverage, a contractor must be awarded at least one nonexempt contract with an award value of at least $7.5 million. Once an initial CAS-covered contract is awarded, all nonexempt contracts with award values of $650,000 or more, awarded after the date of the initial CAS-covered contract, are also CAS covered. In addition, contracts awarded to contractors whose backlog of other CAS-covered contracts is less than $50 million in award value may be subject to "modified CAS," which requires compliance with only four of the 19 standards (CAS 401, 402, 405, and 406). Determining the CAS-coverage status of a contract or contractor can be complicated. The decision chart included as Exhibit 8-4 (as obtained from the Defense Contract Audit Manual[19]) summarizes CAS coverage exemptions and thresholds.

Even if a contractor is not subject to the rules and regulations of CAS, it is important to stress that many of the CAS standards are also incorporated into the provisions of the FAR Part 31 Cost Principles; for example, as noted in the self-insurance discussion above, FAR 31.205-19 incorporates CAS 416, Accounting for Insurance Costs.

Standards

A brief description of each of the Cost Accounting Standards is provided below:

- 401, Consistency in Estimating, Accumulating, and Reporting Costs, requires that contractors use the same cost accounting practices before and after award of a contract. It requires contractors to maintain cost accounting systems that allow comparison of bid costs to incurred and billed costs.

Exhibit 8-4
CAS Coverage and Disclosure Statement Determination

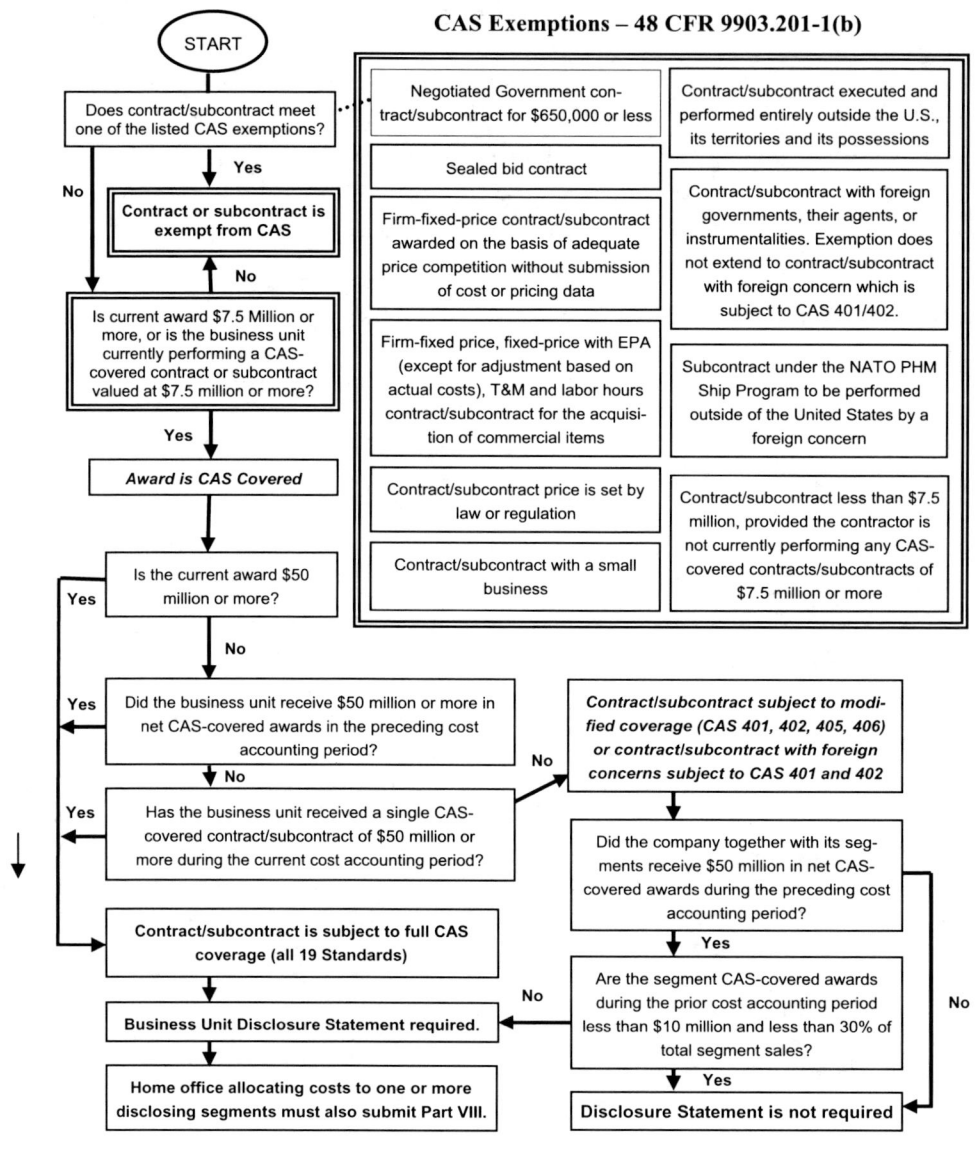

- 402, Consistency in Allocating Costs Incurred for the Same Purpose, requires contractors to classify costs as direct or indirect on a consistent basis. It prevents contractors from allocating the same type of cost as a direct cost to one contract and as an indirect cost to other contracts.
- 403, Allocation of Home Office Expenses to Segments, provides that home office costs must be allocated to operating divisions of a business entity based on a uniform equitable basis, either as direct, homogeneous, or residual costs. A three-factor formula is prescribed for residual costs.
- 404, Capitalization of Tangible Assets, provides criteria regarding which assets should be capitalized and how their capital value should be determined.
- 405, Accounting for Unallowable Costs, requires contractors to identify, segregate, and eliminate unallowable costs from government contract bids and billings.
- 406, Cost Accounting Period, requires that contractors specify a 12-month cost accounting period to be used for assignment of costs. The standard requires consistency in the application of the established cost accounting period to all contracts.
- 407, Use of Standard Costs for Direct Material and Direct Labor, provides criteria regarding the establishment and revision of standard costs, and outlines requirements for the allocation of cost variances.
- 408, Accounting for the Costs of Compensated Personal Absence, requires that the costs of vacations, holidays, sick leave, and other compensated absences be allocated on a pro rata annual basis to all cost objectives.
- 409, Depreciation of Tangible Capital Assets, outlines practices for the assignment of the cost of capital assets to cost accounting periods, and assignment within cost accounting periods to cost objectives. It specifies acceptable depreciation methods and conventions that may be used to assign capital asset costs to government contracts.
- 410, Allocation of Business Unit General Administrative Expenses to Final Cost Objectives, establishes acceptable methods for allocation of business unit general and administrative indirect costs. It clarifies acceptable G&A cost pool practices and specifies acceptable G&A cost allocation bases.
- 411, Accounting for Acquisition Costs of Material, requires written policies and practices regarding material cost charging practices. It contains specific criteria regarding acceptable inventory valuation methodologies.
- 412, Composition and Measurement of Pension Cost, provides guidance for determining and measuring the components of pension costs and the assignment of pension costs to cost accounting periods.

- 413, Adjustment and Allocation of Pension Cost, provides guidance on the measurement and allocation of actuarial gains and losses and the bases for allocation of pension costs to segments.
- 414, Cost of Money as an Element of the Cost of Facilities Capital, provides that the cost of capital committed to facilities is an element of contract cost, and details the methodology for the computation and allocation of that cost.
- 415, Accounting for the Cost of Deferred Compensation, defines when deferred compensation must be recognized, how it should be valued, and to which cost accounting periods it should be allocated.
- 416, Accounting for Insurance Costs, identifies acceptable cost accounting practices for the measurement and allocation of purchased and self-insurance costs. It provides that "projected average loss" should be the measure for each period's self-insurance charge.
- 417, Cost of Money as an Element of the Cost of Capital Assets Under Construction, provides that the cost of capital assets being constructed, fabricated, or developed should be included in cost of money calculations.
- 418, Allocation of Direct and Indirect Costs, provides criteria for the accumulation of costs into cost pools and the selection of allocation bases for those cost pools. It requires that cost pools consist of homogeneous costs and that cost pools be allocated by means of a "causal or beneficial" allocation base.
- 420, Accounting for Independent Research and Development (R&D) and Bid and Proposal (B&P) Costs, requires tracking of R&D and B&P costs by individual projects, and provides guidance on the allocation of R&D and B&P from home offices to specific business segments.

Although not all government construction contractors are subject to the CAS, essentially all government contractors are required to comply with the requirements because, as noted, many of the requirements of the CAS are incorporated into FAR Part 31.

Certification of Indirect Costs and Related Penalties

Under federal government contracting procedures, the contractor is required to provide an annual incurred cost submission (ICS) to the government. The ICS lists the contractor's actual incurred costs, and includes calculations supporting the contractor's various final indirect cost rates (e.g., labor burden, on-site and off-site overhead, and G&A rates).[20]

As part of the ICS, the contractor must certify its asserted indirect cost rates. The certification must be signed by a person at the level of vice-president or chief financial officer or higher. The required certification language is as follows:

FAR 52.242-4, Certification of Final Indirect Costs.

CERTIFICATE OF FINAL INDIRECT COSTS

This is to certify that I have reviewed this proposal to establish final indirect cost rates and to the best of my knowledge and belief:

1. All costs included in this proposal (identify proposal and date) to establish final indirect cost rates for (identify period covered by rate) are allowable in accordance with the cost principles of the Federal Acquisition Regulation (FAR) and its supplements applicable to the contracts to which the final indirect cost rates will apply; and

2. This proposal does not include any costs which are expressly unallowable under applicable cost principles of the FAR or its supplements.

If the contractor certifies an indirect cost rate and it is discovered later during audit that the rate actually included expressly unallowable costs, the FAR prescribes the following penalties:

FAR 52.242-3, Penalties for Unallowable Costs.

(a) *Definition.* "Proposal," as used in this clause means either—

(1) A final indirect cost rate proposal submitted by the contracting officer after the expiration of its fiscal year which—

(i) Relates to any payment made on the basis of billing rates; or

(ii) Will be used in negotiating the final contract price; or

(2) The final statement of costs incurred and estimated to be incurred under the incentive price provision clause (if applicable), which is used to establish the final contract price.

(b) Contractors which include unallowable indirect costs in a proposal may be subject to penalties. The penalties are prescribed in 10 U.S.C. 2324 or 41 U.S.C. 256, as applicable, which is implemented in Section 42.709 of the Federal Acquisition Regulation (FAR).

(c) The Contractor shall not include in any proposal any cost that is unallowable, as defined in Subpart 2.1 of the FAR, or an executive agency supplement to the FAR.

(d) If the Contracting Officer determines that a cost submitted by the Contractor in its proposal is expressly unallowable under a cost principle in the FAR, or an executive agency supplement to the FAR, that defines the allowability of specific selected costs, the Contractor shall be assessed a penalty equal to—

(1) The amount of the disallowed cost allocated to this contract; plus

(2) Simple interest, to be computed—

(i) On the amount the Contractor was paid (whether as a progress or billing payment) in excess of the amount to which the Contractor was entitled; and

(ii) Using the applicable rate effective for each six-month interval prescribed by the Secretary of the Treasury pursuant to Pub. L. 92-41 (85 Stat. 97).

(e) If the Contracting Officer determines that a cost submitted by the Contractor in its proposal includes a cost previously determined to be unallowable for that Contractor, then the Contractor will be assessed a penalty in an amount equal to two times the amount of the disallowed cost allocated to this contract.

(f) Determinations under paragraphs (d) and (e) of this clause are final decisions within the meaning of the Contract Dispute Act of 1978 (41 U.S.C. 601, et seq.).

(g) Pursuant to the criteria in FAR 42.709-5, the Contracting Officer may waive the penalties in paragraph (d) or (e) of this clause.

(h) Payment by the Contractor of any penalty assessed under this clause does not constitute repayment to the government of any unallowable cost which has been paid by the government to the Contractor.

As noted, the "regular" penalty to the contractor for including an unallowable cost is two times the amount improperly paid, plus interest. As the unallowable cost was previously determined to be unallowable for that contractor, the total penalty is then three times the amount in question, plus interest.

Conclusion

The FAR and the CAS are intended to bring order, integrity, and fairness to the government procurement process. While they have succeeded to some extent, they have also created a complex web of rules, disclosures, and certifications that government contractors must deal with on a daily basis, and with which even the most experienced contractors often struggle. When applied to the construction industry, the FAR and CAS present a number of unique challenges. Well-established practices and procedures for preparing commercial bids and for accounting for and charging costs to commercial contracts may nevertheless result in violations of federal laws and regulations when bidding and performing on government contracts. Any number of issues, ranging from the amount of equipment costs to include in bids to the failure to remove interest expenses or unallowable travel costs from indirect cost pools, can lead to noncompliance with these regulations. It is essential that construction contractors understand the responsibilities assigned to them by the FAR and the CAS and develop and follow business practices designed to ensure that they remain in compliance.

Notes

1. FAR 2.101.
2. FAR 15-403.4.
3. As with most areas of compliance in the federal arena, disclosure is critical to avoid or reduce exposure to defective pricing and false claim situations.
4. FAR 31.105(d)(1).
5. Daewoo Eng'g & Constr. Co. v. US, 73 Fed. Cl. 547 (2006), aff'd, 557 F.3d 1332 (Fed. Cir. 2009), Petition For Cert. Filed, 78 U.S.L.W. 3049 (June 26, 2009) (No. 09-3).
6. FAR 31.105(d)(2)(i)(C).
7. FAR 31.205-20.
8. FAR 31.105(d)(3).
9. FAR 31.205-14.
10. FAR 31.205-19(c)(3).
11. FAR 31.205-46.
12. 41 C.F.R. pts. 300–304.
13. FAR 31.205-47.
14. Bill Strong Enters., Inc. v. Shannon, 49 F.3d 1541, 1549–50 (Fed. Civ. 1995); Tecom, Inc. v. United States, 86 Fed. Cl. 437 (2009).
15. 41 U.S.C. § 211.
16. This matter resulted in three separate decisions: Morse Diesel Int'l, Inc. v. United States, 66 Fed. Cl. 788 (2005); Morse Diesel Int'l, Inc. v. United States, 74 Fed. Cl. 601 (2007); Morse Diesel Int'l, Inc. v. United States, 79 Fed. Cl. 116 (2007).
17. FAR 52.232-5(h).
18. FAR 52.232-27, Prompt Payment for Construction Contracts.
19. DCAM, Figure 8-1-1, CAS Coverage and Disclosure Statement Determination.
20. For entities new to the contracting process, the Defense Contract Audit Agency (DCAA) has issued publication DCAAP 7641.90, which provides guidance to contractors on how to properly submit an ICS.

CHAPTER 9

Pricing of Construction Claims

PAUL J. GORMAN
DANIEL KWON
PAUL A. VARELA
DAVID B. WONDERLICK

Introduction

The decision regarding how to price a construction claim presents a vexing dilemma for a contractor. The temptation to simply maximize the amount of the claim in any way possible may be difficult to resist. Contractors frequently advocate such an approach, perceiving that no matter the amount of legitimate damages, the contractor will never recover more than 50 or 60 cents on each dollar of its claim amount. Or contractors may simply desire to jump-start negotiations by signaling to the owner that they are not to be trifled with.

This approach is fraught with pitfalls, however. Under no circumstances should a contractor present a deliberately inflated claim—that is, one that includes costs to which the contractor *knows* it has no entitlement. On a public contract, such conduct exposes the contractor to harsh penalties under the federal False Claims Act,[1] Contract Disputes Act,[2] and Forfeiture of Fraudulent Claims Act,[3] and related state statutes, particularly in light of the recent focus on stricter and more frequent application of those statutes. Additionally, an attorney who approves such a claim may run afoul of Rules of Professional Conduct regarding the presentation of meritorious claims and candor toward courts and other tribunals.[4] Even stretching the boundaries of claimable costs and presenting claims that, in whole or in part, have only marginal support may prompt the government to invoke one or more of the aforementioned statutes and can lead to significant liability and/or the loss of potentially valid claims.[5]

Although these statutes do not apply to private contracts, presenting a claim inflated with easily rebutted costs still can damage the contractor's credibility before the fact finder (whether a court, arbitrator, or jury), as well as during informal negotiations, diminishing the chance of prevailing on the truly legitimate portions of the claims.

Accordingly, the most prudent claim-pricing approach requires presentation of well-supported, well-documented, and legitimate costs that readily can be tied to impacting events on the project. This concept seems simple in a vacuum, but becomes difficult when examining the record for a construction project with thousands of construction activities resulting in hundreds of thousands of accounting transactions to record the cost of material, labor, equipment, subcontractors, and overhead. Furthermore, construction projects almost universally are beset by several simultaneous issues, events, or impacts, some of which are the responsibility of the owner and others the responsibility of the contractor. Claim pricing accordingly requires that accounting systems designed to manage the construction process be adapted to document damages being asserted by the contractor.

This chapter seeks to provide a general understanding of how construction costs are incurred, what circumstances can give rise to increases in construction costs, and the various methods of quantifying the costs for claim purposes. This discussion is based on a variety of experiences in a wide variety of jurisdictions. Practical lessons that have emerged from these experiences are also discussed.

Construction Costs

The job cost report (JCR) is the most frequently utilized vehicle for accounting for individual construction projects. The JCR establishes a detailed set of cost codes for various items of work. It distinguishes between both the type of cost (labor, material, or equipment), and the various elements of the project's scopes of work. These scopes of work may represent physical areas of the project, particular trades, or some combination of these. The JCR also depicts any variances between actual and budgeted costs for these scopes of work.

The costs that appear on the JCR are typically the "direct costs." "Indirect costs," such as home office expenses, usually are not included in this report. The classification of costs as direct or indirect varies widely from company to company and even from project to project within companies. To successfully price a claim, the contractor or claim consultant must identify and distinguish between the direct and indirect costs that have increased, and these variations in categorization often present one of the more challenging aspects of this process.

Costs on construction projects generally fall into one of three categories: activity-related, time-related, or some combination of both. Activity-related costs result directly from construction efforts by craft labor (such as electricians) and the related material (such as drywall and caulk) installed as part of the project. Time-related costs are incurred based upon the duration of a project. Examples include the salaries of project managers and superintendents, which are normally fixed monthly amounts, the job site trailer and related services, rented equipment, and the cost of other support services that may be necessary for a remote project (e.g., operation of an equipment yard). The costs associated with some construction functions result in the incurrence of both activity-related and time-related costs. For example, the rental cost of equipment is a fixed, time-related cost, while the operating costs of that same equipment (e.g., fuel, repairs, maintenance) vary with the level of usage of the equipment and are therefore activity-related costs.

Segregating time-related from activity-related costs becomes critical when pricing a claim, though in no construction claim is it that simple. Claim issues may give rise to both activity-related and time-related costs. For example, overinspection by the owner could hamper both labor productivity and the project schedule, resulting in a claim for both the additional (activity-related) cost per unit of production and the (time-related) cost of extending the project.

Figure 9-1 illustrates the various types of construction costs: time-related, activity-related, and both time/activity related (combined cost).

Figure 9-1

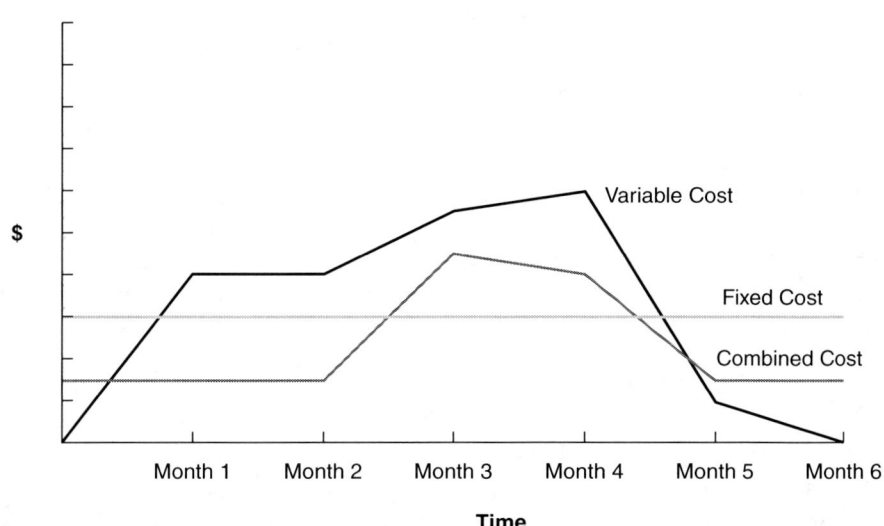

Contractual Considerations in Pricing Claims

Any party attempting to price a claim must analyze the applicable contract very early in the process to determine the appropriate manner in which to proceed. Any entitlement to damages must be grounded in the contract and its various clauses and terms. As always, legal counsel should be consulted for guidance in interpreting the language of the contract itself, relevant statutes, case law, and jurisdictional idiosyncrasies applicable to the particular situation. The pricing of the claim also may turn upon whether the contract is public or private. Although the theories and methodologies of calculating damages are similar in both the public and private sector, additional regulations (such as the Federal Acquisition Regulation) apply to public contracts. By contrast, private contracts may not offer the contractor some protections available in the public realm (such as prompt pay statutes and statutes restricting a public owner's right to limit the contractor's damages for delay).

Additionally, the pricing mechanism of the contract itself must be taken into account. There are two basic categories of contracts: fixed-price/lump-sum type contracts and cost-plus/cost-reimbursement type contracts. The category of pricing mechanism will determine, among other things, how risk is shared among the parties, what costs will be reimbursed, and how payments are made and profits earned.

The pricing of the claim also will depend heavily upon specific terms of the contract. Ideally, the contract will allocate specific risks to the party best able to manage those risks. The following sections discuss some of the key terms that should be evaluated, preferably with the assistance of competent legal counsel.

Changes Clause

Any well-drafted construction contract includes a clause addressing changes to the project. Most frequently, the Changes clause gives the owner the authority to make changes or to order the contractor to perform extra work within the contractor's general scope of work,[6] and provides the formula for compensating the contractor for such changed work. Often, the Changes clause permits a contractor to recover the actual cost of the changed or extra work, plus a predetermined percentage markup to account for the contractor's overhead and profit. Finally, the Changes clause typically requires that the parties memorialize their modification of the contract in a change order signed by both parties.

Force Account

Closely related to the Changes clause, a Force Account provision provides a way of pricing changed or extra work. Typically, such a clause provides for extra work to be accomplished on a "time and materials" basis, and will provide a mechanism for the owner and/or contractor to track the use of labor, materials, and equipment, with a specified markup applied to each cost category. The Force Account provision also provides for tracking costs on a force account basis where the owner and contractor dispute the responsibility for the performance of a certain work item.

Differing Site Conditions

The majority of construction contracts include a separate clause addressing unforeseen or differing site conditions. Some owners may attempt to place all risk of differing site conditions on the contractor. Although such clauses are often enforceable,[7] most owners fear the contingencies that such clauses would prompt contractors to include in their pricing, and therefore include some form of Differing Site Conditions provision allowing for a contract modification in the event differing site conditions are encountered.

The most commonly used clause, modeled after that utilized in federal government contracts, permits the contractor to seek extra compensation or time if it encounters conditions differing materially from either (1) the conditions positively represented by the owner in the contract documents, or (2) the conditions typically encountered in performing work of the character specified in the contract, at the location of the project. In either case, the contractor must provide notice of the allegedly differing conditions to the owner prior to disturbing those conditions. This notice requirement affords the owner the opportunity to verify that the conditions do, in fact, differ from those the contractor should have anticipated and, if so, provides an opportunity for the owner to mitigate the potential impact of the conditions on the project, in terms of both time and money.

Quantity Variations

Particularly in unit-price contracts—those where a contractor bids a specified price for each unit of work, such as a cubic yard of concrete, and is paid based on the actual quantity of such work performed or installed—a variation in the expected quantity of work to be performed can upset the pricing expectations of the contractor or the owner. Accordingly, contracts utilizing unit price items frequently include a clause permitting the contractor to seek an adjustment to the unit price where the actual quantity of a given unit of work varies beyond a certain threshold (e.g., 25 percent) from the quantity estimated and utilized in the bid form for evaluating prices. Such Variation in Estimated Quantity clauses are prevalent in state highway construction contracts, for example, and permit the contractor (or the owner) to apply for an adjustment to the unit price to more accurately reflect the actual costs of performance where the quantity of a unit price item varies significantly from the expected value.

No Damages for Delay

Frequently, owners will attempt to limit their exposure to a contractor's damages for delay (that is, extended job site and home office overhead), as these costs can be quite substantial when a significant compensable delay occurs. The typical vehicle for attempting to accomplish this is a No Damages for Delay clause. This clause typically states that, regardless of the cause of the delay, the contractor's sole remedy will be an extension of contract time, and that the contractor will not be entitled to any delay-related compensation for any delay. Although many courts will apply these clauses as written in private contracts, those same courts generally also have recognized numerous exceptions to these clauses that may nevertheless permit the contractor to recover its delay damages in certain situations.[8] What particular exceptions apply varies from jurisdiction to jurisdiction. Additionally, some states have enacted statutes expressly making such clauses ineffective in public contracts,[9] and at least two states have made such clauses unenforceable in any construction contract, public or private.[10]

Liquidated Damages

Just as extending the time of performance creates increased and extended costs for a contractor, owners also face significant added costs if completion of a project is delayed. These costs may include those incurred from the inability to use an uncompleted facility—such as the inability to generate revenue by selling energy from a newly constructed power plant—or additional interest costs resulting from extending project financing longer than planned. Because the amount of these damages, particularly for a new business, may be highly speculative, many contracts include liquidated damages for delay in completion by the contractor. A liquidated damages provision establishes a certain amount that the contractor is to pay as damages for each day the completion of the project is delayed beyond the date established for completion, assuming there is no basis for obtaining a time extension. The amount of liquidated damages should represent a reasonable attempt to estimate the actual costs the owner will incur as a result of the delay. If the liquidated damage rate does *not* represent a reasonable approximation of the costs likely to be incurred as a result of the delay, the contractor may seek to challenge the rate as an unenforceable penalty.[11] Additionally, a few states permit a contractor to challenge the application of a liquidated damages provision where the owner has not suffered any *actual* damages,[12] or where the amount of liquidated damages assessed would be grossly disproportionate to the amount of actual damages.[13]

Notice of Claim Requirements

The contract typically will also require the contractor to provide notice to the owner of any claims for which the contractor wishes to seek additional compensation or time within a certain time period following the occurrence of the issue giving rise to the claim. Often, such notice requirements are included as part of the Changes clause. The contract may specify the contents to be included in the notice, such as any projected cost or time impacts and supporting documentation detailing those impacts. The contract may also specify that the contractor waives its right to any modification to the contract if it fails to provide timely notice and supporting documentation. Although courts sometimes will recognize exceptions to the need to provide timely notice of claims (such as when the owner had actual notice of the claim[14] or the owner suffered no prejudice as a result of the contractor's failure to provide notice[15]), the best practice for the contractor is to adhere to these requirements as closely as possible.

Disputes Clause

The contract usually also specifies the method for obtaining a binding resolution of any disputes by a neutral third party. If the parties wish to have disputes addressed through litigation, the dispute resolution clause may specify the court before which any disputes may be brought, such as a court with jurisdiction over the location of the project. If the parties prefer not to utilize the court system, the contract will instead specify an alternative dispute resolution method, such as mediation or binding arbitration. The Disputes clause also may include a requirement that the law of a certain jurisdiction will govern any disputes. Both the forum (whether court or some form of alternative dispute resolution) and the law of the jurisdiction may affect a contractor's right to recover. Finally, the Disputes clause may establish a specific venue for any litigation or arbitration, with the location of the project again being the most frequently preferred venue. If another venue is selected, the enforceability of that venue selection clause may be subject to challenge, as some states have laws circumscribing the parties' ability to select the venue contractually[16] or may otherwise hold such clauses unenforceable.

The Project Record

In addition to a comprehensive review of the contract, a thorough review of the available project record should be conducted early in the claim process. This includes the amount, form (electronic versus paper), and condition of project documents available, the specifics of which are discussed in detail later in this chapter. This review also should consider the availability of project personnel to assist the claims team, as it is not unusual for key project players to shift to other projects (either with the same contractor or with a different organization) as a job nears completion. Even if the project personnel remained employed, their ongoing project commitments often hinder their availability to work with the claims team. Obviously, these personnel have critical knowledge, and will be needed to provide their understanding of the issues and events impacting the project and how costs were contemporaneously recorded. Because these personnel may be accessible only within a limited window, preliminary interviews with key project staff should be scheduled as early as possible. Understanding the limitations of the project record and availability of project personnel will both assist the claims team to formulate a plan of action and help prioritize the work to focus upon the most convincing arguments and evidence.

Pricing Methods

The method utilized in pricing the claim may affect whether a court or board will even consider the claim. Broadly, pricing methods can be divided between global (or overall) and discrete methods of presenting the claim. Global pricing methodologies include the total cost method, in which the claimant seeks recovery of all costs in excess of its estimate, and the modified total cost method, in which the contractor claims all costs in excess of its estimate, reduced for discrete costs that are the contractor's fault. Such global approaches are often easily calculated, but also are likely to meet with skepticism by a court or board.

As discussed below, tribunals will examine such claims carefully because the causal link between entitlement and damages is not straightforward. Generally, courts and boards favor and frequently will require discrete pricing methodologies because of the more readily apparent causal link between the contractor's entitlement and the contractor's damages. Discrete pricing approaches generally require more complex analysis, are data intensive, and often rely on estimates. Often, claims take a hybrid approach, pricing certain costs discretely (e.g., extended rental equipment costs) while taking a global approach to another component of the claim (such as utilizing the modified total cost method for labor productivity impacts). The following sections provide an overview of the most commonly seen approaches to claim pricing.

Discrete Pricing Methods

Specific Identification

Contemporaneous identification and tracking of all costs attributable to a specific owner-caused impact or issue is the method most preferred by courts and boards for pricing construction claims. To do this, the contractor creates a unique cost code in its JCR and notifies its field and supervisory personnel to charge all costs (labor, material, equipment, etc.) incurred as a result of a particular owner-caused action to the new cost code.

Despite such efforts to capture the costs of the impact contemporaneously, this approach often presents practical difficulties. First, on a complex construction project a single issue can cause multiple and overlapping effects or impacts, making it difficult to identify, for example, the portion of a labor effort that was inefficient on a particular day. Second, project personnel must shoulder the burden of coding the costs as they are incurred. Project personnel may view this as a nuisance, distracting them from their primary focus upon getting the job built. In a retroactive analysis, this supposed contemporaneous record of the cost effect of a particular action may not capture all the costs actually attributable to that issue. Additionally, the project staff sometimes treat these newly created job cost codes as catch-all codes for which they are not accountable, charging costs to these codes that rightfully should be attributed to base contract work.

Therefore, while establishing separate cost accounts may provide a valuable starting point for quantifying incremental costs, the contractor also should review its other cost codes carefully as a "sanity check" of the costs that have been charged to the special code. For example, additional fuel costs usually will form part of a claim for inefficient use of equipment. Frequently, however, the contractor simply will charge all fuel costs to a job site overhead account. Specific identification of the fuel costs related to the inefficient use of the equipment and charging them to a separate cost code is often difficult, if not impossible. In that case, the job record and interviews with project management may provide the only avenue for identifying the incremental costs of the impact.

Discrete Pricing of Time-Related Costs

Just as with activity-related costs, courts and boards will look more favorably upon efforts to tie time-related costs directly to owner-caused impacts. The typical costs claimed in such a situation include job site overhead, home office overhead, idle equipment, material escalation, and interest. Job site overhead costs primarily present fixed costs incurred daily as the contractor remains on the project (including the salaries of project management and supervisory personnel, the cost of trailers and utilities, etc.). If a delay to the completion of the project occurs, the contractor will incur job site overhead costs beyond those contemplated in its bid. By apportioning responsibility for the delay between the owner and contractor and calculating a daily or monthly rate of job site overhead, the contractor can discretely price its delay claim for job site overhead. Discretely priced, time-related claims are further discussed later in this chapter.

Measured Mile

In most claims for activity-related cost impacts, where the contractor contends an owner-caused event forced it to perform work less efficiently than originally planned, the claim will measure actual performance against some benchmark or baseline of what the performance "should have been," but for the impact. In most projects, accounting records reasonably can establish the actual cost of the work. The "should have been" costs are more difficult to establish. Contractors may be tempted simply to utilize the cost as estimated in their bid as this baseline figure, effectively resulting in a total cost or modified total cost claim, subject to the challenges discussed in later sections. However, the "Measured Mile" approach has emerged over the years as a preferred alternative to a total cost or modified total cost claim.

As compared with total cost and modified total cost methods, courts have received the Measured Mile approach fairly well as a method of pricing inefficiencies related to specific events on a project, and at least one state appellate court has stated explicitly that "[w]hen a contractor alleges a loss of productivity, the measured mile approach is the preferred method of computing damages."[17] This approach compares the performance in an impacted period of the project to the performance in an unimpacted period of the same project by the same contractor.[18] The performance measurement (typically man-hours per unit installed; for example, man-hours per cubic yard of fill placement) is calculated during the unimpacted or Measured Mile period, and then compared to the man-hours per unit installed during the disrupted or impacted period.

The strength of the Measured Mile approach stems from two factors. First, it links the events that occurred on the project to various productivity levels actually realized on that project. Second, establishing the baseline level using actual productivity data avoids use of the bid and consequently heads off a potential challenge to the reasonableness of the contractor's estimate. By using actual productivity data, the contractor demonstrates the productivity levels it presumably could have continued to achieve but for the owner's interference.

Global Pricing Methods

Total Cost Method

Quantification of a claim using the total cost method is relatively simple. The contractor simply subtracts the total revised contract price (i.e., the bid amount adjusted for approved change orders) from the actual costs incurred, to determine the total loss incurred on the project, and then adds to that an amount for profit on the entire contract. The contractor then claims this entire loss as damages caused by the owner. For example, assume that a contractor bid and was awarded a contract for $2 million. The contractor's bid estimate included $1,818,182 of costs, plus a 10 percent markup for overhead and profit. Further assume that there were $200,000 of approved change orders, each including a 10 percent markup for overhead and profit, executed during the project. In performing the work, the contractor's actual costs were $2.7 million. A total cost approach claim for this contract is shown in Table 9-1.

Table 9-1

Total Cost Claim	
Actual costs incurred	$2,700,000
Plus overhead and profit of 10%	270,000
Total	2,970,000
Less revised contract price	(2,200,000)
Claim Amount	$770,000

Although appealing in its simplicity, contractors presenting a total cost method claim bear a heavy burden, primarily because the total cost method attributes *all* responsibility for the cost overrun to the owner without establishing a clear linkage between the owner's alleged actions and the cost overrun. Accordingly, courts have established a four-part test that the contractor must be prepared to satisfy before it will be permitted to proceed on the basis of a total cost claim:

1. The contractor could not prove the actual, direct increased costs for which the owner is responsible;
2. The contractor submitted a reasonable bid with no material errors;

3. The actual costs were accurately recorded to the project and were reasonable; and
4. The contractor bore no responsibility for any of the cost overrun.[19]

The contractor must establish *each* element, or face potentially complete rejection of its total cost method pricing approach.[20] Because the total cost method is so removed from a specific identification of direct costs, courts and boards throughout the country regularly have derided this approach to pricing claims, identifying it as a "last resort," available only where the contractor can demonstrate the impracticability of utilizing other methods.[21] For example, if the owner introduces persuasive evidence that the contractor could have tracked its direct costs as it performed the work, a total cost method claim likely will fail.[22]

Despite the relatively infrequent ultimate success of total cost claims, the method nonetheless has its place in damage calculations. On occasion, the events that occurred on a project may align sufficiently to support the use of this method.[23] More often, the total cost method presents a good starting point for subsequent cost analysis. This high-level calculation can establish parameters for the potential claim amount, while also measuring the reasonableness of a claim amount calculated using more discrete pricing approaches. It also provides the basis for performing a modified total cost calculation as next described.

Modified Total Cost Method

The modified total cost method has evolved in response to the weaknesses of the total cost method. Under this approach, the contractor essentially anticipates some of the challenges to a total cost claim and adjusts the figures included in its calculation accordingly. For example, the contractor may adjust its bid amount upward to account for any estimating errors, or reduce its actual costs to account for problems for which the contractor has accepted responsibility. Even under the modified total cost method, however, the contractor must establish the same four elements required by courts for use of the total cost method discussed above.[24]

By demonstrating that the contractor accepts some responsibility for its overruns and that the bid, at least as adjusted, is reasonable, the contractor's claim can immediately be made more credible than a total cost claim. However, this approach still suffers from the primary flaw of the total cost method, namely, the failure to link the increased costs directly to the owner's actions, and to exclude those costs for which the contractor is responsible.[25] The contractor likely must do more than simply assign itself a percentage of fault for the cost overruns incurred and reduce its claim accordingly.[26] The more precise the calculation, in terms of isolating the cost codes actually impacted by the claim issue and those for which the contractor was responsible, the more credible the calculation of damages and the greater the possibility of its acceptance by the tribunal.

As a result, the modified total cost method may prove most useful not in presenting a global claim for *all* the costs incurred on a project, but rather when applied to a *portion* of the contract costs (such as labor overruns) and/or a specific scope of work (such as steel erection) where no other method of claim quantification is feasible.[27]

Quantum Meruit *and Jury Verdict*

Quantum meruit and "jury verdict" pricing methodologies also fall within the category of global claims, although they differ somewhat from the total cost and modified total cost methods. Recovery in *quantum meruit* is an equitable theory that may be a basis for relief to the contractor when it otherwise might not be available under the contract. For example, if a contract is declared unenforceable based on a failure of the parties to achieve a "meeting of the minds" as to the essential terms of the contract, but the contractor has already performed some work, the court may award equitable relief in the form of compensation for the reasonable value of the contractor's services.[28] The calculation of *quantum meruit* damages differs from a total cost method calculation, because the contractor recovers only the *reasonable value* of its services—that is, fair market value—which may be something different from its actual costs.[29]

To utilize a jury verdict approach, the contractor must establish that (1) it suffered a clear injury as a result of the owner's actions, and (2) presenting precise proof of damages is impossible.[30] The contractor also must supply sufficient evidence for the court, board, or jury to make a reasonable approximation of the damages.[31] Such evidence should include any proof of actual, direct costs, expert testimony on the approximation of the costs, and use of any standards recognized in the industry for the calculation of costs (such as Blue Book equipment rental rates).[32] Like the other global pricing methods, recovery under a jury verdict approach is relatively uncommon, although at least one court has suggested that it would entertain a jury verdict damages calculation more readily than a total cost method claim.[33]

Inefficiency Claims

Labor productivity is generally defined as a measure of output (units installed) compared to the input (labor hours) required to achieve that output. Productivity may be expressed as either labor hours per unit installed (which is also referred to as "labor efficiency") or units installed per labor hour. Productivity can also be expressed as a cost per unit, such as a cost per linear foot of trenching. Contractors and subcontractors typically rely upon their past experience to develop productivity rates on which they base their estimates and bids for new projects (indeed, this is often regarded by contractors as treasured, proprietary information). These estimated productivity rates not only consider the contractor's actual experience on previous projects, they also reflect the contractor's understanding of the nature of the proposed work and the conditions under which that work will be performed. When the contractor is not able to achieve its planned productivity rates (that is, it incurs more hours per unit installed than anticipated), it incurs a cost overrun, sometimes alternately referred to as an unfavorable labor variance. If the cost overrun is significant, it may warrant an investigation to understand why the overrun occurred. Potential causes of labor overruns include, but are not limited to, bid errors (inadequate estimates), poor supervision, quality of the labor force, lack of access to the work, stacking of trades, excessive changes and/or requests for information, overtime and shift work, severe weather, and errors and omissions in the drawings.

When the contractor believes it has experienced labor inefficiency or lost labor productivity as a result of acts or omissions on the part of the owner, the problem then becomes how to quantify the incremental costs resulting from that source of inefficiency. However, the very nature of labor inefficiency makes it difficult if not impossible to specifically track or price contemporaneously. This is because the inefficient component of the work does not usually represent an additional or identifiable scope of work; it simply takes more man hours to complete the work than had been estimated because of the conditions under which the work is performed.

As mentioned above, the contractor could use a total cost or modified total cost method, industry studies, or other methods of pricing claims to quantify a lost productivity claim. However, the Measured Mile approach is widely regarded as the best approach for labor inefficiency claims because it accounts for the contractor's own problems, is based on actual performance on the project at issue, and establishes a link between the cause (claim issue) and the effect (labor inefficiency).[34]

The following is an example of the process typically utilized to quantify labor inefficiency damages using the Measured Mile approach.

Sample Measured Mile Calculation

Measured Mile

The Measured Mile approach compares a contractor's actual productivity rate achieved during an unimpacted period to an actual productivity rate achieved during an impacted period.[35] Typically, a claim for inefficiency is initiated after a cost overrun is observed in a monthly JCR. Figure 9-2 illustrates a typical chart used in a measured mile calculation. In the depicted scenario, installation of 4" schedule 40 stainless steel pipe was measured and plotted against time. The planned level of productivity (approximately 0.41 labor-hours per linear foot installed) is depicted by the dashed line, and the actual level of productivity is shown as a solid line.

Figure 9-2
Plan vs. Actual Productivity of 4" Schedule 40 Stainless Steel Pipe

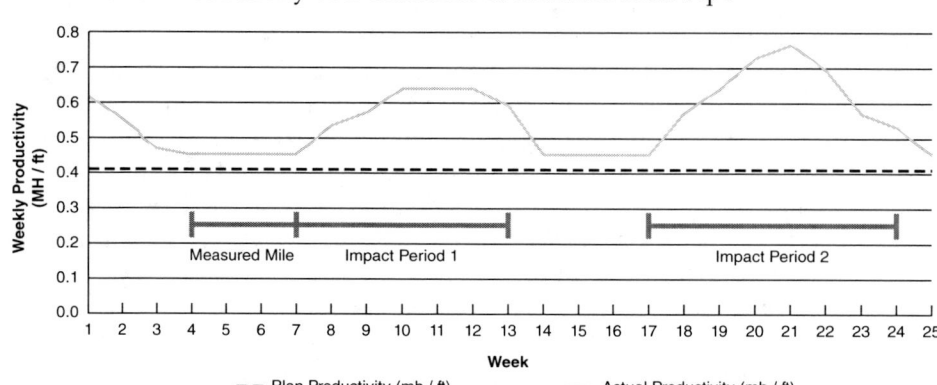

The installation work initially performed experienced a level of productivity significantly lower than planned (that is, more labor-hours per linear foot installed were required than planned). Weeks 1 through 3 show the level of productivity gradually improving. This trend may be the result of new crews coming onto the project and having to become familiar with the project work and the environment. It is common for worker productivity to improve as the workers continue to perform repetitive or similar tasks. This is often referred to as the learning-curve effect, which eventually levels off to a productivity rate that is reasonably achievable and sustainable by the crew.

According to Figure 9-2, after this initial learning curve period, the productivity rate leveled off at approximately 0.45 labor-hours per unit installed and stayed at that rate for four weeks, through week 7. During this four-week period there were no significant impacts and the performance of the activities required to install the 4" pipe during this period were determined to be a reasonably accurate representation of the tasks required to install the remaining 4" pipe scope of work. As a result, the 0.45 man-hours per linear foot provides a good Measured Mile productivity rate to use in a calculation of lost labor productivity. It is important to note that this rate is less efficient than the planned rate of approximately 0.41 labor-hours per linear foot. This may be because, for example, the contractor underestimated the hours required or because the skill level of the tradesmen is not what the contractor anticipated. Whatever the reason, 0.45 man-hours per linear foot becomes the baseline for measuring lost labor productivity during later periods, and the difference between this rate and the estimated rate is absorbed by the contractor because there is no basis to conclude that this loss has been caused by the acts or omissions of the owner.

Impact Period 1 starts in week 8 and continues through week 13. During this period the contractor's work was impacted by problems related to its pipe fabricator/supplier. The pipe was not shipping at a rate to support efficient installation, a problem for which the contractor was responsible. As a result, the productivity during Impact Period 1 averaged 0.60 labor-hours per unit installed. After week 13, the fabricator resolved its problems and adequate amounts of pipe were delivered to the site, allowing the contractor to return to its previously achieved levels of productivity.

The contractor was again impacted starting in week 18 and continuing until the last of the 4" pipe was installed, a period identified as Impact Period 2. During this period, the work of other contractors had been delayed by the owner, but the owner nevertheless directed those other contractors to achieve their original completion date. This resulted in multiple contractors working within the same restricted work space, an impact known as "stacking of trades." The stacking of trades caused the pipe installation workers to be less efficient. Average productivity during this period was 0.63 labor-hours per linear foot installed.

Table 9-2 then illustrates the calculation of cost overruns resulting from the issues associated with Impact Periods 1 and 2 in our example. The Measured Mile calculation is based on the difference between the actual labor hours incurred and the hours that should have been incurred absent the impacts. The "should have been" incurred hours are derived by multiplying the actual number of units installed by the Measured Mile productivity rate of 0.45 hours per linear foot. The difference between actual and "should have been" hours is then multiplied by the actual hourly labor rate to arrive at the additional costs incurred for each impact period.

Table 9-2

	Productivity (mh / ft)	Actual Productivity Installed (ft)	Should Have Been Hours	Actual Hours	Variance in Hours	Actual Hourly Labor Rate	$ Loss
	(A)	(B)	(C) = (B) × 0.4520 hrs	(D)	(E) = (C) − (D)	(F)	(G) = (F) × (E)
Bid	0.4103						
Measured Mile	0.4520	4,956	2,240	2,240			
Impact Period 1	0.6000	5,600	2,531	3,360	(829)	$ 40.33	$ (33,431)
Impact Period 2	0.6328	6,195	2,800	3,920	(1120)	$ 40.33	$ (45,170)
					Total		$ (78,600)

In Table 9-2, the loss incurred during Impact Period 1 ($33,431) was not caused by the owner and therefore needs to be absorbed by the contractor. The loss incurred in Impact Period 2 ($45,170), however, was caused by the owner and therefore would be appropriately included in a claim against the owner.

Challenges to Measured Mile Analyses

Challenges to a Measured Mile analysis typically fall into one of three categories. The first category relates to the nature of the work being performed, and challenges whether the work performed in the Measured Mile "unaffected" performance period is, in fact, comparable to the work done during the allegedly disrupted performance period. The work in both periods need not be identical. For example, one board accepted an electrical contractor's Measured Mile analysis comparing unimpacted electrical feeder installation to impacted branch circuit installation, based on testimony that the nature of the work was functionally similar, and that no unaffected period of branch circuit installations existed.[36] What is appropriately considered to be "comparable" only extends so far, however, and may not include comparing one contractor's impacted work to that of another, unimpacted contractor on the same project, at least absent foundational testimony establishing an appropriate degree of similarity between the two companies.[37]

Similarly, the contractor cannot attempt to reap the benefit of an unaffected performance period consisting of relatively simple work, as compared to an impacted period of more difficult and labor-intensive activities. For example, if the 4" pipe productivity rate during the Measured Mile performance period in the above example involved primarily long, straight runs of pipe in an unencumbered setting, while the impacted period involved work in a cramped above-ceiling space with turns and tight fits, using the productivity rate achieved on the simpler work to quantify the inefficiency due to the owner would be unreasonable, because one would expect less efficiency (even absent the claimed owner interferences) in the work period involving more complex tasks.[38]

The second category of challenges concerns whether the claimed Measured Mile productivity rate represents actual performance over a sufficiently long period to be representative. The actual productivity rate used should not be susceptible to the contention that it is unreasonable and was obtained only in isolated instances, and therefore is not representative of a sustainable actual productivity rate.

Third, if the owner-caused impacts are not in fact the single or at least major cause of the loss of productivity during the impacted period, the Measured Mile calculation of damages may be compromised. Courts will reject a Measured Mile analysis if the contractor fails to adjust its impact period to account for its own inefficiencies.[39] The project record should be carefully reviewed and project personnel interviewed to ensure that no other nonowner issues or events are significantly impacting the labor productivity during the disrupted period, or else adjustments should be made to account for these other issues.

Industry and Academic Studies

Use of academic studies to analyze and quantify inefficiency is generally not a preferred method. When possible, actual measurements of productivity on the construction project at issue are preferred as a means of inefficiency analysis. The primary utility of academic and industry studies lies in bolstering the credibility of a claim prepared using another method, such as a Measured Mile analysis. For example, one state court accepted an electrical contractor's use of its as-bid projection of labor efficiency as a baseline, based on the contractor's use of industry-standard manuals, coupled with its experience on similar prior projects, to formulate this projection.[40] Academic studies also may prove useful during informal negotiations, in attempting to convince an owner of the merit of a lost productivity claim.

However, for various reasons, use of actual cost records is not always possible. If the contractor has no other options, use of industry and academic studies can be helpful, although recovery on a claim based *solely* on such studies can be a daunting proposition, and few court decisions have permitted such claims. The following is a brief discussion of some of the more commonly referenced industry and academic studies.

Trade Organization Studies: Mechanical Contractors Association of America and National Electrical Contractors Association

The Mechanical Contractors Association of America (MCAA) study "Factors Affecting Productivity" is among the most commonly referenced measures of inefficiency.[41] Sixteen individual factors that may cause inefficiency are listed, including trade stacking, overtime, errors and omissions, and learning curve. Each factor is assigned a different percentage of efficiency loss depending on whether the condition is judged to be minor, average, or severe. The efficiency loss percentages range from 5 percent to 50 percent, depending on the factor and its severity. According to the study, "the values are a percentage to add onto labor costs, of change and in some cases, original contract hours."[42] The factors are presented with a disclaimer warning against their use as a general proposition absent more specific information and assessment.[43] Table 9-3 lists some of the inefficiency factors for each of the scenarios.

Table 9-3

Factor	Minor	Average	Severe
Stacking of Trades	10%	20%	30%
Morale and Attitude	5%	15%	30%
Reassignment of Manpower	5%	10%	15%
Crew Size Inefficiency	10%	20%	30%
Concurrent Operations	5%	15%	25%
Dilution of Supervision	10%	15%	25%
Learning Curve	5%	15%	30%

No guidelines are provided in the MCAA study to help the user determine what distinguishes a minor impact from an average or severe impact. The source of data for the factors is also unclear. In addition, many projects suffer impacts from some combination of these factors, but no guidance is provided as to how to combine the effects of multiple factors. Despite these open questions, the MCAA factors are widely encountered in the industry due to their simplicity of application.

The National Electrical Contractors Association (NECA) published a study as early as 1969 titled "Time and Productivity in Electrical Construction," based on responses to a four-question survey that NECA sent to its membership. The results indicated a drop in productivity as higher levels of sporadic overtime were utilized, with differing levels of impact depending on whether the overtime was sporadic by week or by day. The study suffers from significant weaknesses, however, because of a lack of information on the survey, including the percentage of surveys returned and the fact that the conclusions appear to be based upon the survey respondents' own judgments rather than on any empirical data or independent analysis.

Overtime-Related Inefficiency Studies: Army Corps of Engineers and Business Roundtable

Two fairly well-known studies have attempted to assess the impact of sustained overtime upon a contractor's productivity. The Army Corps of Engineers (COE) released its "Modification Impact Evaluation Guide" in 1979, while The Business Roundtable published a report in 1980 titled "Scheduled Overtime Effect on Construction Projects." The COE Guide depicts the relationship between productivity and various amounts of overtime over a four-week period, and the Business Roundtable data illustrates a relationship between the number of weeks worked at 50 or 60 hours worked per week and the resulting level of productivity, compared against a baseline starting point. Both studies show a modest (approximately 5 to 10 percent) decrease in productivity in the first week to two weeks of overtime work, with productivity continuing to decrease thereafter, and precipitously so in situations where both longer hours and additional days are being worked for an extended period.

Neither study provides a description of the data source for the relationships presented, making the range of applicability of the data unknowable. The COE Guide also states, "These data are included merely as information on trends rather than firm rules which might apply to any project,"[44] and the Business Roundtable study notes that the exhibits reflect the averages of many observations, and that tranquil labor relations and excellent field management and direction were experienced on the projects studied. Still, the Court of Federal Claims has found the Business Roundtable study "credible and relevant" in accepting it as support for a lost productivity claim in at least one case.[45] The COE Guide also may prove useful in negotiating lost productivity claims on federal government contracts, particularly those administered by the Army Corps of Engineers.

Change Order-Related Inefficiency Studies: Leonard and Ibbs

Charles Leonard wrote a master's degree thesis in 1988 titled "The Effects of Change Orders on Productivity" that attempted to investigate the link between change orders and productivity.[46] The study considered the effect of the size, frequency, and percentage of overall change order hours on productivity. In general, Leonard noted a correlation between productivity and the overall change order hours as a percentage of total contract hours. He also noted that this correlation seemed to exist only when the overall percentage of change hours to total contract hours exceeded 10 percent.

Criticisms of Leonard's study include the limited nature of the dataset (limited to 57 mostly Canadian projects with an average project size of $4 million) and the inclusion only of projects that had progressed to a dispute. Leonard's curves also do not appear to show reasonable data in situations where there are no change orders. Leonard also combined data from different groups in his data analysis, without providing any cause or justification for doing so. As a result, the Leonard study has not gained wide acceptance, and at least one board flatly has rejected its application.[47]

More recently, William Ibbs has developed similar metrics based on an expanded dataset of 170 projects with a median value of $44 million.[48] Ibbs states that his data is not limited to projects in the disputes phase, and that it includes both public and private projects. Ibbs's conclusions are similar to Leonard's. Because Ibbs's study is relatively new, no court or board has yet had an opportunity to evaluate his study and analyze whether it addressed the flaws of the Leonard study sufficiently to merit judicial consideration. As a result, its usefulness in a trial setting is uncertain. Unless it becomes widely accepted, use of Ibbs's study likely will face many of the same challenges as the Leonard study.

Delay Claims

If the work on a project extends longer than the contractor anticipated at the time of bid, the contractor will continue to incur various time-related costs for a longer period than planned. The amount of damages the contractor suffers will depend upon the cumulative duration of the project delay(s). Accordingly, delay damages frequently are computed by multiplying a daily rate of compensable costs by the number of days of project delay experienced. Determining the length of the delay typically presents the first step in pricing a claim for delay damages. This analysis usually will require the assistance of an expert/consultant to evaluate the as-planned schedule, review the project records (daily reports, diaries, meeting minutes, etc.), develop an as-built schedule depicting the contractor's actual performance on the project, compare the as-planned schedule to the as-built schedule to identify any delays and their duration, and apportion responsibility for these delays between the owner and the contractor.

Delays fall into three general categories: compensable delays, excusable delays, and nonexcusable/noncompensable delays. The General Services Administration Board of Contract Appeals succinctly outlined the distinctions between these types of delays in a 1987 opinion:

> All compensable delays are excusable, but not all excusable delays are compensable. If a delay is excusable no liquidated damages can attach to it. Such delays are usually caused by third parties or circumstances extraneous to the contract. No blame for them attaches to either the Government or the contractor. Both compensable and non-compensable delays involve the issue of fault. If the delay is the Government's fault it is compensable to the contractor. If it is the contractor's fault it is non-compensable, i.e., the contractor has to absorb the delay costs. Similarly, if the delay is the contractor's fault it cannot be excusable so as to vitiate liquidated damages.[49]

There are several types of costs a contractor may seek to recover if it proves a compensable delay, that is, a delay caused solely by the actions of the owner. These include the costs discussed in the following sections.

Extended Field Overhead

Contractors typically charge field office overhead (also referred to as job site overhead or general conditions) as a direct cost of the contract in the JCR. For example, assume the contractor places an office trailer on the job site shortly after receiving notice to proceed, and removes it shortly after substantial completion of the work. In pricing a claim for job site overhead, the rental cost of the trailer, the related utilities such as electricity, heat, phone, Internet access, and office costs (supplies, etc.) would all form part of the field office overhead. Assuming the trailer is fully staffed during the delays, the employment costs of supervisory and administrative personnel who staff the trailer also typically are part of the time-related costs included in field overhead. Even though these costs are time-related, they nevertheless typically fluctuate over the course of the project, particularly the personnel expenses. The field overhead expense tends to ramp up from project start-up, maintain a relatively constant level once the project is fully underway, and then ramp down as the project approaches completion.

Frequently a delay claim is priced without accounting for the "ramp up" and "ramp down" effects. The job site overhead costs are lumped into a single pool and presumed to be incurred at a steady rate over the entire duration of the contract. In pricing a claim for field office overhead, this cost pool is then divided by the days of total performance of the project to establish a daily rate of job site overhead costs. In determining the cost of the delay, the contractor then multiplies this daily rate by the number of compensable days of delay sought.[50] This approach of establishing a constant field overhead rate for the entire project is viewed as relatively conservative.

On some projects, however, segregating the overhead costs into two or more distinct periods may be appropriate. For example, this might be the case in a commercial construction project neatly divided between base building and tenant build-out portions, each of which had different management and cost structures. There, the contractor would establish daily rates for each component of the project, to be multiplied by the number of days of delay associated with each component.

When the contractor believes that it can specifically identify the costs for the delayed period, a more aggressive approach may be taken whereby the field overhead cost actually incurred for that particular period is claimed, in lieu of using a daily rate calculation. This approach often increases the amount claimed for field overhead. This approach may be vulnerable to challenge based on when the delay occurred, however (at the beginning, middle, or end of the project). Also, the timing of the recording of costs and accrual accounting issues will often come into play, in attempting to identify accurately the costs actually incurred or accrued during the delay period.

Finally, there are almost always "one-off" and activity-related costs that must be removed from the field overhead cost pool before calculating the daily rate. For example, a delay likely will not alter the basic cost of bringing the trailer to the job site and setting it up. That cost is simply not affected by the delay; therefore, leaving that cost in the pool would produce an overstated daily rate of ongoing, time-related field overhead costs. Additionally, if some added field overhead costs have been recovered as part of change orders, this must be taken into account and the claim adjusted accordingly.

Home Office Overhead

The ordinary costs necessary to maintain a construction business make up the contractor's home office overhead. The contractor will normally incur these costs at a regional, division, or headquarters office, as opposed to a project site. Ordinarily, the contractor charges these costs to general ledger accounts. Financial statements generally reflect these costs under the category of general and administrative costs. Examples include salaried employees not located at any project (accounting, receptionist, executives not chargeable to a project), and office rent and utilities. These costs are generally a function of time and cannot be attributed directly to any single project.

Under normal circumstances, a contractor "recovers" its home office overhead by successfully completing projects with a gross margin (contract revenues less direct costs) sufficient to pay these home office costs. If the contractor's gross margin cannot cover these costs, then the contractor records a net loss for the period.

When a project is delayed beyond the contractual completion date, the contractor's home office must support that project for a longer period than planned. Contractors often argue that while a project is delayed, that contract produces an inadequate share of gross margin, resulting in "unabsorbed" home office overhead during the delay period, and/or the home office must support the delayed project for a longer period of time, resulting in "extended" home office overhead for the delay period beyond planned completion.[51] Unabsorbed or extended overhead often constitutes a sizable portion of a contractor's delay claim.

The Eichleay Method

On federal government contracts, federal courts and boards of contract appeals will accept only one method of pricing a claim for unabsorbed or extended home office overhead—the Eichleay method, a formula named after a 1960 Armed Services Board of Contract Appeals decision.[52] The formula provides a three-step calculation of extended home office overhead. First, the contractor determines the amount of its total home office overhead that is attributable to the contract during the actual performance period of the contract, with the appropriate share determined as the subject contract's billings divided by the company's total billings. This allocation of home office costs is then divided by the number of days of performance to establish a daily rate of home office overhead, similar to the calculation of job site overhead previously described. In the third step, the daily rate so determined for the contract performance period is multiplied by the compensable days of delay that were experienced. Table 9-4 illustrates this formula.

Table 9-4

Calculation of Home Office Overhead Using the Eichleay Formula				
Contract amount	=	$2,500,000		
Period of delay	=	30 days		
Contract period (including delay)	=	395 days		
Revenues during contract period	=	$15,000,000		
Overhead during contract period	=	$2,000,000		
1. Contract Amount Revenue during contract period	=	$ 2,500,000 $ 15,000,000	=	16.7%
2. 16.7% × Overhead during contract period	=	16.7% × $2,000,000	=	$ 333,333
3. Overhead per day	=	$ 333,333 395 days	=	$843.88
4. 30 days of delay ×$ 843.88/day	=	$25,316.40	=	**Unabsorbed overhead**

The U.S. Court of Appeals for the Federal Circuit has held that the Eichleay formula provides the exclusive method of calculating a claim for unabsorbed home office overhead on a federal government construction contract.[53]

Numerous state courts also have recognized the use of the Eichleay formula.[54] Several states, however, reject the Eichleay formula as a calculation of damages as inherently too speculative, unless the contractor can establish a causal link between the delay and specific home office activities.[55]

To prove entitlement to utilize the formula, a contractor must prove

1. A government-caused delay that was not concurrent with any contractor-caused delay;
2. An extension of the original contract time for performance; and
3. That the delay placed the contractor on "standby."[56]

If the contractor proves these three elements, the government still can rebut the contractor's prima facie case by offering evidence that it was not impractical for the contractor to take on other work to "absorb" some of its home office overhead and thereby mitigate its damages.[57] If the government does provide such evidence, the burden of persuasion shifts to the contractor to establish that it was, in fact, impractical to acquire other work.[58] Although some decisions suggested that the contractor must be *completely* unable to find replacement work, the Federal Circuit has clarified this issue, and the law currently requires that assuming additional work must only be *impractical*.[59]

Numerous court decisions have focused on the third element—when the contractor is considered to be on "standby."[60] In its most recent explanation of the Eichleay formula, the Federal Circuit clarified that "standby" involves the effective suspension of all or most work for an indefinite duration, at the conclusion of which the contractor is expected to resume work immediately.[61] The court then set forth an "exacting" set of questions to be considered by future tribunals evaluating a contractor's request to compute a home office overhead claim according to the Eichleay formula:

> (1) was there a government-caused delay that was not concurrent with another delay caused by some other source; (2) did the contractor demonstrate that it incurred additional overhead (i.e., was the original time frame for completion extended or did the contractor satisfy the *Interstate* three-part test); (3) did the government [contracting officer] issue a suspension or other order expressly putting the contractor on standby; (4) if not, can the contractor prove there was a delay of indefinite duration during which it could not bill substantial amounts of work on the contract and at the end of which it was required to be able to return to work on the contract at full speed and immediately; (5) can the government satisfy its burden of production showing that it was not impractical for the contractor to take on replacement work (i.e., a new contract) and thereby mitigate its damages; and (6) if the government meets its burden of production, can the contractor satisfy its burden of persuasion that it was impractical for it to obtain sufficient replacement work.[62]

In sum, although the Federal Circuit continually has reaffirmed the validity of the Eichleay formula as a general proposition, its decision in *P.J. Dick* appears to limit its application to a quite narrow set of circumstances.

Challenges to Home Office Overhead Costs

As just discussed, most debate over the use of the Eichleay formula focuses upon whether the conditions exist to justify its application. However, it is also important to consider the appropriateness of the data utilized in the calculation. For example, on federal contracts the home office overhead pool must be reviewed to eliminate costs that are not allowable, not reasonable, or not allocable to the project, as defined in the Federal Acquisition Regulation (FAR) section 31.201.[63] The FAR defines allowable costs, in part, as follows:

> A cost is allowable only when the cost complies with all of the following requirements:
>
> a. Reasonableness.
> b. Allocability.
> c. Standards promulgated by the CAS [Cost Accounting Standards] Board, if applicable, otherwise, generally accepted accounting principles and practices appropriate to the circumstances.
> d. Terms of the contract.
> e. Any limitations set forth in this subpart.[64]

Costs that are specifically not allowed to be recovered under federal contracts are identified in FAR 31.205 and include, but are not limited to, bad debts, contributions or donations, entertainment costs, interest on borrowings, losses on other contracts, and certain public relations and advertising costs.[65] Although these costs are typically treated as part of home office overhead, on government contracts they must be removed from the overhead pool utilized in the Eichleay calculation.

In pertinent part, the FAR defines "reasonable" costs as follows: "A cost is reasonable if, in its nature and amount, it does not exceed that which would be incurred by a prudent person in the conduct of a competitive business."[66] The government on this basis may challenge overhead costs it believes to be excessive, such as an extravagant benefits package provided to the owner and/or other staff members.

Finally, the FAR defines "allocable" costs as follows:

> A cost is allocable if it is assignable or chargeable to one or more cost objectives on the basis of relative benefits received or other equitable relationship. Subject to the foregoing, a cost is allocable to a Government contract if it—
>
> a. Is incurred specifically for the contract;
> b. Benefits both the contract and other work, and can be distributed to them in reasonable proportion to the benefits received; or

c. Is necessary to the overall operation of the business, although a direct relationship to any particular cost objective cannot be shown.[67]

In view of this definition, costs incurred by a particular division of a diversified company may need to be excluded from the Eichleay calculation even though the division overhead is a proper part of home office overhead for other purposes. For example, overhead costs associated only with a product research and development division that supports specific cost objectives other than the construction project for which the claim is being prepared should be excluded from the calculation.

In addition to considering just what costs should be included in the home office cost pool used in the Eichleay calculation, the time period for which the cost and billing data is utilized is also important. Home office overhead costs and company billings for the entire contract performance period should be utilized, not just the original contract period or the extended period. Similarly, the project contract amount used in the calculation should be the adjusted contract value, including approved change orders, not the original contract value. The U.S. Court of Federal Claims has ruled that even where a contractor has established entitlement to unabsorbed overhead, if the Eichleay formula is not utilized correctly, the court cannot award damages. In *Orlosky, Inc. v. United States*, the court denied recovery because in its application of the Eichleay formula, the contractor used cost and revenues for the period of April 1, 1996, to March 30, 1997, while the actual contract performance period was from November 23, 1995, to February 4, 1997.[68] In addition, the court said that it would not recalculate the damages even if the contractor had provided the raw data to do so.[69]

Under both federal and private contracts, the question of whether the home office overhead pool should consist only of fixed costs has been debated. The Veterans Administration Board of Contract Appeals addressed this issue in a 1980 case, stating that

> The Eichleay formula, in determining an average daily rate of home office expense, uses the total home office expense incurred during the period of performance. This necessarily includes some costs which may vary during such period. Even those costs which the government defines as "fixed" costs may vary. For example, the rent for office space may increase or decrease, and utility bills certainly vary, but these are, without question, allocable overhead items. It is generally accepted that the Eichleay formula is used primarily for construction contracts, where there is an assumption that almost all overhead is fixed rather than variable, but this is not to say that overhead costs which do not remain constant are to be excluded solely on this basis.[70]

The most widely used standard form construction contract in the private sector, the American Institute of Architects (AIA) Document A-201, General Conditions of the Contract for Construction, effectively precludes use of the Eichleay formula or recovery of extended or unabsorbed home office overhead. This is because the AIA General Conditions preclude recovery of consequential damages by either party, and specifically exclude "damages incurred by the contractor for principal office expenses."[71]

Acceleration Costs

Types of Acceleration Costs

An acceleration claim is in many respects the flip side of a delay claim. If a delay on the project occurs, the contractor may incur additional costs not as a result of extended performance, but rather by attempting to recover the lost time and still complete the project within the required time frame.[72] Such acceleration efforts to overcome a delay may include working overtime, adding a second or third daily shift, or bringing additional crews and/or equipment to the site. As a result of such efforts, the contractor typically will incur some combination of added direct and indirect costs. The direct costs for additional labor, equipment, and supervision usually will be relatively easy to determine. These costs also include the "premium" time a contractor must pay its workers for working overtime above and beyond their ordinary hourly rate, usually either time-and-a-half or double time, depending on the number of hours of overtime worked and when the overtime was worked.

The contractor also is likely to incur a harder to determine added cost, usually in the form of lost efficiency. The addition of crews and equipment may result in stacking of trades and crowded work areas, both of which may hamper the contractor's progress. Labor productivity also may decline as a result of workers consistently exceeding a 40-hour work week, and the fact that a second or third shift—particularly those working overnight—likely will not achieve the same level of performance as their daytime counterparts. The Business Roundtable study discussed previously attempts to quantify the effects on production of sustained overtime efforts as may be involved in an acceleration plan. A Measured Mile analysis of the contractor's production before and after the shift to a 50- or 60-hour work week also may prove effective in quantifying this inefficiency.

Entitlement to Recover for Acceleration

Voluntary acceleration is a contractor's own election to speed up in order to recover delays the contractor itself has caused, likely based on an economic calculus of the cost of accelerating versus the cost of completing late and paying liquidated damages. Voluntary acceleration is not compensable. However, the contractor can recover if the owner issues an express direction to accelerate in order to get the project completed earlier than required.[73]

The gray area is where the contractor believes it has suffered an excusable delay, and thus is due a time extension, but the owner disagrees. In that situation, the owner may make clear that it intends to hold the contractor to the original completion date despite the disputed cause of delay, leading to a claim for "constructive acceleration" when the contractor accelerates as a result of this threat.[74] To recover in such circumstances, the Federal Circuit has held that a contractor must prove

1. The existence of an excusable delay;
2. That the contractor made a timely and sufficient request for an extension of the schedule;
3. The failure or refusal of the owner to grant the requested extension of time;
4. That the owner insisted on completion of the contract within a period shorter than the period to which the contractor would be entitled by taking account of the period of excusable delay, after which the contractor notified the owner that it regarded the alleged order to accelerate as a constructive change in the contract; and
5. That the contractor was required to expend extra resources to compensate for the lost time and remain on schedule.[75]

In *Fraser*, the court stated that these elements had been "compressed" into three essential elements in prior holdings.[76] In particular, the fourth element—notice to the owner that the contractor considered the alleged order to accelerate a constructive change—was not previously articulated, and may not be given significance by later courts because it played no part in the Federal Circuit's decision.

Nonetheless, federal courts have applied this requirement in subsequent cases,[77] although finding it satisfied with relatively insubstantial evidence. In *Ace Constructors*, for example, the Court of Federal Claims appeared to find the contractor's continuous use of overtime to recover time lost as a result of differing site conditions, and notification to the government that the project was 60 days behind schedule, sufficient to comply with this requirement, despite not referencing any communication from the contractor to the owner that explicitly mentioned a "constructive change."[78]

Additionally, other courts have not mentioned any necessity of notice to the government of the contractor's intent to accelerate,[79] and the contractor may likely avoid any such requirement under a federal contract by proving that any lack of such notice did not prejudice the government.[80] In sum, while the specific requirements for constructive acceleration vary somewhat from one jurisdiction to another, the more closely the contractor's proof conforms to the above list of elements, the greater likelihood it has of succeeding on its acceleration claim.

Change Order Claims

Change Order Pricing Generally—Direct Costs and Markup

The first step in pricing a change order is to establish that the work in question actually represents additional work; that is, work that is now required to complete the project but was not included in the original scope of work. Once that is established, pricing the change order work includes identifying the direct and indirect costs of the added work, to which a markup for overhead and profit is then added. Direct and indirect costs include the cost of labor, materials, equipment, subcontractors, and site overhead. The markup is intended to provide an allowance for home office overhead and profit. Frequently, the contract will spell out the allowable costs and markup percentage to be used in pricing of change orders.

Change orders are typically tracked on a project document referred to as a change order log, which lists all the approved, pending, and denied change orders. The direct costs included in approved change orders should be identified and used to update the budgeted costs in the JCR.

Cumulative Impact of Multiple Changes

Change order pricing becomes much more difficult when a multitude of changes on a project causes disruption or inefficiency in the performance of the work that is not impacted directly by the changes. Such a situation may lead the contractor to present a "cumulative impact" claim, also sometimes referred to as "ripple effect."[81] Claims of this type are generally quite difficult to prove, and frequently will be attacked on the ground that a bilateral contract modification previously executed to address the direct cost of the change also encompassed (or released) all later-claimed cumulative impact costs.[82] The contractor may need to demonstrate that it expressly reserved its rights to make a cumulative impact claim,[83] or that the specific circumstances of the execution of the earlier modification made it clear that the contractor did not intend to release such claims.[84]

If the contractor successfully establishes its right to present a cumulative impact claim, the inherently retrospective nature of this type of claim may relax somewhat the level of specificity in establishing cause and effect that is necessary to prove entitlement.[85] Still, the sheer number of changes, standing alone, will not suffice to prove that those changes impacted unchanged work.[86] To prove the amount (quantum) of its damages, the contractor must introduce "testimony and contemporaneous documents evidencing the type and extent of disruption to the work, and a showing that the disruption resulted from [the owner's] actions."[87] The contractor also must take care to segregate those inefficiencies (and related costs) for which it alone is responsible.[88] Even if it cannot pin down the *precise* cost of the cumulative impact of changes, however, the contractor may be able to recover on a jury verdict theory if it presents adequate evidence that it in fact suffered a "ripple effect" impact and introduces sufficient documentation for the fact finder to effectively quantify these costs.[89]

Equipment Cost Claims

Pricing claims for equipment costs can be inherently difficult because they frequently include a hybrid of time- and activity-related cost components. Time-related equipment costs are fixed, consisting of either a rental rate (for rented items) or the ownership costs (for the contractor's own equipment). Activity-related costs for equipment include fuel, filters, oil, and grease (FOG), tires and tracks, and minor repairs. The time- and activity-related components of an equipment cost claim should be segregated when pricing the claim. The next sections primarily address the time-related costs.

Equipment Rental Costs

Contractors often rent a significant portion of the construction equipment they utilize in constructing a project. Equipment rental agreements typically provide for a fixed monthly charge, with a surcharge applied if equipment usage exceeds a certain threshold of hours used in the given month. Because most project delays usually involve some degree of idled equipment, the contractor can use a pool approach to determine the monthly or daily rental cost for its on-site equipment, similar to the manner in which extended job site overhead is calculated. However, if additional operating hours caused the contractor to incur equipment surcharges—in an acceleration situation, for example—those added costs can be included as part of the relevant activity-related claim.

Equipment Ownership Costs

For owned equipment, contractors incur equipment ownership costs regardless of whether the equipment is in use or idle. These ownership costs include depreciation, cost of facilities capital (defined below), major repairs and overhauls, and insurance. One accounting text defines depreciation as "the process of allocating the cost of property plant and equipment as an expense in a systematic and rational manner to those periods expected to benefit from the use of an asset."[90] The allocation of depreciation costs involves the use of estimates, as the actual cost of depreciation often cannot be determined until the particular piece of equipment is sold, scrapped, or destroyed. At that time the "true depreciation cost" can be calculated by subtracting the sale or salvage value from the original cost, augmented by any capital improvements made to the equipment during its lifetime.

Equipment ownership requires significant capital outlay by the contractor, usually funded by some mix of debt and equity, but this varies by contractor. In federal government contracts, the concept of the cost of facilities capital allows contractors to measure this investment and obtain a measure of compensation for it.[91] Although the applicable federal regulations do not apply in the case of state government or private sector contracts, a contractor seeking to recover these costs may attempt to apply the federal definition by analogy.

Additionally, construction companies sometimes establish a separate, affiliated business entity to maintain ownership of its equipment, and this affiliate then rents the equipment to individual projects. Each project is thereby charged an internal rate for the equipment, similar to a third-party rental cost, and derived, with varied levels of precision, from an analysis of the cost of owning it. Care should be taken in utilizing such internal charge rates in a claim, as they are frequently challenged. Before they are used, they should be reviewed carefully to determine if their derivation can be established clearly, if they are clearly tied to the recoupment of the actual costs of the equipment involved, and if they are comparable to the established market rental rate for similar equipment.

Equipment Rate Manuals

Because of the difficulty in determining the true cost of equipment usage, several industry rate manuals are published to provide guidelines for pricing equipment costs.[92] These manuals are compiled from large databases of information on the costs of owned and rented equipment, and also sometimes identify rates for operating costs under a variety of conditions. Often, a construction contract will refer explicitly to one of these manuals as the designated source for use in tracking or pricing equipment costs in claims for changed work (e.g., work done under force account).

Other Claim Elements

In addition to the costs detailed above, contractors typically include claim components for markup (overhead and profit), bond costs, and interest. The contractor may include a percentage markup in its claim to account for profit on the claimed work, as well as overhead. This percentage may be obtained from any number of sources. Sometimes it is the contractor's as-bid margin for the project, or a historical average for either the contractor or the industry on similar projects. The allowable percentage markup also may be specified expressly in the Changes clause of the contract. In claiming markup, however, contractors must take care to distinguish between the portion that is intended to cover home office overhead and the portion that represents profit alone, to avoid being accused of seeking "double recovery" if the contractor also is presenting a claim for time-related home office overhead.

When the construction contract requires the contractor to provide performance and payment bonds from recognized surety companies, the contractor may incur additional bond premium costs as a result of change orders or other owner actions. The premium paid for the bond is usually based on a percentage of the contract price, and will be adjusted periodically if the value of the contract changes. The contractor may appropriately add an amount to the claim to reflect the additional premium it will have to pay if the contract value is revised upward by the amount of the claim. Although disputes over the inclusion of bond premiums are fairly rare, care must be taken, especially in public contracts, to charge only the actual amount paid for the bond, net of any incentive or rebate from the bonding company, as a failure to account properly for this has resulted in a false claim charge in a widely noted case.[93]

Finally, most contractor claims include some amount for interest. Interest *on* a claim must be distinguished from interest *in* a claim. Interest *on* a claim is simply interest running from the time the contractor files the claim to the time it is paid, also referred to as prejudgment or preaward interest. The applicable interest rate may be established by either the contract or a statute. Interest *in* a claim refers to interest included in the claim amount, such as for borrowings the contractor was forced to make to finance extra work in the absence of a change order. This is generally more difficult to recover. For example, a contractor cannot recover interest on borrowings under federal government contracts.[94] To recover such interest costs, contractors must typically tie specific debt (and related interest) directly to owner-caused events.[95]

Documents Required to Support Claimed Costs

Assembling documentation to support the actual costs incurred and the calculation of damages for a claim is an essential part of calculating construction damages. However, the documents are generally not sufficient in themselves to tell the entire story needed to formulate and support the claim. Examination of the documents will typically lead to questions that are best answered by project staff. As a result, it is important to gather key documentation as quickly as possible, in order to be able to review it and identify the appropriate project staff to be interviewed to assist in understanding what happened during the project and the effect that had on the costs incurred by the contractor. The following discussion covers what are typically considered key documents and their relevance to a claim.

Cost Documents

Original Bid Estimate

The original bid estimate, including all detailed take-off sheets and data, should provide the best record of the assumptions and plans with which the contractor started the project. When examining these documents, some questions to investigate include the following:

- Was the bid reasonable? How does it compare to the estimates or bids submitted by other contractors regarding quantities and pricing? Does the bid include all scopes of work reflected in the contract drawings and specifications? If not, this could represent a bid error, and any claim amount may need to be adjusted by at least the amount of the bid error.
- What productivity rates were used to develop the bid and what was the source of those rates? What assumptions, if any, were used to adjust the estimated productivity rates based on conditions under which the work would be performed (e.g., location of the work, availability of skilled labor, union versus nonunion labor)?
- Was overtime included in the bid, and to what extent?
- What general conditions costs were included in the bid and for what period of time?

Change Orders

The change orders issued on a project address changes to the scope of work, both increases and decreases, and changes to the project duration (usually extensions to the project completion date). If a change order log exists that includes all of the change orders related to the project, whether approved, pending, or denied, this greatly eases the task of assessing the existing change orders. Recall that change orders not only add or subtract scope of work, but may also disrupt the prosecution of unchanged contract work as a result of the order of magnitude and frequency of the changes, as well as their timing relative to the progress of the project.

Job Cost Reports

The JCR, as discussed earlier, provides a contemporaneous snapshot of the financial status of the project. Typically issued monthly, it provides the planned or budgeted costs, the actual cost to date, and the projected cost at completion. Most important, it should also show variances between the earned amount (i.e., the budgeted amount adjusted for actual work performed to date) and the actual to date or forecasted total. Examination of these variances can provide project management with an early warning sign of problems while the project is ongoing. Some typical questions regarding JCRs include the following:

- Is the bid accurately reflected in the JCR? That is, has the total estimated direct cost by category (labor, equipment, etc.) that was included in the bid been transferred to the budget in the JCR? If not, artificial negative variances may be reported in the JCR.
- Have approved change orders properly been incorporated into the JCR by adjusting the budgeted amount by the estimated cost of each change?
- Are actual expenditures accurately reflected in the JCR? What procedures are in place to ensure the accuracy of the actual costs and other relevant data included in the JCR?
- How often are the JCRs issued and who receives them?

Detailed Transaction Reports

Detailed transaction reports are support schedules or cost ledgers that identify each individual transaction within each individual cost code in the JCR. Because these reports capture all project transactions, they are typically very lengthy. A review of the detailed transaction report can help provide confidence that the actual cost data summarized in the JCR is accurate and reliable. This report is also useful when analyzing time-related costs to identify both "one-off" and fixed costs in order to develop a daily field overhead rate.

Labor Distribution Reports

Labor distribution reports typically capture and summarize information from individual timesheets. As a result, they provide a summary view of the location by cost code and date as to where and when labor was expended on the project. As with other job cost documents, the first question to consider is whether the cost coding has been accurate and consistent. Labor distribution reports can be very helpful when attempting to isolate and analyze the impact of an issue on specific work, rather than the broader impact on the entirety of the labor expense incurred on the project. For example, the payroll distribution report can be used to determine which individuals actually worked overtime, for how long, and what work they were doing while working on an overtime schedule. Labor distribution reports and payroll reports can also be used to determine the amount of labor turnover the contractor incurred, which may contribute to labor inefficiency, and these reports also document actual labor and burden rates.

Productivity Information
Accurate measurements of productivity are essential to determining if the progress of work has been impacted. Contemporaneous records that reflect actual quantities installed and their location, when combined with labor records such as the payroll distribution report, provide critical productivity data to project management. If the productivity information is gathered and analyzed in a timely manner, the project manager may be able to identify and resolve problems before they cause significant impact. The data can also be used to identify changed work that should be quantified in a change proposal and submitted to the owner as soon as reasonably possible. Finally, if necessary, the same data can be used to support a claim for inefficiency, and is an integral part of establishing a cause-and-effect relationship between the acts or omissions of one party (the cause) and the resultant lost labor productivity (the effect).

Applications for Payment
Applications for payment are submitted periodically by the contractor, typically monthly, and (as they may have been adjusted by the owner) reflect progress payments to the contractor from the owner. This information is an important part of any calculation of damages. Under a lump-sum contract, the pay applications typically consist of a schedule of values that has been modified or supplemented to include approved change orders, as well as the agreed-upon progress (e.g., percent complete) per month by line item in the schedule of values.

Additional Documents
Other documents that can be useful in claim pricing include equipment logs that track equipment dedicated to the project and the status of that equipment (idle or working). Vendor invoices can also establish the actual cost of specific equipment, materials, supplies, and site overhead items. Subcontractor invoices can provide additional insight into the progress of the project and the amount of changes to the subcontractors' scope of work.

Finally, correspondence between the parties, meeting minutes, and diaries kept by project staff can help explain what actually was happening on the project at various times and may reveal the parties' contemporaneous perception of what was causing or contributing to problems occurring on the project.

Schedule Analysis—Related Documents

Findings from a schedule analysis typically become the basis for delay, acceleration, or labor inefficiency damages calculations. The scheduling expert's conclusion as to the amount of compensable delay is a key element of the damages calculation as the compensable delay days found are multiplied by the field overhead daily rate to determine delay damages for site overhead costs. Documents that schedule analysts typically rely upon parallel those relied upon by damages analysts—instead of a bid estimate or JCR, the schedule analyst will typically rely upon the approved baseline schedule and subsequent schedule updates. There is typically some overlap between documents of interest to the schedule analyst and those of concern to the damages analyst. The schedule analyst will also typically be very interested in daily reports, journals, project photos, and change orders.

Conclusion

The process of pricing a construction claim is complex and nuanced, particularly when the claim goes beyond the straightforward pricing of added work scope. It is not a matter of simply presenting the largest conceivable dollar figure and hoping for payment of some percentage of that amount. Such a practice can result in harsh consequences. Whether the project is public or private, the applicable contract provisions (e.g., differing site conditions or "no damages for delay" clauses), the type of impacts (extra work, delays, lost productivity, and acceleration), the cost records available, and numerous other considerations all will significantly affect the pricing of the claim. As a general rule, the most well-documented and thoroughly vetted claims have the greatest chance of success, and this chapter has sought to illuminate the key principles to be considered when seeking to present a well-crafted claim that maximizes the opportunity for favorable resolution.

Notes

1. 31 U.S.C. § 3729. Recently enacted legislation has broadened the scope of the False Claims Act's applicability. *See* Fraud Enforcement and Recovery Act of 2009 (FERA), Pub. L. No. 111-21, § 4(a), 123 Stat. 1617, 1621–23 (2009).

2. 41 U.S.C. § 604 (requiring contractor that submits fraudulent claim to pay penalty equal to the portion of the claim found to be fraudulent).

3. 28 U.S.C. § 2514 (requiring contractor to forfeit entire claim, including any meritorious portions, if any portion of claim is fraudulent).

4. *See* MODEL RULES OF PROF'L CONDUCT R. 3.1, 3.3 (2008).

5. *E.g.*, Daewoo Eng'g & Constr. Co. v. United States, 557 F.3d 1332, 1339 (Fed. Cir. 2009) (affirming trial court's imposition of over $50 million in penalties and forfeiture of $13 million portion of claim that may have had some merit, where court found that contractor submitted large claim as a "negotiating ploy"); Morse Diesel Int'l v. United States, 74 Fed. Cl. 601, 625–34 (2007) (holding that contractor forfeited numerous, unrelated claims where contractor failed to disclose discounted bond premiums it had received, but had charged to government at full price).

6. If the owner exceeds the general scope of work to such a degree that that contractor is required to construct a project fundamentally different from that for which it bargained, the contractor may have a claim that the owner has breached the contract by directing a "cardinal change." *E.g.*, Luria Bros. & Co. v. United States, 369 F.2d 701, 707–09 (Ct. Cl. 1966).

7. *E.g.*, Branna Constr. Corp. v. W. Allegheny Joint Sch. Auth., 242 A.2d 244, 247 (Pa. 1968).

8. *E.g.*, J.A. Jones Constr. Co. v. Lehrer McGovern Bovis, Inc., 89 P.3d 1009, 1014–16 (Nev. 2004) (reviewing case law from other jurisdictions regarding exceptions to No Damages for Delay clauses and adopting exceptions for "(1) delays so unreasonable in length as to amount to project abandonment; (2) delays caused by the other party's fraud, misrepresentation, concealment or other bad faith; and (3) delays caused by the other party's active interference").

9. *E.g.*, CAL. PUB. CONT. CODE § 7102; MO. REV. STAT. § 34.058(2); VA. CODE ANN. § 2.2-4335.

10. OHIO REV. CODE ANN. § 4113.62(C); WASH. REV. CODE § 4.24.360.

11. *E.g.*, Carrothers Constr. Co v. City of S. Hutchinson, 207 P.3d 231, 235 (Kan. 2009) (whether liquidated damages constitute a penalty depends solely upon whether the liquidated damage amount represented a reasonable projection of the actual damages as of the time of contracting).

12. *E.g.*, Grand Bissell Towers, Inc. v. John Gagnon Enters., Inc., 657 S.W.2d 378, 379–80 (Mo. Ct. App. 1983).

13. *E.g.*, RKR Motors, Inc. v. Assoc. Unif. Rental & Linen Supply, Inc., 995 So. 2d 588, 595 (Fla. Dist. Ct. App. 2008); Boots, Inc. v. Singh, 649 S.E.2d 695, 698 (Va. 2007).

14. *E.g.*, Hoel-Steffen Constr. Co. v. United States, 456 F.2d 760, 766–67 (Ct. Cl. 1972); New Pueblo Constructors, Inc. v. State, 696 P.2d 185, 191 (Ariz. 1985); Ga. Dep't of Transp. v. Dalton Paving & Constr., Inc., 489 S.E.2d 329, 337–38 (Ga. Ct. App. 1997); Roger J. Au & Son, Inc. v. N.E. Ohio Reg'l Sewer Dist., 504 N.E.2d 1209, 1216–17 (Ohio Ct. App. 1986); Clark-Fitzpatrick, Inc./Franki Found. Co. v. Gill, 652 A.2d 440, 446–47 (R.I. 1994); Metro. Sewerage Comm'n v. R.W. Constr., Inc., 241 N.W.2d 371, 383 (Wis. 1976).

15. *E.g.*, *New Pueblo Constructors*, 696 P.2d at 191; Leiden Corp., 84-1 B.C.A. (CCH) ¶ 16,947, at 84,297, 1983 WL 13402 (ASBCA 1983).

16. *E.g.*, VA. CODE. ANN. § 8.01-262.1 (voiding any clauses in contracts involving a Virginia contractor that specify a venue anywhere outside Virginia).

17. James Corp. v. N. Allegheny Sch. Dist., 938 A.2d 474, 495 (Pa. Commw. Ct. 2007), *reargument denied* (Jan. 30, 2008); *see also* Luria Bros. & Co. v. United States, 369 F.2d. 701, 713–14 (Ct. Cl. 1966); Bay West, Inc., 07-1 B.C.A. (CCH) ¶ 33,569, at 166,302–03, 2007 WL 1342482 (ASBCA 2007); P.J. Dick, Inc., 01-2 B.C.A. (CCH) ¶ 31,647, at 156,340–41, 2001 WL 1219552 (VABCA 2001) (*citing* U.S. Indus., Inc. v. Blake Constr. Co., 671 F.2d. 539 (D.C. Cir. 1982)), *aff'd in part, rev'd in part on other grounds sub nom.* P.J. Dick, Inc. v. Principi, 324 F.3d 1364 (Fed. Cir. 2003); W. G. Yates & Sons Constr. Co., 01-2 B.C.A. (CCH) ¶ 31,428, 2001 WL 576900 (ASBCA 2001); Clark Concrete Contractors, Inc., 99-1 B.C.A. (CCH) ¶ 30,280, 1999 WL 143977 (GSBCA 1999)).

18. If the contractor cannot identify an unimpacted period during the project, it may seek to utilize an unimpacted period on a previous project of similar size and complexity. Because such a comparison inherently involves more speculation, however, it may not be as readily accepted.

19. *E.g.*, Propellex Corp. v. Brownlee, 342 F.3d 1335, 1339 (Fed. Cir. 2003); Amelco Elec. v. City of Thousand Oaks, 38 P.3d 1120, 1129 (Cal. 2002).

20. *Propellex*, 342 F.3d at 1343 ("The four requirements of the total cost method are distinct requirements and a contractor must prove all of them before it can obtain the benefit of the total cost method.").

21. *E.g.*, Servidone Constr. Corp. v. United States, 931 F.2d 860, 861 (Fed. Cir. 1991) ("A trial court must use the total cost method with caution and as a last resort."); WRB Corp. v. United States, 183 Ct. Cl. 409, 426 (1968) ("This theory has never been favored by the court and has been tolerated only when no other mode was available."); *Amelco*, 38 P.3d at 1130 ("The total cost method of determining damages is generally disfavored."); Glenn H. Haese & Timothy J. Dragelin, *Types of Claims*, in PROVING AND PRICING CONSTRUCTION CLAIMS § 1.05 (Robert F. Cushman et al. eds., 3d ed. 2001 & Supp. 2007) ("Courts, in general are reticent to allow a total cost approach. . . . The total cost approach has by its very nature inherent shortcomings. . . ."); WILLIAM SCHWARTZKOPF & JOHN J. MCNAMARA, CALCULATING CONSTRUCTION DAMAGES § 1.03[C] (2d ed. 2001 & Supp. 2007) ("[T]he courts have often criticized and rejected the total cost method because of the implicit assumption that the contractor did everything right and all cost overruns must be the result of owner actions.").

22. *E.g.*, *Propellex*, 342 F.3d at 1343 (contractor's quantification and removal of costs for which the contractor was responsible implied the ability to track and quantify directly those costs for which the government was responsible as well); Huber, Hunt & Nichols, Inc. v. Moore, 136 Cal. Rptr. 603, 622 (Ct. App. 1977) (declining to permit total cost recovery because "Contractor could have maintained a proper accounting system to establish its alleged damage proximately caused by [the defendant's] alleged negligence, if it had desired to do so. Apparently it simply did not desire to do so.").

23. *E.g.*, Moorhead Constr. Co. v. City of Grand Forks, 508 F.2d 1008, 1016 (8th Cir. 1975).

24. *Propellex*, 342 F.3d at 1339 (under the modified total cost method, the contractor's costs serve as "only a starting point.")

25. Propellex Corp., 02-1 B.C.A. (CCH) ¶ 31,721, at 156,730, 2001 WL 1678757 (ASBCA 2001), *aff'd sub nom.* Propellex Corp. v. Brownlee, 342 F.3d 1335 (Fed. Cir. 2003). *See also* G.M. Harston Constr. Co. v. City of Chicago, 371 F. Supp. 2d 949, 953 (N.D. Ill. 2005) ("[T]he contractor, in a modified total cost methodology, must vigorously exclude any costs it cannot justify. . . ."); *Amelco*, 38 P.3d at 1130 ("The total cost method . . . should be applied only to the smallest affected portion of the contractual relationship that can be clearly identified." (citation omitted)); SCHWARTZKOPF & MCNAMARA, *supra* note 21, § 1.03[D] ("[T]o the extent possible, total cost calculations should be made on separate items or areas of work, allowing further refinements of the calculation, rather than taking all costs as a lump sum."); *id.* § 2.09[F] ("Modified total cost calculations segregate impacted from nonimpacted work activities."); *cf.* PCL Constr. Servs., Inc. v. United States, 96 Fed. Appx. 672, 675 (Fed. Cir. 2004) (unpublished) (contractor excluded from its modified total cost claim items that delay could not have impacted, such as "Parties, Flowers, Donuts & Coffee" and "Site Flat Work").

26. *E.g.*, S. Comfort Builders, Inc. v. United States, 67 Fed. Cl. 124, 146–50 (2005) (refusing to accept contractor's 10 percent reduction in overall claim even where expert testified to the reasonableness of this amount, suggesting that this figure was "randomly chosen"); Amelco Elec. v. City of Thousand Oaks, 38 P.3d 1120, 1132 (Cal. 2002) (rejecting contractor's "apparently arbitrary" 5 percent reduction of its claim).

27. *See* J.D. Hedin Constr. Co. v. United States, 347 F.2d 235, 246–47, 171 Ct. Cl. 70 (1965) (permitting contractor to recover modified total costs of performing foundation work in light of defective specifications, among various other items of recovery calculated

according to traditional methods), *overruled in part on other grounds*, Wilner v. United States, 24 F.3d 1397, 1402 (Fed. Cir. 1994); Amp-Rite Elec. Co. v. Wheaton Sanitary Dist., 580 N.E.2d 622, 641–42 (Ill. App. Ct. 1991) (applying modified total cost method only to contractor's claimed labor overruns, where contractor asserted several other items of damages); Wyo. State Highway Comm'n v. Brasel & Sims Constr. Co., 688 P.2d 871, 877 (Wyo. 1984) (the contractor "isolated the areas of the construction project affected by the [owner's] breach and applied the total-cost method to calculate increased costs with respect to each area").

28. *E.g.*, Costa & Sons Constr. Co. v. Long, 412 S.E.2d 450, 452 (S.C. Ct. App. 1991). Note, however, that if the court declares the contract unenforceable because it is *illegal*—such as where the contractor is not properly licensed to perform the work called for in the contract—*quantum meruit* recovery may be unavailable. Kansas City Cmty. Ctr. v. Heritage Indus., Inc., 773 F. Supp. 181, 185 (W.D. Mo. 1991), *aff'd*, 972 F.2d 185 (8th Cir. 1992).

29. Allan Constr. Co. v. United States, 646 F.2d 487, 494–95 (Ct. Cl. 1981).

30. Joseph Pickard's Sons Co. v. United States, 532 F.2d 739, 742–43 (Ct. Cl. 1976); WRB Corp. v. United States, 183 Ct. Cl. 409, 425 (1968).

31. *E.g.*, *WRB Corp.*, 183 Ct. Cl. at 425.

32. *E.g.*, Meva Corp. v. United States, 511 F.2d 548, 558–59 (Ct. Cl. 1975); Sternberger v. United States, 401 F.2d 1012, 1015–16 (Ct. Cl. 1968); *WRB Corp.*, 183 Ct. Cl. at 424–26.

33. Metro. Sewerage Comm'n v. R.W. Constr., Inc., 255 N.W.2d 293, 298 (Wis. 1977).

34. *Supra* note 17 and accompanying text.

35. *E.g.*, Clark Constr. Group, Inc., 00-1 B.C.A. (CCH) ¶ 30,870, at 152,404, 2000 WL 375542 (VABCA 2000).

36. P.J. Dick, Inc., 01-2 B.C.A. (CCH) ¶ 31,647, at 156,340–41, 2001 WL 1219552 (VABCA 2001) ("[T]he ascertainment of damages for labor inefficiency is not susceptible to absolute exactness. . . . We will accept a comparison if it is between kinds of work which are reasonably alike, such that the approximations it involves will be meaningful." (citation omitted)), *aff'd in part, rev'd in part on other grounds sub nom.* P.J. Dick, Inc. v. Principi, 324 F.3d 1364 (Fed. Cir. 2003).

37. S. Comfort Builders, Inc. v. United States, 67 Fed. Cl. 124, 150 (2005) (rejecting such an attempt where contractor's expert admitted that attempting to compare the two companies was fundamentally flawed).

38. In *P.W. Construction, Inc. v. United States*, 53 Fed. Appx. 555, 557 (Fed. Cir. 2002) (unpublished), the court rejected the contractor's attempt to utilize a "measured mile" consisting of welds that took 15 seconds to two minutes to complete, where the allegedly impacted work involved much more complicated welds that would have taken up to two hours to complete, even under unimpacted conditions.

39. *E.g.*, J.A. Jones Constr. Co., 00-2 B.C.A. ¶ 31,000, at 153,100–01, 2000 WL 1014011 (ENG BCA 2000) (rejecting measured mile analysis that failed to segregate impacted and unimpacted work by, for example, claiming an "impact" to an entire labor crew of eight to 10 workers if only one worker was delayed by the performance of change order work on a given day); *see also* Kit-San-Azusa, J.V. v. United States, 32 Fed. Cl. 647, 654–55 (1995), *aff'd*, 86 F.3d 1175 (Fed. Cir. 1996).

40. Pebble Bldg. Co. v. G.J. Hopkins, Inc., 288 S.E.2d 437 (Va. 1982). Because the contractor utilized its as-bid costs as the baseline, this claim may more accurately be viewed as a Modified Total Cost claim applied to the labor portion of the contractor's costs. Although the court stated that "quantum may be fixed when the facts and circumstances are such as to permit . . . an intelligent and probable estimate thereof," *id.* at 438, it did not analyze whether the contractor had proved that other methods of proof were unavailable.

41. *E.g.*, Hensel Phelps Constr. Co. v. Gen. Servs. Admin., 01-1 B.C.A. ¶ 31,249, at 154,321, 2001 WL 43961 (GSBCA 2001) (accepting use of this study as method of measuring lost labor productivity), *aff'd sub nom.* Perry v. Hensel Phelps Constr. Co., 36 Fed. Appx. 649 (Fed. Cir. 2002); Clark Constr. Group, Inc., 00-1 B.C.A. (CCH) ¶ 30,870, at 152,406–10, 152,419, 2000 WL 375542 (VABCA 2000).

42. Mechanical Contractors Association of America, Bulletin No. CO 1, *Change Orders*, Appendix B: Factors Affecting Productivity, at 31 (1987).

43. "These factors listed are intended to serve as a reference only. Individual cases could prove to be too high or too low. The factors should be tested by your own work experience and modified accordingly in your own use of them, since percentages of increased costs due to the factors listed are necessarily arbitrary and may vary from contractor to contractor, crew to crew and job to job." *Clark Constr. Group*, 00-1 B.C.A. at 152,407 (quoting the MCAA study).

44. U.S. Army Corps of Engineers, *Modification Impact Evaluation Guide*, Engineer Pamphlet 415-1-3, at 4-9 (July 2, 1979).

45. Ace Constructors, Inc. v. United States, 70 Fed. Cl. 253, 281–83 (2006), *aff'd*, 499 F.3d 1357 (Fed. Cir. 2007).

46. Charles A. Leonard, The Effects of Change Orders on Productivity (Feb. 1988) (M.S. thesis, Concordia Univ., Montreal, Quebec) (on file with author).

47. J.A. Jones Constr. Co., 00-1 B.C.A. (CCH) ¶ 31,000, at 153,096–97, 2000 WL 1014011 (ENG BCA 2000).

48. William Ibbs, et al., The Challenges of Lost Productivity: Proving and Quantifying a Claim 1–6 (Constr. Claims Advisor Staff eds., 2008).

49. Pathman Constr. Co., 87-1 B.C.A. (CCH) ¶ 19,643, at 99,440–41, 1987 WL 40846 (GSBCA 1987).

50. *E.g.*, Emerald Maint., Inc., 98-2 B.C.A. (CCH) ¶ 29,903, at 148,051–52, 1998 WL 414697 (ASBCA 1998); Santa Fe Eng'rs, 91-1 B.C.A. (CCH) ¶ 23,571, at 118,196, 1990 WL 235083 (ASBCA 1990).

51. The concepts of unabsorbed versus extended overhead are different conceptually but are often used interchangeably, even in the relevant case law.

52. Eichleay Corp., 60-2 B.C.A. (CCH) ¶ 2688, at 13,568, 1960 WL 538 (ASBCA 1960).

53. Wickham Contracting Co. v. Fischer, 12 F.3d 1574, 1580–81 (Fed. Cir. 1994); *see also* P.J. Dick, Inc. v. Principi, 324 F.3d 1364, 1372–73 (Fed. Cir. 2003); Melka Marine, Inc. v. United States, 187 F.3d 1370, 1376 (Fed. Cir. 1999); West v. All-State Boiler, Inc., 146 F.3d 1368, 1372 (Fed. Cir. 1998).

54. *E.g.*, S. New England Contracting Co. v. State, 345 A.2d 550, 558–60 (Conn. 1974); Cent. Fla. Plastering & Dev. v. Sovran Constr. Co., 679 So. 2d 1226, 1228 & n.1 (Fla. Dist. Ct. App. 1996); Gladwynne Constr. Co. v. Mayor & City Council, 807 A.2d 1141, 1156–58 (Md. Ct. Spec. App. 2002); PDM Plumbing & Heating, Inc. v. Findlen, 431 N.E.2d 594, 595–96 (Mass. Ct. App. 1982); Complete Gen. Constr. Co. v. Ohio Dep't of Transp., 760 N.E.2d 364, 367 (Ohio 2002); Hart Eng'g Co. v. City of Pawtucket Water Supply Bd., 560 A.2d 329, 330 (R.I. 1989); Fairfax County Redev. & Hous. Auth. v. Worcester Bros. Co., 514 S.E.2d 147, 151–52 (Va. 1999); Golf Landscaping, Inc. v. Century Constr. Co., 696 P.2d 590, 593 (Wash. Ct. App. 1984).

55. *E.g.*, Berley Indus., Inc. v. City of New York, 385 N.E.2d 281, 283–84 (N.Y. 1978); Chilton Ins. Co. v. Pate & Pate Enters., Inc., 930 S.W.2d 877, 892–93 (Tex. Ct. App. 1996); *cf.* Paliotta v. Pa. Dep't of Transp., 750 A.2d 388, 390 (Pa. Commw. Ct. 1999) (Pennsylvania Department of Transportation's standard specifications prohibit claims for extended home office overhead, whether computed using the Eichleay method or otherwise).

56. *P.J. Dick*, 324 F.3d at 1370.

57. *Id.*

58. *Id.*

59. *All-State Boiler*, 146 F.3d at 1376.

60. *E.g., Melka Marine*, 187 F.3d at 1376; *All-State Boiler*, 146 F.2d at 1372–73; Altmayer v. Johnson, 79 F.3d 1129, 1134 (Fed. Cir. 1996); Interstate Gen. Gov't Contractors, Inc. v. West, 12 F.3d 1053, 1058–59 (Fed. Cir. 1993).

61. *P.J. Dick*, 324 F.3d at 1372–73.

62. *Id.* at 1373. As part of the second question, the court referred to a three-part test it had established previously for considering delay claims measured against an early completion date. *Interstate*, 12 F.3d at 1059. To maintain such a claim, the contractor must prove "that from the outset of the contract it (1) intended to complete the contract early; (2) had the capability to do so; and (3) actually would have completed early, but for the government's actions." *Id.*

63. The FAR is codified in Title 48 of the Code of Federal Regulations.

64. FAR § 31.201-2(a) (2009).

65. *Id.* § 31.205.

66. *Id.* § 31.201-3(a).

67. *Id.* § 31.201-4.

68. 68 Fed. Cl. 296, 316–18 (2005).

69. *Id.* at 318.

70. Salt City Contractors, Ltd., 80-2 B.C.A. (CCH) ¶ 14,713, at 72,559, 1980 WL 3029 (VABCA 1980).

71. AIA Document A201—2007, General Conditions of the Contract for Construction § 15.1.6.2.

72. *E.g.*, James Corp. v. N. Allegheny Sch. Dist., 938 A.2d 474, 483 & n.8 (Pa. Commw. Ct. 2007), *reargument denied* (2008).

73. *E.g.*, Imperial Constr. & Elec., Inc., 06-1 B.C.A. (CCH) ¶ 33,276, at 164,949, 2006 WL 1313984 (ASBCA 2006); Advanced Eng'g & Planning Corp., 05-1 B.C.A. (CCH) ¶ 32,806, at 162,321, 2004 WL 2677071 (ASBCA 2004), *modified in part on other grounds*, 05-1 B.C.A. (CCH) ¶ 32,935, 2005 WL 874473 (ASBCA 2005).

74. *E.g., James Corp.*, 938 A.2d at 483 n.8.

75. Fraser Constr. Co. v. United States, 384 F.3d 1354, 1361 (Fed. Cir. 2004).

76. *Id.* (citing Norair Eng'g Corp. v. United States, 666 F.2d 546, 548 (Ct. Cl. 1981)).

77. *E.g.*, Ace Constructors, Inc. v. United States, 70 Fed. Cl. 253, 280 (2006), *aff'd*, 499 F.3d 1357 (Fed. Cir. 2007).

78. *Id.* at 281.

79. Elte, Inc. v. S.S. Mullen, Inc., 469 F.2d 1127, 1131–32 (9th Cir. 1972) (permitting subcontractor to recover from contractor for constructive acceleration, without citing notice as a requisite element of proof); *James Corp.*, 938 A.2d at 483 n.8 (stating the elements of a constructive acceleration claim as "(1) [the contractor's] own delays in performance are excusable, (2) the contractor was ordered to accelerate, and (3) the contractor did so and sustained extra costs") (quoting Dep't of Transp. v. Anjo Constr. Co., 66 A.2d 753, 757 (Pa. Commw. Ct. 1995)).

80. Fru-Con Constr. Corp. v. United States, 43 Fed. Cl. 306, 328 (1999). The Court of Federal Claims in *Fru-Con* also made clear that the contractor can make a constructive acceleration claim even if it fails to complete the work within the original contract time. *Id.* (citing *Norair Eng'g*, 666 F.2d at 548).

81. *E.g.*, Jackson Constr. Co. v. United States, 62 Fed. Cl. 84, 103–04 (2004); *see also* Pittman Constr. Co. v. United States, 2 Cl. Ct. 211, 216 (1981); S. Comfort Builders, Inc. v. United States, 67 Fed. Cl. 124, 143–44 (2005); McMillin Bros. Constructors, Inc., 91-1 B.C.A. (CCH) ¶ 23,351, 1990 WL 140900 (EBCA 1990), *aff'd sub nom.* McMillin Bros. Constructors, Inc. v. Watkins, 949 F.2d 403 (Fed. Cir. 1991); Bechtel Nat'l, Inc., 90-1 B.C.A. (CCH) ¶ 22,549, 1989 WL 160470 (NASA BCA 1989); Reginald M. Jones, *Lost Productivity: Claims for the Cumulative Impact of Multiple Change Orders*, 31 PUB. CONT. L.J. 1 (2001).

82. *E.g.*, Bell BCI Co. v. United States, 570 F.3d 1337, 1340–42 (Fed. Cir. 2009); *Jackson Constr.*, 62 Fed. Cl. at 91; King Fisher Marine Serv., Inc. v. United States, 16 Cl. Ct. 231, 237 (1989); Huber, Hunt & Nichols, Inc. v. Moore, 136 Cal. Rptr. 603, 618 (Ct. App. 1977).

83. Care should be taken when attempting to reserve rights, however, as the contractor's attempt to begin reserving its rights later in a project may be viewed as a tacit recogni-

tion that prior modifications *had* addressed impact damages, and that the contractor accordingly had waived its right to make further claims for impacts allegedly related to this earlier work. *See* ILM Sys., Inc. v. Suffolk Constr. Co., 252 F. Supp. 2d 151, 159–60 (E.D. Pa. 2001).

84. *E.g.*, Hensel Phelps Constr. Co. v. Gen. Servs. Admin., 01-1 B.C.A. (CCH) ¶ 31,249, at 154,312–13, 2001 WL 43961 (GSBCA 2001) (government's contracting officer recognized project-wide impact of extensive plumbing changes, and had discussed contractor's intent to later submit claim for this cumulative impact), *aff'd sub nom.* Perry v. Hensel Phelps Constr. Co., 36 Fed. Appx. 649 (Fed. Cir. 2002).

85. *See Bechtel Nat'l*, 90-1 B.C.A. (CCH) at 113,177. At least one state trial-level court, however, has held that this retrospective assessment of a cumulative impact claim renders such claims inherently too speculative to be recognized. *In re* Venetian Lien Litig., Nos. A397391, A413638, 2004 WL 3265025, at *1 (Nev. Dist. Ct. Clark Cty. Sept. 23, 2004).

86. *Bechtel Nat'l*, 90-1 B.C.A. (CCH) at 113,177; *see also Jackson Constr.*, 62 Fed. Cl. at 104. *But see* Ingalls Shipbuilding Div., Litton Sys., Inc., 78-1 B.C.A. (CCH) ¶ 13,038, at 63,000–02, 1978 WL 2301 (ASBCA 1978) (permitting cumulative impact claim based on literally thousands of changes and four-year delay in completion of project). The converse of this argument—i.e., that a small number of changes does not *preclude* the contractor from presenting a cumulative impact claim—is not necessarily true, however, and courts and boards have accepted owners' arguments that a relatively insubstantial number of changes undermined a claim of cumulative impact. *Pittman Constr.*, 2 Cl. Ct. at 216–17 (rejecting cumulative impact claim where 206 changes added roughly 12 percent to the contract's dollar value); *McMillin Bros.*, 91-1 B.C.A. (CCH) at 117,102–03 (noting relatively small number and relatively minor nature of changes in rejecting cumulative impact claim).

87. *Jackson Constr.*, 62 Fed. Cl. at 104 (quoting *McMillin Bros.*, 91-1 B.C.A. (CCH) at 117,105); *see also Bechtel Nat'l*, 90-1 B.C.A. (CCH) at 113,177–78.

88. J.A. Jones Constr. Co., 00-1 B.C.A. (CCH) ¶ 31,000, at 153,107–08, 2000 WL 1014011 (ENG BCA 2000); *Bechtel Nat'l*, 90-1 B.C.A. (CCH) at 113,177.

89. *E.g.*, *Bechtel Nat'l*, 90-1 B.C.A. (CCH) at 113,181 (allowing contractor "jury verdict" recovery of approximately $450,000 on $7.5 million cumulative impact claim).

90. WILLIAMS ET AL., INTERMEDIATE ACCOUNTING 560–61 (3d ed. 1989).

91. FAR § 31.205-10; *see also* 48 C.F.R. § 9904.414-30 (defining CFC as "an imputed cost determined by applying a cost-of-money rate to facilities capital").

92. Examples of these manuals include *The AGC Guide*, published by the Associated General Contractors of America; *The Rental Rate Blue Book*, published by Dataquest; *The Associated Equipment Distributor's Manual, The California Department of Transportation Equipment Manual*, and *Construction Equipment Ownership and Operating Expense Schedule*, published by the Army Corps of Engineers.

93. Morse Diesel Int'l, Inc. v. United States, 74 Fed. Cl. 601, 625–34 (2007) (applying Forfeiture of Fraudulent Claims Act, 28 U.S.C. § 2514, and holding that contractor forfeited numerous claims unrelated to the contractor's fraud in failing to disclose discounted bond premiums it had received, but had charged to government at full price); *modified in part on other grounds*, 2007 WL 5177405 (Fed. Cl. June 29, 2007).

94. FAR § 31.205-20.

95. *E.g.*, S. S. Silberblatt, Inc., 80-1 B.C.A. (CCH) ¶ 14,263, at 70,259–61, 1980 WL 101286 (PSBCA 1980), *aff'd*, 3 Cl. Ct. 644 (1983).

CHAPTER 10

Discovery and Use of Accounting Information and Accounting Experts in Construction Litigation and Arbitration

COLIN A. JOHNS
JOHN W. RALLS

Introduction

Accounting information and accounting and cost experts are routinely used to prove and disprove damages in construction disputes. Accounting information is of central importance in connection with disruption and extra work claims brought by contractors as well as in connection with delay claims brought by contractors and owners. This chapter discusses methods of discovering accounting and cost information, and provides several forms and checklists for use in propounding such discovery. This chapter also discusses the pros and cons of using accounting and cost experts and describes the legal standard for challenging such experts.

Discovery of Accounting Information

Identifying the Need for Discovery

Generally, the need for discovery of accounting information depends on whether the client is bringing or defending a claim. In many construction cases, the party bringing the claim can prove its damages with its own records and personnel, and so has little need for this kind of discovery.

For instance, a contractor bringing a delay, extra work, and disruption claim will be able to price that claim based on its own job cost accounting records and source documents. For a contractor bringing such claims, discovery may be of great value in proving the *merits* of its case, and learning what adverse witnesses will say at the trial or hearings. But the pricing information itself will generally be in the contractor's own possession. The challenge for counsel in these situations is gathering and working with the client's information. Those challenges should not be underestimated.

Of particular note are the potential difficulties associated with the sophistication, or lack thereof, of the client's accounting systems as well as potential difficulties with the volume of data that may be included in the project accounting records, and with ensuring that the accounting data is consistent with the assertions of the client.

The same is true for owner claimants. Generally speaking, when an owner has incurred damages as a result of a contractor's failure to perform, it will have the records needed to price its damages in its possession.

Parties defending construction cases, however, have an important need for discovering the accounting and other cost and damages records of the claimant. Such parties must have a discovery plan.

Developing a Discovery Plan: A Checklist

The most useful vehicles to discover the other side's accounting information, and to learn about the other side's damages case, are document production requests, depositions of fact witnesses, and expert discovery. Interrogatories also have their place. Before firing off such requests, it is useful to develop a discovery plan. The starting point is to consider what information you need, so that the appropriate discovery vehicle can be identified. The following checklist is useful.

- Do I know the exact amount of damages my opponent will present at the trial or hearing? If not, then some combination of interrogatories, depositions, and expert discovery is necessary, and provisions should be made to require the claimant to update its responses.
- Do I have all of the records my opponent will use to prove its damages? If not, a document production request should be made.
- Do I have sufficient information to understand my opponent's actual costs, and how my opponent's actual costs compare to what is being claimed? If not, document production requests are prudent, supplemented by depositions of the organization or of knowledgeable persons who can provide necessary explanations of the cost documentation.
- Do I have sufficient records to test whether the costs being claimed were incurred as a result of the events and circumstances that form the bases for the claim (as opposed to other causes for which my client is not responsible)? If not, then document production requests are in order.
- Do I know whether my opponent will use fact witnesses or expert witnesses (or a combination) to prove its damages case? If not, then interrogatories, depositions, and expert discovery should be used.
- Do I know the methodology by which my opponent is pricing its damages? If not, then some combination of interrogatories, depositions, and expert discovery will be necessary.

The next few sections discuss the use of particular discovery vehicles.

Discovery Vehicles

Document Production Requests

List of Categories of Documents to Request

The vast majority of discovery plans in construction cases should include requests for the claimant's accounting records (both paper and electronic). Such requests will frequently be among the initial discovery requests, as having these records will assist in preparation for depositions and expert analysis. A detailed list of contractors' records to consider requesting in discovery is Appendix A to this chapter. Major categories to request may include the following.

- Bid information
- Project-related accounting information
- Specific cost-related information (e.g., labor costs, material costs)
- Claim information
- General accounting information

Discovery of Electronically Stored Information

Accounting information is frequently stored electronically. In fact, the accounting operations of some businesses are paperless and so all such information is electronic. As suggested above, having such information in electronic form can be extremely useful. As a result, counsel need to understand the evolving rules concerning electronic discovery. This is a body of law unto itself, and one that has undergone dramatic changes in the last 40 years.[1]

In 1970, Rule 34(a) of the Federal Rules of Civil Procedure (FRCP) was amended to include "electronic data compilations" *within* the definition of "documents and things."[2] After this amendment, lawyers sought to obtain all manner of electronic information.[3] Given the new and varied ways in which information is stored and modified electronically, "electronic data compilations" was recognized to be inadequate.[4] In 2006, FRCP 34(a) was amended again, this time to add the more inclusive term "electronically stored information."[5]

The 2006 amendment to FRCP 34 was part of the development of a number of new rules regarding electronic data productions, including rules regarding the form of such productions.[6] Simply producing a print-out of all electronic data, as was suggested by the 1970 amendment to the Federal Rules, would no longer suffice.[7] Since 1970, computing power has grown tremendously while computer size and cost has shrunk.[8] In addition to the physical impracticalities of producing massive quantities of electronically stored information (ESI) in print-outs, converting the data to paper, or even into a more universal electronic format, may decrease the ability of the requesting party to search, organize, or otherwise use the data.[9] A searchable and sortable database of job cost information may offer much more insight into the accounting of a construction project than dozens of reams of job cost report print-outs. Before 2006, however, the lack of any specific rule regarding native-format production requests made the outcome of such requests unpredictable.[10] In an effort to remove the ambiguity, and aid the requesting party, FRCP 34(b) was amended to add a provision granting the requesting party the option to "specify the form or forms in which electronically stored information is to be produced."[11]

By virtue of the 2006 amendment, requesting parties may now decide whether to request documents in their native electronic format.[12] Native format files generally contain the most information, and are viewable in the manner intended by the creator of the file, but a trade-off exists.[13] Both sides may find that ESI produced in nonnative form—either electronic or paper—may present several advantages.[14] The responding party may prefer if all ESI is converted into PDF (portable document format) or TIFF (text-imaged file format)[15] files because these formats make it easier to review and redact for privilege, and concerns over what the metadata[16] may contain are eliminated. The requesting party may also prefer to receive ESI in paper, PDF, or TIFF formats because such data is easier to catalog and Bates stamp.[17] PDF and TIFF files also interface seamlessly with programs such as Concordance or Adobe Reader, software many law firms already own.[18]

When it comes to accounting information, native format is useful because it allows the party to view, search, and sort the ESI in the program in which it was originally created. However, job cost records and other accounting information on a construction project are often far more useful when produced in, or converted to, Microsoft Excel, Microsoft Access, or another common spreadsheet or database program. If data is produced in PDF or TIFF formats, there are various software programs available that can extract the data from those files and convert it into such a common program. Most job cost data is organized into tables. Obtaining files in, or converting files to, Excel or Access allows the requesting party to better search for accounting and other financial data,[19] and also allows the party to discover, analyze, and adjust the various formulas and calculations contained within, in order to better understand the opposing side's records. Frequently, knowing where different figures originate, or how particular numbers are calculated, is critical to a forensic accounting.[20]

Generally, in order to obtain ESI, the document production request should specify (1) that the production of ESI is requested and (2) that all or some of the requested items are to be produced in electronic form and in their native file formats. The following general language might also be inserted into the document production request seeking ESI:

> Please produce all nonprivileged responsive electronic documents in their native file format. This means that you are to produce responsive electronic files in the same format in which the files were created and stored on computer. To the extent technically feasible, each electronic file will be produced with all of its original metadata intact and all original file names and file paths and folder structure will also remain intact.

E-mail documents will be produced in .pst or .msg format and loose electronic files will be produced in their native format except as otherwise provided in this stipulation. The native format documents shall be delivered to opposing counsel on CD, DVD or portable hard drive. Each piece of media will be identified by unique media control number.

Obviously, this language is broad. This language would not be appropriate—at least not in its entirety—where only a discrete category of items are sought in electronic form. In addition, the requesting party should be careful not to request items in their "native file formats" where such formats will be difficult or impossible to use. Where a party is requesting a particular item (say, a final job cost report), knows the information can be exported into Microsoft Excel, and desires to have the information in that format, it would be better off simply specifying that the production is to be made "in electronic form, all information having been exported into Microsoft Excel, in a way that maintains the substance and organization of the data, and on CD, DVD, or portable hard drive."

Utilizing the native files in a document production is not always as simple as requesting their production. Requesting parties may receive files created by unfamiliar software, including software that is proprietary. Such scenarios create several problems. The requesting party may need to purchase or obtain licenses to use the necessary software. In the case of proprietary software, which was intended by the responding party for its use only, the party may refuse to allow use of the software for fear of divulging protected, proprietary information.[21] These problems are common in construction cost accounting because there is no industry-standard accounting software.[22] In such situations, the requesting party should attempt to arrange a licensing agreement, direct-link access to the other party's computer system, or conversion of the data to a more commonly used program such as Microsoft Excel.[23] If the propounding party anticipates this problem, it might add to its document request language such as, "Where files are native to proprietary and/or uncommon software programs, the responding party should, where possible, convert such files to Microsoft Excel or another commonly used file format." In addition, the propounding party might inquire as part of a Rule 26(f) conference, in depositions, or by interrogatories how the other side's accounting information is kept, and whether the requested information can be converted or exported to Microsoft Excel or a similar program.

The 2006 amendments to the Federal Rules not only authorize requests for ESI but also protect responding parties. FRCP 26(b)(2)(B) provides that a party's initial disclosures need not include production of ESI "from sources that the party identifies as not reasonably accessible because of undue burden or cost." Obviously, defining the term "not reasonably accessible" may become a source of dispute. The Advisory Committee Notes acknowledge this fact, and suggest that such disputes be resolved by courts using the factors (generally, a balancing of cost and benefit) set forth in FRCP 26(b)(2)(C).[24]

Questions regarding whether data is "not reasonably accessible" are likely to arise in construction cases, particularly where files have often been created in "legacy" programs that are no longer in use. In such cases, the Advisory Committee suggests that parties approach this situation on a case-by-case basis, applying the factors articulated in FRCP 26(b)(2)(B).[25]

Responding parties must also be aware of their obligations that arise under the 2006 amendments with regard to the way ESI is produced. For example, FRCP 34(b)(2)(E)(i) states that the responding party must produce the documents or ESI "as they are kept in the usual course of business or must organize and label them to correspond to the categories in the request."[26] This rule was added to prevent the responding party from deliberately shuffling the structures of file systems in order to conceal important or damaging documents.[27] The 2006 amendments created a corresponding protection for the responding party. FRCP 34(b)(2)(E)(iii) dictates that a responding party "need not produce the same [ESI] in more than one form."[28] But note that a requesting party may still request the production of different ESI in different forms, since "different forms of production may be appropriate for different types of [ESI]."[29]

Additionally, the responding party must use caution in its response to a request for production that does not specify a desired format. If the request does not specify a form, FRCP 34(b)(2)(E)(ii) gives the responding party the option of producing ESI in the "form . . . [in] which it is ordinarily maintained or in a reasonably usable form."[30] Although the requesting party need not specify the desired form, the Advisory Committee Notes that accompany the Federal Rules caution the responding party against producing ESI in the form it prefers without prior notice.[31] Without notifying the requesting party of the intended form of production, the responding party will risk an objection on the grounds that the production was not in a form that is "reasonably usable."[32] The Advisory Committee Notes promote a fairly stringent standard for the term "reasonably usable." They suggest that technical support and other reasonable assistance may be required, and any conversion of the ESI from its "ordinarily maintained" form must not "make[] it more difficult or burdensome . . . to use," nor "remove[] or significantly degrade[]" any feature, such as the ability to search.[33]

White v. Graceland College Center for Professional Development & Lifelong Learning, Inc. provides an example of a district court that enforced this strict standard.[34] In that case, although the plaintiff had not initially requested a specific form in which to produce the ESI, the court held that the defendant was required to reproduce the data in its native form.[35] The court found that the printed-out e-mails were not in "either the form in which they are ordinarily maintained, or in a 'reasonably usable form,'" particularly as the information contained in the metadata for the e-mails was critical to the plaintiff.[36] The court also chastised the parties for not making a better effort to discuss this issue during their Rule 26(f) conference, suggesting that this dispute might never have arisen had the proper preliminary steps been followed.[37]

Depositions of Fact Witnesses

Depositions of fact witnesses are frequently essential as part of the discovery of accounting information. They are particularly useful to parties defending a claim in order to obtain information about the following: how the adversary's job cost system functions and what it records and does not record; if there is a written claim, and how that claim was put together; what the adversary's actual costs were, and how those costs compare to what is being claimed, particularly where the cost documentation requires explanation; the methodology by which the adversary is pricing its damages; and whether the adversary has in-house personnel with the knowledge to support its damages case.

Generally, depositions are more useful where documents have been obtained in advance. In many cases, based on counsel's review of documents or the client's knowledge from the project, counsel will know exactly who to depose. In other cases, counsel will need to conduct discovery in advance of the deposition to identify the correct witness—such as the identity of the accounting and cost control personnel assigned to the job, as well as the individuals who worked on the written claim, if any.

Where counsel does not know the individuals to depose, he should consider noticing the claimant's "organization" for deposition pursuant to FRCP 30(b)(6) or a state law equivalent.[38] Such deposition notices are also useful because they force corporate opponents to identify individuals whose answers will bind the company.[39] In a notice for deposition directed to an organization under FRCP 30(b)(6), the party requesting the deposition is required to "describe with reasonable particularity the matters for examination." The organization is then required to designate individuals who must testify "about information known *or reasonably available to* the organization." (Emphasis added.) A leading commentator observes, "[S]everal courts have held that the organization has an affirmative duty to prepare the designated deponents so that they can give full, complete, and non-evasive answers to questions posed regarding the relevant subject matter."[40]

This type of notice, also known as a "person most knowledgeable" deposition notice, can be particularly useful in ferreting out how a contractor's job cost system works, including the job cost reports and other documentation that exist, as well as the relationship of source documents, job reports, budgets, and schedules of value. Such a notice of deposition also can be very useful in identifying the methodology used to quantify claim calculations as well as how those relate to the contractor's accounting records.

The following topics are worth considering for designation as "matters for examination" in a notice for deposition of an organization under FRCP 30(b)(6):

- The original estimate for the project
- The original budget for the project
- The procedures and controls used to capture, accumulate, and analyze costs incurred by the organization generally and with respect to the project

- The amount of damages sought (including each and every component)
- The calculation of damages sought (including each and every component and the basis for each calculation)
- The consideration and use of the following in connection with the determination of entitlement and calculation with respect to damages: bid and estimate information; contract documents; project-related accounting information and documents, including job cost information; other accounting information and documents; and change orders, change information, and documentation
- The nature of the accounting systems utilized; how data is captured and organized; whether all data is captured in centrally maintained systems or whether there are other data files maintained on project site computers; how costs are accumulated both on a specific project basis and for the home office; whether non-project-specific costs such as information technology costs are allocated to individual projects and the basis for such allocations; how charges for company-owned equipment are calculated, and so on
- Any written claims for damages, including the preparation of those claims, the individuals involved, the basis for the calculations contained therein, and the documents and other source information used to prepare the claims

Naturally, these are general categories. In any given case, there are likely to be particular claim components that have to be explored and particular project circumstances and events that require specific coverage.

Interrogatories

It is easy to become disillusioned with interrogatories because the responses are frequently evasive. But interrogatories have their place. The following interrogatories are worth considering as part of a discovery plan to gather information about the other party's damages:

- With respect to the damages you seek to recover in this action, please provide the following information: the total amount of damages; a description of each item or category of damages; a description of the nature of the damages sought for each item or category; and the amount of damages sought for each item or category.
- With respect to each item or category of damages you seek to recover in this action, please describe in detail how you calculate each item or category of damages, including, without limitation, an identification of the documents that you utilize or refer to in computing each item or category of damages as well as an identification of the documents that record or reflect the costs, expenditures, and sums and/or dollar amounts associated with each item or category of damages.
- Where you want to focus in on particular types of damages: Please state the dollar amount, if any, of the damages you seek to recover in

this action as a result of [delays/disruptions/extra work/lost profits/ home office overhead/job site or field overhead, etc.]. Please describe in detail how you calculate these damages, including, without limitation, an identification of the documents that you utilize or refer to in computing these damages as well as an identification of the documents that record or reflect these damages and/or costs.
- With respect to the damages you seek to recover in this action as a result of delays, if any, please describe in detail how you calculate these damages, including, without limitation, an identification of the documents that you utilize or refer to in computing these damages as well as an identification of the documents that record or reflect these damages and/or costs.
- If there has been a mechanic's lien, stop notice, and/or notice to withhold: Please describe in detail how you calculated the amount of the mechanic's lien, stop notice, and/or notice to withhold, including, without limitation, an identification of the documents that you utilized or referred to in computing the amount of the mechanic's lien, stop notice, and/or notice to withhold as well as an identification of the documents that record or reflect the costs, expenditures, and sums and/or dollar amounts that constitute the amount of the mechanic's lien, stop notice, and/or notice to withhold.
- If there has been a written claim: Please describe in detail how you calculated your claim for [identify category in the written claim, including dollar amount], including, without limitation, an identification of the documents that you utilized or referred to in computing these damages as well as an identification of the documents that record or reflect these damages and/or costs.

Use of Accounting Records in the Proof and Disproof of Damages

This section discusses the practical aspects of using accounting records to prove or disprove damages in construction cases.

The party bringing the claim should give careful consideration to what documents it has in its possession to prove its claimed damages. While many of the considerations in this area are covered by other chapters in this book, it is worth repeating that the success of a claimant can be severely affected by a failure to meet the evidentiary requirements for proof of damages. The burden of proof lies with the claimant and requires that the claimant demonstrate the fact of loss and that the damages have been calculated with reasonable certainty using the best available evidence.[41]

A wealth of information with respect to the project can be contained in the accounting records. To understand what happened on a project, the old adage of "follow the cash" is a good one. A thorough review of these records should be performed to ensure that the data contained in them supports the theory or story presented in the claim. It should always be assumed that the responding party will also perform a similar review, so if there are inconsistencies or weaknesses in the claim it is better to identify and address them early in the process.

Some of the areas to consider in performing this review and evaluation of the data are comparisons of costs for different aspects of the work to the anticipated costs reflected in the original bid or budget, actual versus planned manning levels and labor rates, turnover rates for the labor force, and timing of the work. Many times such an analysis will identify areas that should be investigated further through interviews with project personnel or analyzing other nonaccounting contemporaneous documents such as daily logs.

In the case of extra work, consideration should also be given to what the capabilities of the accounting system were for tracking such costs, for instance through the use of additional cost codes. The failure of a claimant to utilize such capabilities when available and practical has in some cases limited the ability of the claimant to succeed in the prosecution of its claim.[42]

The ability to analyze the accounting records, by both parties, is greatly aided when the data is available in a usable electronic form. This permits data with respect to particular issues to be extracted and sorted with relative ease. The familiarity of the claimant's accounting staff with the accounting system and its capabilities can be valuable in performing such analyses, but, depending on the sophistication of the claimant and its prior history in terms of involvement in claims, the staff may not be familiar with the intricacies of claim calculations and the presentation of a claim. In those cases the staff can still be extremely important in the generation of the data needed to present the claim under the guidance of, or working together with, an accounting expert.

As stated above, many, if not all, of the analyses that should be performed by the claimant can also be performed by the responding party. Obviously, the focus of the responding party is to identify weaknesses or inconsistencies between the accounting data and the submitted claim. In cases where such items are identified, this can be a powerful source of data to refute or defend the claim either in its entirety or by limiting the amount of the recoverable damages.

Using and Opposing Accountants as Expert Witnesses

This section discusses the practical aspects of using and opposing damages experts in construction cases.

When to Retain an Accounting or Other Cost Expert

There is no general legal requirement that a claimant has to present expert opinion testimony. In fact, many claims are successfully presented without the use of specially retained expert witnesses.

The obvious advantage of using in-house personnel to calculate and present damages evidence is saving the fee that would otherwise be charged by the expert. The cost of retaining a damages expert has to be balanced against a number of other factors, such as the following.

- *Getting the work done.* Will in-house personnel be able to find the time to devote to the claim in addition to their operational responsibilities?
- *Reliance upon the client's own records.* Generally, the more the contractor relies on its own actual cost records, the less the need for a specially retained expert.
- *Presentation of findings.* Does the case require the analysis and presentation of findings about accounting records? If so, then an expert may be required. Generally, parties opposing a claim will have a greater need to hire experts because they will want to make their own presentation about the claimed damages and accounting records, which some courts will not permit unless the presentation is made by an expert.[43]
- *Ability to render opinions (especially when pricing disruption claims).* In order to present the claim, is it necessary or helpful to render and present expert opinions? Some damages methodologies are likely to require expert testimony, especially in connection with the pricing of disruption claims. If methods such as measured mile, total cost, and the application of industry standards and handbooks are utilized, then the need for expert testimony is greater. Such experts can review the available data, and may be allowed to render opinions about the proper methodology to calculate damages as well as the application of that method. Labor productivity and efficiency experts may be allowed to render damages opinions as well.[44]
- *Need to prepare a report.* Under the Federal Rules and many state procedural rules, retained experts have to prepare and issue a written report in order to be able to render opinions at trial. Employees rendering opinions may not have to issue such a report.[45]

These factors have to be weighed in every individual case.

Challenges to Expert Accounting Testimony

Generally, before the testimony of experts is admissible, the trial court must decide that the expert is qualified to testify in accordance with Federal Rule of Evidence (FRE) 702[46] and *Daubert*.[47] If requested, most arbitrators will follow a similar procedure, even if exclusion of expert testimony is rare.

Accounting and other cost experts must overcome these hurdles in order to give expert opinion testimony. As discussed below, the primary challenge for accounting and other cost experts is not whether they are qualified to render opinions, as cost accounting is generally recognized as a valid area of expertise. Rather, the primary challenge for accounting and other cost experts is whether their opinions are sufficiently based on facts, data, and reliable methods of analysis.

Legal Standard

FRE 702, *Daubert*, and *Daubert*'s progeny form the current federal standards for admissibility of expert testimony. In 1993, the *Daubert* factors, developed to determine the reliability of expert scientific testimony, replaced the 1923 *Frye*[48] "general acceptance" test.[49]

In *Daubert v. Merrill Dow Pharmaceuticals*, the U.S. Supreme Court affirmed that FRE 702 was the appropriate standard for admissibility of expert witness testimony, and in dicta stated that it envisioned the Rule 702 inquiry to be flexible, focusing on the relevance and reliability of the proposed expert testimony.[50] The Court identified five factors that can be used to determine the reliability of expert testimony: (1) whether theories and techniques used by expert witnesses have been tested and the extent to which they have been tested; (2) whether the technique has been subject to peer review; (3) whether techniques utilized by expert witnesses have determinable rates of error; (4) general peer acceptance of techniques upon which expert witness testimony is based; and (5) publication records and other scholarly qualifications and activities of expert witnesses.[51] The Court noted that the factors do not constitute a "definitive checklist or test."[52] "*Daubert*'s list of specific factors neither necessarily nor exclusively applies to all experts or in every case. Rather, the law grants a district court [. . .] broad latitude when it decides *how* to determine reliability. . . ."[53]

Additionally, in *Daubert*, the Court reiterated the role of the trial court as the "gatekeeper" for expert testimony. The Court stated that the trial court must ensure that "any and all scientific testimony or evidence admitted is not only relevant, but reliable."[54] The Court limited the scope of its holding in *Daubert* to expert scientific testimony.[55]

Following *Daubert*, two Supreme Court cases, *General Electric Co. v. Joiner*[56] and *Kumho Tire Co., Ltd. v. Carmichael*,[57] influenced the interpretation of the *Daubert* standard. In *Joiner*, the Court held that the applicable standard of review for FRE 702 and *Daubert* decisions is abuse of discretion by the trial court.[58] In *Kumho*, the Court held that the *Daubert* factors could apply to non-scientific experts, thus opening the door for many other disciplines to admit experts under FRE 702 and the *Daubert* standard.[59] In both *Joiner* and *Kumho*, the Court again reiterated the role of the trial court as a "gatekeeper," noting that the Court interpreted FRE 702 and *Daubert* factors to be flexible.[60]

States have taken varying approaches to *Daubert* and its progeny. Some states apply *Daubert* or a similar test to determine admissibility of expert testimony,[61] some states continue to apply the 1923 *Frye* standard,[62] some states have not rejected *Frye* in total but apply *Daubert* factors,[63] and some states have developed their own tests.[64]

Financial Damages Expert Testimony

Generally

Following *Kumho*, financial damages expert witness testimony was regularly admitted under FRE 702 and *Daubert*. Financial damages experts are allowed to compute or rebut a claim for financial losses, provide analysis on liability issues in their area of expertise, and organize financial data.[65]

Generally, a court will first look at whether the expert witness's testimony is relevant to the case. Second, the court will look to whether the expert witness's testimony is reliable. The court can utilize the *Daubert* factors to determine reliability, as well as the FRE 702 factors, including the expert's qualifications, the methodology used by the expert to derive his opinion and information, and the conclusions the expert reached.

Under FRE 702, there are five bases under which an expert can be qualified to provide expert testimony: (1) knowledge, (2) skill, (3) experience, (4) training, and (5) education.[66] It is important to note that although the Court has not stated if more than one basis is necessary for an expert to qualify, most experts fulfill more than one basis of qualification.[67] In particular, financial experts often hold a degree in business or accounting, are licensed as a CPA, and have relevant work experience. While "the mere possession of a CPA certificate does not, by itself, qualify an individual as an expert in any accounting/finance field,"[68] as the expert must have specific knowledge of the topic he is testifying about,[69] experts are not often disqualified from testifying for lack of qualification.[70]

The methodology used and the conclusions reached by an expert in his analysis are also looked at by the court to determine if the expert's testimony is admissible. An expert must be knowledgeable not only about the methodologies he employs, but also about the methodologies customarily used by experts doing a similar analysis, and by experts whose methodologies have been accepted in court.[71] For example, financial damages expert witnesses are often used to testify in construction damages cases to "explain the methodology behind the calculation of the damages and how the available cost records were used in calculating the damages."[72]

Issues with Financial Damages Expert Testimony

In a study conducted between 2000 and 2007, PricewaterhouseCoopers analyzed over 3,600 *Daubert* financial expert witness challenges, and concluded that the jurisdiction, type of expert, and reliability of the expert's work were the keys to successfully passing a *Daubert* challenge.[73] Most of the issues with financial expert testimony were reliability issues, including unreliable methodology, unsupported conclusions, invalid facts or data, relying on others' work, failure to comply with standards, or testifying beyond their expertise.[74]

Recent Cases

There are hundreds of business litigation cases regarding *Daubert* and financial experts, but a much more limited number of construction cases with *Daubert* challenges to financial damages experts.[75]

In *Leon v. Kelly*,[76] a forensic accountant and business valuation expert was used by the defense as an expert witness to analyze the plaintiff's damages calculations in a failed acquisition and development of a shopping mall.[77] The court held a *Daubert* hearing to determine if the expert's testimony would be admissible.[78] The expert explained the scope of his expertise, noting that forensic accounting was the discipline of calculating business interests, intangible assets, and income streams, which could be used in determining economic damages and lost profits.[79] The expert explained the methodology for his analysis as set forth in the American Institute of Certified Public Accountants practice aid, and noted that he also followed accounting standards for litigation services.[80] The expert relied on defense materials and conducted his own independent research.[81] The court allowed the expert's report to be included as admissible evidence because the court was satisfied the expert fulfilled the requirements of FRE 702 and *Daubert*.[82]

In *Shadow Lake Management Co., Inc. v. Landmark American Ins. Co.*,[83] an expert was used to establish the reasonable markup rate for repair work to residential apartment buildings that had suffered storm damage.[84] The expert's report discussed different methods to calculate overhead and profit in construction projects, as well as an opinion about the upper limit for overhead costs that insurers will accept.[85] Although the expert used no scientific methodology to reach his conclusions, his opinions were based on specialized knowledge of the construction industry.[86] The court deemed his expert opinion and report relevant and admissible to the case.[87]

In *MACTEC, Inc. v. Bechtel Jacobs Co., LLC*,[88] the expert was attempting to testify about critical path method analysis, a topic about which the expert had little experience.[89] However, the court noted that because the expert had written a chapter in a construction law textbook regarding the calculation of construction damages and a chapter in another book about disruption claims, and had extensive experience in the development and review of claims for damages caused by schedule delay and disruption, the expert had sufficient experience to provide expert opinion in the case.[90] Additionally, the court held that the expert had sufficient experience to provide expert opinion on the flaws that another expert in the case may have made in his analysis, even though the expert did not have any experience to form his own analysis in that area of expertise.[91]

In *RLI Insurance Company v. Indian River School District*,[92] the defendant wanted to have the plaintiff's designated expert, a president of a construction management firm, excluded from giving expert opinion testimony on damages and delay.[93] The defendant argued that the expert's report did not properly disclose the basis for the opinions reached and did not comply with the standards set forth in *Daubert*.[94] The court found that the basis for the expert's opinions (both the information relied upon and the expert's methodology) was not apparent from the report.[95] Noting that a trial date had not yet been set, the court allowed the plaintiff an opportunity to cure the deficiencies in the report so that it complied with FRCP 26 and the *Daubert* standard.[96] Among other things, the court required the plaintiff to provide a report containing "a straightforward statement of the data or other information considered" and "identifying with greater clarity and precision the analysis methodology." Otherwise, the expert would not be allowed to testify at trial.[97]

In *Carlisle Corp. d/b/a/ Carlisle Syntec Systems v. Medical City Dallas, Ltd.*,[98] the expert witness was a licensed commercial property adjuster with at least 14 years of experience inspecting buildings and writing and reviewing estimates of damages to commercial buildings, including roofs.[99] He had inspected about 250 commercial roofs, and written over 225 roof repair or replacement estimates, using estimating software and his own experience.[100] The appellate court held that the trial court did not err in allowing the expert witness to testify as to the replacement cost of a new foam roof.[101]

In *Jefferson v. Jefferson*,[102] the plaintiff's brother was allowed to testify as an expert in residential construction in a case regarding the cost and repairs needed to the plaintiff's house after a fire.[103] The plaintiff's brother had over 27 years of experience in residential and commercial building, was a member of a local union, and was a supervisor for a licensed contractor.[104] His job was to estimate costs of new construction or renovations on potential jobs.[105] The court held that his expertise was sufficient to testify as to the cost and repairs needed on the plaintiff's house.

Deposing Accounting Experts

In many construction cases, the deposition of an accounting expert is one of the most important depositions in the entire case. There are number of excellent, practical guides to expert depositions.[106] Many experienced practitioners consider expert depositions to be among the easiest to take because the witness has to answer questions about what opinions he intends to present at the trial or hearing as well as the basis for those opinions. This is consistent with a primary goal of counsel in taking an expert deposition, which is to determine all of the opinions the expert is going to offer at trial or hearing, and the basis for those opinions. At the same time, the following topics are worth covering in most expert depositions.

- A thorough coverage of the expert's experience and expertise
- Whether the expert has been challenged or was the subject of prior *Daubert* challenges[107]
- Prior testimony of the expert, including prior use of the methods being used or attacked in the particular case
- The amount of work performed
- The precise scope of anticipated testimony, including whether the expert will be testifying about related topics such as delay and whether the expert will be relying upon fact witnesses for particular facts in support of his opinions
- Accounting records considered and not considered
- Reliance on other experts
- An identification of the methodology employed
- Interaction with project personnel

The above list of topics also serves as a useful list in preparing one's own expert for deposition and testimony.

Conclusion

Construction cases that are good on the merits can fall apart for failure to prove damages. This fact creates challenges for parties bringing claims and opportunities for those defending claims. These challenges and opportunities are best met with careful, advance planning. Such planning might include discovery (especially document discovery and depositions), the review and analysis of accounting records (gathered through discovery or within the client's control), and the retention of accounting and cost experts.

Notes

1. For an excellent, thorough, and practical discussion of the discovery of electronic evidence, see Gil Keteltas and John Rosenthal, *Discovery of Electronic Evidence*, in ELECTRONIC EVIDENCE LAW AND PRACTICE 1, 1–77 (2d. ed. 2008). Focusing on the Federal Rules, the authors review a host of issues surrounding the discovery of electronic evidence, including the extent to which electronic evidence must be a part of initial disclosures, approaches to cost allocation, the right to "test and sample" the other side's electronically stored information, privilege, the use of document production requests and interrogatories, spoliation, document retention, and the use of vendors.
2. FED. R. CIV. P. 34(a) advisory committee's note (2006 Amendment).
3. Id.
4. Id.
5. Id.
6. 8A CHARLES ALAN WRIGHT ET AL., FEDERAL PRACTICE AND PROCEDURE § 2218 (2d Supp. 2009).
7. Id. at (1970 Amendment).
8. One author used an excellent visual representation: "The average personal computer hard drive can easily store 60 gigabytes of data—the equivalent of 60 stacks of paper 85 feet high." MICHAEL T. BRAMBLE & BARRY B. BRAMBLE, DISCOVERY IN CONSTRUCTION LITIGATION 4-4(C)(1) (4th ed. Supp. 2008).
9. NEAL J. SWEENEY ET AL., CONSTRUCTION LAW UPDATE § 7.03(B) (Aspen 2007).
10. BRAMBLE & BRAMBLE, *supra* note 8.
11. FED. R. CIV. P. 34(b)(1)(C).
12. "Native format" refers to "electronic records that are produced with the file structure assigned to the document's application intact." Common examples of this are productions that include Microsoft Word or Excel files, or PST ("personal storage table") files of a user's e-mail messages in their original Microsoft Outlook format. SWEENEY ET AL., *supra* note 9, at § 7.03.
13. Id.
14. Id.
15. Portable document format (PDF) and text-imaged file format (TIFF) are two of the most common formats used to create exact digital pictures of original files in a universal format that is easily accessible. *See* SWEENEY ET AL., *supra* note 9, at § 7.03.
16. Metadata is the hidden, embedded data containing files that, if properly accessed, give the reader information regarding various details about the creation and life of the file. *See* FED. R. CIV. P. 26(f) advisory committee's note (2006 Amendment); SWEENEY ET AL., *supra* note 9, at § 7.03(A).
17. SWEENEY ET AL., *supra* note 9, at § 7.03.

18. *Id.* In other instances, native format ESI is essential to good discovery and litigation. Sometimes, the native format ESI is sought purely for what is contained in the metadata, which might be of immense value, for example, if the date of an internal memorandum, or the identity of blind recipients of an e-mail, is at issue. *See, e.g.*, White v. Graceland Coll. Ctr. for Prof'l Dev. & Lifelong Learning, Inc., 586 F. Supp. 2d 1250 (D. Kan. 2009).

19. Optical character recognition (OCR) software is often used to enable word searches in PDF and TIFF files; however, the technology is not always reliable, and may encounter problems with spreadsheets and numerical charts in particular. *See* SWEENEY ET AL., *supra* note 9, at § 7.03.

20. *Id.*

21. *See id.* at § 7.03(D).

22. *Id.*

23. *Id.*

24. FED. R. CIV. P. 26(b) advisory committee's note (2006 Amendment). The factors contained in Rule 26(b)(2)(C) include whether the information is available through alternate means; whether the requesting party has had "ample opportunity to obtain the information by discovery"; and whether the "burden or expense . . . outweighs its likely benefit" given factors such as the "needs of the case, the amount in controversy, the parties' resources, the importance of the issues at stake in the action, and the importance of the discovery in resolving the issues." FED. R. CIV. P. 34(b)(2)(C)(i)–(iii).

25. FED. R. CIV. P. 34(b) advisory committee's note (2006 Amendment).

26. FED. R. CIV. P. 34(b)(2)(E)(i).

27. 8A CHARLES ALAN WRIGHT ET AL., FEDERAL PRACTICE AND PROCEDURE § 2219 (2d Supp. 2009).

28. FED. R. CIV. P. 34(b)(2)(E)(iii).

29. FED. R. CIV. P. 34(b) advisory committee's note (2006 Amendment).

30. FED. R. CIV. P. 34(b)(2)(E)(ii).

31. FED. R. CIV. P. 34(b) advisory committee's note (2006 Amendment).

32. FED. R. CIV. P. 34(b) advisory committee's note (2006 Amendment); FED. R. CIV. P. 34(b)(2)(E)(ii).

33. FED. R. CIV. P. 34(b) advisory committee's note (2006 Amendment).

34. White v. Graceland Coll. Ctr. for Prof'l Dev. & Lifelong Learning, Inc., 586 F. Supp. 2d 1250 (D. Kan. 2009).

35. *Id.* at 1263–64.

36. *Id.* at. 1264.

37. *Id.*

38. Many states authorize depositions of "persons most knowledgeable" on enumerated topics. *See, e.g.*, CAL. CIV. PROC. CODE § 2025.230; FLA. RULES OF CIV. PROC. § 1.310(b)(6); ILL. SUPREME COURT R. 206(a)(1); N.J. RULE OF COURT 4:14-2(c); VA. RULE OF COURT 4:5(b)(6).

39. "It should be kept in mind that a Rule 30(b)(6) designee testifies on behalf of the corporation, and binds the entity with its testimony." 7 JAMES WM. MOORE ET AL., MOORE'S FEDERAL PRACTICE ¶ 30.25[3] (3d ed. 2009) (citing Sigmund v. Starwood Urban Retail VI, LLC, 236 F.R.D. 43, 45 (D.D.C. 2006)). "The answers given by the person designated by the corporation under Rule 30(b)(6) are admissions by the corporation: 'The designated witness is speaking for the corporation.'" SCHWARZER ET AL., FEDERAL CIVIL PROCEDURE BEFORE TRIAL ¶ 11:1414 (The Rutter Group 2009) (citing United States v. Taylor, 166 F.R.D. 356, 361 (M.D.N.C. 1996); Sprint Commc'ns Co., L.P. v. Theglobe.com, Inc., 236 F.R.D. 524, 527 (D. Kan. 2006); Reilly v. NatWest Markets Group Inc., 181. F.3d 253, 268 (2d Cir. 1999); Rainey v. Am. Forest & Paper Ass'n, Inc., 26 F. Supp. 2d 82, 95 (D.D.C. 1998).

40. MOORE ET AL., *supra* note 39 (citing Mitsui & Co. v. P.R. Water Res. Auth., 93 F.R.D. 62, 67 (D.P.R. 1981); Bank of New York v. Meridien Biao Bank Tanzania, Ltd., 171 F.R.D. 135, 151 (S.D.N.Y. 1997); S.E.C. v. Morelli, 143 F.R.D. 42, 45 (S.D.N.Y. 1992); Wilson v. Lakner, 228 F.R.D. 524, 528 (D. Md. 2005); Marker v. Union Fid. Life Ins. Co., 125 F.R.D. 121, 126 (M.D.N.C. 1989); Brazos River Auth. v. GE Ionics, Inc., 469 F.3d 416, 433 (5th Cir. 2006); Fed. Deposit Ins. Corp. v. Butcher, 116 F.R.D. 196, 199 (E.D. Tenn. 1986); Dravo Corp. v. Liberty Mut. Ins. Co., 164 F.R.D. 70, 75 (D. Neb. 1995); Quantachrome Corp. v. Micrometrics Instrument Corp., 189 F.R.D. 697, 699 (S.D. Fla. 1999); Alexander v. FBI, 186 F.R.D. 137, 141 (D.D.C. 1998)). "If necessary, the corporation owes a duty to 'educate' its designees; i.e., to prepare them so that they can answer fully questions posed as to the designated subject matters." SCHWARZER ET AL., *supra* note 39 (citing Sony Elecs., Inc. v. Soundview Techs., Inc., 217 F.R.D. 104, 112 (D. Ct. 2002)).

41. M & R Contractors & Builders v. Michael, 138 A.2d 350, 355 (Md. 1958).

42. Propellex Corp. v. Brownlee, 342 F.3d 1335, 1341 (Fed. Cir. 2003) (modified total cost claim properly denied in toto where the contractor "failed to demonstrate the impracticability of proofing its actual losses directly. The evidence shows that [the contractor] could have set up its accounting system to track the [extra] costs...."); Boyajian v. United States, 423 F.2d 1231, 1233–34 (Fed. Cir. 1970); *but see* E.C. Ernst, Inc. v. Koppers Co., Inc., 626 F.2d 324, 329 (3d Cir. 1980) ("[T]he [trial] court's opinion [denying recovery] has the effect of finding liability with no damages even though it recognized that the plaintiff had suffered some damage and that the defendant was entirely responsible for the damage."); *see also* Appeal of Grumman Aerospace Corp., 06-1 BCA ¶ 33,216 at 164,607 (2006) ("GAC [the claimant and appellant] had an accounting and cost-tracking system that was technically capable of tracking out-of-scope work activities.... In a few instances GAC sought to track certain claimed out-of-scope costs through use of secondary job numbers.... However, many of appellant's claims impacted identical WBS [work breakdown structure] elements in the same contract performance period.... Given such concurrency, it was difficult to accurately track which costs were attributable to which claims." The Board found that the contractor had "satisfied the first prong of the MTCM [modified total cost method] test, that is, that it was impracticable to prove all its losses directly through actual cost data." However, the Board denied recovery because the contractor was unable to prove the reasonableness of its bid costs or its lack of responsibility for the claimed cost overruns. *Id.* at 164,620–21.

43. Generally, lay witnesses may not give opinions going beyond matters personally perceived. FED. R. EVID. 701.

44. *See* Hensel Phelps Constr. Co., 01-1 BCA ¶ 31,249, 154,321–24 (2001) (discussion of the use of MCAA inefficiency factors and the use of experts to quantify loss of productivity); *see also* Luria Bros. & Co. v. United States, 369 F.2d 701, 713 (Ct. Cl. 1966) ("It is a rare case where loss of productivity can be proven by books and records; almost always it has to be proven by the opinion of expert witnesses. However, the mere expression of an estimate as to the amount of productivity loss by an expert witness with nothing to support it will not establish the fundamental fact of resultant injury nor provide a sufficient basis for making a reasonably correct approximation of damages."); Sunshine Constr. & Eng'g, Inc. v. United States, 64 Fed. Cl. 346, 358–60, 368–71 (2005) (comparing and contrasting the approaches taken by two experts to delay and lost productivity issues).

45. *E.g.*, FED. R. CIV. PROC. 26(a)(2)(A), (B) ("Unless otherwise stipulated or ordered by the court, this disclosure [of witnesses to give opinion testimony] must be accompanied by a written report . . . if the witness is one retained or specially employed to provide expert testimony in the case or one whose duties as the party's employee regularly involve giving expert testimony.").

46. Federal Rule of Evidence 702 provides, "If scientific, technical, or other specialized knowledge will assist the trier of fact to understand the evidence or to determine a fact

in issue, a witness qualified as an expert by knowledge, skill, experience, training, or education, may testify thereto in the form of an opinion or otherwise, if (1) the testimony is based upon sufficient facts or data, (2) the testimony is the product of reliable principles and methods, and (3) the witness has applied the principles and methods reliably to the facts of the case."

47. Daubert v. Merrell Dow Pharms., Inc., 509 U.S. 579 (1993).
48. Frye v. United States, 293 F. 1013 (App. D.C. 1923).
49. *Daubert*, 509 U.S. at 579.
50. *Daubert*, 509 U.S. at 594–95.
51. *Id.* at 595.
52. *Id.* at 593.
53. Kumho Tire Co., Ltd. v. Carmichael, 119 S. Ct. 1167, 1171 (1999).
54. *Daubert*, 509 U.S. at 590.
55. *Id.* at 589.
56. Gen. Elec. Co. v. Joiner, 522 U.S. 136 (1997).
57. *Kumho*, 119 S. Ct. at 1171.
58. *Joiner*, 522 U.S. at 136.
59. *Kumho*, 119 S. Ct. at 1169.
60. *Joiner*, 522 U.S. at 136; *Kumho*, 119 S. Ct. at 1175.
61. Alaska, Arkansas, Colorado, Connecticut, Delaware, Idaho, Indiana, Iowa, Kentucky, Louisiana, Maine, Michigan, Mississippi, Montana, Nebraska, New Mexico, North Carolina, Ohio, Oklahoma, Oregon, Rhode Island, South Carolina, South Dakota, Tennessee, Texas, Vermont, West Virginia, and Wyoming. Alice B. Lustre, Annotation, *Post-Daubert Standards for Admissibility of Scientific and other Expert Evidence in State Courts*, 90 A.L.R. 5th 453 (originally published 2001, updated 2009).
62. Arizona, California, District of Columbia, Florida, Illinois, Kansas, Maryland, Minnesota, Mississippi, Missouri, New York, North Dakota, Pennsylvania, and Washington. *Id.*
63. Alabama, Hawaii, Massachusetts, Nevada, New Hampshire, and New Jersey. *Id.*
64. Georgia, Utah, Virginia, and Wisconsin. *Id.*
65. ROMAN L. WEIL ET AL., LITIGATION SERVICES HANDBOOK: THE ROLE OF THE FINANCIAL EXPERT 1–5 (4th ed. 2007).
66. FED. R. EVID. 702.
67. 29 CHARLES ALAN WRIGHT & ARTHUR R. MILLER, FEDERAL PRACTICE AND PROCEDURE § 6265 (2009).
68. Michael DeCelles et al., *10 Years After* Daubert: *What Accounting Litigation Experts Should Know About Admissibility of Expert Witness Testimony*, TODAY'S CPA, Mar./Apr. 2007, at 22.
69. 29 CHARLES ALAN WRIGHT & ARTHUR R. MILLER, FEDERAL PRACTICE AND PROCEDURE § 6265 (2009).
70. PricewaterhouseCoopers, 2000–2007 Financial Expert Witness *Daubert* Challenge Study (2008), http://www.pwc.com/extweb/pwcpublications.nsf/docid/9082E2EC969ED877852575AF0078ECBF (last visited Dec. 6, 2009). The Web site reports that an update will soon be posted.
71. DeCelles et al., *supra* note 68, at 22.
72. ROBERT CUSHMAN ET AL., PROVING AND PRICING CONSTRUCTION CLAIMS 517 (3d ed. 2001).
73. The 2000–2007 PricewaterhouseCoopers study analyzed 3681 *Daubert* challenges published in written case opinions and found 635 challenges related to financial experts. The study found the exclusion of the witnesses was jurisdictionally specific, as high as 69 percent in the 11th Circuit and as low as 21 percent in the First Circuit; case-type specific,

as 56 percent of financial expert witnesses were excluded in fraud cases, but only 24 percent were excluded in breach of contract/fiduciary duty cases; and dependent on the reliability of the experts' work, which was the reason that 57 percent of financial experts were excluded in 2007. PricewaterhouseCoopers, *supra* note 70.

74. *Id.*

75. *See Daubert*: More Important than You Think in Business Litigation, ABA Annual Meeting, Bus. Law Section, Bus. and Corporate Litig. Comm. (Aug. 2006); *Daubert* on the Web, http://www.daubertontheweb.com/ (last visited Dec. 6, 2009); BRUCE S. SCHAEFFER ET AL., CHALLENGES TO THE ADMISSIBILITY OF EXPERT FINANCIAL TESTIMONY: 2005–2008 (Wolters Kluwer, 2008). One reason for the relatively few number of construction cases is that many construction cases are arbitrated, and so do not result in reported decisions.

76. Leon v. Kelly, 2009 U.S. Dist. LEXIS 39010 (D.N.M. 2009).

77. *Id.* at *4.

78. *Id.* at *12.

79. *Id.* at *13.

80. *Id.* at *14.

81. *Id.*

82. *Id.* at *43.

83. Shadow Lake Mgmt. Co., Inc. v. Landmark Am. Ins. Co., 2008 U.S. Dist. LEXIS 86850 (E.D. La. 2008).

84. *Id.* at *2–3.

85. *Id.* at *9.

86. *Id.*

87. *Id.*

88. MACTEC, Inc. v. Bechtel Jacobs Co., LLC, 2008 U.S. Dist. LEXIS 5968 (E.D. Tenn. 2008).

89. *Id.* at *5.

90. *Id.* at *5–6.

91. *Id.* at 7.

92. RLI Ins. Co. v. Indian River Sch. Dist., 2007 U.S. Dist. LEXIS 89519 (D. Del. 2007).

93. *Id.* at *2

94. *Id.* at *20.

95. *Id.*

96. *Id.*

97. *Id.* at *20–21.

98. Carlisle Corp. d/b/a Carlisle Syntec Sys. v. Med. City Dallas, Ltd., 196 S.W.3d 855 (Tex. App. 5th 2006).

99. *Id.* at 867.

100. *Id.*

101. *Id.*

102. Jefferson v. Jefferson, 946 So. 2d 191 (La. App. 5 Cir. 2006).

103. *Id.* at 195.

104. *Id.* at 195–96.

105. *Id.* at 196.

106. See, e.g., RAOUL D. KENNEDY & JAMES C. MARTIN, CALIFORNIA EXPERT WITNESS GUIDE 505–40 (CEB, rev. ed. 2009) (which contains an excellent, general outline for expert deposition); ROBERT J. MACPHERSON, BUCKNER HINKLE, W. ALEXANDER MOSELEY, JR. & RICHARD F. SMITH, DISCOVERY DESKBOOK FOR CONSTRUCTION DISPUTES 170–72 (ABA 2006).

107. See *Daubert* Tracker, http://www.dauberttracker.com.

APPENDIX

Contractors' Cost and Accounting Records to Consider Requesting in Discovery

1. Bid Information
   a. All workpapers, correspondence, internal memoranda, supporting documents, and assumptions or calculations used to develop the bid estimate for the contract. These documents include, but are not limited to, engineering quantity takeoffs, labor rates, rental rates, efficiency and productivity standards, equipment usage rates, subcontractor bids, material quotes, projected labor usage, material costs, overhead and profit percentages, and other project cost elements used to estimate the bid costs on which this contract award was based.
   b. All documentation, workpapers, estimates, and assumptions used to determine the labor, material, equipment (including hourly rates), overhead, and unit costs used in the compilation of the (Subcontractor) bid.
   c. Planned man loading schedules and/or graphs, as well as materials and equipment usage planning schedules.
   d. Planned overhead absorption schedules and overhead allocation schedules used in the bid development or pricing.
2. Project-Related Accounting Information
   a. Project cost ledger and subsidiary contract cost ledgers.
   b. Project accounts receivable ledgers for all project receipts.
   c. Cash disbursements and receipts journals.
   d. Bank statements, account reconciliations, cancelled checks, and deposit slips.
   e. Contract status reports, job cost status reports or summary reports comparing actual, committed, projected, or incurred costs to bid, and budgeted or targeted costs for each period for which such data was prepared.
   f. List of all backcharge credits and other refunds, credits, reimbursements, or allowances received from vendors, suppliers, insurance companies, or others.

g. Progress or physical status reports of the percentage or stage of physical completion for each pay item for each period for which such reports were prepared.
h. Reports, charts, graphs, or other documents indicating physical units completed for each period for which such data was prepared.
i. Documents, memoranda, instruction, or correspondence relating to accounting procedures for accumulating, charging, or identifying costs on the subject contract.
j. Owned equipment inventory reports listing equipment assigned to this project.
k. Owned equipment reports showing hourly use charges for each item of owned equipment charged to this project. The total of these charges should equal the balance shown for owned equipment in the summary of total project costs.
l. Monthly progress reports for the entire project.
m. Records detailing progress payments received on this contract.
n. Daily force reports, attendance reports, and manning charts or reports (including both "plan" and "actual" data) for the entire project.
o. Change order logs listing all change orders proposed and awarded.
p. Documents describing change order costs, whether incurred or estimated, and related pricing documentation.
q. Analysis of actual cash flows prepared for this project.
r. Daily reports or diaries prepared by the project superintendent(s) or project manager(s).

3. Specific Cost-Related Information
   a. Labor Cost Information.
      (1) Reports identifying labor hours and costs charged to each account, subaccount, labor work order, change order, or cost code within the contract for the entire project period (such reports are commonly referred to as labor or payroll distribution reports).
      (2) Time cards.
      (3) Foreman's daily time and classification reports.
      (4) Schedules detailing composition of labor cost elements included in labor burden including components of fringe benefit pools and methods of allocation to this project.
   b. Material Cost Information.
      (1) Material usage and cost distribution reports that account for materials used on a period-by-period basis by cost area for the entire project.

(2) Purchase journals, voucher registers, invoices, and raw material receiving records indicating the quantity and date of receipt of raw materials.
  c. Equipment Cost Information.
    (1) Equipment records for all equipment used on the project, including acquisition or ownership costs. Ownership costs including fuel, oil, grease, repairs, maintenance, overhaul, depreciation, insurance, tires, and storage.
    (2) Invoices, rental agreements, and purchase orders indicating rental rates and terms for all pieces of equipment used on this project.
  d. Subcontractors.
    (1) Subcontractor cost and distribution reports that account for the subcontractor(s) on a period-by-period basis by cost code for the entire project.
    (2) Progress or performance reports for subcontractors for the entire period.
4. Claim Information
  a. Supporting schedules, working papers, documentation (including computer print-outs, disks, or magnetic tape) and computations detailing the methods used to derive claims arising from this project.
5. General Accounting Information
  a. Chart of accounts providing a complete description of all cost codes used in the project cost system.
  b. Accounting procedures manual.
  c. General ledger for all periods.
  d. Payroll and income tax returns for all relevant years, including supporting schedules and amended returns.
  e. Financial statements prepared for internal and/or external use.
  f. Analysis of (subcontractor's) financial performance, cost performance, or account analysis.
  g. Any computation of bonuses paid to personnel that were in any way based on the financial performance of the company.
  h. Claim documents, working papers, and calculations prepared in connection with other contracts of the company.
  i. Weekly, monthly, quarterly, annual, or other periodic management and/or executive reports that discuss, analyze, or examine:
    (1) Labor contracts.
    (2) Management contracts.
    (3) Personnel performance.

CHAPTER 11

Accounting Issues in Fraud Investigations

BRANDI N. KLEINMAN
STEVEN J. KMIECIAK
ALAN F. NAGORZANSKI
RODNEY W. SOWARDS
DANIEL P. WIERZBA

Introduction

Fraud is becoming an increasingly significant issue in business transactions in both the private and public sectors. The overwhelming majority of the participants in the construction industry, both companies and employees, are honest and competent.[1] Despite that fact, the construction industry suffers from a higher incidence of fraud than other industries.[2] According to recent studies, the cost of construction fraud has grown to 10 percent of gross revenue.[3] In addition, fraud schemes on construction projects are growing more complex.[4] The purpose of this chapter is to introduce the various types of fraudulent accounting activities that can involve companies and activities on construction projects. Understanding fraud from the accounting and legal perspectives will aid in detecting fraudulent accounting activities and preventing them from affecting a company's operations and viability. The consequences for engaging in fraud can be severe. Companies should be especially vigilant now, because scrutiny of accounting activities, particularly by government agencies, has increased significantly in recent years.

Definition of Fraud

Accounting Definition

The American Institute of Certified Public Accountants issued the AICPA Statement on Auditing Standards (SAS) 99, Consideration of Fraud in a Financial Statement Audit, to assist an auditor in identifying risks that may result in material misstatements in financial statements. SAS 99 defines fraud as an intentional act that results in a material misrepresentation in financial statements that are the subject of an audit. Auditors do not make legal determinations of whether fraud has occurred and do not attempt to determine intent of misstatements; however, auditors do employ analytical procedures to investigate potential fraud risks. Although the SAS 99 definition specifically addresses audits of financial statements, the definition can be applied to construction project accounting documents, because these documents affect the total revenues and expenses reported on a construction company's audited financial statements.

Legal Definition

The concept of fraud has developed both in the common law and by statute. Every state and the federal government have enacted criminal statutes to deter and punish fraudulent activity. Additionally, the federal government and some state governments have enacted civil false claims statutes to penalize fraudulent activity on state and federal contracts.[5]

Fraud is often defined as "[a] false representation of a material fact—whether by words or by conduct, by false or misleading allegations, or by concealment of what should have been disclosed—that deceives and is intended to deceive another so that the individual will act upon it to her or his legal injury."[6]

Legal Elements; Penalties for Fraud

The specific requirements of any applicable fraud statute must be analyzed to determine whether certain conduct violates the applicable statute. However, most fraud statutes share the same five elements: (1) a false statement of a material fact, (2) knowledge on the part of the accused that the statement is untrue, (3) intent on the part of the accused to deceive the alleged victim, (4) justifiable reliance by the alleged victim on the statement, and (5) injury to the alleged victim as a result.[7]

These elements all contain nuances that can be difficult to prove. First, a statement of belief is not fraud, because it is not a statement of fact; and not all false statements are actionable as fraud. To satisfy the test for fraud, a false statement must relate to a material fact, which means that the statement must relate to the significant aspects of the transaction at issue. Otherwise, the false statement typically will not be considered to be fraudulent.[8] Second, the accused must know that the statement is untrue. The statement must be made with intent to deceive the victim, and a statement of fact that is simply mistaken is not fraudulent.[9] Third, the false statement must be made with the intent to deprive the victim of some legal right. Fourth, the victim's reliance on the false statement must be reasonable. For example, the alleged victim cannot claim fraud if he relies on a patently absurd false statement.[10] Finally, the false statement must cause the victim some injury that leaves him in a worse position than before the fraud.[11]

Organizational and Performance Fraud

Understanding both how and why a contractor may commit fraud will assist in the prevention and detection of fraud. Common ways that fraud can occur on construction projects include improper timing and valuation of revenue and expenses, related-party transactions, and contract performance. Contractors may commit fraud in order to overcome unanticipated project delays, cost overruns, downturns in the economy, or deficient project management. In addition, a contractor may misrepresent its financial condition or exaggerate financial capacity to satisfy bonding requirements or to bid on larger projects with minimum asset or liquidity requirements.

This chapter addresses two basic categories of fraud that could affect participants in the construction industry. The first category is organizational fraud, or fraud concerning the ability or capacity of a company to do business. Organizational fraud includes fraud related to a company's balance sheet or its financial statements with the intention of deceiving lenders, sureties, and owners about: (1) the company's financial standing; (2) its capacity to perform a volume of work; (3) its creditworthiness or ability to service loans and lines of credit; or (4) its bonding capacity and its ability to indemnify sureties for bonds they issue on the company's behalf. The second category is performance fraud. This category includes preparation of fraudulent invoices, time records, payment applications, and other documents that are relied upon during the performance of a project. Performance fraud also involves a party's attempt to obtain a greater payment than it is entitled to receive under the contract, or to perform less work or work at a lower standard than what is required by the contract.

Organizational Fraud

A variety of state and federal statutes govern fraud with regard to financial reporting and loan applications. The criminal consequences for fraudulent activity can be severe. In addition, the financial consequences can be equally severe. While criminal statutes may target the individuals involved in the fraudulent activity, the financial consequences for the business could force the company into bankruptcy or dissolution.

Misrepresentations regarding a company's financial position on a loan application or a surety bond application can be particularly devastating. Upon learning of the misrepresentations, a lender or surety could cancel the company's line of credit, call the loan for immediate repayment, or terminate the company's bonding capacity.[12] Additionally, to the extent the lender or surety incurs damages as a result of the company's fraud, the lender or surety would be able to recover at least its actual damages, and many states allow the injured party to recover punitive damages that may far exceed the actual damages.[13] Punitive damages compensate the injured party in excess of actual damages and are intended to punish the party who committed the wrong.[14]

Revenue Recognition

Contractors often record revenue on construction projects on either a completed contract or a percent complete revenue recognition method. The rules governing revenue recognition methods for construction projects are contained in AICPA Statement of Position (SOP) 81-1. The collection of cash does not necessarily result in recognition of revenue. Cash collection prior to providing a good or service results in unearned revenue. Since an obligation exists on the part of the company to provide a future good or service, the advance payment received should be recorded as unearned revenue, which is a liability. Underreporting the liabilities associated with unearned revenue serves to overstate revenue and profits, and is therefore a potential fraud risk in construction accounting.

Other potential fraud risks related to revenue recognition on construction projects include fictitious sales, improper timing of recordation, and improper valuation of project revenue. Fictitious sales can result from recording revenue from nonexistent clients and projects or erroneous or nonexistent change orders. Erroneous acceleration of revenue recognition at year-end or just prior to the cutoff date of financial statements is also a timing problem in the construction industry that results in fraudulent overstatement of reported revenue. Improper valuation of revenue can result from the omission of deductive change orders, improperly classifying subsequent phase work as current, or treatment of deposit returns as revenue.

Expense Recognition

The accounting concept known as the matching principle requires the recordation of an expense in the period in which the associated revenue is earned. Similar to revenue recognition, cash payment does not necessarily result in proper recordation of current expenses; nor does the absence of payment indicate that an expense should not be recorded. Because most contractors do not follow a strict cash basis of accounting, contractors can potentially manipulate reported expenses as part of a fraudulent scheme to overstate reimbursement or profit. Labor, material, or overhead expenses can be completely omitted or improperly recorded as capitalized assets. Capitalizing such expenses delays expense recognition, and the ultimate effect is to overstate profits. Contractors can also improperly fail to record properly accrued expenses because payment has not been made. One of the most obvious but potentially most difficult fraud risks to detect is the omission of certain project overhead expenses. For example, job cost reports can be manipulated to reflect overstated profitability by omitting project supervision expenses that are captured and recorded at the corporate level. Alternatively, equipment buydowns or discounts negotiated by the contractor can be applied at the corporate level, but not properly allocated to the project job cost reports. Another type of expense fraud involves failing to estimate properly and record reserves for end-of-project punch list activities or warranty costs. Proper valuation of these accrued expenses is important not only to present the company's financial statements accurately, but also to represent the profitability of the individual jobs affected by these reserves accurately.

Related-Party Transactions

Auditors of financial statements place great emphasis on evaluating or disclosing the existence of related-party transactions. The absence of a third-party, arm's-length transaction, which is the case between related parties, results in a significant fraud risk on construction projects. Recordation of unreasonably high revenue or abnormally low expenses may indicate a potential misrepresentation related to the related-party transaction. Contractors working on a time and material or cost-plus contract for an owner may have less incentive to obtain competitive bids for activities that are performed by a related-party subcontractor. The ability of a contractor to hire and use related parties on a project creates a potential conflict of interest between the owner's desire to minimize cost and the contractor's desire to maximize profit (not only from the contractor's own activities, but also from the services provided by the related companies).[15]

Misappropriation of Assets

Another type of fraud that can occur in the construction industry is the misappropriation of assets. Readers of a construction company's balance sheet often rely on the reported assets as being properly recorded, properly valued, and owned by the company. Through misappropriation of company assets, contractors can siphon cash, tools, and equipment away from appropriate project activities. Receivables can be factored and pledged to a third-party financing company. The owners of the company can pledge company assets to secure unrelated personal or other business loans. All of these activities can deplete or consume the reported assets, causing those assets to be unavailable to support the operations of the construction company. Most typically, the contractor fails to disclose the factoring or pledging of company assets, where a third party has acquired a security interest in (if not outright ownership of) the company's asset. This distorts any financial evaluation of the contractor by making the contractor appear to have more working capital (defined as current assets less current liabilities) or to be more solvent (total assets less total liabilities).

There is no foolproof way to detect the misappropriation of assets, especially at the outset of a proposed relationship with a contractor. Asking a prospective contractor about its practice with respect to pledging fixed assets and factoring of receivables is always advised. Conducting Uniform Commercial Code (UCC) and lien searches is also advisable. Article 9 of the UCC allows equipment dealers (or lenders) to perfect a security interest in equipment that is bought or financed. These security-interest filings are available for review by anyone interested in determining whether third parties have such security interests in equipment or similar property. Searches of UCC filings at the appropriate state agency will reveal the existence of perfected security interests.

Performance Fraud

The most frequent occurrences of fraud in the construction industry occur during contract performance. An audit is the most useful tool to detect fraud, but unlike balance sheets and annual reports that may be subjected to audit, auditors do not routinely review records related to the cost of the performance of a project. Contract provisions may address the consequences of misrepresentations of costs during performance. In addition to actual damages, most states allow the recovery of punitive damages for fraudulent activity.

A contractor may commit fraud on a construction project through a variety of actions, such as labor overcharging, installing substandard materials, billing for unallowable costs, submitting inappropriate or duplicate markups, and using inappropriate labor and equipment rates. Each of these is addressed next.

Labor Overcharging

A contractor may attempt to overcharge labor to a project through several means.[16] Overstating applicable charge rates or misstating employee positions/titles are the most obvious ways of accomplishing this, but several other techniques may be utilized. To the extent the contractor has other, ongoing lump-sum contracts, the contractor may attempt to reassign idle labor from its fixed-price projects to a cost-plus contract project. Evidence of such attempts may include sporadic and partial daily charges for specific individuals to the cost-plus project during a work week. Alternatively, the contractor may simply charge laborers or supervisors who are actually working on other projects to the cost-plus project. To the extent the contractor is using a related-party subcontractor, the contractor may attempt to overbill the subcontractor's labor costs to a particular project. Because the entities are affiliated, such overbilled amounts would not undergo the typical contractor vetting of invoices for labor costs. Lastly, labor costs may be overbilled by using billing rates, in lieu of and in reality higher than actual costs, when negotiating prices for contracts or contract modifications, when charging cost-reimbursement contracts, or when pricing claims.

Substandard or Substituted Materials

A contractor attempting to fraudulently minimize material costs may revert to the use of substandard materials. Such materials are often used in areas or locations that will be out of sight, covered up, or difficult to access due to high temperature, height, or congested spaces. For example, the contractor may use inferior bolts or other such fasteners that do not meet specified strength requirements. In areas that become covered, such as slabs, walls, and above-ceiling locations, a contractor willing to commit fraud to minimize costs may not only use substandard materials, but may also use less reinforcing, conduit, or supports in those hidden locations. Submittal of material certifications should be required to manage this risk. An owner may also require inspections to be conducted before out-of-sight areas are covered in order to control and minimize such fraudulent actions. Additionally, contractors may commit fraud by substituting different materials and equipment for the items specified in the contract. For example, installing reconditioned equipment instead of new equipment, or utilizing different models than those identified in the specifications, may be considered fraud. In these instances, if the contractor certified that it complied with the specifications, then it does not matter if the materials or equipment actually installed are comparable to those specified.[17] Additionally, the contractor could be liable even if it submits material or equipment that conforms to the specifications but that the contractor failed to have tested and inspected prior to delivery as required by the contract.[18] On the other hand, the contractor may be able to provide nonconforming materials if it requests and obtains a waiver of the design requirements from the owner before delivering the materials.[19]

Billing of Unallowable Costs

A contractor seeking to become overcompensated on cost-reimbursement contract work may attempt to bill unreimbursable costs. These attempts may disguise or alter the descriptions of work or costs in order to make the work appear to be reimbursable cost work. For example, descriptions of rework or other work performed due to contractor errors or inefficiencies may be altered when such rework is not reimbursable under the contract. Costs that should be covered by insurance may be portrayed as contractually reimbursable. Where salaries and wages for certain supervisors or management personnel are not reimbursable under the contract, such individuals may be fraudulently identified as tradesmen or working foremen. Labor charges for activities such as "drafting" or "document review" may not be supported by actual time reports. Contractors using generic activity billing descriptions such as these should maintain detailed descriptions of the specific tasks actually being performed in order to provide substantiation and minimize challenges to such charges. In like manner, a generic activity such as "drafting" should occur coincident with design revisions, drawing issuances, as-built drawing production, and other periods of necessary drafting activities.

Inappropriate or Duplicate Markup

The markups used by a contractor in its billing of cost-plus or change order work are another potential area for fraud. Contractors may allow subcontractors to use excessive markups, especially where the general contractor has a long-standing positive relationship with the subcontractor. Unless closely checked, the contractor may duplicate markups, or use markups in excess of those allowed by contract for work performed. Standard labor or equipment rates that already include a markup may be marked up a second time.

Labor burden is the cost of all insurance, taxes, and benefits associated with the direct cost of labor, and is in addition to the amount that the worker receives in his or her paycheck (the paycheck is direct labor cost). Labor burdens should be verified by demonstrating the actual amounts paid by the contractor to prevent use of a labor burden rate that also includes a profit component. For example, the contractor may routinely charge 50 percent labor burden on direct labor costs, although actually incurring burden costs significantly less. With respect to overhead, the contractor may charge overhead costs to a direct cost account, while also applying an overhead percentage markup to other charged costs. Sometimes, labor burden may include small-tools costs or another overhead component that the contractor attempts to also separately charge as a discrete cost of the work.

Use of Labor or Equipment Rates in Excess of Contract Rates

A contractor can defraud the owner by charging labor or equipment rates that are in excess of those allowed by contract. Overtime may be billed at time and one half (1.5 times direct labor plus labor burden), even though overtime labor burden does not increase at the same rate for overtime hours. For example, if a worker earns $20 per hour, labor burden may increase the cost of the worker to the contractor by another $10 per hour, for a total cost of $30 per hour. When that individual works overtime, the company generally will have to compensate the worker at time and a half of direct labor, or $30, before labor burden. If labor burden does not increase during overtime work, the contractor's cost for an hour of overtime work would be $40. However, an aggressive contractor may decide to charge an owner 1.5 times the fully burdened rate of $30, or $45 per hour. This would overstate labor charges by $5 per hour. Additionally, laborers may be billed as higher-skilled workers, whether apprentices or journeymen, without appropriate documentation. Journeymen performing unsupervised tasks could be overbilled as superintendents or foremen, if the contractor believes that such level-creep is likely to go unchallenged.

Contractor-owned equipment is often allowed to be charged at specified equipment rates. To increase billings, the contractor may instead utilize rental rates, which tend to be higher than owned-equipment rates (to account for the profit of the equipment rental company). Or the contractor may ignore required idle equipment charge reductions specified by the contract. The Rental Rate Blue Book for Construction Equipment as it relates to owned equipment provides guidance that standby rates for equipment should approximate the total of depreciation, cost of facilities capital, and indirect cost factors provided for that equipment. For example, the Blue Book provides that the standby rate for a skid steer loader is 41 percent of the Blue Book rate.

Another area where the contractor can abuse equipment rates is the selection among daily, weekly, and monthly rates. Weekly rates tend to be approximately 28 percent to 50 percent more than monthly rates, so equipment utilized for periods in excess of one month should not be charged at weekly or daily rates unless this is permitted under the contract. For example, the Blue Book weekly rates for owned equipment are approximately 28 percent more than the monthly rates. The AED (Associated Equipment Distributors) Green Book, another reference for rental rates for construction equipment, provides weekly rates that are 33 percent to 50 percent more than the monthly rate, depending on the tool or the type of equipment. For example, the 2008 AED Green Book base rental rate for a clay spade air tool accessory is $44 weekly and $88 monthly. If this tool is on a project for a consecutive four-week period, the appropriate charge is the monthly rate of $88, if a contract specifies use of AED Green Book rates. However, if the contractor uses the weekly rate of $44, this is $176 for the four-week period, and the contractor will have inappropriately overcharged the owner by $88.

It is advisable that all projects maintain an equipment log to reduce the opportunity for phantom charging of equipment that is actually not on site. Equipment delivered to the site for use on the project should be logged in and accompanied by delivery receipts and a description of intended use (possibly related to specific schedule activities). Owners need to guard against equipment being stored on the project before or after it is needed for productive work, to assure that the contractor cannot keep charging the equipment to the project while it is stored. For example, as site preparation and grading activities are completed, earth-moving equipment should be removed from the site and not continue to be charged to the owner merely because it is not needed immediately elsewhere.

False Claims Acts

The Federal Criminal False Claims Act and the Federal Civil False Claims Act address fraud committed on federally funded or sponsored projects. The public sector represents one of the most active construction markets.[20] The U.S. government has increased the number of investigations and prosecutions of construction industry participants for false claims. Many states have modeled their own false claims acts on the federal statutes.[21]

Criminal False Claims Act—18 U.S.C. § 287

The two Federal False Claims Acts each provide that a party has made a false claim when it (1) made or presented a false, fictitious, or fraudulent claim to an official, a department, or an agency of the United States; (2) knew such claim was false, fictitious, or fraudulent; and (3) did so with specific intent to violate the law or with a consciousness that what the party was doing was wrong.[22] The penalties for violating the criminal False Claims Act include (1) up to five years' imprisonment, (2) fines, and, (3) for Department of Defense contracts, fines of an additional $1 million. In addition, violations of the criminal False Claims Act generally result in the contractor being suspended or debarred from all federal government contracting.[23] Typically a party is required to disclose its violation and penalty, if any, as well as whether it has been suspended or debarred, as part of its bid or proposal for other federal, state, and local government contracts. Such a disclosure may then disqualify that party from receiving awards under those contracts, and possibly lead to debarment by state or local governments as well.

Civil False Claims Act—31 U.S.C. § 3729

Actions under the civil False Claims Act are initiated in one of two ways. First, the U.S. Department of Justice (DOJ) may file suit in the appropriate U.S. district court having jurisdiction over the defendant. DOJ typically takes this action at the conclusion of an investigation into allegations of improper conduct, often conducted by a contracting agency's Inspector General and related investigative services such as the Department of Criminal Investigative Service (DCIS), or its suit may be the result of an audit performed by the Department of Defense Contract Audit Agency (DCAA). Many times the contractor's receipt of an Inspector General's subpoena or a grand jury subpoena is the first indication that it is under investigation.

Second, an action under the civil False Claims Act can be initiated by a private citizen filing suit against a contractor on behalf of the United States. Such an action is known as a *qui tam* action.[24] In a *qui tam* action, the private citizen, frequently a present or former employee of the contractor, files suit in the appropriate U.S. district court having jurisdiction over the contractor. The case is filed under seal and served on the DOJ. DOJ then has 60 days to decide whether to take over the case from the plaintiff, referred to as the "relator," or to decline to take over the case.[25] DOJ often seeks additional time from the court to conduct its investigation and make this decision. Such leave is usually granted and the case remains under seal pending the DOJ investigation. The courts will usually continue to extend DOJ's deadline so long as DOJ can show that it is pursuing its investigation. Once DOJ makes its decision, the seal is lifted and the suit is served on the defendant. The case then proceeds like any civil case in the appropriate U.S. district court.

If DOJ decides to take over the case, it directs the case.[26] The relator typically is on the sidelines, although the relator is usually a key witness and source of evidence against the contractor. If the relator has included a count alleging that the contractor retaliated against the relator for complaining about the alleged misconduct, the relator will be more actively involved in the case.[27] The relator and its counsel, not DOJ, will be responsible for handling the retaliation count. If DOJ settles or obtains a judgment in favor of the United States on the false claims counts, the relator will receive a share of the award, ranging between 15 percent and 25 percent of the total award. This amount is in addition to any recovery it receives on the retaliation count.[28]

If DOJ declines to take over the case, the relator has the right to prosecute the case on its own, on behalf of the United States. Any settlement or judgment is shared with the U.S. government, but in this instance, the relator's share is higher, between 25 percent and 30 percent.[29] Again, this share is in addition to any recovery on an associated retaliation claim.

A violation of the civil False Claims Act occurs if (1) defendant knowingly presented or caused to be presented to an official, department, or agency of the United States, a false or fraudulent claim for payment or approval; (2) defendant knowingly made, used, or caused to be made or used a false record or statement to get a false or fraudulent claim paid or approved; (3) defendant conspired to defraud the government by getting a false or fraudulent claim allowed or paid; or (4) defendant knowingly made, used, or caused to be made or used, a false record or statement to cancel, avoid, or decrease an obligation to pay or transmit money or property to the government.[30] The defendant can also be found liable for a false claim under the civil Act if the claim was presented with reckless disregard or in deliberate ignorance of its truth or falsity.[31] Unlike the criminal False Claims Act, no specific intent to defraud is necessary to find liability.

In 2009, Congress passed the Fraud Enforcement and Recovery Act of 2009 (FERA).[32] Among other changes, FERA restated Section 3729(a) of the civil False Claims Act to define a claim as any request or demand related to a government program and paid from funds supplied by the government.[33] This provision of FERA overruled the decision of the U.S. Supreme Court in *Allison Engine Co. v. United States ex rel. Sanders*.[34] In *Allison Engine*, the Supreme Court held that a subcontractor was not liable under the civil False Claims Act unless it made a false claim with the specific intent to induce the government to pay or approve payment of a false or fraudulent claim, rather than merely defrauding a prime contractor. Under FERA, subcontractors and suppliers may be liable under the civil False Claims Act if they submit false or fraudulent claims to a prime contractor on a federal project if the U.S. government will provide any portion of the money or property requested or if it will reimburse the contractor for a portion of the money or property that is requested or demanded.[35]

The penalties under the civil False Claims Act may be applied individually or together and include the following: (1) civil fines of $5,500 to $11,000 for each false claim;[36] (2) three times the damage to the government; and (3) costs, including attorney's fees of the government's (and relator's) cost of prosecuting the case.[37] The civil Act allows for liability to be reduced to not more than two times the damages if the company discloses its conduct before the government discovers it and then cooperates in the government's investigation.[38]

Recent Examples of the Consequences of Fraudulent Activity

Two recent decisions illustrate both the symptoms that allow fraud to occur and the devastating consequences of fraudulent behavior. Both cases included the submission of false claims.

The first example is the 2006 decision by the Court of Federal Claims in *Daewoo Engineering & Construction Co, Ltd. v. United States*.[39] Daewoo performed a construction contract in the Republic of Palau for the U.S. Army Corps of Engineers (COE). Daewoo encountered a number of conditions during the project that Daewoo believed entitled it to equitable relief.[40] Daewoo's management also believed that the COE was not taking its claims seriously. As the court described it, Daewoo inflated its claims significantly in an effort to get the COE's attention, with the goal that the COE would then promptly pay Daewoo a considerably smaller, but justifiable, amount for its claims. In a decision that blasted Daewoo's management, consultants, and counsel for pursuing a grossly inflated claim, the court awarded the government a judgment in excess of $50 million, finding that sum to be the amount of Daewoo's false claim.[41] The court also found that by acting as it did, Daewoo forfeited the $13 million claim that was potentially supported by the evidence in the case and that, but for the false claim, might have been recovered from the government. In that case, it appears that Daewoo did not understand the rules and displayed an attitude that the ends justified the means.[42] Both of those factors contributed to the court's decision.

The second significant decision is *Morse Diesel International, Inc. v. United States*.[43] In that case, the Court of Federal Claims found that Morse Diesel had submitted a number of false claims during the performance of several federal courthouse construction contracts.[44] In determining that Morse Diesel had engaged in improper conduct, the court ruled that Morse Diesel had forfeited its right to recover approximately $53 million in claims on those projects.[45] The violations were more procedural than substantive, and it is questionable whether Morse Diesel's conduct actually damaged the government. For example, Morse Diesel billed the government for its bond premiums before it paid for them.[46] Unfortunately, Morse Diesel certified that it was entitled to be paid for those premiums when it billed for them, although the applicable regulations state that a contractor can bill for bond premiums only after they are paid. Apparently, Morse Diesel also billed owners a bond premium surcharge because it relied on financial support from its parent company.[47] However, the surcharge exceeded Morse Diesel's actual costs. In other instances, Morse Diesel certified on its applications for payment that it had paid its subcontractors in accordance with the terms of the Prompt Payment Act, even though it had not done so.[48] The court found these actions to amount to false claims, even though no party appeared to have been harmed by this conduct.[49] In many of these situations, if Morse Diesel had trained its employees properly and then monitored their activities to ensure compliance with the rules, these issues probably could have been avoided.

Uncovering and Detecting Fraud

Opportunities for Fraud in the Construction Industry

Job Cost Reports

Many people view the contractor's job cost report as merely an internal tracking tool. However, there are often instances, in both the commercial and government project arenas, where the contractor uses the job cost report to prepare, submit, and, most importantly, substantiate a claim. On government contracts, the contractor is entitled only to recover its "allowable costs."[50] The contractor can commit fraud in job cost reporting by hiding or redirecting costs to avoid detection through an audit. For example, the contractor may try to inflate its claim on a specific project by adding costs from a separate and totally unrelated project to the job cost report. Evidence of such an occurrence may include the charging of material costs to a work activity line item well after the completion of the related work. In addition, the contractor may try to include unallowable costs by adding them to an allowable cost category. Oftentimes, such cost descriptions will reflect an overly simple description. The key, for contractors and owners alike, is to make sure all costs are properly accounted for and easily traceable to work actually performed on the project in question. Costs applied to a job cost report should be organized by type of work (or work breakdown structure) and should be scrutinized if incurred in a period of time outside the actual period of performance of that work activity. For example, foundation or grade beam labor should be questioned if it was incurred during a period well after the completion of foundations. Distinct gaps of time between the incurrence of costs for a particular category of work may signal that the later charge was rework, if such a break was not originally contemplated. An attempt to pass such anomalies off as valid costs of construction may constitute fraud.

Payment Applications

Contractors may commit fraud in the course of routine tasks such as submitting payment applications. Many commercial projects use the standard forms issued by the American Institute of Architects (AIA), including standard AIA Form G702 for payment applications. Although the contractor may not have even read the payment application prior to signing it, each time it signs an AIA standard form monthly payment application it represents and certifies to the owner that (1) the work covered by the payment application is completed in accordance with the project specifications, (2) prior funds received have been paid to the respective subcontractors, and (3) the amount of the payment application is actually due and owing to the contractor.[51] If any of those statements are not accurate, the contractor may have committed fraud by signing the payment application, which the owner can then raise in any claims or litigation that later arise. The contractor must be fully aware as to what is being certified when it signs a payment application, and most importantly, determine whether these statements are accurate for each and every payment application. The *Morse Diesel* case provides an excellent illustration of a failure to provide accurate and truthful payment applications and the serious consequences that may result.

Contractors may also overstate the percentage-complete identified on the pay application for specific line items of construction work. To counter any such attempts, the owner may subdivide the pay application schedule of values by area or type of work within an area (rough-in versus finish, for example). In the initial preparation of the schedule of values, care should be taken to ensure that the schedule of values reasonably subdivides the contract sum into the appropriate tasks and minimizes the overweighting of initial tasks (front-end-loading). Another manner of implementing a front-end-loading strategy is to include a large-dollar-amount "mobilization" activity in the schedule of values. Upon moving equipment, a job trailer, and some staff to the site, the contractor may seek payment for the complete mobilization sum, even if actual costs at that point are far less. Stored materials may also be an area of overstatement unless the owner implements a procedure or ability to verify that the project has actually received the stored materials. To minimize pay application fraud, the owner may utilize a schedule of values breakdown by units, areas of work, or similarly countable categories. The owner can also minimize fraudulent pay application overstatements by timely reviewing pay applications and timely authorizing fair payments.

Bonding Process

The bonding process is an important preconstruction activity that also presents opportunity for contractor fraud. Owners rely on the bonding process to insure that the contractor has the financial ability to complete the project, or has a surety lined up to step in to take over the project if problems arise. However, contractors sometimes misrepresent their bonding capacity, and sometimes a contractor will use the bonding capacity of a parent company as its own. In the *Morse Diesel* case, Morse Diesel's parent agreed to indemnify the sureties when they issued bonds to Morse Diesel. The parent charged Morse Diesel for this indemnity in an amount equal to the bond premium that Morse Diesel paid to the surety. Morse Diesel billed the government the total of the bond premium and the parent company charge, but represented to the government that the amount it was billing was only the bond premium, in effect charging the government twice the actual bond premium. Morse Diesel then compounded its difficulties by certifying to the government in its payment application that it had paid the bond premium (as required by the contract) even though Morse Diesel knew that the premium had not actually been paid as yet. In fact, Morse Diesel directed its broker to issue paid invoices that it could submit to the government to substantiate payment, even though no premium payment had been made. The court also found that Morse Diesel had changed its bond broker and agreed that the new broker would be its exclusive broker in exchange for a split of the broker's commissions on the bonds purchased—a kickback in violation of the Anti-Kickback Act of 1986, 41 U.S.C. §§ 51–58.

Although relying on a parent company's financial strength for bonding purposes is not fraud per se, and even if the contractor does not engage in the type of conduct that Morse Diesel engaged in, courts nevertheless sometimes use the contractor's reliance on the parent's financial strength in support of a ruling against the contractor on other grounds. For example, in *Old Dominion Electric Cooperative v. Ragnar Benson, Inc.*,[52] the court provided a litany of reasons why the contractor was not entitled to any recovery for delays to a project, but was instead liable to the project owner. Specifically, the court noted that the contractor was not entitled to any consequential damages due to owner delays because, among other things, it relied on the financial standing of its parent company to obtain bonds and, therefore, did not suffer the claimed consequential damages because the delays in completing the project did not affect the subsidiary company's bonding capacity.[53]

In addition to the denial of the contractor's claim for consequential damages, this case also illustrates a number of problems that a contractor can encounter when it or its employees misrepresent the company's financial condition or its financial position on the project. In *Ragnar Benson*, the contractor also claimed that the owner's failure to pay for extra work and the owner's delays to the project impaired or diminished its bonding capacity, preventing it from obtaining future work and causing loss of the profits it would have earned on those other projects. The court found, however, that the misrepresentations of the contractor's employees actually caused these losses. First, the court found that in its efforts to convince the owner to award the contract, the contractor represented that it, in combination with its parent, had an unlimited bonding capacity and average annual sales exceeding $600 million. The court found that neither of those statements was true, and because of those representations, the owner could not foresee that its failure to pay for changes could have the effect of limiting the contractor's bonding capacity. Since the claimed consequential damages could not have been foreseen at the time of entry into the contract, they were not recoverable.

The court further found that the contractor had actually lost its bonding capacity because it had lost its line of credit, and that the contractor lost its line of credit because its vice president inflated the profits on the project to show that planned profit budgets would be met, even though, according to the court, he knew that those profits could not be achieved. The vice president received a bonus for "demonstrating" that the budgeted profits would be achieved. In short, the court determined that misrepresentations made by the contractor in order to get the contract precluded its recovery of consequential damages because its misrepresentations made those damages unforeseeable. Worse, the court determined the vice president's knowing misrepresentations regarding the profitability of a project, motivated by a desire to report better than actual performance on financial statements and a personal desire to earn a bonus, cost the company its line of credit and its entire bonding capacity.

Contract Performance

In general, a lump-sum, fixed-price contract provides the owner the greatest insulation from contractor fraud. The contractor must perform the specified work for a fixed, defined sum. However, even lump-sum contracts are not immune from fraudulent activity. Often the owner's requirements for all phases of the work cannot be defined with exactness or specificity. For portions of the work scope lacking specificity, the owner will often provide for "allowances," or preliminary budgets, for those undefined portions of the work. Additionally, lump-sum contracts still require change orders for alterations in the scope of the contract or specifications. Work subject to allowances or change orders both provide areas where fraud can occur. And in any type of contract, the failure to perform and supply materials in accordance with the requirements of the specifications provides opportunities for fraud.

The structure of cost-plus contracts and guaranteed maximum price (GMP) arrangements provide a higher risk to the owner of contractor fraud. Although subject to the greatest potential for fraud, closely monitored cost-plus contracts may provide the lowest total cost of performance because the individual, actual costs of work items can be determined, and the amount of profit is typically limited to a percentage of costs incurred. The greatest potential for dispute on a cost-reimbursement or GMP contract is defining what costs are allowed to be billed to the owner. While allowable costs are usually defined in the contract, contractors may try to claim costs outside that definition.

Initial decisions regarding contract structure should consider, among other factors, the potential for fraud and the difficulty of its detection for different contract structures. An owner that is not able to monitor project progress and project records closely during the performance of the project should try to avoid a cost-reimbursable contract structure and stick to lump-sum contracts whenever possible. Defining typical allowances (such as finishes) clearly prior to bid can assist in minimizing opportunities for fraud. If a cost-plus arrangement is needed, proper controls should be implemented to enable the owner to timely verify the actual allowable costs incurred by the contractor.

Red Flags or Badges of Fraud

Although fraud can occur in many areas of a project, the following situations or events tend to have the greatest likelihood for instances of construction fraud.

Off-site Storage or Delivery of Materials

The contractor may need to avoid delivering all of its materials and equipment to the job site in advance of installation. Good reasons for this hesitation include the potential for theft, damage, exposure to adverse weather, limited storage areas, and a limited ability to protect the materials or equipment. For these reasons, the contractor may instead deliver materials or equipment to off-site locations or to a multiproject-shared warehouse. When materials are stored off site, the potential for these materials to disappear or be utilized on other projects becomes more likely and more difficult for the owner to detect. If materials and equipment become intermingled with materials slated for other projects, the assurance that those materials will eventually make it to the owner's project becomes very difficult to monitor.

Should the owner's project be the only (or one of a limited number of) cost-plus project among otherwise lump-sum contracts being performed by the contractor, a shared storage facility provides an opportunity for the contractor to bill more delivered materials to the cost-plus contract than were actually used or required. For example, where the contractor has three projects, each requiring 1,000 sheets of drywall, all 3,000 sheets may be purchased at one time to optimize a quantity discount. If the contractor then accepts delivery and stores all 3,000 sheets at a common inventory site, the delivery tickets and invoices will show 3,000 sheets of drywall delivered to a common location. If two of the projects are lump sum, they generally will require no specific documentation of the drywall quantities withdrawn from inventory for use at those projects, since the price for the work has been fixed in advance. Only the cost-reimbursement project requires detailed invoices and delivery tickets to substantiate charges to the contract. The contractor may accordingly submit the delivery tickets and invoices for up to all 3,000 sheets of drywall for reimbursement, up to 2,000 sheets in excess of the quantity actually used. The owner must accordingly institute precautions against this, such as by forbidding common inventory storage, requiring specific documentation of delivery to the site from the common storage area, and testing for overcharging by obtaining a clear understanding of the estimated quantities of the materials needed for the project. The contractor's supporting invoices should identify the location of the material deliveries, dates of deliveries, and the quantity of delivered materials. Multiproject-shared storage locations should be discouraged or prohibited. In some cases, the owner may realize a net cost benefit by providing single project storage location for the contractor's use.

Excessive Front-End-Loading

Contractors desire to receive as much money as possible early in the contract in order to avoid financing the cost of the work themselves and to remain cash flow positive. The most common method that contractors may use to accelerate early payments is to front-end-load the schedule of values used by the owner to evaluate progress and make payments. Front-end-loading assigns a greater share of the contract price to work items performed during the earlier time periods of the contract's duration. When carried to excess, this practice can have serious adverse consequences to the owner. Later portions of the project likely will cost more for the contractor to perform than it will be paid for that work. As a consequence, the contractor may lose its incentive to complete the later work properly or timely, or to perform punch list work. If the owner terminates the contractor for default, the unpaid balance of the contract price may not be sufficient to cover the cost of completing the remaining work. Items that may be front-end-loaded are items of work typically performed early in the project schedule, such as excavation, foundations, grade beams, drilled piers, structural steel, metal decks, underslab mechanical, electrical, and plumbing (MEP) work, and concrete slabs. As stated earlier, another means of accomplishing front-end loading is to establish an excessive mobilization line item.

Out-of-Sequence Work

On a cost-reimbursement contract, the billing of work in an out-of-sequence manner can be an opportunity for fraudulent activity. To the extent out-of-sequence work is billed, such work may not have been performed. For example, in-wall conduit work generally needs to be performed prior to the installation of drywall. The billing of the drywall installation in a work area prior to the performance of a needed predecessor activity may signal the occurrence of fraudulent billing for work performed incompletely or not at all. Another example of fraudulent billing occurs when the contractor bills corrective work to the regular billing number, instead of absorbing the cost of corrective work (when this is required by the contract). The owner can often utilize project schedule updates to assess the timing of such out-of-sequence billings. To the extent work has not been represented as having started in the project schedule update, no portion of that line item in the schedule of values should be included in the pay application. As such, it often is advantageous from the owner's standpoint to make the schedule of values line-item breakdowns closely match the project schedule activity descriptions. In this manner, the payments applied for by the contractor should track to a schedule activity and provide a check of the completeness of that work. Rework may be identified via meeting minutes, punch lists, or nonconformance reports, and this documentation can be reviewed to assess the timing and categories of such rework.

Excessive Productivity

A progress payment billing that implies a productivity rate in excess of typical productivity may signal a fraudulent billing. For example, a billing that claims completion of a large quantity of work in an overly short time period, or via utilization of minimal man-hours, may signal fraud. Such billings may point to the failure of the contractor to perform the required scope of work. Billing reviews may uncover that the contractor has failed to dig a foundation to the appropriate depth, to use conduit in covered wall locations, or to appropriately support mechanical installations.

For example, the contractor may fail to install conduit and wiring in walls, but be careful enough to install electrical outlet faceplates on the finished drywall. Through such a fraud attempt, the contractor seeks to save the time and cost of actually installing the in-wall work. Because the fraud would otherwise soon be detected, such problems are more prevalent in situations where the in-wall installations are planned to remain unused pending future expansion or acquiring additional funding. A review of timesheets or payrolls would likely identify only a small number of electrical installation hours actually recorded, although the contractor billed for the completion of the electrical work. Similarly, inserting inspection hold points prior to covering-up work into the schedule is often prudent for installations that will not be put into service until after the contractor had completed the project.

Related Business Entities

The contractor's use of related entities for the supply of labor or materials provides another opportunity for fraud. On a cost-plus contract, an affiliated or wholly owned entity related to the contractor may overcharge labor rates or material unit prices in a situation where the contractor has no incentive to challenge the overcharges. For example, a wholly owned drywall subcontractor may overcharge labor hours, rates, material quantities, or material prices to the related general contractor. Due to the affiliation, the general contractor may be motivated to increase its profits by ignoring the overcharges, whereas in an arm's-length relationship such situations would be routinely challenged. Similarly, if there is insufficient work on other projects for a wholly owned subcontractor, the contractor also will have an incentive to oversupply or overcharge labor or materials to the cost-reimbursable project.

Questionable Journal Entries
Whether the contractor's operations are being funded by a bank, surety, or the project owner, the uncontrolled supply of funds to the contractor provides an opportunity for fraud. Such fraud is often identified through erroneous or inconsistent accounting journal entries.

Prepayments to payees such as vendors or subcontractors can be a sign of fraud. If such payments are not yet due, the contractor likely receives no benefit from the early payment, meaning there may be a hidden, fraudulent benefit flowing to the contractor. For example, a prepayment of six months' rent may provide the contractor with a lower cost of operations on a future project. So, if a surety has agreed to pay the contractor's home office costs for a two-month period per a performance bond obligation, an unscrupulous contractor may disguise a longer stream of rent payments as liabilities accruing during the two-month period paid for by the surety. Instead of a $1,000 monthly rent payment, the contractor may represent a $6,000 cost, thereby covering its rent for four additional months. Prepayments to credit card companies or friendly vendors overstate expenses and provide a pool of cash for unrelated future use. Typical vendors that may accept prepayments include equipment suppliers, phone companies, office supply vendors, gas or fuel stations, temporary labor suppliers, contract employees, employee benefits providers, and the Internal Revenue Service. Left unchecked, the contractor may build up large credit balances that it can utilize on other projects, or obtain refunds at a later point in time. Appropriate controls include requiring that invoices match payments to verify that only current, appropriate expenses have been paid with project funds.

Payments made in round dollar amounts may constitute another warning sign of fraudulent payments. From an accounting perspective, prepayments should be appropriately recorded as an increase in an asset account, with a corresponding decrease in a cash account. Other account debits, such as to expense accounts, may indicate fraud.

Increased payments to non-project entities are another sign of potential fraud. Payments to country clubs, fictitious organizations, marketing entities, and employee reimbursable accounts should be scrutinized for this reason. Deposits to investment accounts should be similarly scrutinized. Further, the reimbursement of employees or affiliated entities for project materials should be closely reviewed. Appropriate controls include requiring and closely reviewing submitted documentation including vendor invoices for any such proposed cost or payment.

Another fraudulent technique is to make payments to individuals or entities via an accounting transaction that creates an "account receivable" from that entity. Such newly created receivables may never be reimbursed, and typically fall under nonproject uses of cash. Reimbursement of the fraudulently created account receivable is then avoided by a fraudulent write-off of the amount owed. Accounts receivable are typically only validly created for work performed that has not yet been paid by the owner or general contractor. If accounts receivable are being created via payments to vendors, employees, or subcontractors, close scrutiny should be applied to such transactions. Unfortunately, the typical job cost report only provides identification of the payee, and the contractor's general ledger must be consulted to obtain the accounting transaction description or reason for such payment. As such, analysis of the contractor's general ledger is often critical in uncovering fraud.

One example of this abuse, on a surety-funded project, involved the use of project funds to purchase a sizable certificate of deposit—a fully insured, short-term investment instrument. The general ledger later reported that the certificate of deposit was written off as a bad debt, erasing the value of the certificate of deposit from the contractor's books. Any creation of new account descriptions, stockholder share repurchases, or other investment activities should accordingly be scrutinized. Adjusting entries may be used in attempts to disguise financial improprieties and should be carefully reviewed.

Fraudulent contractors typically want to leave as little a documentation trail as possible. This may lead the contractor to utilize credit cards, bank counter checks, or direct bank cash withdrawals to facilitate payments. Credit card receipts often are accepted as sufficient documentation, even though they provide only very limited documentation or itemization of the underlying transaction. Similarly, bank withdrawals merely remove cash from bank accounts and do not reveal the true uses of the cash. The fraudulent accounting is accomplished when the contractor withdraws cash (an accounting credit to a cash account) and debits a project expense account (real or contrived), while diverting the cash to other purposes.

Inappropriate or illogical account transactions should be closely reviewed when inspecting an accounting general ledger. An increase of a balance sheet asset account is a debit, while an increase of a liability is a credit. On the income statement, an expense transaction will be a debit, while a revenue transaction will be a credit. Any reversal of these standard designations is a red flag for potential fraudulent activity. For example, if a large cash outflow (balance sheet credit) corresponds to a reversed debit designation of "income" (since an income sheet debit would be an expense), it should be closely scrutinized.

Reimbursements to employees for items disallowed by employee benefit handbooks should be carefully reviewed. The transfer or sale of assets should be closely monitored. If an asset is sold (such as a piece of equipment), the typical transaction will credit a balance sheet asset account (reflecting the removal of the asset), and debit an account receivable or similar asset account. To the extent the corresponding debit entry is an expense designation (an unusual occurrence), or other income sheet account, careful review is called for.

Numerous Bank Accounts

The use of a multiplicity of bank accounts can signal an attempt to move funds away from project or creditor control. Contractors often have operating, investment, and payroll accounts. To the extent the existence or location of such accounts changes numerous times, moves overseas, or increases in number, fraud may be the explanation for this activity. With proper audit rights, owners should have the ability to obtain bank account information during random and periodic forensic audits. To the extent that bank account information is not reviewed during the project, it should be requested as part of discovery in resulting litigation.

Fraud Prevention and Detection

Preventing and detecting fraud require knowledge as to how and why a contractor or an individual can manipulate financial information. Effective prevention of fraud also involves establishing adequate precontract project controls and performing basic analytical procedures throughout the project duration. The old adage "if it sounds too good to be true, it probably is," is a good rule of thumb when reviewing financial statements, bid proposals, and payment applications. Understanding and using the available information wisely is vital to prevention and early detection of fraud.

Precontract Project Controls

Compliance and ethics programs that regulate every aspect of each project are an important tool, but one of the most effective project controls is an attitude and practice pervading all levels of management to deter fraud. Owners should implement project controls prior to contract execution in order to evaluate potential contractors. Prescreening potential contractors is a vital exercise that helps reduce the risk of fraud and provides valuable information about contractors and their vendors. Attorneys and their clients should exercise common sense and professional skepticism in employing the following suggested precontract project controls:

- Investigate each company's standing with the Secretary of State's Office and local Better Business Bureau. Review legal filings to identify any proceedings initiated against the contractor. Check for subcontractor liens for nonpayment.
- Obtain several years of historical financial statements, and note occurrences of rapid growth in revenue or assets. This can be a sign of false inflation of financials, as well as an area of concern regarding

the quality and depth of management to oversee an apparent rapid expansion of projects.
- Inquire regarding the accounting system and process in place to account for specific project and company assets. Determine the number of people working in the accounting department and their qualifications. Proper separation of duties between various accounting functions will decrease the risk of fraud. Also, inquire whether independent accountants evaluate or process accounting or tax information.
- To the extent available, obtain and evaluate transaction histories showing dates and timing of reported revenues. Inquire as to the revenue recognition methodology and whether there have been any changes in accounting principles used to record revenue and expenses. Note and inquire about quarter-end, year-end, or significant transactions immediately before the presented financial statements.
- Inquire as to credit facilities and factoring arrangements in place to finance operations. Understand financial performance criteria that are included in debt covenants. Review and analyze historical financial information to evaluate if interest expense has increased over prior years. Evaluate alleged profitability against increasing financing charges.
- Inquire as to the available bonding capacity of the company. Inquire about changes in bonding companies or bonds being called on projects.
- Inquire about related companies performing work or services for the contractor. Understand the scope and magnitude of financial transactions with related companies. If possible, understand the parameters of other entities owned by the company or its principals.
- To the extent available, obtain and evaluate journal entries made by the company into its accounting system.

Ongoing Project Analytical Procedures

In addition to precontract project controls, parties to construction contracts should frequently analyze ongoing projects to deter and detect fraud in a timely manner. As previously mentioned, the AICPA issued the AICPA Statement on Auditing Standards (SAS) 99, Consideration of Fraud in a Financial Statement Audit, to assist an auditor identifying risks that may result in material misstatements in financial statements. SAS 99 changed and strengthened the audit procedures recommended to be performed in assessing the risk of fraud. SAS 99 specifically requires auditors to perform analytical procedures to identify unusual or unexpected relationships that may point to fraudulent accounting. Some of these same procedures can be used during the course of a project by project staff to identify potential fraud risks. In addition, attorneys and their clients may perform these analyses if fraud is suspected on a project.

- Identify changes in schedules of values over time.
- Compile a single summary of payment applications.

- Compare actual and budgeted costs for each area of work.
- Compare payment applications to actual payments to date.
- Reconcile payment applications to job cost reports.
- Review changes in the allowances and contingency accounts.
- Carefully review timing of change orders relative to the dates that work was performed.
- Conduct supplier confirmations.
- Review subcontractor invoices and payment applications relative to contractor's applications for payment.
- Carefully review subcontractor bid documents.

Conclusion

The English author Samuel Johnson said that "fraud and falsehood only dread examination. Truth invites it." Assessing the "truth" in construction accounting requires both knowledge and skill: knowledge to understand the types of fraudulent schemes employed to manipulate financial information, and the skills and techniques to prevent and detect fraudulent activity. These resources, coupled with vigilance in examining accounting information provided prior to and throughout a construction project, will help to minimize the risk and impact of fraud on construction projects.

Fraud can be classified as organizational fraud (fraud concerning the ability or capacity of a company to do business) or performance fraud (fraud that occurs during the performance of a contract). This chapter has mainly focused on performance fraud and outlined numerous schemes and manipulation techniques employed to misrepresent financial information. Understanding how and why contractors and companies engage in fraudulent activity is essential to detecting and preventing fraud. Several indicators of potential fraud are red flags to be aware of prior to and throughout a construction project. These indicators include off-site storage or delivery of materials, excessive front-end loading, out-of-sequence work, excessive productivity, use of related entities, questionable journal entries, and numerous bank accounts.

Fraud allegations can seriously damage a company's reputation, result in serious civil and criminal penalties, and impair the company's ability to obtain public and, perhaps, commercial contracts. Companies must be vigilant, both in their corporate conduct and in controlling and monitoring the conduct of their employees. Even when basic corporate practices and attitudes are fundamentally sound, controls must be in place to prevent improper conduct by rogue employees.

Finally, project controls and analytical procedures both precontract and throughout the project can be used to help detect and prevent fraud. The information here provides some basic knowledge and techniques to help engage in the examination and, hopefully, prevention of fraud in the construction industry.

Notes

1. Although this chapter identifies fraudulent activities committed by contractors, similar behavior occurs for every participant in the industry—no category of party is immune from such activity.

2. Kroll, Economic Intelligence Unit, *EIU Survey*, 2007/2008 GLOBAL FRAUD REPORT.

3. Blake Coppotelli, *Audits, Screening, and Expertise Help to Build Integrity*, 2007/2008 GLOBAL FRAUD REPORT.

4. Gary Goldman, James T. Schmid & Carol S. Esselink, Top Ten Construction Project Fraud Schemes (Mar. 12, 2009) (On Demand Webcast *available at* https://university.learnlivetech.com/CourseDesc.aspx?brandingid=1085&course_id=11645).

5. *E.g.*, 18 U.S.C. § 287; 31 U.S.C. § 3729; CAL. GOV'T CODE §§ 12650 *et seq.*; 740 ILL. COMP. STAT. 175/1 *et seq.*; MASS. GEN. LAWS ch. 12, §§ 5A *et seq.*, N.Y. FIN. LAW § 187 *et seq.*; United States v. Adams Mgmt. Group, Inc., Case No. 1:09-cr-10137 (D. Mass. 2009) (subcontractor on Boston's Big Dig Project pled guilty to conspiracy to make false claims related to work performed on a time and materials basis). One of the government's allegations in *Adams Management* was that the subcontractor engaged in a scheme to overbill the Big Dig Project by falsely categorizing apprentice workers as journeymen.

6. 4 WEST'S ENCYCLOPEDIA OF AMERICAN LAW 487 (2d ed. 2005).

7. *Id.*

8. *Id.*

9. *Id.*

10. *Id.*

11. *Id.*

12. A good illustration of such a situation can be found in *Old Dominion Elec. Coop. v. Ragnar Benson, Inc.*, Case No. 3:05-cv-34, 2006 WL 2854444, at *55–57 (E.D. Va. Aug. 4, 2006).

13. *E.g.*, CAL. GOV'T CODE § 12653(c); MINN. STAT. § 15C.14(c).

14. *See* City of Newport v. Fact Concerts, Inc., 453 U.S. 247, 266 (1981) ("Punitive damages by definition are not intended to compensate the injured party, but rather to punish the tortfeasor whose wrongful action was intentional or malicious, and to deter him and others from similar extreme conduct.").

15. *E.g.*, United States *ex rel.* Oliver v. The Parsons Corp., 498 F. Supp. 2d 1260 (C.D. Cal. 2006) (failure to identify a subcontractor as an affiliated company rendered the contractor's disclosure statement false).

16. Examples of labor mischarging on U.S. government contracts in industries other than construction are instructive. United States v. Frequency Elecs., 862 F. Supp. 834 (E.D.N.Y. 1994) (contractor created false and inaccurate time cards and destroyed actual time cards in order to inflate requests for payment); United States *ex rel.* O'Keefe v. McDonnell Douglas Corp., 918 F. Supp. 1338 (E.D. Mo. 1996) (contractor intentionally inflated labor costs by $11 million and instructed employees to charge labor hours to unrelated government contracts); United States v. Newport News Shipbuilding, Inc., 276 F. Supp. 2d 539 (E.D. Va. 2003) (shipbuilder charged time for developing commercial transport vessels to an indirect independent research and development cost account that was allocable to all of its government contracts, rather than as a direct charge to the commercial vessel accounts). The government has frequently prosecuted the individuals involved in the fraud as well as the company, including senior company officials. *E.g.*, United States v. Sys. Architects, Inc., 757 F.2d 373 (1st Cir. 1985); United States v. Martel, 792 F.2d 630 (7th Cir. 1986); United States v. EER Sys. Corp., 950 F. Supp. 130 (D. Md. 1996).

17. This issue has frequently occurred on U.S. government supply contracts, and those decisions are analogous to the situations that arise on construction contracts. *E.g.* Grand Union Co. v. United States, 696 F.2d 888 (11th Cir. 1983); United States v. O'Connell, 890 F.2d 563 (1st Cir. 1989).

18. United States v. Genii Research, Inc., Crim. No. 85-2795 (E.D.N.Y. 1986).

19. Canadian Commercial Corp., ASBCA No. 17187, 76-2 BCA ¶ 12145.

20. This is especially true since the enactment of the American Recovery and Reinvestment Act of 2009 (ARRA), Pub. L. No. 111-5, in February 2009.

21. A detailed discussion of state false claims acts is beyond the scope of this chapter. An excellent survey of the state statutes appears in Chapter 11 of *False Claims in Construction Contracts* (Charles Sink & Krista Pages, eds.; American Bar Ass'n Forum on the Constr. Indus. 2007). The states that have false claims statutes are as follows: California, CAL. GOV'T. CODE §§ 12560 *et seq.;* Delaware, DEL. CODE tit. 6, sub II, ch. 12, §§ 1201, *et seq.;* Florida, FLA. STAT. ANN. §§ 68.081–68.09; Hawaii, HAW. REV. STAT. ANN. §§ 661-21 *et seq.* and §§ 46-171 *et seq.;* Illinois, 740 ILL. COMP. STAT. 175/1 *et seq.* (2006); Indiana, IND. CODE §§ 5-11-55, *et seq.* (2006); Massachusetts, MASS. GEN. LAWS ch. 159, § 18, §§ 5A *et seq.;* Montana, MONT. CODE. ANN. §§ 17-8-401, *et seq.;* Nevada, NEV. REV. STAT. §§ 357.010 *et seq.* (2002); New Hampshire, N.H. REV. STAT. ANN. §§ 167:61-b *et seq.;* Tennessee, TENN. CODE ANN. §§ 4-18-101 *et seq.;* Virginia, VA. CODE ANN. §§ 8.01-216.1 *et seq.* (2006). Additionally, Arizona provides for penalties for anyone making a false claim with regard to a lien or bond claim. ARIZ. REV. STAT. §§ 12-820 to 12-826, 20-463 to 20-466.05, 30-420. Louisiana enacted a false claims statute to punish false claims under hurricane relief programs. LA. REV. STAT. ANN. tit. 39 Public Finance, ch. 22, §§ 2151 *et seq.* (2007).

22. 18 U.S.C. § 287.

23. Two other excellent resources on false claims violations, penalties, compliance programs and fraud avoidance are John T. Boese, *Civil False Claims and Qui Tam Actions* (3d ed. 2006), and Seyfarth Shaw LLP, *The Government Contract Compliance Handbook* (4th ed. 2007).

24. 31 U.S.C. § 3730.

25. 31 U.S.C. § 3730(b).

26. 31 U.S.C. § 3730(b) and (c).

27. 31 U.S.C. § 3730(h).

28. 31 U.S.C. § 3730(d).

29. *Id.*

30. 31 U.S.C. § 3729(a).

31. 31 U.S.C. § 3729(b).

32. Pub. L. No. 111-21, 123 Stat. 1617, S. 386 (2009).

33. 31 U.S.C. § 3729(a)(1), (a)(2).

34. 128 S. Ct. 2123 (2008).

35. 31 U.S.C. § 3729(b)(2).

36. This provision has been interpreted to include, for example, each invoice that contains or depends upon false information. United States v. Mackby, 339 F.3d 1013 (9th Cir. 2003), *cert. denied,* 541 U.S. 936 (2004) ($730,000 penalty for $55,000 in damages was appropriate under the circumstances).

37. 31 U.S.C. § 3729(a).

38. *Id.*

39. 73 Fed. Cl. 547 (2006), *aff'd,* 557 F.3d 1332 (Fed. Cir. 2009).

40. 73 Fed. Cl. at 555–60.

41. *Id.* at 595–97.

42. *Id.* at 568–69 & nn.38–39.

43. 74 Fed. Cl. 601 (2007).
44. *Id.* at 624–25.
45. *Id.* at 626–34.
46. *Id.* at 607–18.
47. *Id.* at 624–25.
48. *See id.* at 615.
49. *Id.* at 729.
50. Allowable costs are addressed in the Federal Acquisition Regulation (FAR) at 48 C.F.R. § 31.205.
51. Contractor's Application for Payment, AIA Form G702.
52. Case No. 3:05-cv-34, 2006 WL 2854444 (E.D. Va. Aug. 4, 2006).
53. *See id.*

TABLE OF AUTHORITIES

Cases

A

Ace Constructors, Inc. v. United States, 70 Fed. Cl. (2006), 243; 254n45, 255nn77–78

Advanced Eng'g & Planning Corp., 05-1 B.C.A. (CCH) ¶ 32,806 (2004), 255n73

Alexander v. FBI, 186 F.R.D. (D.D.C. 1998), 274n40

Allan Constr. Co. v. United States, 646 F.2d 48 (Ct. Cl. 1981), 253n29

Allison Engine Co. v. United States *ex rel.* Sanders, 291, 305n34

All-State Boiler, 146 F.3d, 254nn59, 60

Alpert v. Crain, Caton & James, P.C., 178 S.W.3d (Tex. App 2005), 74n49

Altmayer v. Johnson, 79 F.3d (Fed. Cir. 1996), 254n60

Aluminum Co. of Am. v. Essex Group, Inc., 499 F.Supp 53 (W.D. Pa. 1980), 182n43

Amelco Elec. v. City of Thousand Oaks, 38 P.3d (Cal. 2002), 252nn19, 21, 25, 26

Amp-Rite Elec. Co. v. Wheaton Sanitary Dist., 580 N.E.2d (Ill. App. Ct. 1991), 253n27

Aniero Concrete Co. v. New York City Const. Auth., 308 F.Supp. (S.D.N.Y. 2003), 180n4

Anixter v. Home Stake Prod. Co., 77 F.3d (10th Cir. 1996), 73n19

B

Baker v. Barnard Constr. Co., 146 F.3d (10th Cir. 1998), 182n35

Baker v. Flint Eng'g & Constr. Co, 137 F.3d (10th Cir. 1998), 182n35

Bank of New York v. Meridien Biao Bank Tanzania, Ltd., 171 F.R.D. (S.D.N.Y.1997), 274n40

Barnard Constr. Co. v. City of Lubbock, 457 F.3d (5th Cir. 2006), 181n12

Barnett and Herenchak, Inc. v. N.J. Dep't of Transp., 648 A.2d 256, 276 N.J. Super. (N.J. Super. A.D. 1994), 182n27

Bay West, Inc., 07-1 B. C.A. (CCH) ¶ 33, 569 (2007), 251n17

Bechtel Nat'l, Inc. 90-1 B.C.A. (CCH) ¶ 22,549 (1989), 255n81

Bechtel Nat'l, Inc. 90-1 B.C.A. (CCH) ¶ 113,177 (2004), 256nn85–88

Bell BCI Co. v. United States, 570 F.3d (Fed. Cir. 2009), 255n82

Berley Indus., Inc. v. City of New York, 385 N.E.2d (N.Y.1978), 254n55

Bethlehem Steel Co. v. Turner Cons. Co., 161 N.Y.S.2d 90, 2 N.Y.2d (N.Y. 1957), 180n9

Bethlehem Steel Corp. v. Litton Indus., Inc. 321 Pa. Super. 357, 468 A.2d (Pa. Super 1983), 180n9

Bill Strong Enters, Inc. v. Shannon, 49 F.3d (Fed. Civ. 1995), 215n14

Black v. Colaska Inc., No C07-823JLR, 2008 WL 4681567 (W.D. Wash. 2008), 182n32

Boots, Inc. v. Singh, 649 S.E.2d 695, 698 (Va. 2007), 251n13

Bouten Constr. Co. v. M & L Land Co., 877 P.2d Idaho 957 (Idaho App. 1994), 181n14

Boyajian v. United States, 423 F.2d (Fed. Cir. 1970), 274n42

Branna Constr. Corp. . W. Allegheny Joint Sch. Auth. 242 A.2d (Pa. 1968), 251n7

Brazos River Auth. v. GE Ionics, Inc. 469 F.3d (5th Cir. 2006), 274n40

C

Canadian Commercial Corp., ASBCA No. 17187 B.C.A. ¶ 21145, 305n19
Carlisle Corp. d/b/a/ Carlisle Syntec Systems v. Medical City Dallas, Ltd., 196 S.W.3d (Tex. App. 5th 2006), 271, 276nn98–101
Carrothers Constr. Co. v. City of S. Hutchinson, 207 P.3d (Kan. 2009), 251n11
Cavaralla v. United States, 284 F.3d (2002), 156n19
Cen. Fla. Plastering & Dev. v. Sovran Const. Co., 679 So.2d (Fla. Dist. Ct. App. 1996), 254n54
Cent Bank of Denver, N.A. v. First Interstate Bank of Denver, N.A. 511 U.S. (1994), 74nn50–51
Century 21 Deep S. Props, Ltd. v. Corson, 612 So.2d (Miss. 1992), 74n48
Chem-Age Ind., Inc. v. Glover, 652 N.W.2d (S.D. 2002), 74n48
Chilton Ins. Co. v. Pate & Pate Enters., Inc. 930 S.W.2d (Tex. Ct. App. 1996), 254n55
City of Newport v. Fact Concerts, Inc. 453 U.S. (1981), 304n14
Clark Concrete Contractors, Inc., 99-1 B.C.A. (CCH) ¶ 30, 280 (1999), 251n17
Clark Constr. Group, Inc. 00-1 B.C.A. (CCH) ¶ 30,870 (2000), 253n41, 254n43
Clark Constr. Group, Inc., 001-B.C.A. (CCH) ¶ 31, 647 (2001), 253
Clark-Fitzpatrick, Inc./Franki Found. Co. v. Gill, 652 A.2d (R.I. 1994), 251n14
Commercial Contractors, Inc. v. U.S. Fidelity & Guaranty Co., 524 F.2d (5th Cir. 1975), 180n6
Complete Gen. Constr. Co. v. Ohio Dep't of Transp., 760 N.E.2d (Ohio 2002), 254n54
Cost & Sons Constr. Co. v. Long, 412 S.E.2d (S.C. Ct. App. 1991), 253n28
Cotten v. Hfs-Usa, Inc., 620 F.Supp 2d (M.D. Fla 2009), 182n32
Credit Union Cent. Falls v. Groff, 966 A.2d (R.I. 2009), 74n48
Cuneo v. Schlesinger, 484 F.2d (D.C. 1973), 103n32

D

Daewoo Eng'g & Constr. Co. v. United States, 557 F.3d (Fed. Cir. 2009), 251n5, 291–292, 305nn39–41
Daewoo Eng'g & Constr. Co. v. United States, 73 Fed. Cl. (2006), 215n5
Daubert v. Merrell Dow Pharmaceuticals, Inc., 154, 156nn11–12, 267–268, 269, 275nn47, 49–52, 54–55, 276nn75, 107
Davis v. Sliney, 1988 WL 75331 (Tenn. Ct. App.), 181n14
Dep't of Transp. v. Anjo Constr. Co., 66 A.2d (Pa. Commw. Ct. 1995), 255n79
Dingwall v. Friedman Fisher Assocs, P.C. 3 F.Supp 2d 215 (N.D.N.Y. 1998), 182n34
Dixon Fin. Servs., Ltd. v. Greenberg, 2008 WL 746548 (Tex. App 2008), 74n49
Dravo Corp. v. Liberty Mut. Ins. Co., 164 F.R.D. (D. Neb. 1995), 274n40
Durham v. Guest, 171 P.3d (N.M. Ct. App. 2007), 74n49

E

Eastover Ridge, LLC v. Metric Constructors, Inc. 139 N.C. App. 360, 533 S.E. 2d (La. App. 2003), 182n26
E.C. Ernst, Inc. v. Koppers Co., Inc., 626 F.2d 3d Cir. 1980), 274n42
Eichleay Corp., 60-2 B.C.A. (CCH) ¶ 2688 (1960), 254n52
Emerald Maint., Inc., 98-2 B.C.A. (CCH) ¶ 29,903, (1998), 254n50
Employers Ins. of Wassau v. Musick, Peeler & Garrett, 871 F.Supp. (S.D. Cal 1994), 73n20
Equity Lifestyle Props. v. Fla. Mowing, 556 F.3d (11th Cir. 2009), 182n39

F

Fairfax County Redev. & Hous. Auth. v. Worcester Bros. Co., 514 S.E.2d (Va. 1999), 254n54
Fed. Deposit Ins. Corp. v. Butcher, 116 F.R.D. (E.D. Tenn. 1986), 274n40
Flink/Vulcan v. United States, 63 Fed. Cl. (2004), 103n25

Fraser Constr. Co. v. United States, 384 F.3d (Fed. Cir. 2004), 243, 255nn75–76
Fru-Con Constr. Corp. v. United States, 43 Fed. Cl. (1999), 255n80
Frye v. United States, 293 F. (App. D.C. 1923), 268, 275n48
Fuechtman v. Mastec, Inc., 390 F.Supp 2d (S.D. Fla 2005), 70, 74nn45–47

G

Ga. Dep't of Transp. v. Dalton Paving & Constr., Inc. 489 S.E.2d (Ga. Ct. App. 1997), 251n14
Gen. Const. v. Greater St. Thomas, 107 S.W.3d (Tenn. App. 2002), 180n3
General Electric Co. v. Joiner, 522 U.S., 268, 275n60
Gladwynne Constr. Co. v. Mayor & City Council, 807 A.2d (Md. Ct. Spec. App. 2002), 254n54
G.M. Harston Constr. Co. v. City of Chicago, 371 F.Supp 2d (N.D. Ill. 2005), 252n25
Golf Landscaping, Inc. v. Century Constr. Co., 696 P.2d (Wash. Ct. App. 1984), 254n54
Grand Bissell Towers, Inc. v. John Gagnon Enters., Inc., 657 S.W.2d (Mo. Ct. App. 1983), 251n12
Grand Union Co. v. United States, 696 F.2d (11th Cir. 1983), 305n17
Greebel v. FTP Software, Inc. 194 F.3d (1st Cir. 1999), 74n41
Greycas, Inv. v. Proud, 826 F.2d (7th Cir. 1987), 74n48
Grumman Aerospace Corp., 06-1 B.C.A. ¶ 33,216 (2006), 274n42

H

Hart Eng'g Co. v. City of Pawtucket Water Supply Bd., 560 A.2d (R.I. 1989), 254n54
Hensel Phelps Constr. Co. v. Gen Servs. Admin., 01-1 B.C.A. (CCH) ¶ 31,249 (2001), 253n41, 256n84, 274n44
Hickman v. Kralicek Realty & Const. Co., 129 S.W.3d Ark. App. 61 (Ark. App. 2003), 182n40

Hickman v. Taylor, 329 U.S. (1947), 156n23
Hoel-Steffen Constr. Co. v. United States, 456 F.2d (Ct. Cl. 1972), 251n14
Holder Const. Group v. Ga. Tech, 640 S.E.2d (Ga. App. 2006), 182n42
Hopkins v. Texas Mast Climbers, LLC (S.D. Tex. 2005), 182n35
Huber, Hunt & Nichols, Inc. v. Moore, 136 Cal. Rptr. (Ct. App. 1977), 252n22, 255n82

I

ILM Sys., Inc. v. Suffolk Constr. Co., 252 F.Supp.2d (E.D. Pa. 2001), 256n83
Imperial Constr. & Elec., Inc., 06-1 B.C.A. (CCH) ¶ 33, 276 (2006), 255n73
Ingalls Shipbuilding Div., Litton Sys., Inc., 78-1 B.C.A. (CCH) ¶ 13,038 (1978), 256n86
In re Raytheon Securities Litigation Sec Litig., 157 F. Supp.2d (2008), 69–70, 73nn13, 36–40, 74nn41–44
In re Software Toolworks, Inc. Sec Litig. v Painewebber, 50 F.3d 615, 628 n.3 (9th Cir. 1994), 73n20
In re ZZZZ Best Sec. Litig., 864 F.Supp. (C.D. Cal 1994), 73nn20–21
Insterstate Gen. Gov't Contractors, Inc. v. West, 12 F3d (Fed. Cir. 1993), 254n60

J

J.A. Jones Constr. Co., 00-1 B.C.A. (CCH) ¶ 19,643 (1987), 254n47, 256n88
J.A. Jones Constr. Co., 00-2 B.C.A. ¶ 31,000 (2000), 253n39
J.A. Jones Constr. Co. v. Lehrer McGovern Bovis, Inc. 89 P.3d (Nev. 2004), 251n8
Jackson Constr. Co. v. United States, 62 Fed. Cl. (2004), 255nn81–82, 256nn86, 87
James Corp. v. N. Allegheny Sch. Dist., 938 A.2d (Pa. Commw. Ct. 2007), 251n17; 255nn72, 74
J.D. Hedin Constr. Co. v. United States, 347 F.2d 171 Ct. Cl. 70 (1965), 252n27
J.E. Hathman, Inc. v. Sigma Alpha Epsilon Club, 491 S.W.2d (Mo. 1973), 181n14

Jefferson v. Jefferson, 946 So. 2d (La. App. 5 Cir. 2006), 271, 276nn102–1015
Johnson v. Big Lots Stores, Inc., 604 F.Supp 2d (E.D. La. 2009), 182n33
Jones v. J. H. Hiser Construction Co., 484 A.2d (Md. Spec. App. 1984), 161, 181n23
Joseph Pickard's Sons Co. v. United States, 532 F.2d 739, (Ct. Cl. 1976), 253n30

K

Kahle v. John McDonough Builders, Inc., 582 A.2d (Md. Spec. App. 1991), 161, 181n24
Kansas City Cmty Ctr. v. Heritage Indus., Inc., 773 F.Supp. 1(W.D. Mo. 1998), 253n28
King Fisher Marine Serv., Inc. v. United States, 16 Cl. Ct. (1989), 255n82
Kit-San-Azusa, J.V. v. United States, 32 Fed. Cl. (1995), 253n39
Kumho Tire Company v. Carmichael, 526 U.S. (1999), 154, 156nn13–15, 268, 275nn53, 57, 59

L

Leiden Corp., 84-1 B.C.A. (CCH) ¶ 16,947 (1983), 251n15
Leon v. Kelly, 2009 U.S. Dist., 269–270, 276nn76–82
Luria Bros. & Co. v. United States, 369 F.2d (Ct. Cl. 1966), 251n6; 251n17, 274n44

M

MACTEC, Inc. v. Bechtel Jacobs Co., LLC, 2008 U.S. Dist., 270m, 276nn88–91
Malcolm Pirnie, Inc. v. Martin, 506 U.S. 905, 113 S. Ct. 298, 121 L. Ed 2d 222 (1992), 182n34
Marker v. Union Fid. Life Ins. Co., 125 F.R.D. (M.D.N.C. 1898), 274n40
Marshall Contractors, Inc. v. Brown Univ., A.2d 665 (R.I. 1997), 181n13
Martin v. Malcom Pirnie, Inc., 949 F.2d (2d Cir. 1991), 182n34
McCamish, Martin, Brown & Loeffler v. F.E. Appling Interests, 911 S.W.2d (Tex 1999), 74n48
McMillin Bros. Constructors, Inc. 91-1 B.C.A. (CCH) ¶ 23,351 (1990), 255n81, 256n86
McMillin Bros. Constructors, Inc. v. Watkins, 949 F.2d (Fed. Cir. 1991), 255n81
McNamara Constr. Co. v. United States, 509 F2.d (Ct. Cl. 1975), 180n6
Md. State Highway Admin v. David A. Bramble, Inc. 351 Md. 226, 717 A.2d 943 (Md. 1998), 181n12
Melka Marine, Inc. v. United States, 187 F.3d (Fed. Cir. 1999), 254nn53, 60
Metro Sewerage Comm'n v. R.W. Constr. Inc., 241 N.W.2d (Wis. 1976), 251n14
Meva Corp. v. United States, 511 F.2d (Ct. Cl. 1975), 253n33
Mitsui & Co. v. P.R. Water Res. Auth., 93 F.R.D. (D.P.R. 1981), 274n40
Moorhead Constr. Co. v. City of Grand Forks, 508 F.2d (8th Cir. 1975), 252n23
Moreau v. Klevenhagan, 508 U.S. 22, 23, 113 S. Ct. 1905, 123 L. Ed. 2d 584 (1993), 182n36
Morse Diesel International, Inc. v. United States, 66 Fed. Cl. (2005), 208, 215n16
Morse Diesel International, Inc. v. United States, 74 Fed. Cl. (2007), 208, 215n16; 251n5, 256n93, 292, 293, 294, 306nn43–49
Morse Diesel International, Inc. v. United States, 79 Fed. Cl. (2007), 208, 215n16
M&R Contractors and Builders v. Michael, 138 A.2d (Md. 1958), 2741958
Muschany v. United States, 324 U.S. 49, 62, 65 S.Ct. 442, 449, 89 L.ED 744 (1945), 160

N

N. Ind. Pub Serv. Co. v. Carbon County Coal Co., 799 F.2d (7th Cir. 1986), 180n6
Newport News Shipbuilding & Drydock Co. v. Reed, 655 F. Supp. (E.D. Va. 1987), 103n32
New Pueblo Constructors, Inc. v. State, 696 P.2d (Ariz. 1985), 251nn14–15
Norair Eng'g Corp. v. United States, 666 F.2d (Ct. Cl. 1981), 255nn76, 80

O

Old Dominion Electric Cooperative v. Ragnar Benson, Inc., Case No. 3:05-cv-34, 2006, 294–295, 306nn52–53

Orlosky, Inc. v. United States, 68 Fed. Cl. (2005), 103n25, 241, 255nn68–69

P

Paliotta v. Pa. Dep't of Transp., 750 A.2d (Pa. Commw. Ct. 1999), 254n55
Pathman Constr. Co., 87-1 B.C.A. (CCH) ¶ 19,643 (1987), 254n49
PCL Constr. Servs., Inc. v. United States, 96 Fed. Appx. (Fed. Cir. 2004), 252n25
PDM Plumbing & Heating, Inc. v. Findlen, 431 N.E.2d (Mass. Ct. App. 1982), 254n54
Pebble Bldg. Co. v. G. J. Hopkins, Inc., 288 S.E.2d (Va. 1982), 253n40
Perry v. Hensel Phelps Constr. Co., 36 Fed. Appx. (Fed. Cir. 2002), 253n41; 256n84
Petrillo v. Bachenberg, 655 A.2d (1995), 74n48
Pittman Constr. Co. v. United States, 2 Cl. Ct. (1981), 255n81, 256n86
P.J. Dick, Inc., 01-2 B.C.A. (CCH) ¶ 31,647 (2001), 251n17
P.J. Dick, Inc. v. Principi, 324 F.3d (Fed. Cir. 2003), 251n17; 253n36; 254nn53, 56–58, 61; 255n62
Planning Sys. Corp. v. Murrell, 374 So.2d (La. App 4 Cir. 1979), 181n15
Propellex Corp., 02-1 B.C.A. (CCH) ¶ 31,721 (2001), 252
Propellex Corp. v. Brownlee, 342 F.3d (Fed. Cir. 2003), 252nn19, 20, 22, 24, 25, 274n42
P.T.&L. Constr. Co. v. New York, 578 N.Y.S.2d (App. Div. 1992), 180n6
P.W. Construction, Inc. v. United States, 53 Fed. Appx. (Fed. Cir. 2002), 253n38

Q

Quantachrome Corp. v. Micrometrics Instrument Corp. 189 F.R.D. (S.D. Fla 1999), 274n40

R

R. P. Richards Const. Co. v. United States, 51 Fed. Cl. 116, 125 (2001), 103
Rainey v. Am. Forest & Paper Ass'n, Inc. 26 F.Supp. 2d (D.D.C. 1998), 273n39
Reilly v. NatWest Markets Group Inc., 181 F.3d (2d Cir. 1999), 273n39
Reynolds v. Schrock, 142 P.3d (Or. 2006), 74n49
RKR Motors, Inc. v. Assoc. Unif. Rental & Linen Supply, Inc. 995 So.2d (Fla. Dist. Ct. App. 2008), 251n13
RLI Insurance Company v. Indian River School District, 2007 U.S. Dist, 270, 276nn92–97
Robert McMullan & Son, Inc. ASBCA No. 11998, 68-1 BCA ¶ 7068, 180n6
Roger J. Au & Son, Inc. v. N.E. Ohio Reg'l Seweer Dist., 504 N.E.2d (Ohio Ct. App. 1986), 251n14

S

S. Comfort Builders, Inc. v. United States, 67 Fed. Cl. (2005), 252n26; 253n37; 255n81
S. Dredging Co. ENGBCA No. 5843, 92-2 BCA ¶ 24, 886, 182n41
S. New England Contracting Co. v. State, 354 A.2d (Conn. 1974), 254n54
S. Welding & Mfg. Co. v. United States, 373 F.2d (Ct. Cl. 1967), 182n43
Salt City Contractors, Ltd., 80-2 B.C.A. (CCH) ¶ 14,713 (1980), 255n70
Santa Fe Eng'rs., 91-1 B.C.A. (CCH) ¶ 23,571 (1990), 254n50
Seaboard Lumber Co. v. United States, 308 F.3d (Fed. Cir. 2002), 182n43
S.E.C. v. Durgarian, 477 F. Supp 2d (D. Mass. 2007), 73n20
S.E.C. V. Morelli, 143 F.R.D. (S.D.N.Y. 1992), 274n40
S.E.C. v. Morris, 66, 68–69, 71–72, 72n9, 73nn10–14, 22–35, 74nn53–57
Servidone Constr. Corp. v. United States, 931 F.2d (Fed. Cir. 1991), 252n21
Shadow Lake Managemenet Co., Inc. v. Landmark American Ins. Co., 2008 U.S. Dist., 270, 276nn83–87
Sigmund v. Starwood Urban Retail VI, LLC. 236 F.R.D. (D.D.C. 2006), 273n39
Sony Elecs., Inc. v. Soundview Techs., Inc., 217 F.R.D. (D. Ct. 2002), 274n40
Spirtas Co. v. Div. of Design and Constr., 131 S.W.3d (Mo. App. 2004), 182n40
Sprint Commc'ns Co., L.P. v. Theglobe.com, Inc., 236 F.R.D. (D. Kan 2006), 273n39
S.S. Silberblatt, Inc., 80-1 B.C.A. (CCH) ¶ 14,263 (1980), 256n94

Standard Constr. Co. v. Nat'l Tea Co., 62 N.W.2d Minn. 422 (Minn. 1953), 182n28

Stoneridge Inv. Partners, LLC v. Scientific Atlanta, 128 S. Ct.(2008), 73nn15–17

Sunshine Constr. & Eng'g Inc. v. United States, 64 Fed. Cl. (2005), 274n44

T

Tecom, Inc. v. United States, 66 Fed. Cl. (2005), 103n25

Tecom, Inc. v. United States, 86 Fed. Cl. (2009), 215n14

U

United States *ex rel.* O'Keefe v. McDonnell Douglas Corp. 918 F.Supp (E.D. Mo. 199), 304n16

United States ex rel. Oliver v. The Parsons Corp. 498 F.Supp 2d (C.D. Cal. 2006), 304n15

United States v. Cote, 456 F. (8th Cir. 1972), 156n20

United States v. EER Sys. Corp., 950 F.Supp (D. Md. 1996), 304n16

United States v. Frequency Elecs., 862 F.Supp (E.D.N.Y. 1994), 304n16

United States v. Genii Research Inc., Crim. No. 85-2795 (E.D.N.Y. 1986), 305n18

United States v. Judson, 322 F.2d (9th Cir. 1963), 156n21

United States v. Kovel, 296 F.2d (1961), 154–155, 156nn17–18

United States v. Mackby, 339 F.3d (9th Cir. 2003), 305n36

United States v. Martel, 792 F.2d 630 (7th Cir. 1986), 304n16

United States v. O'Connell, 890 F.2d (1st Cir. 1989), 305n17

United States v. Sys. Architects, Inc. 757 F.2d (1st Cir. 1985), 304n16

United States v. Taylor, 166 F.R.D. (M.D.N.C. 1996), 273n39

United States v. Westinghouse Elect. Co., 788 F.2d (1986), 103n32

United State v. Newport News Shipbuilding, Inc. 276 F.Supp 2d (E.D. Va. 2003), 304n16

Urban Data Systems, Inc. v. United States, 699 F.2d (Fed. Cir. 1983), 159–160, 181nn16–17

U.S. Fid. and Guar. v. Braspetro Oil Servs., 219 F. Supp 2d (S.D.N.Y. 2002), 180n5

U.S. Indus. Inc. v. Blake Constr. Co., 671 F.2d. (D.C. Cir. 1982), 251n17

W

West v. All-State Boiiler, Inc. 146 F.3d (Fed. Cir. 1998), 254n53

W.G. Yates & Sons Constr. Co., 10-2 B.C.A. (CCH) ¶ 31,428 (2001), 251n17

White v. Graceland College Ceneter for Professional Development and Lifelong Learning, 586 F.Supp. 2d (D. Kan. 2009), 262, 273nn34–37

Wickham Contracting Co. v. Fischer, 12 F.3d 1574 (Fed. Cir. 1994), 254n53

Wilner v. United States, 24 F.3d (Fed. Cir. 1994), 253n27

Wilson v. Lakner, 228 F.R.D. (D. Md. 2005), 274n40

Woodward v. Metro Bank of Dallas, 522 F.2d (5th Cir. 1975), 74n56

WRB Corp. v. United States, 183 Ct. Cl. (1968), 252n21; 253nn30–31

Wright v. Ernst & Young LLP, 152 F.3d (2d Cir. 1998), 73n19

Wyo. State Highway Comm'n v. Brasel & Sims Constr. Co., 688 P.2d (Wyo. 1984), 253n27

Z

Ziemba v. Cascade Int'l, Inc., 256 F.3d (11th Cir. 2001), 73n19

Authorities

A

Accounting Research Bulletin
(ARB) No. 45, 60, 61–62
AIA
    A102-2007, 89–90, 97, 98, 104n52,
        104n53, 161, 181n22
        7.1.2, 105n75
        7.2.3, 105n74
        7.2.4, 105n72
        7.2.5, 105n73
        7.4.2, 105n69
        7.5.2, 182n29, 182n37
        7.8.1, 105n83
        7.8.2, 105n82
        11, 104nn55–57
        12.1.7.6, 93, 105n59
        12.1.9, 105n61
    A103-2007, 97
        7.5.4, 105n70
        7.6.10, 105n71
    A111-1997, 181n22
    A114-2001, 181n22
    A133-2009, 160
    A201-2007, 97, 100, 241–242
        2.4, 105n66
        4.2.5, 105n60
        7.6.1, 105n77
        7.6.10, 105n81
        7.6.4, 105n78
        7.6.6, 105n79
        7.6.9, 105n80
        9.1, 105n86
        9.5.1.4, 105n67
        9.6.4, 105n84
        9.7, 105n68
        14.4.3, 105n65
        15.1.6.2, 255n71
    A201-2007 General Conditions, 88, 89
    A305, 42
    B101-2007 5.8, 105n62
AICPA
    Rule 102, 150
    Rule 201, 149
    Rule 202, 149–150
Ariz. Rev. Stat.
    12-820-12-826, 305n21
    20-463-20-466.05, 305n21
    30-420, 305n21
Army Corps of Engineers
    Pamphlet 415-1-3, 254n44

C

Cal. Civ. Proc. Code § 2025.230, 273n38
Cal. Gov't Code
    12560, 305n21
    12650, 304n5
    12653(c), 304n13
Cal. Lab. Code
    § 204.3, 169
    § 513, 169
Cal. Pub. Cont. Code § 7102, 251n9
CAM § 6-902, 104n43
CAS, 414
    31, 190
    401, 209
    402, 209, 211
    403, 211
    404, 211
    405, 209, 211
    406, 211
    407, 209, 211
    408, 211
    409, 211
    410, 211
    411, 211
    412, 211
    413, 212
    414, 212
    415, 212
    416, 204, 212
    417, 212
    418, 212
    420, 212
Code of Federal Regulations. *See* C.F.R.
ConsensusDOCs No. 205, 105n85
Cost Accounting Standards. *See* CAS
C.F.R.
    P 9903, 103n20
    23 C.F.R. § 635.120, 182n38
    29 C.F.R.
        § 541.200(a), 182n31
        § 541.3(a), 182n35
    41 C.F.R. pts. 300-304, 215n12
    48 C.F.R.
        § 31.205, 306n50
        § 9904.414-30, 256n91

D

DBIA 530-2009, 161
DCAA
    Contract Audit Manual ch.4,
        sect.300, 103n15

DCAA (*continued*)
  MRD 006857-09-DPAP.pdf, 104n38
  MRD 08-PAS-843(R), 104n39
  Pamphlet No. 7641.90, 102nn7–11
  Pamphlet No. 7641.90 § 1-301.d, 103n19
  7641.90, 215n20
DCAM
  Figure 8-1-315n191, 215n19
  4-302.1(b)(2), 103n21
  4-702, 102n5
  10-212.2(A), 103N22
  10-212.2(C), 103N23
  7640.1, 81, 102n1
Del. Code tit. 6, sub II, ch12, §§ 1201, 305n21
Department of Defense (DoD)
  Directive No. 7640.2, 83–84
  Directive No. 7650.3, 104n34
  Instruction No. 7640.02, 104n35
  Instruction No. 7640.2, 103n34

E

EJCDC
  C700-2007, 104n58
  C-525-2007, 161, 162
  1.01, 183–187
  1.02, 187
  1.03, 183
Engineers Joint Contract Documents Committee. *See* EJCDC

F

FAR
  P 30, 103n20
  2.1, 213
  2.101, 215n1
  4.700, 102n4
  9.104.1(a), 41
  15, 190–194
  15.403, 191
  15.403.4, 103N24, 215n2
  15.406 .2-(c), 192
  16.203, 180n7
  16.3, 180n1
  30.000.607, 102n3
  31, 160, 190
  31.1015(d)(2)(i)(C), 215n6
  31.105, 199–200
  31.105(d)(1), 215n4
  31.105(d)(3), 215n8
  31.2, 188
  31.201.2, 181n18
  31.201.2(a), 255n64
  31.201.3, 78, 181n19
  31.201.3(a), 255n66
  31.201.4, 181n20, 255n67
  31.205, 195–196, 240–241, 255n65
  31.205.1, 181n21
  31.205.10, 181n21, 256n91
  31.205.14, 181n21, 215n9
  31.205.19, 203–204, 209
  31.205.19(c)(3), 215n10
  31.205.20, 181n21, 215n7, 256n94
  31.205.22, 181n21
  31.205.46, 215n11
  31.205.47, 181n21, 215n13
  31.205.5, 205–206
  32, 190
  32.617(a), 104nn46–48
  36, 190, 206–212
  42.102, 103n31
  42.302, 103n31
  42.709, 213
  42.709.5, 214
  42.801(a), 104n43
  42.803(b)(3), 104n44
  43.102(1) & (b), 103n30
  52, 190
  52.215.2, 76–77, 82
  52.232, 206
  52.232.27, 206, 215n18
  52.232.5, 206
  52.232.5(g), 207–208
  52.232.5(h), 215n17
  52.242.1, 85
  52.242.3, 213–214
  52.242.4, 213
  52.243, 82
FASB Statement No. 168, 2
Federal Acquisition Regulation (FAR). *See* FAR
Federal Rules of Civil Procedure. *See* FRCP
Federal Rules of Evidence
  503, 154
  702, 153–154
FERA § 3729(a), 391
Fla Stat Ann. §§ 68.081-68.09, 305n21
Fla. Rules of Civ. Proc. § 1.310(b)(6), 273n38
FRCP
  26, 152–153
  26(a)(2)(A), 153, 274
  26(a)(2)(B), 156nn8–9, 274
  26(a)(2)(C), 156n10

26(b), 273n24
26(b)(2)(B), 261, 262
26(b)(2)(C), 261, 273n24
26(b)(3), 156n22
26(b)(4)(A), 153
26(f), 272n16
30(b)(6), 263–264, 273n39
34(a), 259, 272nn2–5
34(b), 260, 273nn25–33
34(b)(2)(E)(ii), 262
34(b)(2)(E)(i), 262
FRE 702, 267–268, 269, 274n46, 275n66

H

Haw. Rev. Stat. Ann.
    46-171, 305n21
    661-21, 305n21

I

Ill. Comp. Stat 175/1, 304n5, 305n21
Ill. Supreme Court R. 206(a)(1), 273n38
Ind. Cod §§ 5-11-55, 305n21
IRC § 179, 174

L

La. Rev Stat. Ann. tit. 39 Public
    Finance, ch 22 § 2151, 305n21

M

Mass. Gen. Laws
    18, 305n21
    5A, 304n5, 305n21
    159, 305n21
Minn. Stat. § 15C.14(c), 304n13
Model Rules of Prof'l Conduct
    R.3.1, 3.3 (2008), 250n4
Mont. Code Ann. §§ 17-8-401, 305n21
Mo. Rev. Stat. § 34.058(2), 251n9

N

Nev. Rev. Stat § 357.010, 305n21
N.H. Rev. Stat. Ann. § 167:61-b, 305n21
N.J. Rule of Court 4:14-2(c), 273n38
N.Y. Fin. Law § 187, 304n5

O

Ohio Rev. Code Ann. § 4113.62(C), 251n10
OMB Circular No. A-50, 83

P

Pub. L.
    100-679, 103n20
    111-21, 250n1, 305n32
    92-41 (85 Stat. 97), 214

R

Restatement (Second) of Torts § 876, 71
Restatement (Third) of the Law Governing
    Lawyers § 51(2)(a)(b), 74n58

S

SAS 99, 281–282, 302–303
SOP 81-1, 23–24, 60–61, 72nn3–8, 284
    (.65), 69
SSARS 8, 142

T

Tenn. Code Ann § 1-18-101, 305n21

U

UCC Article 9, 285
U.S.C.
    10 U.S.C. 2324, 213
    18 U.S.C. § 287, 104n49, 289,
        304n5, 305n22
    28 U.S.C. § 2514, 250n2
    29 U.S.C. § 213(a)(1), 182n30
    31 U.S.C. § 3729, 33, 104n49, 250n1,
        280–281, 304n5, 305nn30–31
    31 U.S.C. § 3729(a), 33, 37–38, 305nn30
    31 U.S.C. § 3729(b), 305n31
    31 U.S.C. § 3730, 305nn24–29
    31 U.S.C. § 3730(b), 305nn25–26
    31 U.S.C. § 3730(c), 305n26
    31 U.S.C. § 3730(d), 305nn28–29
    31 U.S.C. § 3730(h), 305n27
    41 U.S.C. § 211, 215n15
    41 U.S.C. § 256, 213
    41 U.S.C. § 422(k), 102n1
    41 U.S.C. § 601, 214
    41 U.S.C. § 604, 250n2
    41 U.S.C. §§ 51-58, 294

V

Va. Code. Ann.
    2.24331, 180n1
    2.2-4335, 251n9
    8.01-216.1, 305n21
    8.01-262.1, 251n16
Va. Rule of Court 4:5(b)(6), 273n38

W

Wash Rev. Code § 4.24.360, 251n10

INDEX

A

Acceleration claims, 242–243
Accountant-client privilege, 154–155
Accountants
    accountant-client privilege, 154–155
    challenges to expert testimony by, 267
    financial damages expert testimony, 268–269
    legal standards for accountant experts, 268
    recent cases on expert testimony by, 269–271
    retention of accountants, reasons for, 266–267
    scope of client representation, liability for statements made in, 66–72
Accounting disclosure disputes, 38
Accounting information, 257–279. *See also* Discovery
    damages, use in proof/disproof of, 265–266
Accounting Standards Codification (ASC). *See* ASC (Accounting Standards Codification)
Accounts payable, Notes to Financial Investments on reporting, 16
Accounts receivable
    Notes to Financial Investments on reporting, 15
    sureties examining, 54
Accrued expenses, Notes to Financial Investments on reporting, 16
Acquisitions, Notes to Financial Investments on reporting, 16
Activity ratios, sureties using, 53, 55
Activity-related costs. *See* Claims
Adobe Reader software, 260
Adverse reports and opinions, 139
Advisory services by CPAs, 150
AED (Associated Equipment Distributors Rental Rates Compilation), 173
    Green Book, 288–289

Agreed-upon procedures reports, 146, 147
AIA (American Institute of Architects) Contractor's Qualification Statement, 42
AICPA (American Institute of Certified Public Accountants), 3–4. *See also* ASC (Accounting Standards Codification); Claims; Construction Audit Guide; SOP 81-1; Statements on Standards for Accounting and Review Services (SSARS)
    Accounting Standards Team, 3–4
    auditing standards, 4–5
    Auditing Standards Board, 4–5
    code of ethics, 135
    fraud, definition of, 281–282
    Technical Standards, 150
Aiding and abetting liability, 71–72
Allen, Dennis L., 1–21
Anti-Kickback Act of 1986, 294
Antitrust defense suits, legal fees for, 205
Application of accounting principles reports, 146, 147–148
Applications for payment. *See* Payment applications
Architects, private auditor's role compared, 94–95
Armed Services Board of Contract Appeals, 194
    Eichleay formula for home office overhead, 238–240
Army Corps of Engineers
    Construction Equipment Ownership and Operating Expense Schedule, 200–201
    equipment pricing guide, 173
    inefficiency claims, overtime-related studies of, 234
    "Modification Impact Evaluation Guide," 234

ASC (Accounting Standards Codification), 2, 23–24, 39nn1. *See also* Claims; Construction Audit Guide
   claims, test for, 32–33
Assets
   balance sheet listing, 9–10
   Notes to Financial Investments on reporting, 16
   sureties examining, 54
Associated Equipment Distributors Rental Rates Compilation (AED), 173
Attest reports, 151
Attorneys
   attorney-client privilege, 155
   claims, attorney opinion letters and, 65–66
   scienter, attorney as, 67
Audit change orders, 88
Audited financial statements, 134–140
   adverse reports and opinions, 139
   comparisons for, 143, 144–145
   disclaimer of opinion, 139–140
   qualified opinions, 137–138
   report types for, 136–137
   typical language in, 138
Audit Guidance and Audit Management Guidance Memorandums for Regional Directors (MRDs), 81
   contents of, 109–117
Audit Guidance Programs (DCAA), 81
Audit Programs (AP), directory of, 119–128
Audits and auditing. *See also* Audited financial statements; GAAS (generally accepted auditing standards); Private audits; Public audits
   contract audits, 8
   cost-reimbursement contracts and, 162
   field work standards, 135–136
   financial statement audits, 6
   fraud audits, 7
   general standards, 135
   government audits, 7–8
   internal audits, 7
   operational audits, 8–9
   project audits, 8
   reporting standards, 136
   standards for, 4–5, 135–136
   suspension of payment after, 85–86
   types of audits, 6–9
Automobile insurance and cost-reimbursement contracts, 171

B

Backlog on existing contracts
   Notes to Financial Investments on reporting, 15
   sureties examining, 45
Balance sheets, 9–11. *See also* financial statements
   completed-contract method, partial balance sheet for, 25–26
   defined, 134
   example of, 10–11, 12
   on unclassified basis, 58n5
Bank accounts, multiplicity of, 301
Beck, John A., 75–131
Benes, Michael R., 157–187
Bernstein, Jay, 41–58
Billing data
   in completed-contract method, 25
   in percentage-of-completion method, 28–29
Billings in excess of costs
   in completed-contract method, 26
   and estimated reviews, 10
Billings in excess of revenue, 58n3
   sureties examining, 45
Blue Book for equipment pricing, 172–173, 288
Boards of Contract Appeals, 194
Bonds, 42–43. *See also* Performance bonds
   fraud in bonding process, 294–295
   premiums reimbursement in government contracts, 207–208
   producers, 43
Bonuses. *See* Incentive compensation
Bright-line test for primary liability, 67
Briglia, Shannon J., 75–131
Bureau of Labor Statistics (BLS), Producer Price Index (PPI), 158–159, 179
Business plan, sureties reviewing, 47
Business Roundtable study of inefficiency claims, 234
Business segment, Notes to Financial Investments on reporting, 16
By specific identification of costs, 224

C

Capacity
   defined, 44

surety's assessing contractor's
capacity, 44–45
Capital
defined, 44
sureties assessing contractor's
capital, 44
CAS (Cost Accounting Standards),
77, 81, 189–190
coverage and disclosure statement, 210
description of, 209–212
for government contracts, 208–212
Cash flow. *See* Statement of cash flows
CFR (Code of Federal Regulations), 189. *See
also* CAS (Cost Accounting Standards)
Change orders. *See also* Claims
audit change orders, 88
GAAP guidelines for revenue on, 62–65
in percentage-of-completion
method, 32–34
reasonableness, consideration of, 64–65
SOP 81-1 guidelines, 63–65
Changes clauses and claims, 220
Character
defined, 44
sureties assessing contractor's
character, 48
Charkow, Jeffrey B., 23–39
Civil actions under False
Claims Act, 290–291
Claims, 217–256
academic studies on
inefficiency, 232–235
acceleration claims, 242–243
entitlement to recover for, 242–243
activity-related costs, 218
Measured Mile approach
and, 225–226
applications for payment
supporting, 249
as-bid margin, claims based on, 246
attorney opinion letters related to
claims, liabilities of, 65–66
bond premiums costs, claims for, 246
booking for reporting purposes, 59–74
Business Roundtable study of
inefficiency claims, 234
change-order claims, 243–244
direct costs and markup,
pricing for, 243–244
documentation, change
orders as, 248

inefficiency claims, studies on, 235
multiple changes, cumulative
impact of, 244
changes clauses and, 220
compensable delays, claims for, 236
contractual issues in pricing, 219–223
correspondence supporting, 249–250
cumulative impact costs, 244
delay claims, 83, 221–222, 235–243
acceleration claims, 242–243
categories of, 236
Eichleay formula for home
office overhead, 238–242
extended field overhead, 236–237
home office overhead
claims, 237–242
differing site conditions and, 220–221
discrete methods for pricing,
223, 224–225
disputes clauses and, 222–223
Eichleay formula, 238–242
determining standby for, 239
equipment cost claims, 244–246
ownership costs, 245–246
rate manuals for equipment, 246
rental costs, 245
equipment logs supporting, 249
excusable delays, claims for, 236
force account provisions and, 220
global pricing of, 223, 226–228
home office overhead
challenges to costs for, 240–242
Eichleay formula for, 238–242
requirements for allowable
costs, 240
inefficiency claims, 228–235
change-order related inefficiency
claims, studies on, 235
industry and academic
studies on, 232–235
Measured Mile approach to, 229–232
overtime-related inefficiency
studies, 234
interest, claims involving, 246–247
jury verdict pricing of, 228
for liquidated damages, 222
Measured Mile approach, 225–226
challenges to, 232–233
industry and academic
studies on, 233
for inefficiency claims, 229–232

Claims, Measured Mile approach (*continued*)
    modified total cost method
        for pricing, 227–228
    National Electrical Contractors
        Association (NECA) study
        on inefficiency claims, 234
    nonexcusable/noncompensable
        delays, claims for, 236
    notice requirements, 222
    overhead
        extended field overhead
            claims, 236–237
        government contracts, field
            overhead costs in, 201–203
        home office overhead
            claims, 237–242
        markup claims, 246
    project record and, 223
    quantity variations and, 221
    quantum meruit pricing of, 228
    subcontractor invoices supporting, 249
    time-related costs, 218–219
        discrete pricing of, 225
    total cost method for pricing, 226–227
    transaction reports as
        documentation, 248
Close-out audits, 88–89
Code of ethics for CPAs, 135
Code of Federal Regulations (CFR), 189
Commercial audits. *See* Private audits
Commitments and contingencies,
    Notes to Financial Investments
    on reporting, 16
Compiled financial statements,
    134, 141–143
    comparisons for, 143, 144–145
Completed-contract method, 25–27
    loss contracts under, 26–27
    revenue under, 23
    scenarios for using, 27
Computer charges in cost-
    reimbursement contracts, 178–179
Concordance software, 260
Conservatism principle, 3
    revenue realization and, 24
Consistency principle, 3
Construction Audit Guide
    on incurred contract costs, 29
    information under, 36–37
    on Notes to Financial Statements, 14–16
    progress, measuring, 34–36
Construction Equipment Ownership and
    Operating Expense Schedule, 200–201

Construction project auditors, 95–97
Construction Specifications Institute, 94
Consulting services, 149–151
    categories of, 150–151
Contract Audit Follow-Up
    (CAFU) system, 104n36
Contract Disputes Act (CDA), 217
    legal fees, 205
Contracting by Negotiation, 190–194
Contractor allowances, private
    audits of, 101
Contracts, 157. *See also* Cost-
    reimbursement contracts;
    Government contracts
    audits, 8, 88
    claims, considerations in
        pricing, 219–223
    firm-fixed-price contracts, 158–159
    Notes to Financial Investments
        on reporting costs, 15
    performance audits, 88
Corporate organization costs,
    legal fees for, 205
Corps Manual, 200
Cost Accounting Standards. *See* CAS
    (Cost Accounting Standards)
Cost Accounting Standards Board, 189
Cost data
    in completed-contract method, 25
    in percentage-of-completion
        method, 28–29
Cost of operations on income
    statement, 11–12
Cost Principles, 160
    company-owned equipment,
        pricing of, 199–201
    entertainment costs, 203
    self-insurance costs, 203–204
    specific cost areas, 199–206
    subparts to, 199
    travel costs, 204
    volume discounts, 205–206
Cost Reference Guide, 173
Cost-reimbursement contracts, 159–162
    audit rights for, 162
    claims, pricing, 220
    computer charges, 178–179
    EJCDC on reimbursable costs,
        183–187
    equipment pricing, 171–177
    FICA taxes, 170
    fringe benefits, 169–170
    government contracts and, 194

increased costs, duty to
    notify owner of, 161
insurance coverages, 170–171
labor costs under, 162–170
out-of-sequence work and
    fraud, 297–298
overtime premiums, 166–169
selected forms of, 160–161
shift differentials, 166–167
small tools, charges for, 177–178
state taxes and, 170
unemployment taxes and, 170
Costs in excess of billings, 10
in completed-contract method, 26
sureties examining, 45
CPAs (certified public accountants),
    133. *See also* Audited financial
    statements; Expert witnesses;
    Financial statements
agreed-upon procedures
    reports, 146, 147
AICPA (American Institute of Certified
    Public Accountants) rules for, 135
application of accounting principles
    reports, 146, 147–148
consulting services, 149–151
going-concern issues, 143–144, 146
privilege of communications
    by, 154–155
restricted use reports, 149
Criminal actions under False
    Claims Act, 289
Current assets on balance sheet, 9
Current liabilities on balance sheet, 10
Current ratio calculation, 53

D

Daigle, Colin A., 75–131
Damages. *See also* Claims; Discovery
    accounting information for proof/
        disproof of, 265–266
    for organizational fraud, 283
DCAA (Defense Contracting Audit
    Agency), 75. *See also* DCAM
    (DCAA Contract Audit Manual)
Audit Guidance Memorandum, 81
Audit Guidance Programs, 81
Corps Manual and, 200
description of, 79–80
examples of situations for audits by, 80
False Claims Act, civil
    actions under, 290

GAGAS (generally accepted
    government auditing standards),
    compliance with, 84–85
headquarters of, 80
procedures for audits, 81–82
REAs (Requests for Equitable
    Adjustments), audit of, 82–83
DCAM (DCAA Contract Audit
    Manual), 75, 107–108
procedures for audits in, 81–82
Defective Pricing audits, 77
Defense Contracting Audit Agency
    (DCAA). *See* DCAA (Defense
    Contracting Audit Agency)
Defense Federal Acquisition
    Regulations Supplement, 84
Deferred costs and revenue, Notes
    to Financial Investments
    on reporting, 15
Delay claims. *See* Claims
Dennis, Kevin D., 59–74
Department of Criminal Investigative
    Services (DCIS), 290
Department of Defense (DoD).
    See also DCAA (Defense
    Contracting Audit Agency)
DCAA auditor, role of, 83–84
Federal Acquisition Regulation
    Supplement, 81
resolution of contract disagreements,
    policy for, 129–131
Department of Energy Acquisition
    Regulations, 194
Department of Justice False
    Claims Act, 290
Depositions
    of accounting experts, 271
    of fact witnesses, 263–264
Depreciation and equipment pricing, 174
Differing site conditions and
    claims, 220–221
Direct costs and markup,
    pricing for, 243–244
Disclaimer of opinion, 139–140
Discounts
    private audits of, 101
    volume discounts in government
        contracts, 205–206
Discovery, 257–265. *See also*
    Accountants; Depositions
categories of documents to
    request, list of, 259
checklist for discovery plan, 258

Discovery (*continued*)
   of electronically stored information, 259–262
   of expert witnesses, 152–153
   interrogatories, 264–265
   list of records to request in, 277–279
   need for discovery, identifying, 257–258
Discrete methods for pricing claims, 223, 224–225
Disputes clauses and claims, 222–223
Documentation. *See also* Claims; Discovery
   additional documentation, 249–250
   applications for payment as, 249
   change orders as, 248
   cost documents, 247–250
   EJCDC requirements, 183
   fraud and, 300
   job cost reports as, 248
   labor distribution reports as, 248–249
   original bid estimate, 247
   productivity information as, 249
   schedule analysis documents, 250
   transaction reports as, 248
Dun & Bradstreet, sureties reviewing reports by, 48

E

EAC (estimated costs at completion), 29, 30
   percentage-of-completion method and, 36
Earnings per share, Notes to Financial Investments on reporting, 15
Economic price adjustment for firm-fixed-price contracts, 158–159
"The Effects of Change Orders on Productivity" (Leonard), 235
Eichleay formula for home office overhead, 238–242
EJCDC (Engineers Joint Contract Documents Committee), 89
   allowances under, 186
   contractor's fee under, 186
   cost of work under, 183–186
   documentation under, 186
   excluded costs under, 182–183
   reimbursable costs, Article 11 on, 183–187
   small tools, contract charges for, 178
   supplemental costs under, 183–184
   unit price of work, 187
Electronically stored information, discovery of, 259–262
Employees. *See also* Labor costs
   overtime, entitlement to, 167–168
Engineers Joint Contract Documents Committee. *See* EJCDC (Engineers Joint Contract Documents Committee)
Enron, 66
Entertainment costs in government contracts, 203
Equipment, 171–177. *See also* Claims; Fraud
   accelerated depreciation for, 174
   actual contractor cost, 173–176
   book value and, 175
   cost of funds and, 175
   cost-reimbursement contracts and equipment floaters, 171
   depreciation and, 174
   and firm-fixed-price contracts, 158
   as fixed-time-related costs, 218–219
   government contracts, pricing company-owned equipment for, 199–201
   heavy construction, investment for, 57n2
   indirect cost of ownership, 175
   Notes to Financial Investments on reporting, 16
   operating expenses and, 175–176
   ownership cost, 173–176
   pricing sheets or lists, 176–177
   private audits of equipment costs, 99–100
   rate books, 172–173
   standard language related to, 172
   sureties examining, 46
Estimated costs at completion (EAC). *See* EAC (estimated costs at completion)
Excess productivity and fraud, 298
Expert witnesses, 151–155. *See also* Accountants
   admissibility of evidence, 153–154
   attorney-client privilege, 155
   disclosure requirements for, 153
   discovery of experts, 152
   privileged communications by, 154–155
   scope of discovery, 153
   topics addressed by, 152
Extended field overhead claims, 236–237

F

Facilities capital cost of money (COM), 201
False Claims Act, 86, 217, 289–291
   civil actions under, 290–291
   criminal actions under, 289
FAR (Federal Acquisition Regulations), 8, 194–199. *See also* Cost Principles; Public audits
   Audit and Records clause, 85
   Department of Energy Acquisition Regulations, 194
   and government contracts, 189
   legal fees, 204–205
   specific cost areas, 199–206
   travel costs, 204
   volume discounts, 205–206
FASB (Financial Accounting Standards Board), 1–3
Federal government contracts. *See* Government contracts
Federal Rules of Civil Procedure (FRCP) on expert witnesses, 152
Federal Travel Regulations (FTRs), 204
FICA and cost-reimbursement contracts, 170
Field work standards for audits, 135–136
Financial Accounting Standards Board (FASB), 1–3
Financial statements, 133–149. *See also* Audited financial statements; Balance sheets; Income statements; Statement of cash flows
   agreed-upon procedures reports, 146, 147
   application of accounting principles reports, 146, 147–148
   audits, 6
   basic financial statements, 9–17
   cash flows statement, 12–14
      example of, 13–14
   compiled financial statements, 134, 141–143
   "Fundamental Principles" for, 2–3
   going-concern issues, 143–144, 146
   home office overheads in, 237
   income statement, 11–12
   litigation strategy, disclosure of, 38–39
   notes to, 14–16
   restricted use reports, 149
   reviewed financial statements, 134, 140–141
   special reports by CPAs, 146–149
   supplemental schedules, 16
      contract revenues, costs and earnings, supplemental schedule of, 18–19
      contracts, supplemental schedule of, 20–21
      sureties reviewing, 48–51
   sureties
      review by, 48–51
      sample analysis by, 55–57
      supplementary schedules, review of, 48–51
   for surety bonds, 43
   unqualified reports and opinions, 136–137
Financing activities, cash flows from, 13
Firm-fixed-price contracts, 158–159
Fixed assets on balance sheet, 10
Force account provisions and claims, 220
Forfeiture of Fraudulent Claims Act, 217
Fraud
   accounting issues, 281–306
   audits, 7
   bank accounts, multiplicity of, 301
   in bonding process, 294–295
   claims, liability for fraudulent, 86
   in contract performance, 295–296
   definitions of, 281–282
   detection of, 301–303
   excess productivity and, 298
   False Claims Act, 289–291
   front-end loading and, 293–294, 297
   job cost reports and, 292–293
   journal entries, questionable, 299–300
   legal elements of, 282
   off-site storage or delivery and, 296–297
   organizational fraud, 283–285
      expense recognition, 284–285
      misappropriation of assets, 285
      related-party transactions, 285
      revenue recognition and, 284
   out-of-sequence work and, 297–298
   in payment applications, 293–294
   penalties for, 282
   performance fraud, 283, 286–289
      excess of contract rates, use of rates in, 288–289

Fraud, performance fraud (*continued*)
    inappropriate/duplicate markup, 287–288
    labor overcharging, 286
    substandard/substituted materials, 286–287
    unallowable costs, billing of, 287
  precontract project controls for, 301–302
  prepayments and, 299
  prevention of, 301–303
  primary liability and, 67
  project analytical procedures and, 302–303
  questionable payments, 299–301
  recent cases on, 291–292
  red flags for, 296–301
  related business entities, use of, 298–299
Fraud Enforcement and Recovery Act of 2009, 291
Fraudulent claims, liability for, 86
Fringe benefits, 169–170
Front-end loading, 293–294, 297
Frye standard, 268
Fuchs, Jeffrey E., 41–58
Full disclosure principle, 3

G

GAAP (generally accepted accounting principles), 1, 136. *See also* Claims; Construction Audit Guide; percentage-of-completion method
  alternative standards, 4
  change orders, recognizing revenue on, 62–65
  claims, recognizing revenue on, 62–65
  and compiled financial statements, 142
  for construction contractors, 23–24
  FAST Statement No. 168 and, 2
  qualified opinions and, 137–138
  Raytheon case and, 69–70
  and reviewed financial statements, 140–141
GAAS (generally accepted auditing standards), 4, 5–6
  field work standards, 5
  list of standards, 5–6
  reporting standards, 5
G&A expenses on income statement, 12
GAGAS (generally accepted government auditing standards), 7–8
  DCAA following, 81
  noncompliance, consequences of, 84–85
GAO (Government Accountability Office) Yellow Book, 7–8
Gavin, Richard E., 1–21
General liability insurance, cost-reimbursement contracts and, 171
General Services Administration Board of Contract Appeals on delay claims, 236
Giddings, Edwin C., 189–215
Gilmore, Jeffrey G., 157–187
Global pricing of claims, 223, 226–228
Going-concern principle, 3, 143–144, 146
Gorman, Paul J., 217–256
Government audits, 7–8
Government contracts, 189–215. *See also* CAS (Cost Accounting Standards); Cost Principles
  adequate competition exception, 191
  architect-engineer contracts, FAR Part 36 on, 206
  bond premiums, reimbursement for, 207–208
  certification of cost or pricing data, 192
  checklist of allowable and unallowable costs, 196–198
  construction contracts, FAR Part 36 on, 206
  contracting by negotiation, 190–194
  Cost or Pricing Data, 191
  cost sweeps, 192–193
  coverage under CAS, 209
  cutoff dates, 192–193
  defective pricing actions in, 193–194
  entertainment costs, 203
  equipment, pricing company-owned, 199–201
  exemptions from CAS, 209
  final indirect costs, certification of, 213
  final payment provisions, 208
  incurred cost submission (ICS) for, 323–325
  indirect costs, certification of, 212–214
  Information Other than Cost or Pricing Data, 191
  itemization of progress payment amounts, 206–207
  legal fees in, 204–205
  methods for, 190
  overhead costs in, 201–203
  payment provisions, 206–208
  penalties for unallowable costs, 213–214
  practical considerations for, 193–194
  progress payments, 206–208

prompt payment provisions, 208
retainage requirement for
    progress payments, 207
self-insurance costs, 203–204
specific cost areas, 199–206
subcontractor information for
    progress payments, 207
TINA sweeps, 192–193
travel costs, 204
unallowable costs, 194–199
    penalties for, 213–214
volume discounts, 205–206
Gray, Scott D., 59–74
Green Book (AED), 288–289
Guaranteed maximum price (GMP)
    cost-reimbursement contracts and, 159
    fraud in contracts, 296
    incurred cost audits for, 88
Guernier, William D., 23–39

H

Halliburton case, 68–69
High-risk areas subject to audits, 97–101
Home office overhead claims, 237–242
Horgan, Kathleen, 41

I

Ibbs, William, 235
Implementation services by CPAs, 150–151
Incentive compensation
    cost-reimbursement contracts and, 170
    private audits of, 98–99
Income statements, 11–12
    defined, 134
Income taxes, Notes to Financial
    Investments on reporting, 15, 16
Incurred contract costs in percentage-
    of-completion method, 29
Incurred costs
    audits, 88
    government contracts, incurred cost
        submission (ICS) for, 212–214
Indirect costs, DCAA compliance
    audits on, 79
Industry studies on inefficiency, 232–235
Inefficiency claims. *See* Claims
Inflated claims, 217
Inspector General, DCAA reporting to, 78
Insurance. *See also* Self-insurance
    cost-reimbursement contracts
        and, 170–171

equipment insurance premium, 175
self-insurance, private audit of, 100
Intangible assets, Notes to Financial
    Investments on reporting, 16
Integrity of contractor, sureties
    reviewing, 48
Interest
    claims involving, 246–247
    government contracts, interest
        expenses in, 201
    prompt pay interest rate history, 202
    public audits, interest
        penalties after, 85
Internal audits, 7
Internal Revenue Service, cost
    segregation reviewed by, 86
Interrogatories, 264–265
Investing activities, cash flows from, 13
Invitation for Bids (IFBs), 190

J

James, Paul M., 133–156
Job cost reports (JCRs), 218. *See also* Claims
    fraud in, 292–293
    sureties reviewing, 45–46
Job cost reports documents required, 248
Johns, Colin A., 257–279
Johnson, Samuel, 303
Joint ventures
    legal fees for, 205
    Notes to Financial Investments
        on reporting, 15
Journal entries, questionable, 299–300
Jury verdict pricing of claims, 228

K

Kickbacks, 294
Krafft, Matthew R., 189–215
Kwon, Daniel, 217–256

L

Laboratory test fees, private audits of, 100
Labor costs. *See also* Fraud
    base wages, 165
    claims, labor distribution reports
        supporting, 248–249
    cost-reimbursement contracts
        and, 162–170
    DCAA compliance audits on, 79
    elements of, 163

Labor costs. (*continued*)
    fringe benefits, 169–170
    home office personnel, 165–166
    inefficiency claims and, 228–229
    Measured Mile approach and, 229–231
    off-site personnel, 164–165
    on-site construction workers, 163–164
    on-site supervision/administrative personnel, 164
    overtime premiums, 166–169
    private audits of, 98
    wages and benefits, consideration of, 166–167
Labor distribution reports supporting, 248–249
Legal fees, FAR regulation of, 204–205
Leonard, Charles, 235
Letters of recommendation, sureties reviewing, 48
Leverage ratios, sureties using, 52, 54–55
Liabilities, on balance sheet, 10
Liability. *See also* Primary liability
    claims, liabilities for attorney opinion letters related to, 65–66
    scope of client representation, liability for statements made in, 66–72
    secondary liability, 66, 71–72
Lines of credit, sureties reviewing, 47
Liquidated damages, claims for, 222
Liquidity ratios, sureties using, 52, 53–54
Litigation strategy, disclosure of, 38–39
Living allowances, audit of costs for, 100
Long-term construction contracts, 60–62, 72n2
Long-term liabilities on balance sheet, 10
Lump-sum contracts, fraud in, 295–296
Lynch, Thomas R., 59–74

M

Management team, sureties reviewing, 46–47
Marketable securities, sureties examining, 54
Markup claims, 246
Matching principle, 3
    revenue realization and, 24
Materiality concept, 39n3
Material misstatements, defined, 6
Materials and firm-fixed-price contracts, 158
McGeehin, Patrick A., 189–215

Measured Mile approach. *See* Claims
Mechanical Contractors Association of America (MCAA) study on inefficiency claims, 233–234
Methods for pricing, 223–228
Microsoft Excel, discovery of documents in, 261
"Modification Impact Evaluation Guide" (Army Corps of Engineers), 234
Modified total cost method for pricing claims, 227–228
MRDs. *See* Audit Guidance and Audit Management Guidance Memorandums for Regional Directors (MRDs)
Multiple changes, cumulative impact of, 244

N

National Electrical Contractors Association (NECA)
    inefficiency claims, study on, 234
    "Tool and Equipment Rental Schedule," 173
Net increase (decrease) in cash, 13
Net working capital ratio, 53
Net worth ratio, 54
No damages for delay clauses, 221–222
North American Industry Classification System (NAICS) code, 158
Notes payable, Notes to Financial Investments on reporting, 16
Notes to Financial Statements, 14–16
Notices
    claims, requirements for, 222
    Intent to Disallow Costs, Notice of, 85

O

OCBOA (Other Comprehensive Bases of Accounting), 4
Off-site labor, private audits of, 99
Off-site storage or delivery and fraud, 296–297
One-off projects, 86
Operating activities, cash flows from, 12–13
Operational audits, 8–9
Organizational fraud. *See* Fraud
Original bid estimate document, 247

Other Audit Guidance (OAG)
documents, director of, 119–128
Out-of-sequence work and fraud, 297–298
Overbillings. *See* Billings in
excess of revenue
Overhead. *See also* Claims
DCAA compliance audits on, 79
Overruns. *See* Claims
Overtime, 166–169
authorization of, 169
base for payment of, 168
entitlement to, 167–168
inefficiency claims, overtime-related
inefficiency studies on, 234
multiple projects, overtime
for work on, 168
Owner audits. *See* Private audits
Owners and ownership
balance sheet, owner's equity on, 10
contractor finances, concerns
about, 41–43
equipment ownership costs,
claims for, 245–246

P

Payment applications
claims, support for, 249
fraud in, 293–294
Payment bonds, 42
claims for costs, 246
Payroll distribution reports
supporting, 249
PCAOB (Public Company Accounting
Oversight Board), 4–5
PDF files for discovery, 260
Penalties. *See also* Interest
False Claims Act violations, 291
for fraud, 282
government contracts, unallowable
costs under, 213–214
public audits, penalties after, 85
Percentage-of-completion
method, 28–36, 32–34
ARB No. 45 recommending, 60
change orders, unpriced, 32–34
claims, accounting for, 32–34
estimated cost-to-complete, 30–31
incurred contract costs in, 29
progress, measuring, 34–36
prohibited methods under, 62
revenue, 23

revenue, determining, 31–32
SOP 81-1 recommending, 60
Performance bonds, 42
costs, claims for, 246
Performance fraud. *See* Fraud
Personnel team, sureties reviewing,
46–47
Prepaid assets, sureties examining, 54
PricewaterhouseCoopers (PwC), 69–70
Pricing claims. *See* Claims
Pricing sheets or lists for
equipment, 176–177
Primary liability, 66, 67–71
under federal securities laws, 67–70
state law on, 70–71
Private audits, 86–101, 89
architects and auditors, roles of,
94–95
audit team, selecting, 96
of bonuses, 98–99
claim audits, 89
close-out audits, 88–89
construction project auditors,
95–97
contractor allowances, 101
contract performance audits, 88
contractual provisions for, 89–90
of discounts, 101
documentation, requests for, 92
employees, interviews of, 91–92
equipment costs, 99–100
frequency of, 93
high-risk areas subject to, 97–101
incurred cost audits, 88
informational requests by
auditors, 91–92
job cost systems and, 93–94
labor costs, 98
miscellaneous costs subject to, 100
of off-site labor, 99
public audits compared, 87
reasonable costs, determining, 97
of rebates, 101
of refunds, 101
related parties, costs of
work by, 100–101
rights clauses, implications of, 90–91
subcontractor costs, 101
Privileged communications
by experts, 154–155
Procurement, audits and, 83–84
Producer Price Index (PPI), 158–159, 179

Productivity
    and Measured Mile approach, 229–230
    records supporting, 249
Product services by CPAs, 151
Professional liability insurance, cost-
    reimbursement contracts and, 171
Profit, sureties examining, 45
Profitability ratios, sureties
    using, 52–53, 55
Profit and loss statements (P&Ls).
    See Income statements
Progress
    input method of measuring, 35
    output methods of measuring, 35
    percentage-of-completion method,
        measuring progress in, 34–36
Progress payments in government
    contracts, 206–208
Project record, claims and, 223
Property and Notes to Financial
    Investments on reporting, 16
Property taxes and equipment pricing, 175
Public audits. *See also* DCAA (Defense
        Contracting Audit Agency); REAs
        (Requests for Equitable Adjustments)
    of claims, 82–83
    cost or pricing data, evaluation of, 77
    Defective Pricing audits, 77
    Department of Defense
        (DoD) and, 83–84
    examination of costs, 76–77
    exit conference after, 82
    FAR (Federal Acquisition
        Regulations) on, 76–79
    fraudulent claims, liability for, 86
    Inspector General, DCAA
        reporting to, 78
    interest penalties after, 85
    interim meetings during, 81–82
    major emphasis in, 79
    noncompliance, consequences of, 84–85
    Notice of Intent to Disallow Costs, 85
    penalties after, 85
    private audits compared, 87
    procurement, role of DCAA
        audit in, 83–84
Public audits of, 82–83
Punitive damages for
    organizational fraud, 283
Purchase price disputes, 37

Q

Quantity variations and claims, 221
Quantum meruit pricing of claims, 228
Quick ratio calculation, 53
Qui tam actions, 290

R

Ralls, John W., 257–279
Ramp up/ramp down effects,
    delay claims and, 236
Rate books for equipment pricing, 172–173
Ratios, sureties using, 52–55
Realization principle, 2
REAs (Requests for Equitable
        Adjustments), 77, 82–83
    government contracts and, 194
    legal fees in government
        contracts, 204–205
Reasonable costs
    auditors determining, 97
    defined, 78
Reasonableness, consideration of, 64–65
Rebates, private audits of, 101
Refco, 66
References, sureties reviewing, 48
Refunds, private audits of, 101
Related business entities, use of, 298–299
Related parties
    government contracts and, 193
    organizational fraud and, 285
    private audits of, 100–101
Relocation of personnel, audit
    of costs for, 100
Rental Rate Blue Book, 172–173, 288
Requests for Equitable Adjustments
    (REAs). *See* REAs (Requests
    for Equitable Adjustments)
Restricted use reports, 149
Revenue, 239–29. *See also* Completed-
        contract method; Percentage-
        of-completion method
    conservatism principle and, 24
    on income statement, 11
    on long-term construction
        contracts, 60–62
    matching principle and, 24
    percentage-of-completion method,
        determining revenue in, 31–32

Revenue recognition principle, 3
Reviewed financial statements,
    134, 140–141
    comparisons for, 143, 144–145
Revised estimates, Notes to Financial
    Investments on reporting, 15
Rules of Professional Conduct
    on inflated claims, 217

S

Salaries and wages. *See also*
    Incentive compensation
    cost-reimbursement contracts
        considering, 166–167
Sarbanes-Oxley Act of 2002, 4–5. *See
    also* Construction Audit Guide
Schedule analysis documents
    supporting, 250
Scienter, attorney as, 67
Scope of client representation, liability
    for statements made in, 66–72
Sealed Bidding, 190
SEC (Securities and Exchange
    Commission). *See also*
    Construction Audit Guide
    aiding and abetting liability
        under, 71–72
    FASB (Financial Accounting
        Standards Board) and, 1–2
    Halliburton and, 68–69
Secondary liability, 66, 71–72
Self-insurance
    cost-reimbursement contracts and, 171
    FAR Cost Principles on, 203–204
    private audit of, 100
Separate entity assumption principle, 3
Shapiro, Stephen B., 133–156
Sheckells, Anita M., 133–156
Shift differentials, 166–167
Site conditions and claims, 220
Small tools, contract charges for, 177–178
Software
    in discovery, 260–262
    private audit of costs, 100
SOP 81-1, 23–24
    change orders, guidelines for, 63–65
    claims, guidelines for, 63–65
    primary liability guidelines, 68
Staff services by CPAs, 151

Standard Audit Programs,
    directory of, 119–128
Standby under Eichleay formula,
    determining, 239
Statement of cash flows, 12–14
    defined, 134
Statement of Position (SOP)
    81-1. *See* SOP 81-1
Statements on Standards for Accounting
    and Review Services (SSARS)
    and compiled financial statements,
        142
    for reviewed financial
        statements, 140–141
State taxes, cost-reimbursement
    contracts and, 170
Stockholder's equity
    on balance sheet, 10
    Notes to Financial Investments
        on reporting, 16
    statement of stockholder's
        equity, defined, 134
Straight line depreciation for
    equipment, 174
Subcontractors
    claims, invoices supporting, 249
    government contract progress
        payments, information for, 207
    private audits of costs of, 101
Subsequent events, Notes to Financial
    Investments on reporting, 16
Substantial participation test for
    primary liability, 67
Supplemental schedules. *See*
    Financial statements
Sureties. *See also* Bonds
    capital of contractor, assessing, 44
    character of contractor,
        assessment of, 47
    contractor finances, concerns
        about, 41–43
    financial analysis ratios used by,
        52–55
    financial tests by, 51–55
    integrity of contractor, perception of, 48
    letters or recommendation and
        references, review of, 48
    third-party reports, review of, 48
Suspension of payment after audit, 85–86
Symon, Robert J., 59–74

T

Third-party reports, sureties reviewing, 48
TIFF files for discovery, 260
Time-related costs. *See* Claims
TINA sweeps, 193
Tools. *See also* Equipment
  small tools, contract charges for, 177–178
Total cost method for pricing claims, 226–227
Trade organization studies on inefficiency claims, 233–234
Transaction reports as claims documentation, 248
Transaction services by CPAs, 151
Trueheart, Douglas A., 157–187

U

Unallowable costs. *See also* Government contracts
  performance fraud by billing, 287
Underbillings. *See* Costs in excess of billings
Unemployment taxes and cost-reimbursement contracts, 170
Uniform Commercial Code, sureties reviewing filings under, 48
Uniform CPA Exam, 3–4
Unqualified reports and opinions, 136–137

V

Varela, Paul A., 217–256
Variation in estimated quantity clauses, 221
Vendor invoices supporting, 249
Veterans Administration Board of Contract Appeals on Eichleay formula, 241

W

Weather delays, contract provisions for, 165
Widget business, 24
Witnesses. *See also* Expert witnesses
  fact witnesses, deposition of, 263–264
Wolter, Claudia R., 133–156
Wonderlick, David B., 217–256
Woodcock, Jeanette, 41
Work Breakdown Structure (WBS), 94
Workers' compensation and cost-reimbursement contracts, 171
Work history, sureties reviewing, 47
Work in progress (WIP), sureties examining, 45
Wright, Wiley R., III, 133–156

Y

Yellow Book, 7–8